FLORIDA STATE
UNIVERSITY LIBRARIES

AUG 30 1993

TALLAHASSEE, FLORIDA

The late
ARTHUR ADAMS, Ph. D.
President Emeritus of the American Society of Genealogists

GENEALOGICAL RESEARCH METHODS AND SOURCES

By

THE AMERICAN SOCIETY OF GENEALOGISTS

Editor
MILTON RUBINCAM

Associate Editor
JEAN STEPHENSON

Committee on Publication
ARTHUR ADAMS
MEREDITH B. COLKET, JR.
DONALD LINES JACOBUS

Washington, D. C.
1960

Copyright 1960

by

THE AMERICAN SOCIETY OF GENEALOGISTS

Second printing . . . 1961

Third printing . . . 1966

Fourth printing . . . 1969

Fifth printing . . . 1972

Sixth printing . . . 1973

This volume may be ordered from
Mrs. Donna R. Hotaling, Agent
2255 Cedar Lane
Vienna, Va. 22180
$6.50, payable to
The American Society of Genealogists

FOREWORD

Soon after the founding of the American Society of Genealogists its Fellows agreed to embark on the project of producing and presenting to the genealogical public a handbook to be written as a joint effort by a group of experts in their respective fields. Mr. Rubincam was appointed editor and, little knowing the trials which lay before him, he accepted the task.

If there be any one among our readers who has struggled to whip a stable of some thirty volunteer and sometimes temperamental authors into getting on with their work and observing a deadline, he will bestow on Mr. Rubincam the deep sympathy which he so justly deserves. It is the sad fact that deadline succeeded deadline as the recalcitrant failed to produce. Our satisfaction is, therefore, the greater that the handbook is finally a reality.

The majority of the chapters herein are the work of Fellows of the Society. In some cases, however, it was found that we had no available expert in a specialized field and, in such cases, others of high authority have been drafted. For their cooperation the editor and the Society are most grateful.

We sincerely regret that four of our Fellows who have contributed chapters to the book, Mrs. Hiden, Sir Francis Grant, Mr. Ewen and Mr. Hoffman, have died during the progress of the work and will not see the product in which they were keenly interested.

It is our collective hope that the book may prove of interest to the experienced genealogist and that it will guide the tyro into the methods which his predecessors have investigated and found sound.

WALTER G. DAVIS

CONTENTS

	PAGE
Foreword	iii

Walter Goodwin Davis, President,
American Society of Genealogists.

Introduction 1
    Arthur Adams, President Emeritus,
    American Society of Genealogists.

PART 1

GENERAL CONSIDERATIONS

CHAPTER
 I. Adventures in Genealogy. *Milton Rubincam* 5
 II. Tradition and Family History 14
    Donald Lines Jacobus.
 III. Interpreting Genealogical Records 19
    Donald Lines Jacobus.
 IV. Genealogy and Chronology 28
    Donald Lines Jacobus.
 V. The Rules of Evidence: A Standard for
    Proving Pedigrees. *Noel C. Stevenson* 37
 VI. Preparing Genealogical Manuscripts for
    Publication. *Donald Lines Jacobus* 49

PART 2

MATERIALS FOR RESEARCH

I. Original Sources.
   A. Family Records. *Walter Lee Sheppard, Jr.* ... 55
      Family Bibles and Family Vital Records.
      Correspondence.
      Memoirs and Diaries.
      Unrecorded Deeds and Wills.
      Diplomas, Certificates, and Testimonials.

CHAPTER   PAGE
    B. Public Records.
        The Census. *Edward H. West* _____ 64
        Federal Pensions. *Edward H. West* _____ 66
        Military Records. *Edward H. West* _____ 68
        Naval Records. *Edward H. West* _____ 70
        Marine Corps Records. *Edward H. West* _____ 71
        Coast Guard Records. *Edward H. West* _____ 72
        Registration of American
          Citizens Abroad. *Meredith B. Colket, Jr.* _____ 72
        Passport Applications. *Meredith B. Colket, Jr.* 73
        Passenger Lists. *Meredith B. Colket, Jr.* _____ 74
        Original "Grants". *Meredith B. Colket, Jr.* ___ 78
        Records of Entry. *Meredith B. Colket, Jr.* ____ 78
        Local Records. *Meredith B. Colket, Jr.* _____ 79
        Probate Records. *Milton Rubincam* _____ 81

    C. Institutional Records. *Walter Lee Sheppard, Jr.* 83
        Church Records.
        Cemetery Records and Inscriptions.
        Educational Institutions.
        Societies and Fraternal Organizations.

II. Secondary Materials. *Milton Rubincam* _____ 91
    A. Manuscripts.
    B. Printed Materials.
        Family Histories.
        Collected Genealogies.
        Source Materials.
        Local Histories.
        Other Printed Materials.

PART 3

REGIONAL GENEALOGY

I. New England.
    A. Maine and New Hampshire. *Walter G. Davis* 99
    B. Vermont. *Jean Stephenson* _____ 105
    C. Massachusetts. *Winifred Lovering Holman* __ 113
    D. Connecticut. *Donald Lines Jacobus* _____ 124
    E. Rhode Island. *Edward H. West* _____ 134

CHAPTER	PAGE
II. New York.	
A. New York City. *Milton Rubincam*	139
B. Upstate New York. *Mary J. Sibley*	145
C. Long Island. *Herbert F. Seversmith*	172
III. New Jersey. *Milton Rubincam*	182
IV. Pennsylvania. *Milton Rubincam*	189
V. Delaware. *Leon deValinger, Jr.*	198
VI. Maryland. *John Frederick Dorman*	203
VII. Virginia. *Martha W. Hiden*	212
VIII. North and South Carolina. *Jean Stephenson*	221
IX. Georgia. *Mary G. Bryan*	235
X. The Westward Expansion. *David C. Duniway*	246
XI. Canada.	
A. Bibliography. *Milton Rubincam*	261
B. Quebec. *Gérard Malchelosse*	265
C. Ontario. *James J. Talman*	277
D. Nova Scotia and New Brunswick. *Edward H. West*	283

PART 4
PRE-AMERICAN ANCESTRY

I. Feudal Genealogy. *G. Andrews Moriarty*	291
II. Royal and Noble Genealogy. *John Insley Coddington*	299
III. England and Wales. *Anthony R. Wagner*	320
IV. Scotland. *Sir Francis J. Grant*	335
V. Ireland. *Margaret D. Falley*	344
VI. Germany. *Milton Rubincam*	375
VII. The Netherlands. *William J. Hoffman*	382
VIII. France. *Milton Rubincam*	391
IX. Switzerland. *Milton Rubincam*	396
X. Scandinavia. *Amandus Johnson and Milton Rubincam*	402

Part 5

SPECIAL FIELDS OF INVESTIGATION

CHAPTER	PAGE
I. Heraldry. *Harold Bowditch*	411
II. Genealogy and the Law: Court Reports. *Noel C. Stevenson*	428
III. A Study of Surnames.	
A. British Surnames. *C. L'Estrange Ewen*	436
B. European Surnames. *Milton Rubincam*	445
The Authors	451
The American Society of Genealogists: *Roll of Fellows.*	455

INTRODUCTION

This book had its origin and inspiration in the needs of a group of genealogists, amateur and professional, making up the membership of the American Society of Genealogists.

All felt the need of recapturing and passing on the spell cast on them by that classic of genealogical literature, Donald Lines Jacobus' *Genealogy as Pastime and Profession,* and by his articles in the early volumes of *The American Genealogist.*

Each one had felt the need for a general introduction to fields of genealogy in which his own experience had been limited, but in which he was interested, for one reason or another, and of which he wanted to know more before he began work in that field and made use of highly specialized handbooks devoted to the particular field of interest.

This special interest might be merely another American State in which he had not worked. For, in spite of the fact that records related to the descent of real estate form the backbone of all genealogy, these records take different forms in different countries and in different periods.

For example, a person might be a competent genealogist in Massachusetts or Connecticut, and yet feel almost lost when confronted with a call to write the history of a family in New York, Pennsylvania or Virginia. A little guidance as to the nature and extent and places of deposit of different kinds of records in these states might be invaluable and save him much time and expense in needless travel and correspondence.

He might assume, not unnaturally, that he would find public records, vital records in Pennsylvania, for example, and might be hard put to it to proceed with his task without them, when he learned that they do not exist, at least for periods back of the last half-century or less.

He might have a German or a Swiss or even an English problem and so come to feel the need of knowing about records and depositories in those countries. He would probably be surprised that nothing like our registries of deeds exists, even in England, or wonder what records could be used to supply their lack.

Or, he might have a problem involving a Magna Charta or a royal descent, and so come to feel the need of some knowledge of medieval genealogy or royal descents.

The purpose of this book is to give inspiration and a justification for genealogical study—if any justification be needed—and to answer these questions, or at least to put one in the way to finding further and more nearly adequate information.

The reading of the President's "Foreword" and a study of the table of contents, will indicate how the Editor has gone about his task.

The book is not the work of any one person. The answers to the questions are the work of a group, informed by one spirit and purpose.

We believe that this book differs sufficiently from any other existing "handbook", "manual", or "textbook", to justify its existence abundantly.

It is the hope of the Editor and of the contributors that the book will meet the "felt need", which gave the suggestions for its preparation and publication.

If it does, then they will feel amply rewarded, and the American Society of Genealogists will feel that it has made a contribution to the science and art of genealogy, which it exists to serve.

ARTHUR ADAMS

Part 1
GENERAL CONSIDERATIONS

CHAPTER I

ADVENTURES IN GENEALOGY *

The desire to know about one's family is as old as recorded history. The Bible, the most sacred volume in Christendom, is replete with descents of individuals and nations. The opening paragraphs of the autobiography of Flavius Josephus, the Jewish historian, is an account of his descent from a family belonging to the sacerdotal order. The monuments that have withstood the storms and ravages of fifty centuries in the Valley of the Nile reveal that the upper-class families of Ancient Egypt took pride in their lineages. Indeed, the world's first critical genealogist was an Egyptian nobleman, Prince Khnumhotep II who, with dignity and simplicity, recorded on the walls of his tomb at Beni Hassan: "I have kept alive the names of my fathers, which I found obliterated upon the doorways [making them] legible in form, accurate in reading, not putting one in the place of another." In the second century of our era the Roman writer, Suetonius, commenced several of his biographies of the Caesars with a critical account of their families, often tracing them to the very dawn of Roman history.

All of the Oriental nations pay particular attention to their ancestral origins. The Chinese have perfected a system of genealogy to a greater degree than any other people. Their family histories are used as references for compiling dynastic histories, local histories, and literary works. Considerable care is exercised by the family associations to preserve their records and many of their genealogies are revised and brought up-to-date every fifty years. Clan and family doctrines regulating the deportment of the members of the family are printed in much detail. The Chinese do not regard themselves as ancestor-worshippers. Their venera-

---

* Originally published, in longer form, as "The Lure and Value of Genealogy", *The Pennsylvania Genealogical Magazine*, XVII, June 1949, 33-44. (See that article for complete footnote documentation of the statements made herein.)

tion of their forebears is an attempt to emulate their more honorable ancestors and to avoid the ignominious conduct of their less worthy progenitors. In other words, they use family records to perpetuate the best phases of their character, civilization, and culture.

In Europe and the British Isles the study of genealogy was not cultivated to any considerable extent until the 16th century. During the Middle Ages few private families possessed such things as ancestral lists. The famous case of Scrope *vs.* Grosvenor in 1385 was fought in the King's courts without any pedigree being exhibited to support the claims of the contestants. In the Tudor and Stuart periods of English history many of the proud old noble houses which had swayed the destinies of the Nation since the Norman Conquest began to be supplanted by the *nouveaux riches*; the families then rising to power began to make fantastic claims, many of them daring even to attach themselves to the First Family in the Garden of Eden. Other families, more modest, were content to trace their origins only to pagan deities or early Christian saints.

On the Continent the trade of pedigree-making flourished to an alarming degree. Especially was this true in France and Italy, where well-to-do patrons were provided with desirable ancestors—at a suitable price, of course. As examples, the houses of Lévis-Mirepoix deduced its origin from the priestly tribe of Levi, Cesarini claimed descent from the omnipotent Caesars, and Massimo heralded far and and wide its mythical progenitors, the family of Fabius Maximus. But it goes without saying that the proudest claim of all was made by the noble and puissant House of Esterházy of Hungary. No family, not even here in America where we often jump blindly into the genealogical abyss, aspires to the glory of the Esterházy origins; not even in the Bible does a family claim an antiquity so remote, for we are told that its history began with:

"Adam Esterházy, first of the name; Adam, his son, second of the name; Adam, his son, third of the name; under whom God created the world"!

Germany was the first European nation to develop the scientific aspect of genealogy. In the 17th and 18th centuries such scholars as Nicolaus Rittershausen, Philipp Jakob Spener, Georg Christian Crollius, and others made far-reaching contributions to our knowledge of European family history.

Real progress has been made possible only within the last century. In England such hard-hitting *savants* as J. Horace Round, Oswald Barron, G. E. Cokayne, and Walter Rye have demonstrated the fallacy of fabricating pedigrees and the necessity for adhering strictly to documentary evidence in reconstructing family history. Round, indeed, was the founder of the modern school of genealogy. One of his biographers wrote that "his insistence on the importance of family history gave a new value to genealogical studies, and it is probable that no other scholar has made so many or such valuable contributions to his subject." One of the neatest examples of genealogical dissections is Round's exposure of the Habsburg origin claimed by the Feildings, Earls of Denbigh and Desmond. In all of his writings he pulled no punches; his humor was biting—and effective.

We Americans, following in the footsteps of our British cousins, have not been backward in claiming fabulous origins. The Rittenhouses of Pennsylvania fondly believe themselves to be sprung from the House of Habsburg. The Springers of Delaware boast of their descent, *in the lineal male line* (!), from Charlemagne. The Howards of Lower Norfolk County, Virginia, claim the House of Arundell of Wardour as their stem—and what does it matter if the alleged ancestor of the American family died in England seventeen years before he set foot in America? These claims die hard, in spite of the fact that they have all been repeatedly exposed by competent genealogists.

Serious genealogical investigation has made as great progress in the United States during the present century as in England. Under the leadership of Donald Lines Jacobus, Editor-in-Chief of *The American Genealogist,* of New Haven, Conn., Dr. Arthur Adams, President of the American Society of Genealogists and Editor of the *New England Historical and Genealogical Register,* and others, a school of research has grown up in this country which sheds all claim to pretense. It is as hard-hitting as the school founded by Round and Barron; it exposes unequivocally the false and ridiculous allegations that continue to find their way into print; on the ruins of the pedigrees thus demolished, it endeavors to reconstruct accurately lines of descent that sometimes extend well beyond the earliest period of American colonization. In the last century we had a few good genealogists, including Col. Joseph L. Chester, who spent many years in England tracing the pre-American connections of New England families; Henry F. Waters, whose *Genealogical Gleanings* are basic sources for the English origins of American families; and Gilbert Cope, of Pennsylvania, whose activities covered also the early part of the present century. Today, we have many specialists, such as G. Andrews Moriarty, the foremost American authority on English feudal genealogy; the late William J. Hoffman, a native of Rotterdam who made the settlements and settlers of New Netherland his own particular field of investigation; Dr. Albert H. Gerberich, whose knowledge of Pennsylvania German genealogy is probably unexcelled; Margaret F. Falley, who has taught us more about Irish genealogical sources than we ever knew existed; and the regional authorities, Walter Goodwin Davis, co-editor of the *Genealogical Dictionary of Maine and New Hampshire;* Charles Carroll Gardner and the late Russell Bruce Rankin, editors of the *Genealogical Magazine of New Jersey;* Herbert F. Seversmith, whose knowledge of Long Island genealogy is second to none; Rosalie Fellows Bailey, author of a *Guide* to New York City sources which will long be the standard work on the subject; and many others.

The most exciting genealogical discoveries are made accidentally. Years ago, while reading an English translation of Gustav Freytag's *Pictures of German Life in the XVth, XVIth and XVIIth Centuries,* the author of this chapter came across excerpts from the autobiography of Friedrich Lucä, a Reformed clergyman who held several important posts in

17th century Germany. He described in entertaining fashion his courtship with Miss Elizabeth Mercer, a Scottish lass whose family had been driven to the Continent by the events which culminated in the first dethronement of the House of Stuart. Pastor Lucä mentioned several members of his lady love's family, and among them was a sister who, he said, "was married in London to a nephew of Cromwell, of the noble family of Cleipold". The significance of this passage escaped us at first, but then a sudden flash of memory made the whole picture clear. Mrs. Graff, in her *Genealogy of the Claypoole Family of Philadelphia* (1893), showed that James Claypoole, the founder of the Pennsylvania family, had married Helena Merces in Bremen, Germany (not in London) in 1658. She also showed that James' brother, John Claypoole, M.P., had married a daughter of the Protector, Oliver Cromwell, which connection was incorrectly reported by Lucä. Moreover, the Claypoole ancestry was traced to a family that had a grant of arms in 1583—a circumstance which would cause a German writer to describe it as "noble". The name *Cleipold* obviously was a German corruption of the English *Claypoole*. Furthermore, an examination (made at the author's request by Meredith Colket) of James Claypoole's personal memorandum of his marriage, preserved in the Claypoole papers in the Historical Society of Pennsylvania, revealed that Mrs. Graff had misread the name Merc*er* as Merc*es*, and so printed it in her book. In an article published in *The American Genealogist* in 1942, the present writer was thus able to demonstrate that James Claypoole, founder of a distinguished Philadelphia family, married in 1658 at Bremen, Germany, Helena, daughter of Balthasar Mercer, formerly parliamentary assessor at Edinburgh, Scotland, who fled to Germany in 1644 with his family, which consisted of his wife (born a Kennedy), several sons who are said to have gone later to India and the Canary Islands, and three daughters, of whom one was the mother of the Claypooles, another was Pastor Lucä's wife, and the third the wife of a merchant named Uckermann, of Wanfried, in Hessen-Rheinfels, Germany.

The history of a family is one continuous adventure. If properly investigated, it is not a mere record of births, marriages, and deaths. A published genealogy that contains only vital statistics makes dull reading indeed. But letters, diaries, memoirs, court records, etc., clothe the bones with flesh and blood, revivify them, and make our long-dead ancestors distinct personalities. The Tuttle family of New Haven, for instance, is famous for its diverse characters, ranging from the insane, the moronic, and the murderous, to the brilliant and public-spirited members whose whole lives were consecrated to selfless service in the cause of humanity. The story of the Wistar-Wister family of Philadelphia is that of heroic men and gracious ladies, of philanthropists and scholars, of soldiers and authors, and of men and women who labored unceasingly for the civic betterment of the community. Successive generations of the Morris family have rendered notable service to the city, state, and nation, holding high political, diplomatic, military and ecclesiastical offices. The contributions which the presidential family of Adams and the Lee family of Virginia have made to our national development are too well-known to need repetition here. Each of our states has its families, great or small, which in their own way have contributed to American progress through the centuries. It is the genealogist's job to ferret out the facts and to show how families have influenced their times and have been influenced by their times.

One of the finest examples of the contributions which a genealogist can make to our knowledge of history was provided by Meredith B. Colket, Jr. A notable fighter for freedom of conscience in 17th century New England was Anne Hutchinson. A great reference work, *The Encyclopaedia Britannica,* states (13th edition, vol. XIV, p. 12) that she was born "about 1600, . . . the daughter of a clergyman named Francis Marbury, and according to tradition, . . . a cousin of John Dryden." So much for the researches of biographers. Mr. Colket, a competent genealogist, dug into the problem. He proved that Mrs. Hutchinson was baptized 20 July 1591, some nine years prior to the estimated date of her birth.

He confirmed the "tradition" of her kinship to the Poet
Laureate of England by showing that she was his first cousin
once removed, as the granddaughter of his great-grandfather.
And what of her father, who was dismissed so casually by
the *Britannica* as "a clergyman named Francis Marbury"?
He was the author of an Elizabethan play, *The Contract of
Marriage Between Wit and Wisdom*. A card cataloguer of
the Library of Congress identified him simply as one who
"flourished" in 1579, the year in which his play was written. The genealogist proved he "flourished" all over the
place, by showing that this same Francis Marbury was baptized 27 October 1555, ordained deacon 7 January 1577-8,
ordained priest 24 June 1605, was tried before the Bishop
of London for his courageous protest over the existing order
of things, enjoyed the favor of William Cecil, Lord Burghley,
was quoted with appreciation by Sir Francis Bacon, died
shortly before 11 February 1610-11, was twice married, and
fathered *at least* 18 children!

The genealogist can render invaluable service to the
eugenicist. Dr. Arthur Adams, in an address before the Conference of Historical Studies, at the meeting of the American
Historical Association in 1922, observed: "The new interest
in heredity and the larger knowledge of its laws are being
found of value and usefulness in ways never dreamed of
by those who compiled them. Data not heretofore thought
worth including in regard to physical characteristics and
mental traits are being industriously compiled and carefully
recorded. The great regret is that so often biological data
of the kind desired cannot be obtained. Color of hair and
eyes, characteristic features, height and weight, etc., too
often now cannot be ascertained; but for present generations and for generations within the memory of those now
living such facts may be learned. If genealogists begin
at once to record such data, within a relatively short time
an adequate amount of material for the statistical and
scientific study of heredity and eugenics will have been
accumulated." Some years ago John I. Coddington discovered, in the possession of a member of the Woollens family

of Lower Dublin Township, Philadelphia Co., Pa., an album containing daguerreotypes and photographs, opposite each of which were *complete descriptions of the subjects*, such as the names, birthplaces, dates of birth, descent ("English" in all cases), names of parents, brothers and sisters (enumerated but not named), education, occupation, politics, religion, dates of marriage, stature, weight, habit (described as "average" in all cases except one, whose habit was given as "full"), complexion, color of hair and eyes, health and, in one case, date of death. These records were published in the *National Genealogical Society Quarterly* in 1942, and amply illustrate the methods whereby the genealogist may contribute to our knowledge of the personal characteristics of the American people.

Dr. Amandus Johnson, the noted authority on the Swedish settlements in the Delaware Valley, once told the National Genealogical Society in a lecture: "History is based upon biography, and biography is based upon genealogy." As the family produces the man or the woman who exerts influence for good or evil on the course of events, so the family is a contributing factor to events that may be world-shaking in importance. Whenever a man rises to prominence in public life a general interest is manifested in his antecedants. A knowledge of his genealogical background is often necessary for an understanding of his character and actions. The trained genealogist has facilities at his command that are not always known to students in other fields of learning. Consequently, he is in a position to make his printed genealogy of a given family a valuable source-book for local or national history. Cases in point are Dr. Robert C. Moon's *The Morris Family of Philadelphia,* published in five stately volumes from 1898 to 1909, and Howard Barclay French's *Genealogy of the Descendants of Thomas French* (2 vols., 1909). These works, and others like them, rise above the strictly genealogical, and are real contributions to an understanding of our historic past.

And lastly, a study of genealogy instills in us an appreciation of the American way of life. The newspaper headlines sometimes frighten us into the belief that the end of the world is at hand. But so long as we remember the principles upon which the Republic was founded, so long as we follow the example of the Chinese and emulate the traits and characteristics of our more honorable ancestors, just so long will we Americans—as the heirs of a great tradition—endure as a free people.

CHAPTER II

TRADITION AND FAMILY HISTORY *

Tradition is a chronic deceiver, and those who put faith in it are self-deceivers. This is not to say that tradition is invariably false. Sometimes a modicum of fact lies almost hidden at its base. The probability of its falsehood increases in geometric ratio as the lineage claimed increases in grandeur.

Every Rogers family has a tradition of descent from John Rogers, the Martyr; every Adams family links itself traditionally with the Braintree stem which produced two presidents. There is nothing surprising in this. It is human nature to be vain, and belief in the importance of one's family is merely an extension of personal vanity. We all prefer to hide the skeleton in the closet, and to display the heraldic device which we would fain believe our knightly ancestors sanctified with their blood.

To show how quickly and easily a tradition emerges out of nothing, let us invent a story. During the presidency of the first Adams, a humble Adams family is living in a frontier settlement. The Adams boy is asked by another whether he is related to the great man. The boy is intrigued; if a kinship can be claimed, he will be able to hold his own against the Sheriff's son when boasts of parental importance are made. So he takes the question to old "Granther" Adams, as the most likely to know. The aged man, his own days of activity over, becomes animated when thus appealed to as an authority on the family history. Well, now, he doesn't rightly know, but when he was living as a young blade back in New England, he once met a man named Adams in a tavern, and come to talk things over, they were related somehow, and he had heard it said as how this man he was talking with was connected with the Braintree Adamses.

---

* Reprinted from *The American Genealogist*, IX, July, 1932, 1-4.

Come to think of it, there probably was a connection way back. Yes, sir, he wouldn't be surprised if there was.

The elated youngster next day, when exchanging boasts with the Sheriff's son, proudly announces that he is related to President Adams. Way back, of course, but it was the same family. His grandfather told him, and he guessed his grandfather knew what he was talking about.

Twenty-five years later, the Adams youngster is a man of affairs, with boys of his own. The Adams myth, from constant retelling in his own boyhood, has become fixed in his mind as an implacable fact, true as gospel. He could not repeat exactly, if asked to do so, the maundering words of his grandfather, but he was certainly left with a distinct impression that a relationship existed. In all these years, the reality of the claim never has been disproved, probably not even challenged. When he pridefully tells his own boys about the Adams family, he believes he is telling the strict truth. Yes, boys, we belong to the same family as President Adams; I had it straight from my grandfather's own lips.

Thus, in a quarter of a century, a strong, enduring tradition has completed its miraculous growth. Thus do the tiny seeds of vanity germinate and produce the towering trees of an illustrious Family History.

While our example is entirely fictitious, every experienced genealogist knows of erroneous and thoroughly disproved traditions which must have originated in some such way. Nor are such erroneous traditions restricted to claims of exalted lineage or connection. They may refer merely to the nationality of the immigrant ancestor, or to the original place of residence in this country, or to any other detail of the family history.

Among families whose surnames are of French origin, or are similar to French names, there is likely to be the French Huguenot tradition. Genealogists who realize how many Norman-French names were carried into England with the Conqueror, do well to view such claims with suspicion until proved. Traditions of Welsh origin of early colonial families are seldom verified.

In one family it was understood that an ancestor was French, came over with Lafayette and served under him in the Revolutionary War. But this ancestor's birth and death records were actually found in his father's family Bible, and the ancestry in this country went back to 1644; he did serve in the Revolution, and his son married a woman whose ancestry was originally French. There had been here some mingling of tradition from different sides of the family.

It was supposed in another family that the first known male line ancestor (born in 1767) came from Martha's Vineyard. Investigation revealed not a single occurrence of the surname in the vital records of the Vineyard prior to 1850. The ancestry was eventually located elsewhere. But this ancestor married a girl who was born on Martha's Vineyard. Here the tradition was correct, except that it had become associated with the wrong ancestral line.

We all recognize the fallibility of tradition when the traditions of some other person's family are questioned. When our own are at stake, it is a different matter. Our grandmother had a marvelous memory, and we *know* that every word she told us was gospel truth. After all, she was *our* grandmother, and it is asking a great deal to suggest that we give up one detail of her cherished memoirs.

The present writer had a great-uncle who took an interest in the family history, and my mother wrote down his account. He started with his great-grandfather, who was one of three brothers who came over. Actually, he *was* one of three brothers, but they were of the fourth generation in America. Did my great-uncle merely assume that the first ancestor he knew about was the original settler, or did my mother misunderstand him? They both possessed good minds for details, yet this much of error crept into the account.

Just why so many traditions center around three brothers who came over, is a problem that has never been solved. Brothers often did come to America, but there were instances of two brothers, and even of four and five, as well as of **three**.

The dear old aunt of the writer was born a Wilmot, and firmly believed in the high, even titled, connections of the family. She had, indeed, a detailed account which on slight provocation she could be induced to relate. We were of the same blood as the notorious John Wilmot, Earl of Rochester. Parenthetically, it should be explained that the old lady did not know of Rochester's reputation for profligacy, and the writer never enlightened her. The last descendant of Rochester, according to her story, had died leaving a large property, including an entire square in London. The nearest heir was a maiden lady named Wilmot who had come to this country from England and lived in the same city with my aunt's brother. She died before taking possession of the property. My uncle had met her and discussed the family history with her, and they were agreed that our branch of Wilmots were "next in line."

In vain did I protest that the Earl of Rochester's only son died a minor, and that the title died with him, while the family estates descended to the daughters who carried them by marriage into other familes. She merely set her lips in a firm line and said, "Well, I'm not lying about it; I guess I know what I know."

Of course she was not lying. Just how this story originated can only be surmised. Quite likely the Wilmot lady from England was deluded by an "inheritance mania" and imagined much of what she told to my relatives; and it is not impossible that my aunt in part misunderstood or misinterpreted the story.

Again, on the writer's paternal side, there was a story of a lost inheritance. My grandfather, early in life, joined an association of Anneke Jans heirs, as he understood that his Doremus grandmother was a descendant. The marriage certificate of his parents was turned over to the association's lawyer, and never recovered, and it was believed that the lawyer "sold out" to the opposing interests. This was the story as it came to me from my grandfather's lips. But so far as my own investigations have gone, I have failed to find a scrap of evidence to prove that my Doremus ancestress descended from Anneke Jans at all. Perhaps she did, but it is very doubtful, and until and unless record proof is forthcoming, I shall not claim the line.

It is natural for people to feel that a special sanctity inheres in the traditions of their own family. To doubt them is to doubt the veracity of their parents and grandparents. The genealogist should therefore be gentle and tactful when his investigations run counter to the cherished traditions. Those who employ genealogists, on the other hand, should realize that their genealogist gets no pleasure out of destroying their traditions. He is employed to ascertain the truth, and it is his duty to report what the records reveal.

Although few traditions prove to be true in every particular, the genealogist should not, with a superior air, dismiss a tradition as unworthy of consideration. Occasionally, a traditional statement is found to be very close to the truth. The majority of them contain some element of truth, however misapplied or encircled with error. Therefore, traditions should be sifted and tested, and utilized as clues, but not accepted as true until verified from contemporary documentary sources.

CHAPTER III

INTERPRETING GENEALOGICAL RECORDS *

Before we have handled genealogical records very long, we discover that considerable special knowledge is required to enable us to interpret the records we find. It is not merely, if we seek out ancient public records, that there is a difficulty in reading the script of three centuries ago, and that considerable practice is required before we are able to read it fluently. But even if we limit ourselves to printed copies of ancient records, we find many terms used which we do not understand, and we are particularly puzzled when words that are entirely familiar are used in a different sense from that which they possess today. A few of these we shall explain here.

The terms "Mr." and "Mrs." in the 17th century were reserved for persons of social position, and the early colonial settlers used these terms in the same sense to which they had been accustomed in England. They denoted people of "gentle" birth; and a "gentleman" in the English sense was a man who did not perform useful labor but derived his living from the income received from the rental of lands. They might be very wealthy, or they might have to scrimp to make both ends meet, but these people, the landed gentry, constituted the aristrocracy.

If younger sons became ministers or barristers, they remained "gentlemen," but it did very often happen that the younger sons of the less wealthy families entered a trade. Conversely, it often happened that a tradesman of ability, or a merchant, acquired wealth; then, if he cared for social recognition, he would buy an estate from some impoverished gentleman, pay the heralds' fee for a coat-of-arms, and perhaps even buy a fabricated pedigree to prove his gentility. Thus, although there were families which had held an as-

---

* Reprinted (with modifications) from *The American Genealogist*, X, July 1933, 2-6, XI, July 1934, 9-11, XIX, July 1942, 8-10.

sured position for many generations, there was in fact much moving up and down the social scale. Social position, then as always in human history, depended on the possession of some form of material wealth.

The colonists were very strict, at first, in limiting the use of the term "Mr." to those whose families belonged to the landed gentry, to ministers, and to those whose official position entitled them to it. In assigning seats in the church or meeting house, great attention was paid to social importance, though some concession was made to people who were hard of hearing. Otherwise, the gentlemen had the first pews, then came the respectable tradesmen and farmers, and lastly the servants and those of low social rating.

The term "Mrs." was applied to both married and unmarried gentlewomen, a fact of genealogical significance which is too often overlooked.

Substantial citizens who were not entitled to the prefix of gentility were formally addressed as "Goodman Jones" or "Goodwife Morris," and the feminine title was often shortened to "Goody." In determining the social position of an ancestor, it is well to scrutinize every record to see what terms of respect were applied to him, how closely he was seated to the pulpit in the meeting house, and who were his intimate friends and associates.

Ignorance of these rudimentary principles has been responsible for the printing of a great deal of nonsense by amateur family historians. Some have recklessly identified an immigrant ancestor as younger son of an English knight or peer, when the appellation of "Goodman" and similar considerations clearly demonstrate that his ancestry should be sought in the yeoman or tradesman class. The compiler of a Dunham genealogy evolved the fantastic theory that the first John Dunham, who was referred to in certain records as "Goodman" Dunham, was identical with John Goodman of the *Mayflower*. He could not have considered the prefix "Goodman" as evidential if he had known the frequency with which it was applied.

The term "servant" did not necessarily imply social inferiority, but merely "one who serves." That is to say, there was no fixed and permanent servant class among the colonial settlers of New England. A boy was often apprenticed, most generally at about the age of fourteen for seven years, to learn a trade. While serving his apprenticeship, he was the "servant" of the man to whom he was apprenticed who during that term was his "master". The master was obliged by the "articles" of apprenticeship to supply the boy with food and clothing and often a certain amount of education, besides teaching him his trade, and sometimes it was provided that the boy upon attaining his majority should receive a modest amount of money or its equivalent in land or livestock. Whatever the boy could earn beyond that, belonged to his "master".

Sometimes a boy was apprenticed to an uncle or other relative, and more often than not, his family belonged to the same social class as the family of his master. It was no unusual thing for an attachment to spring up between an apprentice and a daughter of his master, culminating in a marriage alliance. A family in which there were too many girls might arrange for one of the daughters to enter the household of a neighboring family in which there were too many boys. Such domestic service did not lower the girl's social status below that of the family in which she worked, unless she entered the service of a "gentleman's" family who even without such service were already her social superiors.

The primitive economic conditions of the country in colonial days should be recognized, and those who are inexperienced in genealogical research should abandon all preconceived ideas of social distinctions and study conditions as they actually were; otherwise, they are certain to misinterpret the records they find.

Terms used to denote degrees of relationship had somewhat different meanings than they have today, and this too is a stumbling-block to amateurs. First of all, husband and wife were identified as one person. Hence, when a man writes in his will of "my brother Jones" and "my sister Jones," he may be referring to his own sister and her husband, to his wife's sister and her husband, or to his wife's brother and that brother's spouse.

It is not always possible to decide, in the will of a Puritan around 1650, whether the "Brother Peck" and "Brother Perkins" whom he appointed overseers of his estate were relations by marriage or merely brothers in the church. The expression "*my* Brother Peck" makes it sound a little more like relationship, but is not conclusive. The same uncertainty attaches to the use of the term "sister" in these early wills.

The term "in law" implies a kinship that came about through marriage rather than through lineal or blood connection. The term "brother-in-law" nearly always means either a sister's husband or a wife's brother; which it means has to be determined through other considerations. A man's father-in-law was either his wife's father or his own mother's second husband. Amateurs are sometimes bewildered by a record which states that a boy of fourteen chose his father-in-law for guardian; of course, "stepfather" is meant. In the same way, "mother-in-law" meant either a man's stepmother or his wife's mother. When, in the settlement of an estate, the widow and children of the deceased made an agreement, and the children made provision for their mother-in-law, this proves that she was a second or later wife and not the mother of the children. The terms "son-in-law" and "daughter-in-law" had also the same double meanings.

Many errors in books prepared by compilers of insufficient knowledge are caused by such misinterpretations of records. A Hitchcock Genealogy, for example, suggests that two daughters of John Hitchcock married two Lines brothers, though upon investigation we find that they were well provided with wives without such a Hitchcock alliance. The explanation is simple. John Hitchcock had married the mother of the Lines brothers and hence was referred to in a record as their father-in-law.

The term "cousin" is perhaps the one which is most puzzling to the untrained searcher. It was applied loosely to almost any type of relationship outside the immediate

family circle. It was most frequently used to denote a
nephew or niece, but it could also be applied to a first cousin
or more distant cousin, or to the marital spouse of any of
these relatives, and sometimes to other indirect connections
who were not even related by blood. The first guess should
be that a nephew or niece was meant; if this does not work
out, then try to prove that a cousin in our sense of the word
was meant; if this also proves impossible, it may require
long and profound study to determine just what the connection was. This applies, generally speaking, to the use
of the term in the colonies prior to 1750. No definite and
exact date can be fixed, for the terms nephew and niece
gradually supplanted cousin to denote that form of relationship.

The word "nephew" is derived from the Latin *nepos* which
meant grandson. Sometimes it meant the father's grandson,
hence a man's nephew. The original meaning of the word
survived many centuries, and the writer has seen wills in
this country in which grandchildren, both boys and girls,
were called nephews. But for the most part, even in early
colonial days, it was used, as at present, to denote the son
of a brother or sister; or occasionally, the daughter of a
brother or sister.

In the 17th century, the expression "my natural son" or
"my natural brother" usually meant a son or brother by
blood as opposed to a son or brother by marriage or adoption,
and did not imply illegitimacy. In English wills of the 17th
century or earlier, an illegitimate child would be described
as "my base son" (or daughter) or even "my bastard son"
(or daughter), the latter term being then merely descriptive
and not opprobrious.

Perhaps no phrase has caused more confusion, not only
to amateur-searchers but even to very experienced genealogists, than that of "my now wife" or "my present wife".
Almost invariably it is taken to mean that the testator or
grantor must have had a former wife before the one named
or referred to in the document. It need not mean anything
of the sort, unless the maker of the document is drawing a

distinction between the children he had by a former wife and those he had by his present wife. Ordinarily, it was merely a legal phrase, precautionary rather than explanatory. A man could leave nothing to a former, dead wife. But he could marry a second wife if his "now wife" should die, and the specified bequests were intended for the wife to whom he was married at the time, not for some wife he might marry in the unknown future.

Now a man's wife might be the only wife he had ever had, and the mother of his children. He might wish to make unusually generous provision for her. If after making his will she should die and he should marry again, and he should die without having made a new will, he might not wish this second, later wife to have more than her legal dower, or such provision as might be made for her in a prenuptial contract. If his will made the more generous provision simply for "my wife", there might be a bare chance that a later wife could claim that he intended this provision for the benefit of whoever happened to be his wife when he died. Hence the scribes or notaries who wrote the wills and deeds often employed these phrases, "my present wife" and "my now wife," to provide against such a contingency. Sometimes, of course, it happened that the man had been married before; often he had not. But in either event, this phrase was not necessary to protect his heirs against a former, dead wife, who never could make any claim, but against a possible future wife.

Those who consult 17th century records should be familiar with an odd substitute for the possessive case of nouns, then prevalent. Instead of writing "Jones's brother Smith," the early scribe frequently wrote, "Jones his brother Smith". Or, he might write, "Smith his house," or "the widow Johnson her son". The use of the pronoun in place of the possessive case is confusing to those who have not familiarized themselves with it, and sometimes leads to incorrect interpretations of early records.

The use of two surnames, joined by the word "alias", is puzzling to the novice. There were several causes for the adoption of two surnames. Sometimes in England, when a man had married an heiress and the children inherited her estates, they were known both by the father's and the mother's names. Sometimes a child whose father died early was known in youth by a stepfather's name, and later adopted the alias to make his identity clear, joining the own father's surname to that of the stepfather. Again, in cases of adoption, the original name and that of the foster parent were both retained and joined with an "alias". But when we find in early American records a man referred to as "John Noon alias Night," the most usual explanation is that John was of illegitimate birth, that Noon was the name of his reputed father, and that Night was his mother's name. However, in case of other possible reasons for the alias, illegitimacy should not be assumed without investigation of the specific circumstances.

The terms "senior" and "junior" did not as a rule imply the relationship of father and son until we reach the 19th century. In a day when middle names were not generally given to children, the rapid increase of the early colonial families quite naturally produced many individuals with identical names. Such individuals found it necessary to adopt some method of distinction, to avoid confusion, when signing deeds or other documents. The elder was called "Sr." and the younger "Jr." whether they were father and son, uncle and nephew, or cousins. Serious mistakes are found in many family histories because of the failures of the compilers to inform themselves in this matter, and their insistence that "Jr." must have been son of "Sr."

For example, Gerard or Jarard Spencer of Haddam, Conn., in his will dated 6 June 1738, proved 15 Jan. 1744/5, gave lands to his "sons Jarrard Spencer Junr Benjamin Spencer Daniel Spencer Junr Ephraim Spencer" and to the children of his eldest son John Spencer deceased.[1] It will be seen that he had two sons whom he called "Jr.", one of them obviously because named after himself. But what about the son whom he called Daniel, Jr.? Gerard had a first

---
[1] Colchester Probate District, File No. 2827.

cousin Daniel, much younger than himself and not much older than Gerard's son Daniel, and this cousin, because of seniority of age, was known as "Sr."

Those who search documentary sources encounter this phenomenon constantly. In one town, five men named John Hall lived contemporaneously, and they were strictly labeled, according to age, Sr., Jr., 3d, 4th, and 5th. When Sr. died, each stepped up a notch, Jr. becoming Sr., and so on; for these appellations did not remain attached permanently to the same individual, but were applied to distinguish between *living* men of the same name in the *same township*. If John Hall 4th moved to some other town, he was no longer of Wallingford, hence John Hall, formerly 5th, would automatically become "John Hall, 4th, of the town of Wallingford". The writer has actually seen deeds in which a man called himself "John Doe, Jr., formerly 3d." The novice becomes hopelessly confused in his efforts to determine the identity of the John Doe who was his ancestor when confronted with a perfect labyrinth of John Does.

It has often been observed that the early land records, unlike those of later date, contain much genealogical information. After 1800, the deeds only rarely show more than that a man bought and sold, unless a group of heirs convey inherited property, either singly or as a group. Even these later deeds are useful, for sometimes a man bought land in a place before he came there to live, and the purchase deed states his former habitat. Also, a man sometimes removed from a town before he had disposed of all his land there, and his last sale then shows his new place of residence. Identity is frequently established in this way during the period of migration to the West.

But even in the colonial period there is much variation in the amount of genealogical data contained in the deeds in different places. In some towns it is very apparent that the justice or notary who drew most of the deeds over a term of years had the type of mind which likes to be specific and to give every relevant detail. Deeds drawn by such men are a boon to the genealogist. The writer has seen them specify that the land belonged to a great-grandfather of the grantors, with the descent of the land (or the right to it) traced with full names and relationships through the intervening generations In other towns, the magistrate who drew the deeds seemed to delight in withholding all the information he could, and would merely have the grantors assert that they had right and title to convey the land in question, with no explanation of how they acquired the right and title.

Once an argument arose that B was not son of A, because A in conveying land to B failed to call him his son, although, so the local genealogist claimed, it was then customary in that town at that period to mention such relationships when they existed. The writer examined the deeds recorded in that town with some care, and made this discovery. When a man conveyed to his son "for love and affection," the deed specifically says "to my son," that being the consideration for the conveyance of the land. But when, as occasionally happened, a son bought land from his father, the consideration was the amount of money paid, and in such cases no relationship was stated, and for all the deeds show, the grantor and grantee might have been utter strangers who happened to have the same surname.

If we must draw a moral, the moral is that conditions and practices varied in different places and at different times, and that it is not always safe to draw general conclusions from limited experience or from research in a limited territory.

CHAPTER IV

GENEALOGY AND CHRONOLOGY *

Dates

Names, dates and places are the working material of the genealogist, and for ease and accuracy in handling dates the genealogist should possess or develop a mathematical mind. He should see at a glance that a man born in 1738 was too young to marry in 1751; and that he probably did not marry a woman born in 1724. Experience teaches him to weigh problems of dates and to draw conclusions from them almost instantaneously.

When very few positive dates are available, and the genealogist desires to check the probability of an alleged pedigree or a series of relationships, it is helpful to assign "guessed" dates of births. If the children of given parents are known, but not their birth dates, these can be guessed from known dates. If the age at death of one of the children is found stated, then for this one we have an approximate date of birth, probably not more than a year away from fact in either direction. We thus can work from the known towards the unknown, and group the other children about the one with the fixed date. The marriage dates of some of the children may be known, and birth dates may be guessed from these, on the basis that a boy married at from 22 to 26, and a girl at from 18 to 24. When one of the girls had recorded children born from 1721 to 1745, for example, then at a glance we can set down 1700-1701 almost with certainty as the approximate time of her birth, because here we have the known limits of the period of child-bearing to guide us.

Such "guessed" dates should be clearly marked in some way to avoid confusion with positive dates that have record authority. They can be placed in brackets, thus: [say 1700].

---

* Originally published under the title, "Dates and the Calendar", in *The American Genealogist*, vol. IX, Jan. 1933.

Or the date can be preceded by the word "circa", Latin meaning "about", or its abbreviation, "c." or "ca."

When we have arrived at such approximate dates for the births of all the children, the advantage is the picture it gives us of the family as a whole. Perhaps our problem is the parentage of one Charles Evans, and we suspect that he belonged in the family group whose approximate ages we have been working out. We know, let us say, from his age at death, that he was born about 1685. Let us suppose that the births of this group of children we worked out can be placed with extreme probability between 1698 and 1715. It then appears that our Charles, born about 1685, was more probably of the previous generation, possibly an uncle of the children whose ages we guessed.

For many reasons it is advantageous in doing genealogical research to consider *the family group,* not to look upon each ancestor as an isolated individual, or as a mere link in a chain of descent. One of the most important reasons is, that it enables us to check the chronology. Very often, the relations of dates determine or negate the possibility of an alleged line of descent, or provide clues which might otherwise elude detection. It is a good idea to write out the full family history, or chart the relationships, while working, inclusive of "guessed" dates where positive dates are not known. It is a great aid to the memory as well as to the imagination, if the eye can see the members of the family grouped together.

There is one technical matter that affects dates and needs to be studied in some detail if the genealogist is to understand and properly interpret the Old Style dates; this is the important calendar change of 1752. As few things are more confusing to the inexperienced searcher, a complete explanation of it will be given.

The Calendar

The Julian calendar was used throughout the Middle Ages in Europe. Its inaccuracy amounted to about three days in every four centuries. By the time the Gregorian

Calendar (named after Pope Gregory XIII) was adopted in 1582, calendar dates were ahead of actual time by ten days. Since actual time is the time it takes the earth for one complete revolution about the sun (a year), if the calendar had been left uncorrected, in the course of centuries the present summer months would have come in the winter, and vice versa.

Although the Roman Catholic countries adopted the Gregorian calendar in 1582, the conservatism of the English, and the fact that the new calendar was sponsored by a Pope, delayed the acceptance of it in Great Britain and her colonies until after the passage of an Act of Parliament in 1751.[1] By this time, the old calendar was eleven days ahead of sun time, so the Act provided that in 1752, the second day of September should be followed by the fourteenth day of September. In other words, what would have been September 3rd was called the 14th, exactly eleven days being thus dropped out of the year.

The cause of the error was the addition of a day to the calendar each fourth year (Leap Year). This very nearly made the average year correspond with sun time, but not quite. In every 400 years, as above stated, the calendar went three days ahead of sun time. The dropping of the eleven days in 1752 brought the calendar back into harmony with sun time; and to provide against a recurrence of the trouble, it was also provided that on the even centuries, no Leap Year day should be added except in a century divisible by 400. Thus, 1800 and 1900 were not Leap Years, but the year 2000 will be. In this way, in the 400 years beginning with 1752, there will be three days less than there were in each 400 years preceding 1752, hence the old error will not be repeated.

So little did the people understand the need for the calendar revision that an angry mob gathered outside the Houses of Parliament, demanding that the eleven days

---

[1] The Greek Church did not approve the calendar revision and consequently Greece, Bulgaria and Russia were on the Old Style calendar until the first World War, when they were thirteen days ahead of sun time.

filched out of their lives be restored to them. Actually, calling the third day of September the fourteenth day did not deprive any person of eleven days of his life, any more than changing a man's name from Bill to Tom would make him a different person. The real effect was to make every person born on or before 2 September 1752 eleven days older (by the new calendar) than the record of his birth (in Old Style) would indicate. A child born on 2 September 1752 (the last day of the Old Style) would be, by the calendar, twelve days old on the following day, 14 September 1752 (the first day of the New Style).

People do not like to be considered older than they really are, not even eleven days older. It was natural that those living in 1752 should "rectify" their birth dates. George Washington was born 11 February 1731/2. In 1752, the calendar change automatically made him eleven days older, so like most men of his generation, he rectified his birth date, making it 22 February 1732. The latter is the date on which he *would have been born* if the New Style calendar had been in effect in 1732—which it was not.

Although it was (and is) incorrect to change the dates prior to September, 1752, to New Style, it was done to such an extent by those living in 1752 that the genealogist has to make allowance for it. Suppose, for example, that a group of brothers and sisters were born between the years 1743 and 1760. The older children were born before the calendar change, and in the town records the Old Style dates were therefore used in entering their births. The first child was born, let us say, 25 May 1743. Now, after all the children had been born, the parents bought a Bible, say about 1765, and entered in it their own marriage and the births of the children, giving *New Style* dates for *all* the children, including those born before 1752 whose birth days should properly have been entered Old Style. As a result, we find that the eldest child (whose birth in the contemporary town records had been entered as 25 May 1743) was entered in the Bible as born 5 June 1743. Both dates are correct, but the former is the date that *ought* to be used, unless the latter has the words "New Style" added to indicate that it is a "rectified" date.

A further effect of this change must be mentioned. When a man died after 1752, assuming that he was born before September, 1752, and his age at death was stated exactly in years, months and days, the resultant date of birth (figured from the age at death) is the New Style date of birth, and therefore eleven days later than the recorded Old Style date of birth.

For example, Ephraim Burr, by his gravestone, died 29 April 1776, aged 76 years and 13 days. Subtracting the age gives us 16 April 1700 for his birth, but of course to get the Old Style date then in use we must subtract eleven days more. His birth was not recorded, but he was *baptized* 14 April 1700, two days before his New Style date of birth. After subtracting the eleven days, we find that his real date of birth, in accordance with the Old Style calendar then in use, was 5 April 1700, which was nine days *before* he was baptized. Obviously, he could not have been born two days *after* baptism, which is the result we get if we fail to make allowance for the calendar change.

It is very necessary that the genealogist, professional or amateur, should thoroughly understand this calendar change, or he will miss proofs of identity furnished by the comparison of birth records with stated ages at death.

When a child was born before 1752, and the birth was recorded contemporaneously, add eleven days to the date to obtain the New Style equivalent.

When a person born prior to September, 1752 died after that date and the death record states the *exact* age, subtract the age from the date of death, and then subtract eleven days more to obtain the Old Style equivalent.

Exact ages were not always stated, and unless the *days* are specified, the presumption is that the age is not exact. When the record states that a man died aged fifty years and eight months, he may have been that age to a day, but he may have been a few days over the fifty years and eight months. Recorders did not always bother to specify the age to a day, nor did those who had gravestones erected always so specify.

In order to make quite clear the effect of the calendar change, to those who have difficulty in grasping it, the following was the order of days in 1752 beginning with August 30.

30 August
31 August
1 September
2 September
14 September
15 September

New Year's Day

One other change was made in 1752, and that was the date of beginning the New Year. It is understood by everyone that between one spring and the next a year has elapsed, similarly between one autumn and the next. But when we assign numbers to the years for convenience in referring to them, it is necessary to begin the new year on a particular day. The succession of seasons and years is entirely natural, caused by the orbit of the earth about the sun. But selecting one certain day on which to start a new year is an artificial and an arbitrary thing. Consequently, various peoples in various ages have celebrated different New Year's Days. Some of the ancient races ended their year with a Harvest Festival, and the Jews still retain that season. Others began the year with the Vernal Equinox, and since Easter fell near that season, the date quite generally used for the religious New Year's Day by Christians was 25 March. There was no uniformity in the early centuries, and some began the year on 25 December, the traditional birthday of Christ.

The only dates for New Year's Day which were in use in American colonial days among the English settlers were 25 March and 1 January. The latter was the beginning of the legal year, while the former, as we have seen, had more religious significance. The Act of Parliament in 1751 established 1 January as New Year's Day for 1752 and subsequent years. Thereafter, we are not bothered by the confusion that existed when the year had two possible beginnings.

Now, this change did not, like the dropping of eleven days, have any effect on the ages of persons then living. This will be seen if we suppose that it should be decided hereafter to celebrate the Fourth of July on Armistice Day. A person born 4 May would still be born on 4 May; and when New Year's Day was shifted from 25 March to 1 January, it did not affect the birthday of a man born on 4 May. His birthday was still 4 May, Old Style, or 15 May, New Style.

Some have misunderstood the effects of the change in New Year's Day, and have supposed that it caused a difference of nearly three months in people's ages.[2] When the names of the months of birth were entered, such a notion is unthinkable. Before 1700, the early recorders sometimes used the *number* of the month instead of its *name*. This was the practice of the Quakers, and occasionally survived until a later period. Of course, March was then numbered as the first month, since New Year's Day fell in it, and dates before the 25th were considered as belonging to the first month, as well as dates after the 25th. April was the second month, and May the third. The early Quaker records were often very precise, stating that an event occurred "on the 10th of the 5th month which is called July."

When the *number* of the month was stated in any record prior to 1752, the genealogist should reckon March as the first month, and February as the twelfth.

If a record states that John Jones was born on the 10th of the fifth month, 1710, this must be Old Style, and means that he was born in July. After 1752, July became the seventh instead of the fifth month, but this does not affect the fact that John Jones was born in July.

Before 1752, there is likely to be some confusion with

---

[2] See, for example, the explanatory notes prefaced to the recent *Coolidge Genealogy*, for the expression of such a misunderstanding.

regard to dates between 1 January and 24 March, unless we know what New Year's Day a particular recorder used. It is apparent that if the year began 25 March, a man born on 20 February was born before the new year began, hence a year earlier than it would be by New Style. If 1710 began on 25 March, then a man born on 20 February following was born in 1710, since 1711 did not begin until the next month. Dates between 1 January and 24 March fell in the preceding year if Old Style was used; but if New Style was used, this threw all dates after 1 January into the new year.

The only problem in this connection is the *year* in which a man was born, and we always run the chance of an error of *exactly a year* if we do not know which calendar the recorder used. Back of 1700, we can usually assume that the year began on 25 March, and this is true of most church registers until 1752. But after 1700, the use of 1 January was gradually coming into favor, especially in legal documents and town records.

Careful recorders used a double date, and when this was done all confusion or uncertainty is eliminated. George Washington was born 11 February 1731/2, which means that the year was still 1731 if the New Year was reckoned as not beginning until 25 March, but that the year was already 1732 if it had begun 1 January. That is, it was 1731 Old Style, or 1732 New Style. Genealogists should always copy the double date when it is given in the records for the single date is an uncertain one. The date 11 February 1731, Old Style, is identical with 22 February 1732, New Style.

Sometimes records in Old Style look peculiar to us. In Norwich, Conn., vital records, we read that Robert Wade married 11 March 1691, and the eldest child was born January 1691. We may assume that the marriage occurred 11 March 1690/1, this recorder happening to use the later year date here because he was thinking of March as the first month of the new year; the child was born January 1691/2, ten months later. It was still 1691, Old Style.

Remember that this confusion, before 1752, of year dates,

applies only to dates between 1 January and 24 March, since all other dates belong to the same year regardless of when New Year's Day was celebrated.

CHAPTER V

THE RULES OF EVIDENCE: A STANDARD FOR PROVING PEDIGREES

"But now instead of records, the upshot is a little lousy history .... Is a printed history, written by I know not who, an evidence in a court of law?"
                                       LORD CHIEF JUSTICE JEFFREYS [1]

During the Revolutionary War a young woman named Jennie McRae was murdered and mutilated by Indians. This sad event has resulted in 122 separate accounts of Jennie's death. When a twentieth century historian made a comparison of these 122 versions, he was amazed to find these accounts agreed only in one particular, namely, that Jennie had been murdered.

The case of Jennie McRae is illustrative of the necessity of a body of rules to guide the genealogist. There has never been a suitable standard devised by genealogists for accepting or rejecting genealogical facts. Every genealogist has been a law unto himself, operating with his own set of rules. Genealogists of recognized standing compile pedigrees with the same care as if they were to be presented in a court proceeding. On the other hand, there is the rank amateur whose only standard is that the information came from some printed source.

Considerable confusion can be eliminated if everyone engaged in genealogical research followed one body of rules in accepting or rejecting genealogical facts. The advantages are two-fold: (1) Genealogists will compile more accurate pedigrees because it will be necessary for them to apply strict rules in evaluating source material; (2) by applying a recognized standard of proof, it will be possible to assign logical and objective reasons for the acceptance or rejection of genealogical facts, instead of one's own personal rules.

What body of rules should be adopted? Fortunately, there is a body of rules already in existence that applies to gene-

---

[1] *Mossam* v. *Ivy*, 10 How. St. Tr. 555, 625 (1684).

alogy. These are the rules of evidence applied in courts of general jurisdiction. On those occasions when a matter of pedigree, ancestry, or heirship is in issue in a court proceeding, these rules of evidence are in force. For that reason there is no body of rules more applicable to genealogy.

Of course, it is seldom that the results of a genealogist's search become the subject matter of a trial in court, but in a very practical manner every genealogist in passing on the truth or falsity of genealogical data is acting as a court or jury.

The rules of evidence that follow are those that are applicable to genealogy and their application should result in genealogical compilations of the most accurate type.

Standard of Proof

What standard of proof should apply to genealogy? First, it must be clear that genealogical facts, except in rare instances, cannot be proven to an *absolute certainty*. There are few things in life that can be so proven and matters of pedigree are no exception, unless it is possible to produce an eyewitness to such an event as a birth, marriage, or death. For example, a doctor who delivered an infant is competent to testify of his own personal knowledge as to the identity of the child's mother. The doctor's testimony cannot be used to prove the child's paternity to an absolute certainty because the doctor cannot know of his own personal knowledge who the child's father is.

Therefore, if a pedigree cannot be proven to an *absolute certainty*, what standard is applied? In civil matters before the courts, the requirement is that the party seeking to establish facts or prove the case, must do so by a *preponderance of the evidence*. *Preponderance of the evidence* simply means proving a case by a greater weight of the evidence, or offering such proof as to convince the court or jury that the party producing the proof is right.

It is often said by researchers that they have conclusively proven a genealogical connection to be true. Such a statement is seldom correct, except in the rare cases where living eye-witnesses are available who have personal knowledge of the facts. Even in the case of an eye-witness, proof to an absolute certainty may fail if the credibility of the eye-witness is doubted. For these reasons, the courts do not require the high standard of proof of *absolute certainty*. The law only requires that the parties to a controversy involving a pedigree prove their case by a preponderance of the evidence, and that is not always easy!

What is Evidence?

Evidence is information. It may be correct or false, but it is that which the mind considers in respect to an inquiry. We should distinguish between evidence and proof. Evidence is the information received, whereas proof is the effect produced by this information. When sufficient evidence is presented, proof is established.

The rules of evidence are the laws which govern the admission or exclusion of evidence. *Just because certain evidence is admitted, that is, permitted to be considered (such as specific facts contained in a printed family history), does not mean that proof is the automatic result.* The proponent of the family history is subject to examination and it may be shown that the family genealogy, county history, or other matter may not be correct. It is then up to the court or jury to make the final decision. After evidence is admitted, it is the function of the court or jury to pass on the credibility, weight, and authenticity of the evidence and accept or reject it.

A genealogist is performing the functions of a court or jury when he sits in judgment on the evidence to prove specific genelogical facts. He passes on its admissibility, considers the weight and credibilty of the evidence, and then makes a decision based on that evidence.

The Nature of Evidence

The nature of evidence should not be confused with its forms, which will be discussed later. Evidence is either direct or circumstantial. Direct evidence is information which directly and instantaneously brings about a conclusion on a disputed issue. Direct evidence is always relevant. Whether circumstantial evidence is admissible depends on whether or not it is relevant.

Circumstantial Evidence

Circumstantial evidence does not make an instant and automatic inference upon the issue. It raises a thought or idea in the mind, and imparts information from which something in respect to the question may be inferred.

The application of the rule of circumstantial evidence in genealogy is best illustrated by a hypothetical case. Assume you were tracing the ancestry of Titus Tumblebug Thompson. You found that John Thompson married Elizabeth Tumblebug, daughter of Titus Tumblebug. Furthermore, the Thompson and Tumblebug families lived on adjoining farms. Stipulate there are no other records available. Assume you were called to testify. If you testified to the above facts in that manner you would be testifying as a lay witness. As such you could just testify to those facts; you could not testify he was a son, as that would be a conclusion on your part. Your testimony would be circumstantial evidence. The possibility that Titus Tumblebug Thompson was the son of John and Elizabeth and grandson of Titus Tumblebug is an inference for the court or jury to make from your testimony, not you.

If you were called to testify as an expert witness, your qualifications would be brought out on direct examination, they would meet the test, and you would testify as an expert. In answer to a hypothetical question, you would state that, in your opinion, Titus Tumblebug Thompson was a son of John and Elizabeth and a grandson of Titus Tumblebug, and you would give your reasons for your opinion. This would be direct evidence, because the evidence would act on the minds of the jury directly.

Relevancy

In the law of evidence, two requirements of relevancy must exist. Logical relevancy: There must be a relationship between the evidence and the controversy. Legal relevancy:

The proposed evidence must be of sufficient probative value.

Material and Competent Evidence

Immaterial evidence means that the proposed evidence goes to prove a fact not properly in issue. Competency really means that a person is qualified to testify. However, the term has been used to describe the character of the evidence offered. A person, in order to qualify as a witness, must be intelligent enough to receive and impart facts and must not suffer from certain mental or physical disabilities that would render him imcompetent as a witness.

Opinion Evidence

The general rule is that a witness must state only facts which he has acquired through the use of his own senses. An opinion is a *conclusion* formed by the mind. Generally, opinion evidence is not admissible. There are, however, exceptions to this rule. A lay witness, for example, may testify to the mental and physical condition of another person, values with which he is familiar, and the speed of various things. The testimony of an expert witness is admissible under some conditions. Before a genealogist would be allowed to testify as an expert witness, it would be necessary to examine him on the witness stand to show that he can qualify as an expert in his field. This is done by his answering questions relative to his education, training, and experience.

Forms of Evidence

The forms of evidence should not be confused with its nature nor with the method of introduction of evidence. Evidence may be classified into the following forms: (1) Testimony of witnesses; (2) Documents or writings; (3) Real evidence, such as photographs, sound recordings, or view (such as by the jury).

TESTIMONY OF WITNESSES.—A test of competency is whether the witness has received and can impart correct information.

DOCUMENTARY EVIDENCE.—includes any writing, documents

of any kind, books, papers, accounts, etc. The requirements of relevancy and materiality must be complied with. Documentary evidence is subject to the rules applicable to hearsay evidence.

ANCIENT DOCUMENT RULE.—In law, an "ancient document" is a paper, map, book, or other writing over thirty years of age. Examples of ancient documents are: Wills, ancient deed recitals, family Bible records, newspapers, family genealogies, diaries, or letters. In order for ancient documents to be admitted as evidence they must be authenticated by proving the following elements: (1) Age; (2) Unsuspicious appearance; (3) Contents; (4) Natural custody, that is, a satisfactory explanation of the custody of the document over the years; (5) Signature and handwriting if these are involved.

AUTHENTICATION OF OTHER DOCUMENTS.—Original documents acknowledged before a notary public or other qualified officer do not require further authentication.

Real Evidence

Real or Demonstrative Evidence is evidence other than the testimony of witnesses or writings, consisting of objects, such as a tombstone or pedigree chart.

The Hearsay Evidence Rule

Hearsay evidence applies to both documentary and testimonial evidence. "Evidence, *oral* or *written,* is hearsay when its probative force depends in whole or in part on the competency and credibility of a person other than the witness." Hearsay evidence is that species of testimony given by a witness who relates, not what he knows personally, but what others have told him, or what he had heard said by others.

OBJECTIONS TO HEARSAY EVIDENCE.—The primary objection to hearsay evidence is that it is not trustworthy. It is also objectionable because there is no opportunity for cross-examination of the person who was primarily responsible for the statements made by the witness.

Hearsay under some circumstances might be so likely to be true that if trustworthiness is satisfied and there is a practical necessity for it, the evidence might be admitted. "Trustworthiness may be furnished by special circumstances which operate as a substitute for the test of cross-examination."

METHOD OF PROVING FACTS UNDER THE HEARSAY EVIDENCE RULE.—Thus there are exceptions to the general rule and hearsay evidence may sometimes be admitted, provided certain conditions are complied with. These conditions are: (1) If there is a special guarantee of trustworthiness that the evidence is correct; (2) if the evidence cannot be obtained any other way so it becomes a practical necessity to obtain it from the testimony of a person who has no personal knowledge (this is generally referred to as the "Necessity Principle"; necessity arises when the information should be considered, and the person who made the statement is dead, beyond the jurisdiction of the court, or is incompetent to testify); (3) if the information originated ante litem motam, or before the purpose for which it is now needed was known. If these three conditions are met, hearsay evidence is admissible for *consideration.*

Exceptions to the Hearsay Rule

REPUTATION.—Although general reputation existing in a community is hearsay, it may, under certain conditions be introduced. The necessity principle is satisfied because this is the only means whereby the information may be obtained. The evidence is considered trustworthy because it is based on the general observation of the community.

Due to the paucity of marriage records, the necessity arose for proving a marriage by the general reputation in the neighborhood that a man and woman were in fact husband and wife.

Some courts admit reputation of other facts of family history, such as reputation to prove a person's name or identity, birth, death, relationship, and genealogical facts appearing on gravestones and monuments in public places.

There has been much data given to compilers, past and present, orally and in writing, and also found in such sources as newspapers, documents, letters, printed place and family histories, based on community reputation. This information could not be proven by living witnesses, but may be admitted *for consideration* under the ancient document rule and the declarations of pedigree and family history exception to the hearsay rule.

ENTRIES MADE IN THE REGULAR COURSE OF BUSINESS, such as account books, records of corporations, stores and shops, are admissible under certain conditions. They are considered trustworthy because of the necessity that business records and accounts be kept accurately. In court, a proper foundation must be laid before they can be introduced.

OFFICIAL RECORDS are hearsay evidence, but this type of hearsay is generally considered the most reliable. When official records are presented in court, they must be authenticated to show they are what they purport to be. It must be shown that the whole document is introduced to satisfy the Rule of Completeness. Example: Vital, land and probate records; church records and ship registers when kept as required by law; assessors books, electoral registers, military and naval registers; inquisitions of escheat and postmortem; inquisitions of population (census); officially printed court decisions, session laws and statutes at large. For genealogical purposes other than in court, the authenticity of the record may be determined by examination of the original or by a copy duly prepared and certified by a credible person.

DECLARATIONS OF PEDIGREE AND FAMILY HISTORY.—If the original declarant is unavailable, that is, deceased, incompetent, or beyond the jurisdiction of the court, statement by another person of what such declarant said will be admitted for consideration. The declaration must have been made ante litem motam, or before the controversy arose. There must be no interest or motive on the part of the declarant to deceive. He must have been possessed of the usual testimonial qualification, and must have had fair opportunities for acquiring the knowledge.

Declarations of pedigree and family history may be in any form, oral or written. The declaration may consist of words or conduct, in the declarant's own handwriting or by assenting to or adopting the writing of another. Examples: Family Bible records, printed and manuscript family genealogies, declarations in place histories, oral declarations made by a relative, gravestone inscriptions, letters and diaries.

Affidavits

In the absence of statutory provisions, affidavits are generally not admissible as competent evidence, except in accordance with the rules pertaining to ancient documents, and as declarations of pedigree and family history, if the affidavit can qualify as such.

For the "Expert Witness"

As a further aid in judging genealogical facts, and to assist a genealogist in the presentation of his testimony if called on as an expert witness, the following brief summary of trial procedure should prove helpful:

PRESENTATION OF EVIDENCE.—The order of proof and order of trial is within the discretion of the trial court, but is generally as follows:

(1) The proponent or plaintiff should exhaust all of his evidence in attempting to prove his case.

(2) The opponent, contestant of a will, or defendant in a court proceeding, should then present all the evidence he has to prove his case.

(3) The proponent may, as rebuttal, introduce evidence to try and contradict the proof offered in evidence by the opponent.

(4) The opponent may offer evidence, which is termed "Surrebuttal". This process may be continued, subject to the discretion of the court.

EXAMINATION OF WITNESSES.—After a witness is placed under oath or affirmation, the party that calls him commences what is known as "direct examination", in which the witness is asked questions that must conform to the rules of evidence;

otherwise the questions will be objected to by opposing counsel. Following direct examination, opposing counsel then has the right to cross-examine the witness. The purpose of cross-examination, among other things, is to test the truthfulness, memory, bias or prejudice of the witness. After cross-examination, counsel for the party who called the witness has the right to try and repair any damage done on cross-examination. This is called "Redirect Examination". Following re-direct examination, opposing counsel is privileged to re-examine the witness. This is called "re-cross-examination". Re-direct and re-cross-examination could continue indefinitely except that the court has the right to cut it short if the evidence elicited is immaterial, irrelevant, or merely cumulative.

LEADING QUESTIONS.—A leading question is one so framed that it suggests the answer the interrogator desires. For this reason, the general rule is that leading questions are objectionable. Leading questions are permitted to obtain preliminary information, during direct examination under certain conditions when the witness does not recall information, and during cross-examination, and when the witness is hostile.

Presumptions

Presumptions are not evidence; they are conclusions made from evidence.

Presumptions are of two kinds, rebuttable and conclusive. Rebuttable presumptions are those that continue in force until overcome by evidence that is strong enough to rebut them. For instance, the cohabitation of a man and woman reputedly as husband and wife raises a presumption of marriage. This presumption is rebuttable, but the burden of disproving the marriage rests with the party raising the question in issue. A conclusive presumption is a legal fiction. It is considered true only because the law says it is true. An example of a conclusive presumption is: "The issue of a wife cohabiting with her husband, who is not impotent, is indisputably presumed to be legitimate."

RULES OF EVIDENCE 47

General Rules for Judging the Reliability of Genealogical Evidence

Class or Category	Source of Evidence	Type of Evidence	Rating of the Evidence
1st	Testimony of Witnesses: Evidence from a witness who has personal knowledge of the facts sought to be proven. An "eye-witness".	Testimonial: Personal knowledge.	Excellent — depending on the competency and credibility of the witness.
2nd	Official records, such as vital, land, probate and other court records.	Hearsay.	Excellent, but still hearsay. Nevertheless, apt to be correct in most cases.
3rd	Testimony of Witnesses: Evidence from a witness who does *not* know the facts from his own personal knowledge. (Testimonial family declarations.)	Testimonial: Hearsay.	Excellent, but still hearsay. In isolated cases more reliable than Class 2.
4th	Unofficial records, such as church, corporation and other business records.	Hearsay.	Reliability varies greatly but generally good to excellent.
5th	Family records: Diaries, journals, letters, Bible records, and any other records compiled by a member of a family. (Documentary Family Declarations.)	Hearsay.	Reliability varies from poor to good. If it is a contemporary record made by one having personal knowledge, rate it excellent.
6th	Newspaper files: Contemporary accounts of births, marriages, and deaths.	Hearsay.	Good. The hazard here is the informant and printers' errors.
7th	Family genealogies: Printed and manuscript works.	Hearsay.	Good. The test is who compiled the work and when, and from what sources.

Class or Category	Source of Evidence	Type of Evidence	Rating of the Evidence
8th	General printed works: County and other local histories. Newspaper accounts: Obituaries, biographies, genealogies which are not contemporary accounts.	Hearsay.	Fair. Often unreliable, but there are exceptions.
9th	Traditions: Stories or information presumably passed from one generation to another.	Hearsay.	Unreliable
10th	Folklore: Legends, stories and other information not originating in the family.	Hearsay.	Very unreliable.

The foregoing rules for judging reliability of genealogical data are subject to the application of the rules of evidence and are further subject to the possibility that occasionally what is generally considered the least reliable source may be true and the most reliable evidence false.

Although it has not been possible to give thorough consideration to many phases of the rules of evidence in this chapter because of space limitations, it is hoped it will assist genealogists to judge genealogical facts in an objective manner. If you are able to do so, you are in effect a judge presiding in a court of genealogy. The responsibility of a judge is great, so you will consider your decisions carefully.

CHAPTER VI

PREPARING GENEALOGICAL MANUSCRIPTS FOR PUBLICATION *

Sooner or later, most genealogists, whether professional or amateur, wish to have some of their collected data printed; perhaps in pamphlet or book form by themselves or members of the family, or in an article contributed to a periodical. A few practical hints as to the preparation of their material may therefore prove helpful.

Material for the printers to use in setting type is known as "copy". The copy should be written or typed on one side of the page only; the standard size of typewriter paper is best. Do not use too large a sheet, as it is more difficult for the compositors to handle. Legible handwriting is better than *poor* typing, because inexpert typists make more inadvertent errors ("type errors") than they do when writing long-hand. If these are not found and corrected, the errors may appear in the book, or if caught during the proofreading the printers will make an extra charge for corrections after the type is set.

If typing is employed, be sure to double-space *everything* and to leave good margins, particularly on the left of the page. If the copy is written by hand, the same rule against crowding applies. You may want different sections set in different sizes of type, but do not attempt to show this by double-spacing some sections and single-spacing others. The copy should be properly marked in the left-hand margin, to inform the printers what size of type is desired.

The men who actually set the type are called compositors. When you are having your compilation printed personally and call on a printer, he will show you books in which different sizes of type may be seen, and after you have made your selection he will tell you how to mark the copy; or if you explain to him your wishes, he will mark the copy for the

---

* Reprinted from *The American Genealogist*, XII, July 1935, 2-4.

compositors. Standard sizes in general use are ten-point for the body of a book, and eight-point for lists of children, long quotations, or any section where smaller type is desired. In books with pages larger than the ordinary library size and with wide margins, eleven and nine-point type are sometimes employed. The advice of an experienced printer is to be valued in the selection of type and binding. The size of type chosen should, in general, be proportionate to the size of the page.

The simple rules above are important in submitting articles for publication in magazines. Every periodical has its own "style" and the editors need space in which to mark the copy with instructions for the compositors. They also need space in which to make corrections if the copy contains obvious "type errors." Furthermore, many writers—some of them excellent writers in some respects—are guilty of occasional misspellings or fail to follow the standard system of punctuation. Most genealogical magazines are understaffed, and considerable labor is required of the editors in preparing copy for publication. Is it any wonder that they "shy away" from manuscripts so crowded that it will be almost impossible for them to make the proper annotations and corrections? Your manuscript therefore has a much greater chance of acceptance if it is properly typed.

Never use capitals in typing your copy except for the initial letters of sentences and of proper nouns. The typewriter has only small letters (which printers call "lower case"), and capital letters. The font of the printers has both small and large capitals; the small capitals are of the same height as the small letters, while the large capitals are a trifle higher. When you type a name entirely in capitals, most compositors will think this calls for their large capitals. These, for most uses, stand out and hit the eye too much on the printed page. There are places where you may want them, but in most places you will prefer small capitals with only the initial letter in large capitals. Therefore, do not type in capitals; type the ordinary way, and draw two pencil lines under the name for small capitals, or three lines if you really want large capitals.

The appearance of many a book has been injured by ignorance of this bit of information; and you can imagine the burden it places on editors when they have to mark over your capitals. This is the way a name appears in print if you type it in capitals: JOHN SMITH. This is probably the way you wanted it to appear: JOHN SMITH.

Never type or draw a single line under a word unless you want it set up in *italics*, for that is the standard way of designating italics.

In submitting material for publication in a magazine, it is better not to mark the copy for the compositors, even though you may be thoroughly familiar with the symbols employed; for there is always a possibility that the font of type used in printing the magazines may not contain precisely what your directions call for.

If you have typed a line to the margin which should have been indented, place the mark "]" in the left-hand margin at the beginning of the line. If you have indented a line which should have been brought out to the margin, place the sign "[" against it. To designate the beginning of a paragraph where you have typed solidly, insert the symbol "¶" directly to the left of the word which you wish to have begin a new paragraph. If you have started a new paragraph and change your mind, write "No ¶" in the margin to the left, and the compositors will not begin a new paragraph there. If a letter has jumped up in typing, and you do not want it raised, place " I—I " directly under the letter. Turn this jigger over, with the two prongs pointing down, if you want a letter raised.

Part 2
MATERIALS FOR RESEARCH

CHAPTER I

ORIGINAL SOURCES

A. FAMILY RECORDS

Family Bibles and Family Vital Records

In the early days of our country many families, if they bought no other books, purchased a Family Bible. In these old Bibles there were blank pages, often headed "Births", "Marriages", and "Deaths", on which the head of the house kept the vital records of his family, writing in each event as it occurred. The Bible usually passed on his death to his eldest son who kept the record going, while younger sons started similar records of their own.

As will readily be seen, these old Family Bibles provide some of the most important records available to us of the early years of our country. Municipal and state records are often made up at a later date than the Bible entries and may contain inaccuracies that stem from (1) clerical errors, (2) errors of transcription, (3) errors due to second-hand or word of mouth reports, or may omit entries entirely. (Even currently, the state vital records are not complete. For instance, though the author was born in Philadelphia, Pa., in 1911, and his birth is recorded in his church, school, college, and in several Family Bibles, and though he possesses a valid passport, is a voter, and holds a reserve commission in the Army, still his birth is not recorded in the vital records of the State of Pennsylvania.)

In the colonial days, many towns kept no vital records, and the records of others were destroyed by fire or in some other manner. In such cases, the Bible records often provide the only information available to us.

When the actual Family Bible record was not kept, there are many cases where a member of the family made a record of the family's vital statistics on a scrap of paper and saved his record for posterity just as the Family Bible was saved.

These records are, of course, important for the same reason.

In analyzing the accuracy of Bible records or similar family papers: First check the printer's date on the title page against the earliest dates shown in the record. Second, the student must consider whether the record was contemporary with the event recorded. If the record shows evidence of being made piecemeal (one entry at a time) the chances are excellent that it is accurate. Inaccuracy increases with the time lag between occurrence and entry. At the beginning of all such entries, the head of the family or other person making the record usually put in all the known facts about his family, many times years after the event. A man might already have a grown family before he could afford a Bible and make his first entry. He might then make his initial entries—his marriage, children's birth dates, death dates, all from memory, and though his own and his wife's birth and marriage dates would probably be correct, yet all his children might not be correctly recorded. If his initial entries were copied from an earlier record, his chances of accuracy naturally increased.

As an example of the differences to be noted between Family Bible and Vital Records, refer to *The American Genealogist*, vol. XIX, p. 106. See the reference note under Moses Fifield, and note that the Vital Records of New Hampshire show Moses' wife as "Mary, of Billerica." Actually, as shown by the Family Bible record, and verified by the marriage and birth records of Billerica, we know that her name was Lucy. The Vital Records also give the wrong year for the birth of the daughter, Mary. Note similar differences between the Bible and Vital Records in the case of the family of John Fifield, *ibid*, vol. XVI, p. 174.

Where there is disagreement between the Vital Records and the Bible entries, confirmation of one or the other should be sought from a third source; failing this, probabilities must be considered in deciding which entry is correct. For instance, if the children listed in the Bible are spaced at regular intervals, except for the date in question, and the vital record entry fits better into the pattern, then the vital record entry is more probably the correct one.

Bible entries are sometimes counterfeited by unscrupulous persons who are selling a spurious pedigree either to flatter or for profit. This type of record is easier to counterfeit than a vital record entry and, if there is any doubt of authenticity, the Bible references should be carefully examined in the original. One example of a very doubtful entry is that given for Nicholas Frost's family and quoted in Stackpole's *Families of Old Kittery*, p. 414. Note that Stackpole himself does not accept this reference, though he has quoted it.

Family Bible entries have been, and still are, accepted as supporting evidence in proofs of relationship for legal purposes. In the pension files in the National Archives and in the passport office of the Department of State are many papers that employ such records for support of claims.

Correspondence

Much important genealogical material is lost every year with the destruction of old family letters. To be uninitiated, the newsy letters of our forefathers have interest only for their "queer" spelling, punctuation, and unusual words. However, far from being worthless, properly studied they often provide keys to descent that are otherwise unobtainable. Happy, indeed, is the experienced genealogist if he can dip his hands into the old letter boxes of the families whose connections he is seeking.

To show how such letters are used, let us examine the invaluable Wansboro-Shepherd correspondence that appears in the article, "Sheppards of Fenwick's Colony", *The American Genealogist*, vol. XV, p. 15. Here we find a group of nine letters between these Irish and Colonial American families. The first is a letter dated 4 May 1700, from James Wansboro in Ireland to his sister's husband, Thomas Shepherd at Cohansey, West Jersey. The second, dated 9 April 1716, and the third dated 20 April 1716, have the same addressee and addressor. The fourth (2 April 1724) and the fifth (10 April 1724) are from Joseph and Esther Armitage and Samson and Rachel Bascorfield in Ireland to Mrs. Ann Shepherd, wife of Thomas. The sixth (26 January 1726) is from Thomas

Shepherd in Ireland to his Aunt Ann Shepherd, widow of Thomas, and the seventh (18 April 1729) from James Wansboro to the same addressee—his sister. The eighth and ninth letters are from Robert Dawson to Moses Shepherd in Cohansey. The eighth is dated 23 July 1732 and from England. The ninth is dated 3 April 1741 from Philadelphia (in America).

From the information furnished in these letters, the charts on pp. 28 and 29 of the same volume of *The American Genealogist* are made up. Thus, it was possible to show the relationships of all these people to each other accurately and determine the maiden names and relationships of a number of the wives. In addition, clues are provided to the domiciles in Ireland, not only of the Shepherd and Wansboro families, but of a great many others. It will be appreciated that this type of identification of a colonist with an old world town is by far the best proof that can be obtained for former residents. Although mention in wills and deeds occur infrequently, even when they do, they are usually rather indefinite as to locale as "so and so in America", or "so and so in New England."

The "lost" or "difficult" period for many researchers today is that directly following the Revolution and up to about 1850. This is because in printing family sketches, collecting and compiling old records, and in writing up definitive articles on confused lines, emphasis is always placed on pre-Revolutionary work, for its more general interest, and greater reader appeal and salability. This means that the toughest leg of the genealogist's course lies in this period of great, twice-great and thrice-great grandfathers. Except for New England, records often exist but not in collected form. Church records are fair, but usually in the hands of the churches, and we may be uncertain as to denomination. Careless legal work may have resulted in absence of deeds and wills. Census reports are often lost or incomplete. Here is the real spot for old letters to come to the rescue—and often they do. Let us take a typical example.

There are in existence a series of letters written by Elizabeth Shinnick, daughter of Lewis and Mary (Blake) Shinnick, to her cousin George Shinnick of Zanesville, Ohio, and subsequently, upon his marriage, to his wife, Mary. The first is dated 18 February 1839 and the last 16 May 1858. This covers a period of nearly twenty years. Aside from giving a clear picture of customs and atmosphere of the period and, from 1843 when Mary Shinnick started writing the women's fashions, they provide invaluable genealogical information. During the period covered, there were little or no vital statistics recorded in Philadelphia and Baltimore, the cities concerned, and unless church or other records were available, no real information of some of the people named could be obtained. Add to this the fact that this was the period of movement to the West, and it was often difficult to follow a family's migrations except by supposition. As an example, let us quote some of the information provided:

In her letters of 1839, Elizabeth mentions her cousin, David Parr of Baltimore. Cousin William Shinnick has gone from Baltimore to Zanesville, Ohio. In 1840, a cousin, "Pine" is named, and Elizabeth names "Monday, the 31st of August" as "my birthday." In 1841, she stayed at Mrs. Parr's in Baltimore and Frances returned (to Philadelphia) with her. Two other brothers of Frances, and Miltiades Parr, a younger brother, are mentioned. "Cousin David Parr married since Frances left us." Cecelia James has married an Edward Starr. "Mr. James died three days after the marriage, so Cecelia is a mourning bride." She mentions her aunt, Sophia Lentz, and her cousin, Sophia Lentz. Uncle John Justice, Uncle Jacob Shinnick, of Baltimore, Uncle Michael Knorr of Philadelphia, Cousin Louisa Brunner are mentioned. Mr. James Parr is a Mason, "took Frances and me to the encampment." Cousin John called on me in Baltimore. Cousin James was married in Washington. Did not see Uncle Jacob. In a later letter, we gather that Uncle Jacob died before 27 September 1842. Aunt Betsey Bryant has been ill. Emanuel Mann of Baltimore has married a Miss Taylor. In 1843, William Milligan, son of Charles, died of dropsy at the age of 16. A description of the wedding of her friend, Ellen Berrell to Joe Burr occupies a whole letter. Ellen and Joe have moved west to some place near Zanesville. George marries during this year. In 1844, she mentions that the Burrs live in Cincinnati. Ellen Burr is having a baby. Cousin John, brother of George, has been very ill (in Baltimore). George and Mary have had a son. In 1846 (she is now writing only to Mary), George and Mary have had a daughter named Elizabeth after her. The daughter was six months old by 23 March 1846, and the son less than two years old. This spring, Miltiades Parr marries a Miss Pope.

In 1848, William (in Zanesville) is engaged to a Matilda, and Mary and George have another son, William. (During the summer, Elizabeth visits Zanesville. One letter from Cincinnati, while on her way home mentions "Miss Price, now Mrs. Wilkins, was here. They were married last January, and live somewhere along the river." She sends her love to Sarah (later identified as Mary's sister) and to the three children. From Philadelphia, she writes that "Cousin David Parr's eldest daughter, Margaret Ann, is coming to visit." She is prevented, however, by the illness of her mother after the birth of a son. Miss Boraeff was married during the summer and her younger sister, about 19, died during the summer. Mary and George have another child, Charles. In 1849, William and Matilda are now married. Mr. and Mrs. Ladd who are still in Zanesville have another child; William Derr's (of Philadelphia) wife is dead. "Father's little nephew, Lewis S. Justis, who lived with us" is dead. He was in his 13th year and his sister, Elizabeth, was with him when he died. Aunt Sophia Lentz is sick and so is Elizabeth Taylor, who is pregnant. In 1852, Elizabeth has now married Jesse Lee, and on 5 April, her son is "five weeks old last Friday", named Lewis Shinnick Lee. "My grandmother, mother's stepmother, nursed me." Mary and George have another child. Mrs. Norman of Zanesville is now housekeeping in Philadelphia. Mrs. Woods of Zanesville is now living in Pittsburgh. In 1858, Elizabeth's daughter, Mary Ellen, is sick. Also, she (Elizabeth S. Lee) entered confinement on 7 September and had a daughter on the 10th, born with spasms, named Julia, who died on October 3. Elizabeth has four charms made from "Father's, Mr. Lee's and my children's hair"—hence has only two living children.

The foregoing is a good example of the information available in carefully scrutinized correspondence. At the time these letters were written, no records of any comprehensive nature were available in Philadelphia, and much of the information given is available in no other place.

Memoirs and Diaries

Memoirs and diaries provide source material of great value, which is becoming better understood and more frequently used by genealogists. Unfortunately, bibliographies of this type of book are rare, and their indices are usually imperfect, necessitating exhaustive searches for particular facts.[1] The

---

[1] Two bibliographies that may be helpful are *An Annotated Bibliography of American Diaries Written Prior to the Year 1861*, by William Matthews, and *New England Diaries, 1602-1800*, by Harriette M. Forbes. Others may be located through use of *Index to the Writings on American History, 1902-1940*.

FAMILY RECORDS

types of material obtained from such sources include relationships (often very important in identifying two persons of the same name), location of properties, births, marriages, deaths, and interesting biographical and human interest material. Proof necessary for membership in patriotic societies frequently is found.

Diaries of the more important public figures have been published and are valuable for the detailed information available in them regarding the places and persons that they visited. The diary of Governor John Winthrop of Massachusetts, published as *Winthrop's Journal*, edited by Hosmer, is a case in point. Relationships of many New England families have been proved from statements that he made. Even his mention of a colonist's house has value in proving that a certain man lived in a certain area. Sometimes these statements are all that remain as evidence of such a man's existence.

Many less known and relatively unimportant figures left diaries or records of value, many available in manuscript only; some doctors left case books, a New Jersey mid-wife left a record of deliveries *(Vineland Historical Magazine)*, some ministers left personal records of their activities. In Lovell, Maine, one resident as a hobby kept a record of deaths which has great value in supplementing the local records. The diary of Ephraim Bateman of Cumberland Co., New Jersey (published in the *Vineland Historical Magazine*) contains much important information regarding the families of local residents in his neighborhood during his lifetime, information not available elsewhere.

Many old diaries and memoirs are buried among the papers that collect in the family garret and are destroyed each year when housecleaning time comes around. Such papers frequently contain data of incalculable value to the genealogist, and which he cannot find elsewhere. The proper repository for such material is, of course, the nearest Historical Society, where they can be safely kept and made available to searchers.

Most societies that maintain manuscript collections index these collections only by title. Investigating such documents for use in solving a specific problem is a slow task. Obtain, if possible, the assistance of a person who knows the collection or has used it before. Consider the geographic location and employment, as well as the period, of the writer of the documents to determine if it is possible or likely that the writer came into contact with your subject or his relatives. It should be remembered that the subject's relatives may, even at a subsequent date, have become involved in litigation or some event of historical importance, so that the subject's relationship may be reported in diaries or memoirs of a later period than that in which he lived.

Unrecorded Deeds and Wills

The use of deeds and wills in tracing pedigrees will be discussed in detail later. However, it should be brought out that many deeds and wills have never been recorded, and may be found in the accumulation of papers among family possessions and in historical societies.

In the days when our country was founded, with communications poor, and many of our pioneer ancestors engaged in a real struggle for survival, not as much time was taken with legal formalities as now. Carelessness in filing deeds and wills was common. Even when wills were filed, distribution and executors' accounts were conspicuous by their absence. Occasionally, deeds found their way into the records some forty or fifty years after the transfers of property were effected; many were never recorded at all. Obviously, the genealogical information provided by deed recitations is of equal importance whether the deed ends up in the court house or remains in the family or historical society files. And such unrecorded material frequently supplements that which is available in the records. Today, and over the past fifty or more years, very few deeds are unrecorded; but for the early years of our country such documents are valuable in the extreme.

As in the case of deeds, many early wills were never probated, and remain in the possession of families or historical collections. Many, of course, have been lost or destroyed. Such wills are of inestimable value to the genealogist. Sometimes, an unrecorded will provides the key information which has defied searchers, and gives the final proof on a descent. As with the unrecorded deed, the proper repository of such documents is the nearest historical society, where others may also have access to them.

The value of unrecorded wills, unlike unrecorded deeds, is not limited to the early years of the country. It applies equally well to contemporary pedigrees. When a person makes a will he states that it is his "last will and testament" and supersedes all others. This wording suggests the value of the earlier and hence unrecorded will of the present day, which may not have been destroyed and may be sometimes found among old family papers. The earlier testament may mention children or relatives who were dead and so unmentioned in the later and final will. Perhaps a member of the family is cut off and unmentioned in the final version for offending the testator. Sometimes the name of the wife in the early version is different from that in the final, disclosing an earlier marriage. Often, much information about the testator's family and his personal history may be gleaned. An increase or decline in his property and fortunes, interests in other communities than that in which he lived, birth place, earlier places of residence, travels—all these things may be shown. The value of these earlier versions is often neglected, yet they should always be borne in mind by the biographer or genealogist.

Diplomas, Certificates and Testimonials

Among the papers in the family archives, little understood sources of information are the diplomas, certificates and testimonials. Examples of these might include graduation diplomas from schools or colleges. These would indicate courses studied and years of instruction, and would help us to work out ages and determine places and residence.

Certificates of membership, such as are provided by fraternal organizations and clubs, are not so useful as age indications (except in the case of college fraternities), but they also are the keys to other sources of information. Certificates are also granted for discharge from military and other government service and state the duration of, often together with entry and separation dates, and type of service. Such certificates may provide a physical description of the subject, including such items as height, weight, color of hair and eyes, scars, etc. Of course, this is very useful to the biographer, and also a key to government records. (As an example, see *The American Genealogist,* vol. XVII, p. 80.) Old passports, government orders, social security cards, and so on, are also keys to federal records, and provide date and period data.

Testimonials are often given to persons retiring from business, clubs, government offices, etc., by their associates. These testimonials, frequently illuminated, contain such information as date, period and nature of activity, and sometimes personal or biographical information of value. Again, a key is provided to other records which would possibly assist the genealogist or biographer.

With the few statements above, the searcher will see how the smallest fragment of personal history may guide him to records of value. The items listed above are but a few of the "heirlooms" that may be expected to assist him in his search.

B. PUBLIC RECORDS

The Census

Probably no one set of records contains as much information about people living in the 19th century as the Federal Census. Starting in 1790, a complete census of the inhabitants of the United States was taken every ten years but only the records up to 1880 are open to public inspection. These books must be searched page by page as they are not indexed and only in rare instances are the names alphabetically arranged. These records are divided by counties, the large cities divided by wards.

In the 1790 census there are three items of interest to the searcher—all males over 16 years of age, all males under 16 and all females. The 1800 and 1810 records are classified for males and females in five groups each. They are under 10, 10 to 16, 16 to 26, 26 to 45, and over 45. The 1820 records are the same with the exception of an added column of 16 to 18 for males only. The males in this column are also in the 16 to 26 group. The 1830 and 1840 records have more columns for ages. They run every five years up to 20 years and then every ten years to 100, both for male and female. The 1840 census also lists all those who were United States pensioners. Slaves and free colored persons are also listed in all these records. Only one name is given in each family, that of the head, either male or female.

The inexperienced census searcher may sometimes wonder at the size of the family, which is often much larger than it was supposed to be. One must remember that not only the family, but servants, lodgers and any person living in the household were included at the time the census was taken.

Beginning with the 1850 census, all names in the household are recorded together with the age, occupation and the state or country in which the person was born. In the 1880 census besides the birthplace of the subject there is also the state or country in which the parents were born. The relationship of the various members of the household is for the first time in this census.

Often in following a person through the census years it will be found that the recorded age of a person does not agree in the various records. This is due to the fact that the information may have been given by different persons. In fact, there are cases in which the family was absent from home and the enumerator obtained what he could from some neighbor.

Every state was supposed to have retained a copy of each census taken within its borders, but many of these records have been lost. Even in Washington, the files are not complete. In addition, many states had their own census taken between the dates of the Federal Census. These give information which differs in many cases from the Federal Census, but these state records are in the possession of the state in which they were taken and, therefore, are often easier of access.

Copies of the 1790 census, which has been printed and indexed, may be found in many libraries. The 1800 to 1830 census may be consulted at the National Archives in Washington, as well as the original records from 1830 to 1870. The paper on which the 1880 census was recorded is of such poor quality that the entire census of that year has been withdrawn from public use. Microfilms of this census are now at the National Archives.[2] Some states, libraries, and societies have purchased copies of the films, from 1840 to 1880, and these may be consulted in such places where they are on file.

Federal Pensions [3]

Of all the sources of genealogical information, probably more real interest is shown in the pensions than in any other. This interest is activated not only by a desire to gain membership in some patriotic society, but also by family pride, for in the claim there is often a description of service done by an ancestor, sometimes an interesting one. Nor is there any one subject which has come before Congress so many times. From 1776, when the Continental Congress passed the first pension act, up to the present time there have been many heated debates in Congress, some saying that the veteran did not receive enough, others saying that he received too much. Then too, there were many applicants whose proof of service was not thought sufficient by those in charge of the pensions. These claims were then given to the proper Congressman, taken before that body and generally granted. The missing records which are not in the Office of the Adjutant General and which the present day searcher bewails often kept a man from receiving a pension to which he was rightfully entitled.

The first pension law passed in 1776 granted relief only to the maimed who were unable to support themselves. In 1818, another law was passed by which a man had to show that he was in actual want. That this seemed possible can be seen by the report of the Secretary of War, who claimed that by

---

[2] See *List of National Archives Microfilm Publications* (1953), and *Federal Population Censuses, 1840-80*, issued by The National Archives.

[3] All pension laws applicable to service prior to the Civil War are enumerated and briefly described in *Is That Lineage Right?*, issued by the National Society, Daughters of the American Revolution, in 1958.

22 December 1819, 16,270 claims had been granted.

In 1820, a new law was enacted requiring the soldier to include a schedule of his whole estate, clothing and bedding excepted. Often with these papers were copies of deeds which showed that the soldier had disposed of his property. Most of the copies of these claims are still in existence, although some have been destroyed by fire, or otherwise.

In 1828, a law was passed granting pensions to all surviving soldiers of the Continental Army. This act required the Treasury Department to receive applications and make payments to those who proved their claim. This they did until 1835, when the administration of all pensions was transferred to the newly formed Pension Department. During these seven years, each pensioner was required to make a deposition before he received payment (twice yearly) and all these papers, together with probate papers and others were bound in books, one being filed in the Library of Congress, the others in The National Archives.

The National Archives now has the Last Payments of Pensions of the Revolution, which are being filed with the pension papers. Not all of these records give the date of death of the pensioner; only the period in which the last payment was made. Others contain family records, when the money due at the death of the pensioner was divided among his heirs.

In 1836, the Widow's Act was passed by which the widow of a Revolutionary soldier could receive a pension. Generally, proof of the marriage was given by town or church records or by deposition. Some of the Revolutionary claims were rejected for want of sufficient proof of service, but in most cases these claims give more information about the soldier's service than he could have used if he had absolute proof of service.

The survivors and widows of the War of 1812 did not receive pensions until 1871 unless the survivor was maimed. That the act was popular is shown by the fact that within eight months after its passage about 32,000 claims were filed, among them those of 7,000 widows.

Another valuable set of records connected with the War of 1812 are the Bounty Land Claims. Many of these were made by widows whose husbands were not pensioners and who not only gave the service record of their husband, but some sort of proof of their marriage. Some of these have been interfiled with the pension records; others are in a separate series.

The pension claims of the Indian and Mexican Wars all contain some information, while those of the Civil War often contain the marriage records and lists of the children.

One never knows just what will be found in these pension papers, sometimes it will be a marriage certificate and occasionally there is a page torn from the family Bible. This sometimes contains several generations and is extremely valuable. In one Revolutionary pension of a sailor was a letter written by John Paul Jones which ordered the sailor to take charge of a prize taken while they were on their way to France.

Several books have been issued by the Government, containing lists of pensioners and they are accurate except for the year 1840. These lists were taken from the census records of that year which were supposed to contain the names of all United States pensioners. Some of the men listed in these records have no trace of a pension while others who are known to have received pensions are not listed. Much care should be used in connection with this book.

In March 1943 the National Genealogical Society began the publication of an *Index of Revolutionary War Pension Applications* as a "Supplement" to its *Quarterly*. This gives the name of the pensioner, state from which he served and designating number of the pension file. When completed this will constitute a complete index of the Revolutionary War pensioners. By June 1959 this index had reached the letter "S".

Military Records

Anyone who has never searched the personnel records of the War Department will be surprised to find the number of classifications into which the records of the different wars are divided. Besides the well-known wars—the Revolution, 1812,

Mexican, Civil, and Spanish-American Wars— there are also lists of the Post Revolutionary Wars, 1798-1812, and many Indian Wars from 1818 to 1858, occurring in the South and West. There are also files of militiamen who, on account of some local trouble, were mustered into Federal service, sometimes only for a single day. All of these are records of volunteer or drafted men.

Extending over all these years covered by the above records are the files of the Regular Army. The personnel records of early enlistments give very little genealogical data aside from the name of the soldier and the organization to which he belonged, but gradually the records are broadened and more and more information is given. In a quest for a soldier, it is almost necessary to know the name of the state from which he served as many names are duplicated and it is easy to pick out the wrong man. An error such as this, if not detected quickly, may lead to a long and useless search.

The personnel records of the Revolution are not complete as this was fought before the country was organized and many of the muster rolls were kept by the officers as their personal property. Some of these missing rolls have been destroyed by carelessness, while others have been returned to the War Department. All records are carded, both by a general index and one by states. Besides the name of the soldier and the organization in which he served, there is little genealogical information on these cards, though sometimes it is noted that he was taken prisoner. To supplement these records, there is a special index of items taken from various records, and the cards may show that the man worked as a teamster hauling supplies and cannon while those who supplied forage and other necessities are also listed. These records do not include the names of men who served only in the militia. Information about these soldiers must be procured from the state in which they served.

The post Revolutionary War records are about the same as those of the Revolution but have no Special Index.

The records of the War of 1812 give a little more information than the previous records as sometimes the distance between the place of discharge and the soldier's residence is given. There is also a Special Index which gives the names of those who gave service to the Army but were not of it.

The records of the Indian and Mexican Wars give little more information, but it is generally possible to prove that a man served during one of these wars.

The Civil War records give still more information. It seemed to rest with the enlisting officer whether the town or only the state is given as the birthplace of the soldier. If the soldier was confined in a hospital there is frequently a "bed card" which gives the name of the next of kin. As a general thing, these records are satisfactory and give the full service of the soldier, his age, and his birthplace.

The Confederate records are far from complete, but some of them give the age and birthplace. Others say that the man was taken prisoner or paroled on such a date.

The records of the Spanish-American War give the man's age, birthplace and name of next of kin.

World War I records are now in St. Louis, Missouri, but are not open to the public. Information may be procured from the Office of the Adjutant General of the state from which the man served.

One of the best sources of information about men of modern times is to be found in the Selective Service Cards of World War I. In these cards are to be found the birthplace, age, residence, next of kin, and the marital status of every man of draft age in the country in 1918. These cards are now in the custody of the Federal Records Center, East Point, Georgia, and the information may be procured from that office at a nominal charge provided that the state and city in which the man registered is known.

Microfilms have now been made of the records of the soldiers in the Regular Army. The Confederate records are now also on microfilm. These films are in The National Archives.

Naval Records

The genealogist in search of sailors of the Continental or the United States Navy will find his task a disappointing one;

the reason being that no records were filed in the department for more than forty years after the organization of this country. During this time, the only records of the enlisted man were those inscribed on the ship's roll. Many of these rolls were not filed, but were kept by the master or some other officer of the ship and, of course, some of them were destroyed.

If we know the ship in which the man sailed in the early days of the Navy, his name and rating (the only information) can be found on the roll of that ship, provided that roll is in the Navy files, which are to be found in The National Archives. If the name of the ship is not known, it is still possible to find the man by going painstakingly through roll after roll. If the name is a common one, it may be duplicated, which creates the problem for the searcher of deciding which of the men is the one he wants. Then there is always the possibility that the name of the man wanted is on one of the missing rolls.

In the case of officers, there is additional information to be found. The file of "Acceptances" gives the age, birthplace and the place where the officer was at the time of his acceptance of the appointment. "Orders and Resignations" and "Honorable Discharges" give officers' addresses while "ZB" file gives further information about prominent officers.

The records of enlisted men after 1846 are in the custody of The National Archives. These records give the age, birthplace and next of kin to the man enlisting and with this information the search can generally be completed.

Marine Corps Records

The American or Continental Marines were established by the Act of 10 November 1775, the present United States Marine Corps was established by the Act of 11 July 1798. The Historical Division, Headquarters, U. S. Marine Corps, was established in September 1919, for the purpose of servicing the archives and writing a history of the Corps.

The original records of the Marines are no better than those of the Navy, but the Historical Division has collected a great deal of material from printed books, manuscripts and state records which are on file at this division. On these cards are many names which are not on the original rolls that have been preserved. These records include only those who served in the American Revolution.

Enlistment records from 1798 to and including 30 December 1895 are on file at The National Archives. Records from that date are on file at Headquarters, U. S. Marine Corps.

Coast Guard Records

This organization was established in 1915, from the former Revenue Cutter Service and later the Light House Service was taken over by them. The personnel records from 1915 are on file at their Headquarters in Washington.

The Revenue Cutter Service was founded in 1790, and had various names, but no statutory designation. Incomplete records of officers from 1792 to 1914 and muster rolls from 1833 to 1914 are on file at The National Archives, where are also personnel records of those in the Light House Service. These records have never been carded or indexed, and unless one knows the name of the vessel on which the man served, only searching roll after roll will produce the wanted result. This, of course, cannot be done by those in charge of the records but must be done by personal search or by a professional searcher. The National Archives has a list of searchers which they will send upon request.

Registrations of American Citizens Abroad

An order of 1906 required each consular post to maintain a record book for the registration of American citizens who were temporarily domiciled abroad. Each page consisted of a form to be filled out by an applicant. It provided spaces for such information as to the name of the citizen, the date and place of his birth, the identification of his wife, and the names, and dates and places of birth of his children. Each record book was provided with an index.

Registration books prior to 1935 for the most part are deposited in The National Archives, Washington, D. C.

Records of a foreign post now in The National Archives occasionally include an informal register of American residents made by the consul prior to 1907.

Passport Applications

Passport applications are documents addressed to appropriate civil authorities requesting the privilege of traveling. Prior to the Revolution some of the colonies issued such documents permitting travel into other colonies and elsewhere. After the Revolution some states and other local agencies issued similar permissions in certain types of cases. Georgia was one state that, in view of various arrangements with intervening Indian Nations, issued documents authorizing the bearer to pass through such lands for travel into areas claimed by it that extended westward to the Mississippi River and in the Floridas. Extant for the years 1785-1820, many of the earlier ones have been abstracted by Mrs. Mary G. Bryan, and published by the National Genealogical Society under the title, *Passports Issued by Governors of Georgia, 1785 to 1809,* as its Special Publication No. 21. To a considerable extent they are in the form of testimonials as to the identity and character of applicants. They are particularly useful in a study of pioneers who settled in the area that became Alabama, Mississippi and Louisiana.

Passport applications received by the Department of State begin about 1791 and are deposited in The National Archives, Washington 25, D. C., down through the years 1905. Initially, a passport application was simply a letter containing a minimum of family information. After the passage of a few decades, passport applications were filled-out forms. As time progressed these forms required more and more data. They show such details as the name of the applicant, his age, or date of birth, the place of his residence, and a personal description. If the applicant was a naturalized citizen, it shows the date and port of arrival in the United States and the Court in which naturalization records were filed. There are rough indexes for the period 1834-59, card indexes 1860-80, and book indexes 1881-1905.

Passports were normally not required by the United States

during the 19th century for foreign travel except during the Civil War. Persons of quality commonly requested them for the added protection they might afford. Naturalized citizens returning to their homelands normally applied for them particularly when their homelands were in central European countries where adult males might otherwise be subject to compulsory military service.

Passenger Lists

A passenger list is a document identifying persons who travel by ship. Such lists are of especial interest to Americans in so far as they identify founders of American families who came to this country from Europe during the 17th, 18th, and 19th centuries.

Early passenger lists are almost entirely government records rather than records of ship companies. Information in the list varies considerably depending upon the laws under which they were created, upon local custom, or upon the idiosyncrasies of ship captains who were required to make them. A list shows such information as the name of the vessel that transported the passengers, the name of its captain, the date and port of its arrival, the name of the port of embarkation, and sometimes the date of embarkation. It also showed the name of each adult male passenger; or, more often, the name, age, and occupation of each passenger.

Some passenger lists relate to emigration from a specific foreign port. Other lists relate to immigrants coming to a specific American port. Official lists were not prepared for all passenger vessels; and, in certain instances, where lists were prepared, they were not permanently retained. It is, therefore, important to know something about what lists have been preserved, and what lists are printed.

The British, French, Spanish, and certain German governments maintained records of outgoing passengers. Most of the British passenger lists down to the 1890s, however, have been destroyed. Certain 17th century lists, particularly for the years 1634 and 1635, were published by John Camden Hotten, *The Original Lists of Persons of Quality* . . . (London,

1874). (Some British passenger lists for a few specified later years are extant and have been published. These lists are for 1775-77 (England only), 1774-76 (Scotland only), and 1803-1806).

Many of the French were Huguenots who embarked from ports outside France secretly in ships that maintained no lists. Some lists of Catholic French who migrated to Louisiana during the years 1718-23 have been preserved. Transcripts in the Louisiana Historical Society for the years 1719-20 have been printed in issues of the *Louisiana Historical Quarterly* between vol. 14, p. 516, and vol. 21, p. 978. The Spanish maintained excellent records of passengers who migrated from Spain between 1509 and 1790. They relate to passengers en route for the Indies (including Florida and Louisiana, which for a time were under Spanish sovereignty). These records are particularly detailed for they show places of origin. The original records are in the Archivo de Indias, Seville, Spain. Those for 1509-59 were published between 1940 and 1946 in three volumes, entitled *Catalogo de pasajeros a Indias durante los siglos XVI, XVII, XVIII,* under the direction of the Archivo General de Indias.

During our colonial period, the regulations governing emigration in eastern and northern German states were severe and greatly restricted. Persons from Germanic areas emigrated through Dutch coastal ports, but the Netherlands kept only a statistical record of the numbers of the persons emigrating. Voluminous lists of passengers who embarked for London during 1708 and 1709 are in the Public Record Office, London. These lists, which are important because they contain the names of many who later came to America, were transcribed in Walter Allen Knittle's *Early Eighteenth Century Palatinate Emigration* (1937). Later, Germans emigrated through the German ports of Bremen and Hamburg. Extensive Hamburg lists dated 1840-1873 are very detailed for the period 1850-73. Microfilm copies of the Hamburg lists 1850-73, and rough indexes to them are in the Division of Manuscripts, Library of Congress, Washington 25, D. C.

Those from 1850 on are particularly detailed and show information about places of origin.

American colonial officials normally did not keep records of incoming passengers. There are some exceptions, and the best illustration is for the port of Philadelphia. There, under legislation effective in 1727, ship captains were required to make lists of alien passengers. The great majority of these alien passengers, of course, were of Germanic origin. These lists have been carefully transcribed by William John Hinke and published in: Ralph Beaver Strassburger, *Pennsylvania German Pioneers: A Publication of the Original Lists of Arrivals in the Port of Philadelphia from 1727 to 1808* . . . ed. by William John Hinke, Norristown, Penna., 1934, 3 vols. (Also published as vols. 42-44 of the *Proceedings* of the Pennsylvania German Society.)

With minor exceptions which have been noted in vol 102, pp. 203-5, of the *New England Historical and Genealogical Register,* Federal records of incoming passengers do not antedate 1820. Practically all extant 19th Century Federal passenger lists or microfilms thereof are in The National Archives, Washington, D. C. These lists invariably show the name of each passenger, the date and port of arrival of the vessel, and the name of the port of embarkation. They are very voluminous. As many as 300,000 people arrived in a single year before the Civil War. Although most of the passengers arrived through the port of New York, the ports of Boston, New Orleans, and Philadelphia received many loads of passengers. Indexes are incomplete, defective or non-existent except for lists for the ports of Baltimore and Philadelphia. Because of the volume of the lists, their fragile nature, and the inadequacy of extant indexes, searches in the original records are no longer permitted. The lists are in the process, however, of being microfilmed. At the time of writing, microfilm rolls covering most of the New York and New Orleans lists are available for consultation and may be purchased.

Practically no passenger lists of persons arriving by way of Pacific Coast ports or the Great Lakes are extant for the 18th century. It might be added that there is similarly lack of record of entrances of persons by land from Mexico and Canada.

Because of the incompleteness of the passenger lists, many other records relating to our immigrant ancestors have been sought for to aid us in determining approximated dates of arrival. Such records include license to pass overseas, naturalization records, emigration tax records, records of indentured servants, land records, and church records.

Some licenses to pass overseas have been included in John Camden Hotten's *The Original Lists of Persons of Quality . . .* (London 1874). Perhaps the best publication dealing with 18th century colonial naturalization (of non-British subjects) is M. S. Giuseppi, ed., "Naturalizations of Foreign Protestants in the American Colonies Pursuant to Statute 13 George II, C. 7," *The Publications of the Huguenot Society of London*, Manchester, 1921, vol. 24. An excellent book describing emigration tax records relates to Switzerland: Albert Bernhardt Faust, *Lists of Swiss Emigrants in the Eighteenth Century to the American Colonies . . .* Washington, D. C., 1920-25, 2 vols. Lists of indentured persons who embarked from the British port of Bristol are named in R. S. Glover's *Bristol And America; A Record of the First Settlers in the Colonies of North America 1654-1685*, London (1929?).

Important lists of indentured persons who came to this country from the London area are extant, but for the most part they are unpublished. Some colonies gave away land in return for an individual bringing over settlers and the settlers were often named. The best printed example of lists of early come-overers from land records is Nell Marion Nugent's *Cavaliers and Pioneers, A Calendar of Virginia Land Grants, 1623-1666*, Richmond, 1934. The archivist at Speyer, Germany prepared a book identifying a number of 18th century Germans whose plan to migrate was recorded in local church records.[4]

An excellent bibliography of passenger lists is Adlore Harold Lancour's *Passenger Lists of Ships Coming to North*

---

[4] *Emigrants from the Palatinate to the American Colonies in the Eighteenth Century.* (1953)

America, 1607-1825, A Bibliography . . . New York Public Library Bulletin, vol. 41, No. 5, May, 1937. Reprints of this bulletin are reportedly out of print.

Original "Grants"

Records describing actions that affect the title to land fall into two basic categories. One category relates to land initially alienated by the government or sovereign. Such records are records of entry. They are normally filed with the Colony, State, or Federal Government. The other category relates to land after it has been alienated by the sovereign. Such records are local land records. They are normally filed in the county courthouses but in the case of some New England states they are filed in the offices of the town clerks.

Records of Entry

In colonial times, provincial and other governments distributed land to individuals under many varying conditions. Some land was given away to actual settlers, or in return for military service or for bringing over persons from Europe; some land was sold.

The proprietary governments, Pennsylvania and Maryland, and some of the other colonies, maintained central land offices where all initial transfers were recorded.

The documents relating to such transfers of land are sometimes divided into three groups: The warrant or right to a specific number of acres in an unspecified location; the survey or map showing the exact location of the land to be transferred; and the patent or grant.

The Maryland records of entry are particularly interesting because each patentee was given the opportunity to select a name for a tract of land, and in the case of early settlers, one sometimes obtains a clue as to the settler's place of origin.

Occasionally, efforts have been made to reconstruct the patentees in a particular county. For example, a series of maps in Vol. III of the Horn Papers (the first two volumes are not recommended for use[5]) identifies each original patentee in

---

[5] See *William and Mary Quarterly*, 3rd Series, vol. 4, pp. 409, 428, 444.

Washington County, Pennsylvania, shows where his land was located, how many acres it contained, and when it was acquired. There is a master index of names.

In the thirteen original states and the states carved immediately from them—Maine, Vermont, West Virginia, Kentucky, Tennessee—the records of the original grant or distribution of the land are in the states or local divisions thereof.

Records of entry for the other states in the United States (exclusive of Texas which maintains its own entry records) concern public domain. They are Federal records deposited in Washington. The papers relating to cash entry, credit entry, homestead application, Oregon and Washington donations; bound land entry; and private land claims are in The National Archives. Of particular interest are the homestead application files and private land claims. The homestead application files were created by an Act of Congress of 1862, under the tenure of which 160 acre tracts were given to millions of persons who satisfied certain conditions of tenure and development. The private land claims relate to land formerly claimed by Great Britain, France, Spain and Mexico; and located in the Northwest Territory, Louisiana Territory, Mississippi Territory, Florida, Orleans Territory, Missouri Territory, Arizona, New Mexico, Colorado and California.

The land entry papers in The National Archives are dated chiefly 1800-1950. Those dated before 1 July 1908 are unindexed or partially indexed. It is usually necessary, therefore, to have a description of the land in terms of sub-division, section, township, and range before an effective search in the records can be made. Such information can sometimes be obtained from the clerk of the court in the county where the land was located.

The record copies of patents to the land in the public domain are in patent books deposited in the Bureau of Land Management, Washington 25, D. C.

Local Records

The local land records are normally filed in the office of the Recorder of Deeds or similar custodian in the county courthouses. In some New England states, such as Connecticut and Rhode Island, the local land records are filed in the towns. In some other states, such as Maryland, Pennsylvania, Virginia, North and South Carolina and Georgia, certain early land records or microfilm copies of them have been deposited in the State Archival Depository.

The nature and method of filing these records and the amount of genealogical detail vary considerably, but there are certain principles that are generally characteristic.

The records, copied from the original instruments in private hands, are in folio size bound volumes, called libers. The individual instruments are copied chronologically into a long series of libers. Usually, the recording is shortly after the completion of a transaction, but occasionally instruments are recorded years later (and many instruments are never recorded at all).

There are often two series of bound volumes that serve as indexes. Entries in one series are arranged by name of grantor or seller. Entries in the other series are arranged by name of grantee or buyer. Entries in each series are normally arranged alphabetically to the first letter of the surname, thereunder to the first letter of the given name. Searches, therefore, are sometimes difficult unless the full name of the individual and an approximate date are known.

Local land records are very useful genealogically. Some show the date when a person first came to a county and the name and state of the county from which he came. When land is divided among the heirs of a decedent information often appears as to the names of all the children, the places of their residence, and the names of the husbands of the married daughters.

When a married man sells property, his wife (except in early days in South Carolina) joins in the transaction or releases her dower rights, so her given name appears. In some colonies and sometimes in the states, this information is not recorded in the deed book but is in the County Court Minutes.

By noting the date the deed was proved before the court, the entry can readily be located in the court minutes.

Some instruments recite how the grantors acquired a tract and actually trace a generation or more of ancestors.

Probate Records

One of the most important documents used by genealogists in reconstructing families is "the last will and testament" of a deceased person. This is the instrument whereby the testator (the person making the will) distributes his real and personal estate among members of his family and friends, to take effect after his death. Strictly speaking, the term "will" denotes a document which disposes of real estate, while the "testament" is a document which disposes of personal property.

Many wills are valuable for the light they throw on families. A man may be precise in naming his wife, children, grandchildren, and even his collateral relatives. Unmarried and childless men often name their brothers and sisters, uncles, aunts, and cousins. But sometimes wills are keenly disappointing, for the testators give exasperatingly few details concerning their kinship with their beneficiaries. When this happens, it is necessary to dig into other sources for the desired information about a given family.

There are two types of wills, namely: The written will, signed by the testator and witnessed by two or three persons (the number varies according to the laws of the different states), and the nuncupative will, which is a verbal statement (made in the presence of witnesses) concerning the disposition of property after the testator's death. When a person dies leaving a will, he is said to have died testate. If he does not leave a will, he is then said to have died intestate.

After the testator's death the executor or executors (the persons named in the will to settle the decedent's estate) go before the court in their locality to "prove" (probate) the will. The witnesses appear before the court to testify that the will was signed in their presence. In the case of a nuncupative will the witnesses testify concerning the oral statement made to them about the decedent's testamentary intentions. Letters testamentary are then granted authorizing the executors to proceed with the task of distributing the property in accordance with the testator's wishes.

In intestate cases, the court appoints a person to serve as administrator to distribute the property among the heirs at law according to the intestate laws of the state where the decedent resided.

A whole series of documents make up the group of records known as probate records. These include, besides the will itself, the petition for probate of will, the petition for letters of administration if there is no will, letters testamentary granted by the court to the executors appointed to carry out the testator's wishes, letters of administration granted to the court-appointed administrators when no will has been executed, inventories and appraisements of the personal estates of the decedents, affidavits, etc. Copies of wills are usually entered in record volumes in the custody of the county court houses.

The courts having jurisdiction over probate matters bear different names in different states. Thus, Alabama and Arkansas have Probate Courts, New York and New Jersey Surrogate's Courts, and a number of states have placed probate matters in the hands of Superior or Circuit Courts. Connecticut and Vermont are divided into Probate Districts, although in the case of Connecticut most of the original probate records have been deposited with the State Library at Hartford. Cities such as New York, Philadelphia and Baltimore have Registers of Wills. In Pennsylvania and a few other states the Orphans' Court is devoted largely to probate matters; the clerk of the Orphans' Court is called the prothonotary.

A quick and convenient reference for determining the proper name of the courts in our states is contained in Noel C. Stevenson's *Search and Research: The Researcher's Handbook*, Revised Edition, 1959. The states are arranged alphabetically in this work. In each state appears the heading, "Official Records", and under the sub-heading, "Court Records", the name of that state's court for handling probate matters

(Probate, Surrogate, Superior, Circuit, etc.) is given.

For more extensive information on probate matters, the reader is referred to Stevenson's *Search and Research*, pp. 30-31; Donald Lines Jacobus, "Probate Law and Customs", *The American Genealogist*, vol. 9, July 1932, pp. 4 ff. (reprinted in *The Genealogical Reader*, edited by Noel C. Stevenson, 1958, pp. 61-67); Derek Harland, *A Basic Course in Genealogy*, vol. 2, *Research Procedure and Evaluation of Evidence* (1958), pp. 272-301; Gilbert Harry Doane, *Searching for Your Ancestors* (3rd printing, 1957), pp. 84-94; and E. Kay Kirkham, *The ABC's of American Genealogical Research* (1955), pp. 38-42.

C. INSTITUTIONAL RECORDS

In this section we will examine the records provided by religious groups, societies, and other non-governmental organizations. These can roughly be broken down into the following classifications.

1. Church records
2. Cemetery records and inscriptions
3. Educational institutions
4. Societies and fraternal organizations

Church Records

The records of religious groups vary considerably, both with denomination and the type of person or persons maintaining the records. Generally speaking, they provide the following types of information:

(a) Dates of baptism, often with names of parents, sometimes with names of sponsors and witnesses, sometimes including date and place of birth.

(b) Dates of marriage, sometimes including names of parents (especially in the cases of marriages of young persons). Witnesses are sometimes named.

(c) Dates of burial, sometimes including date of death. (Some such records include a short genealogical sketch of the deceased.)

(d) Date of confirmation, or of admission or acceptance to the church, or date of dismissal to another parish. (Such records frequently show prior affiliations and residence in case of admissions, and the destination in the case of dismissals.)

(e) Record of church activities, such as punishments of individuals for infractions of church rules, names of delegates to various meetings, church officers, etc.

There is little doubt that if the records of all the religious groups of Colonial America were available today the great majority of our genealogical problems would be solved. But many have been lost or destroyed through fire, war or other causes, and others were written so badly or were so poorly cared for as to be almost illegible. Even so, a wealth of this material is available to the searcher, much of it in the hands of active church organizations, some in the keeping of historical societies, or in private hands.

The records kept by the Quakers and the Lutherans are, generally speaking, the most complete. The Lutheran burial records often give the names of the parents of the decedent, marital history and much information about children. The Quakers recorded births rather than baptisms and were much concerned with church government. Their records of admissions and dismissals are very useful in following the travels of the early colonists and often tie them in directly with their British forebears.

The Baptists, from their habit of baptizing adults, only rarely give parentage of those baptized. Their records are perhaps the least useful of all the early church records.

In seeking the original church records, try first the pastor of the church, or the congregational officials, if the church is still in operation. These people will usually have these records, or know where they may be found.[°]

Records of inactive or defunct congregations should be

[°] *Check List of Historical Records Survey Publications*, by Sargent B. Child and Dorothy P. Holmes, contains "List of Church Archives Publications" and "Church Directories". Although not all states nor all denominations are covered, it may be helpful.

sought first at the local or nearest historical society. If no trace of the records is found, apply to the central governing body of the denomination. Most church bodies maintain an historical section or society which acts as a depository of the records of deceased congregations, and frequently also holds the old records of active ones. The Presbyterians and the Baptists, for instance, maintain excellent historical libraries in the Philadelphia area where their records may be examined and assistance may be given the searcher.

Sometimes very old church records are in the hands of the municipal authorities or library. This situation is found where in the early town only one denomination was acceptable and the church was active in the local government.

The accuracy of church records as a rule ranks high. Where conflict is discovered, the church record usually has the highest incidence of reliability. In general, entries are made by the minister himself as events occur or as they become known to him. Gaps in the old records occur during periods of absence of the minister or at times when no minister was available to fill the charge. On the minister's return or the appointment of a new one, an effort was sometimes made to bring the records up-to-date. And at this point, errors are more likely to creep in than at other times.

Although many church records, especially old ones, have been printed in recent years, it is well to remember that misreading a name or date may alter completely the genealogical picture. Therefore, the original records should be checked where absolute accuracy is desired. This is especially true of foreign language records and of the very old ones.

Cemetery Records and Inscriptions

Graveyard prowling has been a genealogical pastime for generations. The amateur and professional alike know that valuable data is given on old tombstones which may not be recorded elsewhere. Where church burial records and municipal death records have been lost or destroyed, the cemetery often provides the only source of this information.

Tombstones themselves may yield, in addition to the year of

death (the most brief type of inscription), the day and even the hour. They may give, in the case of women, her husband's name (sometimes even the name of a former husband). The names of parents may appear in a child's inscription. The association of the grave with others may be very useful knowledge since a family will usually bury its dead together.

Not usually appreciated is the information that may be obtained from the cemetery office. The name of the purchaser of the lot may be shown (and perhaps present owner and relationship), together with records of payment for upkeep, and who made the payments. These are often important in determining relationships. In addition, the office will have a complete record of burials, showing the location of each grave, and the dates. This is a very important file because of the (contrary to common belief) perishable nature of gravestones. Some may have become illegible; others were perhaps uprooted or destroyed.

There are many "lost" cemeteries which have been bought up and plowed under, or where roads have been put through. The tombstones in these cases will have been pulled up and destroyed, but sometimes the records of the cemetery or copies of the inscriptions have found their way into historical collections where they are available to the searcher.

In seeking the grave of your subject, first determine approximately when he died. The local historical society usually can tell you which cemeteries were in use at that time. Check first those which were allied with your subject's religious persuasion, and then try the private graveyards. Unfortunately, some religious groups do not believe in marked graves (Quaker grave markers, for example, are often very simple and brief), and in such cases inscriptions will be lacking.

Accept dates from gravestones with caution. Stone cutters, like clerks, can and do make mistakes. In the early days of our country, stones were very expensive and so a stone would be erected even when it displayed easily recognizable errors, rather than destroy the stone and get a new one. Additional errors creep in when a new stone is erected to replace

INSTITUTIONAL RECORDS 87

an old, worn one or erected on an unmarked grave or a grave marked with a wooden marker. Frequently the dates on these new stones were supplied from memory.

This does not mean that where the dates on tombstones vary from those obtained elsewhere, the gravestone is always wrong. In the case of John Fifield and Phebe Frye, his wife, buried at Menotomy, Oxford County, Maine, the town records have the death dates of both confused, and the tombstone dates are correct. A critical searcher will look for supporting evidence before he states that one source is right and another wrong.

Educational Institutions

Schools and colleges have existed in the Americas as long as have the early settlers and their descendants. Frequently, in the administration of early estates, we come upon records of expense for schooling, or for school clothes or supplies. Since the schools that the children attended were often community supported or church supported, the records of their school boards and of their attendance are frequently kept with a fullness most satisying to a genealogist.

Among the earlier schools in the colonies, to name but a few, were the Boston Latin School, Boston; the Roxbury Latin School, Roxbury; the William Penn Charter School, Philadelphia; the Public School of Germantown (now Germantown Academy) in Germantown. Many of the records of the early schools are still in existence and may be searched to determine parentage, for the records usually show who are the parents or foster parents of a student, and his address.

The colleges and universities also provide a source of information, though often not as complete as the school records. Among the older colleges are found, of course, Harvard, William and Mary, Yale and Dartmouth. Their yearbooks and enrollment records are easily searched and may provide valuable information.

In using school or college records, the following procedure of search is recommended:

(a) If possible, determine the general location of residence of the subject.

(b) If possible, determine subject's religious background.

(c) Check against best local history of the area to determine which schools were in existence at that time.

(d) Check first the records of the nearest schools of the correct religious persuasion, then all other school records, starting with nearest and continuing to most distant in the area.

(e) If schools are indicated which are now extinct, try for their records at (1) the nearest headquarters of the religious order that sponsored the school, (2) the state archives or collection of historical records (especially if community sponsored), (3) the historical society of that state, (4) The National Archives or other department of the U. S. Government in Washington.

Reference works to assist in locating appropriate schools or colleges for study are: Patterson's *American Educational Dictionary* (especially good for schools), Carter V. Good's Guide to Colleges, *Universities and Professional Schools in the United States* and, most recent, Marsh's *American Colleges and Universities*.

Societies and Fraternal Organizations

Few investigators realize the amount of genealogical material available to them in the archives of societies, fraternal organizations and sometimes even in clubs. Yet, most such organizations maintain membership records that include some or all of the following items:

Name of member and place and date of joining; date and place of birth; places of residence; names of children, and sometimes birth dates; names of wives and parents; religious and other affiliations; education; business; personal descriptions; photographs.

Patriotic societies (lists available in any state historical society), in addition, maintain records of descent from an important ancestor.

Some of the older organizations of a strictly fraternal nature having such records are the Masons, Shrine, Odd Fellows, Knights of Columbus, Elks, Moose. Clubs which main-

INSTITUTIONAL RECORDS 89

tain partial records, frequently of use to searchers are the Rotary, Kiwanis, Lions, and others.

If you have indication that your subject was a member of any social organization, it will frequently repay you to get in touch with the local secretary of the organization to ascertain which records they have concerning him. In one instance, it was possible to locate the birth place of a man who came from England to the United States through the records concerning him in the archives of the Odd Fellows.

In the last few years the rise in importance of the professional societies, including such organizations as the American Chemical Society, American Society of Mechancal Engineers, and so on, have opened up new sources of information for the genealogists of the next generation.

Greek letter fraternities, especially college fraternities, also provide good records. The fraternity system in the United States stems basically from Phi Beta Kappa, whose records go back to the year 1776. The oldest of the living social college fraternities is the Kappa Alpha Society, which dates from 1825 at Union College, New York.

Since fraternities are careful to follow "legacies", that is, children of members, to consider them for membership, it will be obvious that good membership lists will be maintained. It is a talking point that "so-and-so" is the son of a member, brother-in-law of another member, has two cousins who are members and a son who is a member. One frequently notes such statements and they are usually documented with places, dates and names.

The best book for the study of the fraternity system is Baird's *Manual of American College Fraternities.* In addition to showing the list of active fraternities, those inactive are also listed. Colleges where they are represented are also shown, and an index of colleges shows what fraternities are or were in existence at the college in question.

Suppose the person under investigation was known to have attended Princeton University in 1850. We turn to Baird's *Manual,* p. 702 (1930 edition), and note that the following fraternities were in existence at Princeton in that year: Delta Kappa Epsilon and Zeta Psi. In addition, Delta Psi and Chi Phi were there the following year, and Kappa Alpha in 1852. We may now write to the secretaries of these fraternities and ask them to examine their records for our man. If they find him, they will probably be able to advise us where he lived, perhaps also his birth and death dates, possibly his marriage record and the names of his parents and children.

Among the effects of a person under investigation, you may find a fraternity pin. Recourse to Baird's *Manual*, then to the secretary of that fraternity will show at once where he joined, and probably his school, age, and place of residence. The rest may follow directly or indirectly from that information.

To obtain the records of extinct fraternities is difficult, but not always impossible. First, the searcher should get in touch with the National Interfraternity Conference. (See the latest issue of Baird's *Manual*.) The secretary may be able to advise the location of the records, or if not, may be able to put the searcher in touch with a member who knows their whereabouts. If this source fails, reference to Baird will indicate the location of chapters of the fraternity, and reference to yearbooks of the colleges where it was represented will provide the names of members, from which names the search may be continued.

The same methods as noted above apply to searches in the records of other fraternal orders and clubs.

The University Clubs require college education for membership. Their membership lists and records will be sure to yield the educational background of your subject if he is a member.

It should also be noted that the rise of women's organizations (including sororities) is providing similar records for the genealogists of the future to use in the search of maternal lines. Since name changes will show in these records, they may prove invaluable for proof of marriages.

CHAPTER II

SECONDARY MATERIALS

Manuscripts

Many historical and genealogical societies possess collections of family records and notes assembled by various genealogists. For instance, the Genealogical Society of Pennsylvania in Philadelphia has the vast collections of Gilbert Cope, William M. Mervine, and May Atherton Leach, all valuable for students of Pennsylvania family history. One of the prized collections of the New Jersey Historical Society at Newark is the tremendous amount of material relating to families of that state gathered together during a long lifetime of research by Charles Carroll Gardner, F. A. S. G. In Washington, the National Genealogical Society owns the genealogical papers of Robert Atwater Smith (New England families), Florence Bridges Culver (Maryland and Virginia), and Gaius M. Brumbaugh (Revolutionary War records, tax lists, Bible records, probate records, etc., relating chiefly to Pennsylvania, Maryland, and Virginia). Such collections are valuable for the researcher, because the compilers have pulled together from a variety of sources information which could be obtained by other interested persons only after long and arduous searches in many states and communities. It should be remembered, however, that no one is infallible, and even the best genealogists make mistakes and misinterpret records. It is always preferable, whenever one has the opportunity, to examine the primary sources for oneself. But collections such as those mentioned above frequently provide short cuts in genealogical research.

In addition to collections of genealogies, historical and genealogical societies and state libraries have assembled other manuscript materials of value for the researcher. The Virginia State Library at Richmond, Virginia, has transcripts of many church registers in that state.. The Library of the National Society of Daughters of the American Revolution has copies of tombstone records, vital statistics, Bible records, church registers, etc., made by D. A. R. chapters all over the country and sent to their national headquarters in Washington. The Manuscripts Department of the Historical Society of Pennsylvania owns such family archives as the Pemberton Papers, to mention one of many; it also has part of Gilbert Cope's tremendous collection of historical and genealogical papers, the other part being in the Genealogical Society of Pennsylvania. A wealth of information awaits the researcher who ferrets out the repositories that contain records of his areas of interest.

Printed Materials

The printed works frequently used by genealogists are family histories, collected genealogies, source materials, and local histories:

FAMILY HISTORIES.—Family histories vary in quality. Donald Lines Jacobus has commented in one of his articles that such histories "are in general the least trustworthy sources for establishing lines of descent". A published genealogy is based on many sources, such as primary records (wills, deeds, pensions, church registers, etc.), the memory (sometimes faulty) of various members of the family, and printed books which may or may not have been carefully compiled. Some books, such as Moon's *The Morris Family of Philadelphia* (5 vols., 1898-1909), Ferris' *Dawes-Gates Ancestral Lines* (1931), French's *Genealogy of the Descendants of Thomas French* (2 vols., 1909), Jacobus' *Hale, House, and Related Families* (1952), Davis's *The Ancestry of Mary Isaac* (1955), and Holman's *Descendants of Samuel Hills* (1957), are models of painstaking genealogical research and careful compilation.

Many works, unfortunately, are not worth the paper on which they are printed. They are carelessly done, their compilers being untrained and inexperienced in methods of genealogical research and presentation. Such persons often arrived at erroneous conclusions as, for instance, the Rittenhouse genealogy of 1893 in which the origin of that famous Pennsylvania family was falsely deduced from the noble von

Rittershausen family and earlier from the Imperial House of Habsburg, and the slender book on the Haines family of Burlington County, New Jersey, in which it was claimed that the founder, Richard Haines, was a grandson of Governor John Haynes, of Connecticut and his wife, Mabel Harlakenden—which, *if it were true,* would mean that Mabel was only about 21 years old when her alleged *grandson* was born! Other cases could be cited to demonstrate that one must be careful in weighing printed statements. A useful little manual, *Is That Lineage Right?*, put out in 1958 by the National Society Daughters of the American Revolution, succinctly expresses it (p. 19): "In evaluating a genealogy, certain criteria may be considered: (1) the author's reputation as a careful and critical genealogist, and (2) the attention paid by the compiler to source materials, at least for the early generations".

COLLECTED GENEALOGIES.—This type of genealogical literature, illustrated by Mackenzie's *Colonial Families of the United States* (7 vols.), Jordan's *Colonial and Revolutionary Families of Pennsylvania* (19 volumes to date), Lee's *Genealogical and Memorial History of the State of New Jersey* (4 vols.), and Virkus's *The Compendium of American Genealogy* (7 vols.), are based on information provided by members of the families discussed in those works. Consequently, many errors and false assumptions are perpetuated; the data must be verified by an independent investigation. As in the case of family histories, they are useful for providing clues for further research.

SOURCE MATERIALS.—Printed source materials are valuable for the researcher who cannot afford to travel long distances for the purpose of personally examining court records, wills, deeds, marriage records, etc., in the places where his family lived. Their value depends, of course, on the accuracy with which the records have been transcribed, and the copyist's knowledge of the handwriting of the period in which he is working. Due allowance must also be made for typographical errors made while the books are in the press.

LOCAL HISTORIES.—Printed histories of states, counties, and

localities often contain much genealogical information. But here a word of caution again must be given, for they, too, vary in quality. Many local histories indulge in eulogies of the families discussed, and errors are frequently made with respect to early generations. Local histories published prior to 1885 are *generally* accurate for the family history of the Revolutionary and post-Revolutionary period; they are based, for the most part, on statements made by members of the family who had knowledge of the persons and events of the period.

OTHER PRINTED MATERIALS.[1]—Reference works, newspapers, and directories are other important published materials frequently used in genealogical research. Reference works include *The National Cyclopaedia of American Biography*, the *Dictionary of American Biography*, various *Who's Who* publications *(Who's Who in America, Who's Who in the Theatre, Who's Who Among North American Authors*, etc.). The record of the arts is not so well defined but biographical studies of artists, even of craftsmen, are common, and it would be wise to check such records for areas from which the family may have come. Similar biographical studies of soldiers and other professions are helpful. Such accounts are basically laudatory and in many instances the data were furnished by the subject or his family. If a searcher knows that his subject was closely associated with some man of local prominence, it may well pay him to check not only for the biography of his subject, but for a biography of that associate who may have been a boyhood friend. The Library of Congress, State libraries, historical societies, and local history sections of larger public libraries have created indexes to such materials relating to their areas.

Newspapers, of course, are invaluable for providing information on marriages and deaths; the older newspapers did not contain birth notices. Obituaries are not always accurate, even at the present time. For example, a Philadelphian who died in 1916 at the age of 56, was described by one newspaper as being 53 years old, and by another as being a flattering 48;

---

[1] This paragraph was contributed, in part, by David C. Duniway.

his only child, a seven-year-old son, was given as seventeen in one of the papers, while in the other he was described as the decedent's *daughter*. In general, however, obituaries can be relied upon for the basic outlines of the subject's life.

Directories, such as city, telephone, trade and professional, are important for locating families and individuals at certain periods of time, and for providing information on their occupations. In the case of large cities, such as New York and Philadelphia, the city directory can often be used for identifying the wards in which families lived, thus facilitating researches to be made later in census schedules.

Part 3

REGIONAL GENEALOGY

CHAPTER I

NEW ENGLAND

A. MAINE AND NEW HAMPSHIRE

The economic urge was the dominating factor in the first colonization of both Maine and New Hampshire, in distinction to the religious impulse which was so powerful in Massachusetts and the other New England colonies. Merchants and ambitious scions of the gentry class obtained large grants of land from the Lord Proprietors, and sent over or brought with them groups of fishermen and laborers to settle in the harbors from the Kennebec to the Piscataqua Valley. Both the upper and lower classes were, generally speaking, loyalist and conformist, and the solid middle class yeomen and artisans, so important in the Puritan colonies, were largely lacking. The bulk of these emigrants came from the southwestern counties of England—Cornwall, Devon, Dorset, Somerset. There were, of course, individual and group exceptions. The town of Hampton in New Hampshire was f om the first a typical Puritan settlement, while Exeter was the home of exiled Bostonians. By the middle of the 17th century, however, the Maine and New Hampshire towns were being reinforced by a stream of East Anglian Congregationalists from Massachusetts which continued to flow until after the Revolutionary War. New Hampshire maintained its political identity, but Maine became an integral part of Massachusetts and so remained until 1820. Against this solid Anglo-Saxon 17th century background, a few exotics stand out, a lone Greek in New Castle, N. H., a Walloon in York, Maine, a few Irish and Jersey boys, probably here against their wills, in the Piscataqua towns, and a group of Scotch prisoners, captured at the battle of Dunbar, at York.

In the first quarter of the 18th century, both New Hampshire and Maine received a strong infusion of blood from the Ulster Scots. In New Hampshire, their chief settlement was the new town of Londonderry, while in Maine they are found in all of the coast towns, with particular emphasis on Wells, Falmouth, and the lower reaches of the Kennebec. Colonel Waldo's large colony of Germans from the Palatinate, with the addition of a group of French Protestants, settled farther to the eastward in the 1750's, and after the Revolution a single Pole turned up in Pownalborough. The majority of pioneers in the newer inland towns of both New Hampshire and Maine were, however, of native or Massachusetts stock. This continued to be the case until, in the middle years of the 19th century, the heavy influx of Irish began, soon followed by thousands of French Canadians, to be absorbed in the great mills and factories on the power-producing rivers of both states. So much for a general statement of racial origins.

For the 17th century and the greater part of the 18th century, the labors of the genealogist have been made less difficult by the great body of original material published by the Maine and New Hampshire Historical Societies or under their auspices. New Hampshire has led the way with its splendid series of *Provincial, Town and State Papers, New Hampshire*, forty volumes to date. All New Hampshire probate records from 1635 to 1771—wills, administrations, inventories and related papers—are printed in vols. 31 to 39 of this series. New Hampshire was not divided into counties until the Act of 29 April 1769, when Rockingham, Strafford, Hillsborough, Cheshire and Grafton were created, and all land and probate business was transacted before that date at the provincial capitol. The lag of two years between 1769 and 1771 was presumably due to the time required in setting up county offices and officers. Vol. XXXX (sic) of the series contains court records (1640-1692) and court papers (1652-1658). The original probate and court material from which these volumes were transcribed, also all deeds recorded before 1771, are to be found in the state archives room at the library of the New Hampshire Historical Society in Concord. For land and probate business after 1771, the records must be searched at the several county seats.

Present day Maine was York County, Massachusetts, until 1760, when two new counties—Cumberland and Lincoln—

were carved from it. York, Cumberland and Lincoln have since undergone further subdivision. *York Deeds,* covering the period from 1632 to 1737, have been published *verbatim* in 18 volumes and are of great genealogical value. The library of the Maine Historical Society in Portland has microfilm carrying the York Deeds to 1860. *Maine Wills,* printed in 1887, contains every will proved in the province from 1640 to 1760, again *verbatim.* Unfortunately, administrations, inventories and other probate papers were not included in this volume and must be sought at Alfred, the York County seat, or on microfilm at the Maine Historical Society in Portland, where York Probate records are available to 1860.

When he edited *Lincoln Probate,* covering the years 1760 to 1800, William Davis Patterson wisely included all probate records. Cumberland County has twice seen its county offices burned to the ground, first in 1866 and again in 1910, and in both fires the probate records were completely destroyed, but the record books of the registry of deeds were providentially saved. All Maine court records from 1636 to 1711 are in print in the four volumes of *Province and Court Records of Maine,* in which will be found much genealogical information. For the newer counties, their record offices must be searched for deeds, wills and court records.

The genealogist working on Maine ancestry should remind himself often that Maine was not separated from Massachusetts until 1820 and that, therefore, certain classes of records must be sought in Boston. The pleadings, depositions and documents in evidence in court cases which were appealed from the Maine county courts to the Supreme Judicial Court of Massachusetts, mounted in scrap books and indexed, are to be found in the Suffolk County Court House and often contain the solution of a difficult problem. Ability to read the old handwriting is a requisite. Many, perhaps the majority, of the papers in the Massachusetts Archives in the State House which deal wholly with Maine have been published, to the year 1791, in *Collections of the Maine Historical Society, Documentary Series,* 24 volumes. The claims made to lands in Maine after the Indian Wars by Maine exiles and Massachusetts speculators have been printed, possibly only in part, in the *Maine Historical & Genealogical Recorder.*

Town and church vital records of the 17th century are fragmentary except in a few towns, such as York, Kittery and Hampton. Some books were undoubtedly destroyed during the Indian Wars (roughly 1675-1677, 1689-1713) when most of the Maine towns were deserted, the inhabitants retiring to New Hampshire or Massachusetts where, with luck, their birth, marriage and death records for the period of their exile may be picked up. Even in the 18th century, the average standard of recording fell below that of the Massachusetts towns, and it continued to fall in the 19th century. Farmhouse fires have taken an appalling toll of town and church records, and in Maine, at any rate, in spite of laws providing for their deposit in safes, record books still repose on grocery shelves, in farmhouse kitchens and in damp cellars of town offices. Maine has made a half-hearted and New Hampshire a somewhat more effective effort to gather vital statistics from the entire state on cards, alphabetically arranged, at the state capitol. New Hampshire births, marriages and deaths from the town clerks' records, but not church records, are at the bureau of Vital Statistics at the State House, Concord. A Maine statute authorizes the publication of vital records in accordance with the system which has been so widely used in Massachusetts, but the legislature has implemented it with appropriations with extreme reluctance. Volumes for Augusta, Belfast, Bowdoin, Farmingdale, Gardiner, Georgetown, Hallowell, Lebanon, Otisfield, Pittston, Randolph, Topsham and Winslow have been issued. New Hampshire has officially taken no such step, but carefully transcribed and beautifully typewritten copies of the town and church vital records of many of the towns in the southeastern part of the state, the work of Miss Priscilla Hammond, may be found on the shelves of the Historical Society and other libraries. Some original record books, also, have found their way to the historical societies. *The New England Historical and Genealogical Register, New Hampshire Genealogical Record,* 1903-1909, *Bangor Historical Magazine* 1886-1894, and the 9 volumes of

Maine Historical & Genealogical Recorder, 1884-1898, contain the town and church records and gravestone inscriptions of many communities of both states, to which the D. A. R. have added many transcriptions, typewritten and bound in volumes which may be found in the larger genealogical libraries. The Maine State Library at Augusta has copies of the Maine section of U. S. Censuses of 1850, 1860, and 1870, and the Maine Historical Society those of 1800, 1830, 1850 and part of 1880 on microfilm, and the New Hampshire Historical Society has a manuscript copy of the U. S. Census of 1800.

Military service by New Hampshire men is admirably covered by the *Adjutant General's Report* for the years 1866 and 1868 which volumes, unfortunately not indexed, contain "The Military History of New Hampshire", including a vast collection of Muster Rolls, etc. *New Hampshire State Papers,* vols. 14 to 17, are devoted to the Revolutionary rolls. The New Hampshire Historical Society also has a typewritten and indexed manuscript containing the record of every Revolutionary pensioner (soldier or widow), copied from the pension records in Washington. Maine's Revolutionary record is covered in the 17 volumes of *Massachusetts Soldiers and Sailors of the Revolutionary War.*[1] For both states, in which King Philip's War is very important, not only because part of it was fought on their soil but because of the great land grants to its veterans, *Soldiers in King Philip's War,* by G. M. Bodge (3d edition, Boston, 1906) is invaluable. Service by Maine men in the other Indian Wars, however, demands search in the Massachusetts Archives. Maine soldiers in the War of 1812 will be found in *Records of the Massachusetts Volunteer Militia.* To its shame, Maine is one of the seven states which have no state archives department.

New Hampshire has been particularly productive, Maine somewhat less so, of local histories containing genealogical

---

[1] It has recently developed that subsequent to the publication of these volumes many additional muster rolls were discovered. Names on these (some 30,000) have been transcribed on cards and are in the office of the Secretary of the Commonwealth. A comparison of them with the published volumes indicates they contain approximately 20,000 names not appearing in the printed lists. Some of these may be Maine men.

and record information. Their great value lies in the contemporary data gathered by the compiler from living members of the families dealt with. In few cases, however, did the authors go to the probate and land records and, particularly in the early generations, there is much traditional chaff to be separated from that which is genealogically sound. The principal MAINE town histories with family material are: Augusta, Belfast, Boothbay, Brunswick, Durham, Eliot, Farmington, Gorham, Greene, Harrison, Industry, Islesborough, Kennebunkport (1837), Kittery, Lincoln, Litchfield, Livermore, Machias, Monmouth, North Yarmouth, Norway, Oxford, Paris, Parsonsfield, Rumford, Saco and Biddleford (1830), *Saco Valley Settlements and Families,* Sanford, Thomaston, Union, Warren, Waterford, Wayne, Windham, Winthrop, Woodstock.[2] NEW HAMPSHIRE: Acworth, Amherst, Andover, Antrim, Bedford, Boscawen, Bristol, Brookline, Canaan, Canterbury, Charlestown, Chester, Concord, Cornish, Coventry, Dover, Dublin, Durham, Exeter, Fitzwilliam, Francestown, Gilmanton, Gilsum, Goffstown, Hampstead, Hampton, Hancock, Haverhill, Henniker, Hillsborough, Hollis, Hopkinton, Jeffrey, Langdon, Littleton, Londonderry, Lyndeborough, Marlborough, Meredith, Milford, Mount Vernon, Newfields, New Ipswich, New London, Newport, Northfield, Nottingham, Pembroke, Penacook, Peterborough, Plymouth, Raymond, Richmond, Rindge, Rye, Salem, Salisbury, Sanbornton, Stratford, Sullivan, Surry, Sutton, Swanzey, Temple, Troy, Walpole, Washington, Weare, West Dunstable, Wilton, Windham, Wolfeborough. In many of these books families from neighboring towns are also included.

In the field of collective genealogy, both provinces are covered by *The Genealogical Dictionary of Maine and New Hampshire* which attempts to give the genealogical and important biographical facts concerning every family which was established by 1699, and in so doing carries many of them well into the 18th century. The book is the result of many

---

[2] Useful in determining the former names of towns and location of streams and mountains mentioned in records is Stanley B. Attwood's *The Length and Breadth of Maine* (1946).

years of research—a long lifetime in the case of Mr. Libby—
but the authors assure the researcher that more exhaustive
work on individual families may produce both *errata* and
addenda. Nor have they material on later generations in reserve, which fact, if sufficiently disseminated, would save
much fruitless correspondence!

B. VERMONT *

Vermont is the northwesternmost state in New England.
Much of the area comprising the state was in dispute between
its neighbors, New York being particularly insistent on asserting jurisdiction over it. This is important, as it means that
sometimes when known early settlers do not appear in the
Vermont records, they *may* be found in records of New York,
New Hampshire or Massachusetts.

The most comprehensive reference work in print is Abby
M. Hemenway's *Vermont Historical Gazetteer,* a sort of quarterly magazine issued over a long period of years. Miss Hemenway was an indefatigable worker who spent the best years
of her life traveling over the state gathering at first hand the
information which she worked into her history. Many of the
town histories were written by local people at Miss Hemenway's request; many of her records were taken from original
documents some of which have been since lost or burned.
Some years ago, the Vermont Legislature, inspired by someone who realized the value of a properly made index, authorized the publication of a thorough index to be made at state
expense. The index now forms the sixth volume, and has
greatly increased the value of the set. Miss Hemenway, at
the time of her sudden death in 1890, had projected a sixth
volume which was never published, so the *Gazetteer* does not
cover the entire state. It must be remembered that Miss
Hemenway is not always accurate, as few histories of that
period are accurate for, as already mentioned, much of her

---

* Based on Gilbert H. Doane's article, "Vermont: A Stumbling Block in
Midwestern Genealogy", *Indiana Magazine of History*, XXIV, March
1938, brought up-to-date by Jean Stephenson with data supplied by
Richard Wood, Director, Vermont Historical Society.

material was secured by interviewing "old settlers", a source of greatly varying reliability. In general, however, she can be relied upon to furnish a workable clue. As she worked between 1865 and 1885 gathering information, much of it came from people who were actually pioneers in the state, and much of it is available in no other place for, as in many young communities, pioneer records were poorly kept.

Another important collection, which to most genealogists is little known, is the *Records of the Council of Safety and Governor and Council of the State of Vermont, 1775-1836*.[1] As the title indicates, these volumes comprise original records of the various state councils and committees for their first half century, the earlier volumes being the official journals of the pre-legislative assemblies such as that at Westminster at which was declared the independence of the province. Like many public records, these are of inestimable value to the genealogist. As an example of their usefulness: The earliest record of the settlement of one branch of the Gilbert family in Vermont was in 1794, according to a deed which was the first dated record to be found. In one of the volumes (IV, 37) of this set is found, under date of 7 November, 1792, a record that Nathan Gilbert was made a member of a Committee on Road Tax in Smithfield (now part of Fairfield), thus carrying back the date of their settlement two years. Genealogically, much may happen in two or three years, especially when such a record indicates that Nathan Gilbert was sufficiently well known to the town's assemblyman to warrant his recommendation to the Governor's Council for such an appointment. Incidentally, there are many, probably about five hundred, biographical sketches of Vermonters of this period scattered throughout these eight volumes. An index to these sketches is found in Volume III (pp. 459-64), and all the names of persons are adequately indexed in each volume.

Of equal importance is *Vermont State Papers* (1918-1958). These contain many names and the last four volumes are petitions which are most helpful from a genealogical standpoint.

Unlike the other New England states, Vermont has made no

---

[1] Eliakim Persons Walton (editor), 8 vols., Montpelier, 1873-1880.

effort to publish the vital statistics of the towns making up the state. However, many town and county histories have been written and some of them include vital statistics.

Many years ago an enterprising individual in Burlington commenced the publication of Vermont marriage records, but only one volume was ever published.[2] That contained the records for Montpelier, Burlington and Berlin.

There are always the records of the first census, that of 1790. The user should remember that town lines and town and county names have changed a great deal since 1790; moreover, the 1790's were moving days, so the location of a man in one town according to the census does not mean that he could not be living fifty miles away, or even farther, the next year. In using the Vermont volume one should know that this census was not taken in Vermont until 1791, so many families may appear in two different volumes of the 1790 census. For instance, one Soule is listed as a resident of Pawling in the New York volume for 1790; and again in the Vermont volume as an inhabitant of Fairfield. Because of the date of this census in Vermont, one can sometimes calculate to within a year the date of migration to Vermont from any of the other states in which the census was taken in 1790.

Copies of the 1790 census are available in most of the larger libraries in the United States.

The Vermont Historical Society has published the U. S. Census for Vermont taken in 1800, which also is available in many libraries. The Vermont State Library has on microfilm the census returns of 1810 to 1870, and manuscript returns of those of 1850 to 1880, inclusive. The National Archives has the originals of those from 1790 to 1870, inclusive, and microfilm of that of 1880. Microfilms of those from 1830 to 1880 may be purchased from The National Archives.

A very valuable source of information as to names of early Vermonters is to be found in Volume XXVI of the *New Hampshire State Papers*. These are the records of the New Hampshire Grants made by Benning Wentworth; appended to

---
[2] *Vermont Marriages* (1903).

the grant of each township is the list of the grantees. It must be remembered that not all the grantees settled in the town, but many of them did, and one obtains from this list a valuable record.

Many of the petitions of the New York grantees may be found in the papers relating to the New Hampshire Grants in the fourth volume of E. B. O'Callaghan's *Documentary History of the State of New York,* where are to be found over five hundred pages of Vermont records, many of them of great genealogical importance. For instance, some of the petitions printed in full in this collection constitute virtual censuses of the several towns. Unfortunately, there is no index.

For Revolutionary rolls there has been published John E. Goodrich's compilation of *Rolls of Soldiers in the Revolutionary War, 1775-1783* (Rutland, 1904). These are not necessarily complete, for every little while a new roll of some company comes to light and has to be added to the others.

These records of Revolutionary men should be supplemented by another important list of "Soldiers of the Revolutionary War Buried in Vermont," published in the Vermont Historical Society *Proceedings, 1903-1904* (pp. 93-106, 114-165). This not only lists all known Revolutionary soldiers who are buried in the state, but also lists the names of various invalid pensioners of that war, resident in the state. This list was supplemented by another in the *Proceedings, 1905-1906* (pp. 189-203). Unfortunately both of these lists are arranged by towns, rather than by surnames, and there is no index, so they are difficult to use unless one knows the locality of the individual for whom he is searching.

The pension records in Washington are important to genealogists. The first major attempt to print the names of pensioners of the Revolutionary War, and certain data about them, was in 1835, when a report of the Secretary of War, ordered by Congress, was printed in three volumes as *Senate Executive Document,* No. 514, first session, twenty-third Congress. For the present purpose but a portion of Volume I, devoted to New England pensioners arranged by states, is of interest. There are one hundred sixty-four pages of Vermont pensioners, arranged by counties. With each name on the roll, are listed the man's rank, annual allowance, sums received, description of service, date when placed on pension roll, commencement of pension, age and remarks (which often constitute the date of death). The second major attempt was after the data of the 1840 census were available, for this census included by name each pensioner then living. This list was published by the Department of State in 1841, and constitutes a quarto volume of one hundred ninety-five pages, again arranged by states, so it is simple enough to get at the Vermont records. Unfortunately there is no index.

The National Genealogical Society has been publishing since March 1943 in its *Quarterly* an Index to the Revolutionary Pensions, the letter "S" having been reached in the June 1959 issue. While this index gives the state from which the pensioner served, rather than the state in which he lived when his pension was allowed, if the name of the soldier is known it can readily be determined if one appearing therein is the man who later lived in Vermont.

The Adjutant General of Vermont published in 1935 a *Roster of the War of 1812,* in which are listed all known Vermont soldiers in that war. The list has been compiled from various sources, and no name has been omitted of which a record has been found. The compiler had all names checked with the pension records in Washington, so pensioners and widows receiving pensions are indicated, and the number of the pension record is cited.

As for state, county and town histories, there are many in print. The worth of these varies greatly. The usual critical appraisal must be made before statements in them can be accepted. All too often such works are unindexed, particularly in the case of old or general histories.

An important index to be found in the *Proceedings* of the Vermont Historical Society for 1911-1912 (pp. 165-226) is that to Zadock Thompson's *History of Vermont* (edition of 1842), a book published at the time when indexes were not considered necessary.

Incidentally, it should be remembered that the New York counties of Cumberland (established 1768), Gloucester (established 1770) and Charlotte (established in 1772, name changed to Washington in 1784) embraced the area now in Vermont, so in tracing families in Vermont prior to 1791 it is well to consult New York records.

Genealogical students are familiar with the distressingly inaccurate and unreliable "genealogical and family" histories published during the last two decades of the 19th century and on into the 20th. Vermont was not slighted, for Hiram Carleton published such a work for the state, which is just as unreliable as dozens of other publications of that time.[3] However, not infrequently these very books furnish an enterprising genealogist with workable clues, so they must not be disregarded entirely. They should not, however, be accepted without thorough checking as *bona fide* proof of a descent. It is doubtful if any of the more important patriotic societies will accept a reference to one of them without substantiating evidence.

Those interested in families who lived near the New York line may find useful *Vermont Once No Man's Land*, by Merritt Clarke Barden (1928).

Every year for twenty-five years the Genealogical Records Committee of the Vermont Daughters of the American Revolution has prepared one or more indexed and bound volumes of genealogical records, usually cemetery inscriptions or church records. The original is in the D. A. R. Library in Washington, and a copy in the Vermont Historical Society Library in Montpelier.

In looking for unpublished records dealing with a genealogical problem, the first thought of the searcher is vital records. The Legislature of Vermont passed an act years ago requiring that each town clerk copy all vital records to be found among his office records and send them to the office of the Secretary of State. These copies were made on cards, and the cards are now filed alphabetically in Montpelier.

---

[3] *Genealogical and Family History of the State of Vermont* (2 vols., New York and Chicago, 1903).

Thus, the Secretary of State has supposedly all vital records from 1770 to date. A letter to the Department of Vital Statistics, Office of the Secretary of State, Montpelier, will bring an answer and certified copies will be furnished for a fee.

Theoretically, all cemetery inscriptions and church records were to be copied by the town clerks, but actually this was done in very few towns. In many towns the records had been destroyed by fire or flood before the act became effective, and, probably, in one or two places, the clerk was careless and didn't get all the records even in the town books. Since the records in Montpelier are by no means complete, failure to find a record there must not discourage the searcher.

The Vermont Historical Society in Montpelier has a large collection of manuscript as well as printed genealogies, and also housed with its collection is that of the Vermont Society of Colonial Dames. There also may be found many of the small locally printed accounts of "centennial celebrations" of churches, settlements, etc., which often provide needed information to the genealogist.

As to the use of vital records, all know that clues can be developed by analogy and from records which are not those of the individual sought, as for instance from the birth record of his brother or sister whose name is known to the searcher.

Failing vital records, and sometimes to establish relationships indicated in vital records, one must turn to probate records. Vermont is rather peculiar in this respect, for the probate district boundary does not always correspond to county lines. There are twenty probate districts in Vermont and only fourteen counties. A list of these districts may be found in the *Vermont Year Book* (formerly called *Walton's Register*). A good description of "Vermont Probate Districts", by Grace W. W. Reed and Winifred Lovering Holman, appeared in *The American Genealogist,* vol. 27, April 1951. It gives the location of each office, area covered, and date of the earliest record.

Land records in Vermont are kept in the offices of the town clerks. Fortunately, because of their value in preparing abstracts of title, indexes of grantees and grantors have been made in most offices, even if witnesses of deeds and others mentioned in the body of the deed are not listed. Land records are especially valuable in tracing a migration, and sometimes valuable in determining a relationship. John Doe of Sandwich, Massachusetts, may buy a piece of land in Bennington, Vermont, and fifteen years later, calling himself John Doe of Canton, New York, deed that same land to someone else. Thus, there is a record of two of his moves, from Sandwich to Bennington and from Bennington to Canton. Or, he may deed that same land "for the natural love I bear him" to his son, Thomas Doe, and in a later deed Thomas Doe of Richmond, Indiana, may dispose of that land in Bennington, thus definitely placing Thomas Doe of Richmond, Indiana, as the son of John Doe of Bennington, Vermont, formerly of Sandwich, Massachusetts.

Church records, another important mass of unpublished records, are more difficult to trace. The clerkship of the church changes, records get lost, ministers move away and sometimes take the records with them. Houses burn and the records perish. But the genealogist of ingenuity will find them, if possible, for in them are sometimes records which are missing from the town books—baptisms, admissions (sometimes by letter from another church a hundred miles away), dismissals (especially those by letter to another church), and burials. Try the yearbooks of the various denominations, such as the Congregational Yearbook, as the first source of information concerning the individual to whom it is desired to write about such records. It will save postage and grief if the letter is written directly to somebody, rather than to the postmaster who has to be asked to give the letter to the proper person—such letters the writer has seen accumulate in one small post office in Vermont!

C. MASSACHUSETTS

The question most frequently asked by the public of the librarians at the New England Historic Genealogical Society is a simple one, "Where can I find records of deeds and estates in Massachusetts?" This it is proposed to answer, also to show up the oddities of some of the methods of keeping them, and in the course of this reply to put in some other helpful hints.

First, we must realize that history should be studied for the background of any colony, province or state, in an effort to comprehend fully why such methods arose; such a survey is left to the individual searcher. Massachusetts, unlike Gaul, was divided before 1686 into *two* colonies, the smaller one covering what is now Barnstable, Bristol and Plymouth. Counties, before it was gobbled up by the much larger and always land-hungry Bay Colony. (Just as the latter "acquired" parts of New Hampshire, in 1641-1642, Maine in 1652, and attempted to take over parts of Rhode Island and Connecticut earlier, but failed in the last two attempts.) Eventually, in 1820, Maine became a separate state. The line between Massachusetts and New Hampshire was partly settled in 1741,[1] that with Connecticut in 1749, and with Rhode Island in 1747. An argument over the western boundary, with New York, lasted much longer. When working with towns near these boundaries, one has always to consider the history or the "genealogy" of that section in respect to dates, in order to locate the place of records at a given date. One must learn what is available for the special period and where these records are, one of the A. B. C.'s of all research.

The probate[2] (wills, administrations and guardianships) are kept in each county. There are no orphans courts as such. Since 1888, probate includes divorces, as well as changes of

---

[1] Final settlement, 13 June 1894 (1902 *Report of the Commissioners*, pp. 3,4).

[2] In Massachusetts the word, "probate," is used in the same sense as "probate records" is used elsewhere, i.e., to cover both books and documents or "loose papers", or, in other words, all records relating to settlement of estates.

name; before that year, divorces were filed in the Supreme Judicial Court, under the counties. The land transactions and mortgages (no separate index for the latter) are kept in each county, as are the various types of county court records. The primer for Finding Aids is Wright's 1889 *Report of the Public Records*, first made available in the 1880's, with additional publications from time to time. Especially valuable is that of 1889, as it gives the full story of town, church and court records, and lists extinct towns and churches (the last by denomination as well as by town), etc. However, it is not infallible and has to be annotated and corrected to bring it up to date.

In 1643, the Bay Colony was divided into four counties, Middlesex, Suffolk, Essex and Norfolk. This last was the "old" Norfolk, set up to include the towns of Dover, Exeter, Portsmouth, Salisbury and Hampton. Its deeds and estates, 1649-1714, in 4 volumes, separately indexed, are at Salem, county seat of Essex. The territory now comprising Amesbury, Merrimac, Salisbury, Haverhill, Methuen and the north part of Lawrence, included in this area was set off to Essex in 1680, at which time Norfolk supposedly expired; yet, records run as late as 1714. At the same time, there were two separate deed registries in Essex, the Ipswich Deeds, 1640-1694, in 5 volumes, likewise separately indexed, and the regular Essex Deeds.[3]

The above comments as to records of deeds and probate do not take into consideration fairly modern registries of deeds. Some of our larger counties have a double registry system: Bristol 1837; Essex 1869; Middlesex 1855, and Worcester 1884.

Thus, at Salem, the Registry for Essex, we have three sets of deeds, one of which includes probate, in the 17th century—

---

[3] These records, Ipswich and Norfolk (copy) are in poor condition, the index of the former is ancient (*ante* 1700), both sets should be copied now and properly indexed. Much will come to light when this does happen, as it is probable that not all the names of the grantors and grantees appear in the present indexes.

Norfolk, Ipswich, and the regular and splendidly indexed Essex.⁴ And, of course, the probate.

The date of earliest entry for Suffolk probate is 1636. The early indexes are published and refer to a file number. From this Docket Index, one gets the index to volumes and pages and a list of the extant documents. It is now customary to limit the actual perusal of the documents to those known to the Register, or who bear a letter to him. This is due to a lack of employees, the old files are not easy of access. But, as in all old probate, one has to cover both the records in the copy-books (volumes) and the original papers or documents to get the complete story. Due to the Andros Administration,⁵ in which a much needed revision of probate proceedings was made by that much maligned governor, estates worth over fifty pounds were brought to Boston to be acted upon from all over New England, from New York, and even from New Jersey.

Suffolk deeds were entered from 1639, are now well housed and with a fine descriptive index. The first 14 volumes have been printed and insofar as recording is concerned carry past 1686; the "other person" index in each volume is invaluable. Not many know that a last name index has been made of "other persons" through 1799, and is available for use in that form. Suffolk lost two of its volumes of deeds in 1776, when all the then extant books were carted to Dedham, the British having taken Boston.

Suffolk now has photostat facilities for both probate and deeds, as do most of the Massachusetts counties, Hampshire probate being one of the present (1959) exceptions.

Middlesex probate date from 1654. The printed index is to the files, so if one wishes to check on the copy-books, always a "must", one has to cover the by-the-volume indexes. More-

---

⁴ It is common in Massachusetts, as elsewhere, to give as a date in the index of deeds, the recording and not the actual passing. It is well to take all *three* dates of each deed when abstracting; this is often missed by so-called experts!

⁵ See *American Genealogist*, vols. 12-13, for an article re-same and index of all estates, giving places of residence (which the printed index omits), etc., 1686-1692.

over, there is a single large modern copy of Miscellaneous Records, *ante* 1692, made from the files of the county court[6] at the instigation of the late Mary Lovering Holman; this covers from the beginning of that county until the appointment of a Judge of Probate in 1692. As this book is cross indexed, it is of immense value.

Middlesex deeds commence with 1649. The index is old type before 1800, that is, no place of land cited, and although a modern index was made some 20 years ago on cards, it has not as yet become available to the public. Also, at this Registry are the little-known Hopkinton and Upton Deeds, 1743-1833, 19 volumes, with a separate grantor index, which deal with land owned once by Harvard. A grantee index would be of value, but it has never been made.

Across the street from the Registry, at the Office of the Clerk of Courts, is an index made by the W. P. A. of the Court Files to about 1733; a most intricate system of filing makes it quite a chore to locate the case or paper from this index, but it can be done. The papers are in bundles and were tagged with years and file numbers but the tags in many instances are now lost, and the bundles are no longer in chronological order, there is insufficient space for them, they are crammed together, and are kept in four separate places. Those in authority know little about the "system". All is kept under lock and key as it should be. They have a photostat machine. The copy-books of the court records date from 1686 and are roughly indexed by the volume.

The present Norfolk is a late county, being established in 1793 from Suffolk. The county seat is at Dedham. But bear in mind that many a town *now* part of Boston was formerly within Norfolk, after 1793. Like the Bay Colony, Boston has been a great grabber of territory! There is a printed index to the probate and both probate and deeds are well kept and easily available.

Barnstable, Plymouth and Bristol Counties were all set up in 1686, when the little "Old Colony" (Plymouth) expired

---

[6] By a Mrs. Rusiel; it is handwritten.

and was embraced by the Bay Colony.⁷ Unfortunately, the deeds and probate files of Barnstable, that happy hunting ground for *Mayflower* descendants, were burned in 1827 although a very few deeds have since been recorded.⁸

In 1746, Cumberland, Barrington, Warren, Bristol, Tiverton and Little Compton, formerly in Bristol County, were annexed to Rhode Island. The county seat of Bristol County was then changed from Bristol to Taunton.

The records of Plymouth Colony were printed a century ago; they include one volume of deeds. At the time it was planned to print all the deeds and the probate. Handwritten copies of these are now at the Massachusetts Archives.⁹ Hence, one can obtain in Boston the usual county deeds and probate before 1686 of these three counties, including those towns which, since 1746, are part of Rhode Island.

Dukes County (mainly Martha's Vineyard) dates from 1696 for probate and 1686 for deeds, and Nantucket from 1706 for probate and 1659 for deeds; both are islands, and were formerly under the jurisdiction of New York.

Worcester was set up in 1731 from Suffolk and Middlesex Counties. In a large county such as Middlesex, many of the deeds are late recorded. Some deeds have been recorded 50, 75 and even 100 years late in Middlesex. One Hampshire County town was included in Worcester, namely, Brookfield. Its probate index is in print and one may use both papers and books. Some of the early deeds are now on microfilm but, when necessary, researchers may consult the actual volume.

Turning to Hampshire, Hampden and Franklin Counties, we find that, before 1787, all deeds pertaining to the three counties are at Springfield. In 1787, three Registries of Deeds were set up in old Hampshire at Deerfield, Northampton and Springfield. Franklin was set off in 1811 and Hampden in 1812, with county seats at Greenfield (at which time Deer-

---

⁷ Older probate files of Bristol are not numbered.
⁸ By a miracle the probate records (vols.) of Barnstable survived. From 25 Oct. 1685 until 17 Nov. 1707, Rochester was within Barnstable Co., and then in Plymouth Co. (*Pilgrim Notes and Queries*, April 1917, vol. 5, No. 4, p. 62.)
⁹ *Vide post.*

field Registry was abolished) and Springfield.[10] But all the probate of Hampshire before 1811 (Franklin) and 1812 (Hampden) are at Northampton.[11] So the searcher must work in both Springfield (deeds) and Northampton (probate) before 1811 and 1812. The deeds for the present Hampshire have been at Northampton since 1787. Border towns such as Somers, Enfield, Suffield, now in Connecticut, were, before 1750, in Hampshire County.

In 1788, Berkshire County, which had been erected in 1761 from Hampshire, was divided into three Registries of Deeds, North Adams, Great Barrington and Pittsfield. All three now have identical sets of typed proprietors' records of some of the older towns, fully indexed, made in 1920.[12] Be sure to see these as there is much land evidence within them. Both the northern district (North Adams) and the southern district (Great Barrington), have abstracts of the deeds before 1788, pertaining to its section, but it is well to cover the parent also, (Pittsfield).

The deeds and probate for Woodstock, Connecticut, are in Boston until 1731 as it was part of Suffolk, then in Worcester until 1750. Another curiosity is the town of Hingham. When the present Norfolk was incorporated, 26 March 1793, it included all the original territory of Suffolk, except the towns of Boston and Chelsea (Rumney Marsh). Hingham, Hull and Cohasset were to be a part of the new county, but before this went into operation as such, the law was repealed 20 June 1793 in regard to Hingham and Hull. These two remained within Suffolk until 13 June 1803, when they were annexed to Plymouth. Cohasset, a part of Hingham until 1770, is now in Norfolk and is separated completely from its county by Hingham and Hull which are in Plymouth. Brookline, in

---

[10] In 1812, the town of Chester (whose deeds had been filed at Northampton from 1787) was annexed to Springfield in so far as registration of deeds was concerned (information supplied by the late Ethel Lord Scofield, Longmeadow, Mass.).

[11] In the 1958 *New England Historic Genealogical Register* appeared a Note *re* Probate (1690-1692) in back of Vol. A. of Hampshire Co. Deeds, at Springfield.

[12] In the use of this index, bear in mind that the copyist could not decipher many of the names.

Norfolk, is isolated by Boston, in Suffolk, and by Newton, Watertown and Cambridge in Middlesex, the reason being Boston's West Roxbury, once a part of Norfolk's Dedham.

Thus, we conclude our very quick and general survey of the counties in respect to their probate and deeds.

It may be of help to note that in 1938 when the Quabbin Dam obliterated some of the old Hampshire and Worcester towns, the records of these towns were placed in the Administration Quarters of the Windsor Dam, in Belchertown. Care must be utilized in using these records for they have been rebound in some instances without regard to the original pagination; it is well to leaf through them. Of these former towns, Greenwich was formed 1754, Enfield 1816, Dana 1801 and Prescott 1822. The bounds of the remaining towns in that vicinity have been changed. The situation needs careful study for good work. The Massachusetts D. A. R. is copying the vital records of Greenwich, Enfield and Prescott. Typed copies of the gravestones of these extinct towns are available. The church records have been placed in various repositories.[13]

The various reports of the printed public records, already cited, give the necessary information about town and church records, and have been, more or less, kept up-to-date, in an interleaved and annotated copy at the New England Historic Genealogical Society.

Vital records of about half or more of the older towns have been published, by various individuals, societies and the state. Hence they vary as to content and arrangement. Before using these volumes, one must always evaluate them by a study of the abbreviations which quickly inform one if they are all-inclusive, with town, church, Bible, private and gravestone records being covered. Many of the older books are not so done. And sometimes, as in Lynn, the original records were used plus recent (and incorrect) additions, not placed in brackets, as is done in the case of Duxbury. Most of these

---

[13] It is regrettable that when church records are included in published vital records the admissions and dismissions are generally omitted, even though not pertaining to births, marriages and deaths.

records are printed in the alphabet form. The *Mayflower Descendant* includes vital records of towns in the Cape Cod and Plymouth areas.

With few exceptions, one has to go to the town to consult the town meeting (minutes) and proprietors' records. The former are valuable for their "Warnings Out" and for records about civil and military services during the Colonial and Revolutionary War periods.[14]

Local town libraries and small historical societies should always be visited for town records, such as Woburn, with its Wyman Collection; Pittsfield with the R. D. Cook copies of church, town and cemetery records; New Bedford; Westfield; and so on.

Boston itself should form a separate chapter, if not a volume of considerable pages. There is a well-known hiatus in its vital records, roughly over a century, from about 1740. This period must be covered by use of the copies of the many old Boston Church Records, now at City Hall. As these copies were paid for by the City, they are in its possession and are subject to a small fee for their examination. There is little room for their careful storage and supervision, and no room at all for the searcher; they should be placed elsewhere. They are by the volume and the indexes are last name only. The originals are still in the possession of the various churches, if extant, if not, it is a hunt! It so happens that the records of a few of these churches have been printed, the Brattle Square being one of these exceptions. An effort has been made by the Congregational, the Episcopal and the Unitarian communities to localize these records, especially in the case of defunct churches, in their respective libraries, in Boston.

The Boston Record Commissioners, known as the B. R. C., issued in 39 volumes the available vital records, selectmen's

---

[14] *Warning Out* had nothing to do with the financial or moral status of those so warned. The law read briefly that no strangers were to be entertained in a town above 20 days without giving notice to the selectmen. (13th of William III.) Some towns rigidly enforced the law, for periods, others never did.

minutes, town records and so on, over a period of years.[15] Such old gravestone records as have been printed have been issued privately, *e. g.,* Copps Hill, Central and Granary. More recent ones have been printed by the City, such as Mt. Hope. Many of the Boston *et vic* cemeteries have been copied in typescript under various auspices.

A listing of places in which to work in Boston may be of some aid:

1. SUFFOLK COUNTY COURT HOUSE, for probate and deeds, and also for the old Superior Court of Judicature (since 1785 the Supreme Judicial Court of the Commonwealth), where is the marvelous Murphy cross index to all the files before 1700. This index is arranged as an index to a Docket Index. After 1700, there are indexes to the cases, under various counties.

2. MASSACHUSETTS ARCHIVES. This is probably the richest and most consecutive collection in these United States, and is also probably the most badly housed and neglected. Now (1959), however, the Commonwealth is erecting an Archives building, with proper temperature and humidity control.

In 1836-1846 the various papers in the Archives were pasted in some 242 volumes by J. B. Felt, in a curious system of his own. There is an index in each. Volumes 1-40 and the Town Series, 112-118 inclusive, are cross indexed in the main catalogue. In addition, there is a chronological catalogue in 7 volumes, which covers the entire 242. Volumes 67-80 are indexed in the military series. Volumes 243-326, which begin about 1660, have been arranged since 1885. These do not appear in the main catalogue, or general index, nor have they any index by the volume. A few have a name index but deal mainly with Shays' Rebellion in 1786. But various booklets have been issued by the Archives about their records. Not much has been indexed since 1940. The main card indexes are:

Military, 1643-1774, 14 volumes; Civil, 1686-1744; Shays'

---

[15] Note that B. R. C. 28, entitled *Marriages, 1700-1751*, contains some intentions, 1695-1697, pp. 348-350, and from 1676 a few marriages, p. 327.

Rebellion, 1786; French and Indian War, 1710-1774.[16] General Index or C a t a l o g u e, explained above; Eastern Claims (Maine); Pensioners; Executive Records of the Governor's Council.

Of the colonial era, it might be estimated that about two-thirds of the records are covered by one of these indexes. Some of the records are now on microfilms. At the Archives are also some census records, late lists of immigrants, original wills not found elsewhere, etc.

At the State House, in which are the inadequately (1959) housed Archives, is also the Bureau of Vital Statistics (the vital records for the entire state since 1842), and the Adjutant General's Office, which contains war services since the Revolution (particularly militia records). The State Library has some treasures, such as the Governor Bradford history, on loan, but does not concentrate upon records as such; it does have files of old newspapers which are helpful.

3. THE BOSTON PUBLIC LIBRARY has newspapers and also the W. P. A. Index to the genealogical pages of the late *Boston Transcript*. THE BOSTON ATHENAEUM, a private library, has newspapers, various published and unpublished sources, including some of the original Suffolk County Court Files, now in print. THE BOSTON MEDICAL LIBRARY is a great help if the ancestor was a doctor. The libraries of various faiths have been cited above; we must also consider those of the colleges and universities in Massachusetts, each with its own specialty, such as Widener at Harvard, with its fine county history collection; Williams, with the original Hutchinson Mss., and so on.

4. FOR CUSTOM HOUSE RECORDS, see Dr. Samuel E. Morison's article, June, 1921, in the *Proceedings of the Massachusetts Historical Society*. There are also two volumes of Maritime Records at the Supreme Judicial Court.

5. THE MASSACHUSETTS HISTORICAL SOCIETY published in

---

[16] This last index is only on cards on which are abstracted the records and it was planned to publish them years ago. But only the Revolutionary and Civil War records have been issued. There are also some additional *unpublished* records of the Revolutionary War available.

1948 a list of their principal manuscript collections, for which they are famed, to which the student is referred. Many of these are now fully cross indexed; they also have the late Miss Thwing's Index to old Boston families and streets, which is sometimes a help to published sources, deeds and probate, and a cross reference.

6. THE NEW ENGLAND HISTORIC GENEALOGICAL SOCIETY is the oldest genealogical library in the United States, and it is especially rich in unpublished material; a continuation, on cards, of the *Munsell Index;* a card index to places, now in process, throughout the United States, for sources within this library; and the *1798 Direct Tax for Massachusetts,* including Maine (see the *New England Historical and Genealogical Register,* vol. 45, 1891, pp. 82-83). Much of the unpublished material is in the vault and no longer available to non-members, but such material on the shelves may be consulted by the public. There is a notable collection of diaries and newspapers. This Society's quarterly, the *New England Historical and Genealogical Register,* now (1959) in its 113th volume, needs no further introduction. Membership, which includes loan of books of which there are duplicates, is essential to those who attempt careful research in Massachusetts.[17]

ADDENDA.

In 1958, the author of this chapter was advised by Mrs. John E. Barclay, F. A. S. G., that the supposed verbatim and complete official copy of the Plymouth Colony deeds and wills, made about 1860 by Shattuck (indexed by the volumes and not cross-indexed), said copy, in some dozen large volumes, being at the Massachusetts Archives, is not complete. (The wills include all types of estates.) Briefly, the original volumes, at Plymouth, Massachusetts, in the Registry of Deeds, for Plymouth County, contain more deeds and many more wills than are given in this "official copy". One would have to compare

---

[17] Grateful acknowledgement is hereby made to Miss M. C. Reed of Brookline, Mass. for her careful reading of this chapter and her valuable suggestions, and to Miss R. E. Thomas, of Medford, Mass., for her scrutiny.

the original indexes of the volumes at Plymouth to see if there were further references for a given family, as to deeds and estates, than in the supposed "copy" at the Archives.

D. CONNECTICUT

Printed Sources

There are histories, more or less full, of most of the Connecticut towns, and some or these contain genealogical data in arranged family form, while others give vital statistics from the town or church records or from both. These books vary greatly as to accuracy and completeness. A bibliography is impossible in limited space, but the following list will serve as a partial guide. After each town, "G" signifies family genealogies, "V" signifies town vital statistics, and "C" signifies church records. An asterisk after the letter means that the records are verbatim or fairly full and accurate copies, or that the genealogies are unusually complete and useful.

Bethany (V, C, G)
Bolton (V*)
Brookfield (G)
Canterbury (C*)
Canton (G*)
Cheshire (V*, C*)
Colchester (early V*)
Cornwall (G)
Coventry (V)
Cromwell (G)[1]
Derby (G)
Durham (V, C)
East Haven (G)
Enfield (V*, C*)
Fairfield (C*, G)[2]
Goshen (G)
Granby (C*)
Greenwich (G)
Haddam (C*)
Hartford (C)[3]
Lebanon (early V)
Ledyard (G)
Litchfield (G)
Mansfield (V)
Meriden (C*)
Montville (G)
New Britain (C, G*)
New Haven (V*)[4]
Newington (C*)
New Milford (G)

---

[1] See title, *Middletown Upper Houses.*
[2] Schenck's *History.* See also Jacobus' *Families of Old Fairfield* (G*); and *Annals of an Old Parish for Southport* (C*).
[3] *Records of the First Church* (C), *Second Church* (C*), and *Episcopal Church* (C*), in three separate publications.
[4] See also Jacobus' *Families of Ancient New Haven* (G*).

New London (C*)[5]
Norfolk (C*)
Norwalk (V)
Norwich (V*)[6]
Oxford (V, C, G)
Preston (C*)
Reading (C, G)
Ridgefield (V)
Salisbury (V)
Saybrook (V*)
Seymour (V)[7]
Sharon (V, C)
Simsbury (V*)
Southbury (C, G)[8]
Southington (C*, G)
Stamford (V)
Stonington (C*, G)
Stratford (G*)
Suffield (C*)
Torrington (G)
Union (G)
Vernon (V)[9]
Wallingford (G)
Waterbury (V*, G)[10]
Wethersfield (G*)
Winchester (G*)
Windham (G)[11]
Windsor (G*)[12]
Wolcott (G)
Woodbury (V, C, G)
Woodstock (V*)[13]

In addition, Bailey's *Early Connecticut Marriages* (7 vols.) gives marriage records before 1800 from a large number of churches and is useful despite many errors in transcribing the records of some of the churches. A list of records in the entire set will be found in the front of the seventh volume. Early vital and church records from a number of towns have appeared in the *New England Historical and Genealogical Reg-*

---

[5] *The Diary of Joshua Hempstead* is a valuable source for New London. Caulkins' *History* has some early genealogy.

[6] Also, Caulkins' *History* has some early genealogy; the Perkins genealogies cover only "A" to "Bingham" in print.

[7] Also, genealogies in *Seymour Past and Present*.

[8] In Sharpe's *South Britain;* see also, Cothren's *Ancient Woodbury*, vol. 3.

[9] Published in the same volume with Bolton Vital Records.

[10] Genealogies in Bronson's *History;* vital statistics, with additions, in Anderson's *History*, vol. 1, appendix.

[11] The printed part of Weaver's *Windham Families* halts in the letter "B", but his manuscripts are at the Connecticut Historical Society, Hartford.

[12] Also, early vital records in *Some Early Records and Documents of ... Windsor* (1930), and in *Births, Marriages and Deaths Returned from Hartford, Windsor and Fairfield* (1898), which are very largely Windsor records.

[13] Also Bowen's *History of Woodstock* (G*).

ister and in *The American Genealogist*.[14] These periodicals and also some of the town histories mentioned, contain inscriptions from gravestones in a number of cemeteries.

The *Colonial Records of Connecticut* (1635-1776) have been printed in fifteen volumes, and also several volumes of State Records covering the Revolutionary period and beyond. The first volume of records of the separate New Haven Colony (with jurisdiction from 1643) is lost, but the second volume (1653-1663) is in print, also the first volume of New Haven town or plantation records (from 1638), mistakenly labeled as the first volume of Colony records. Two additional volumes of New Haven town records have been published, also the book of Hartford land distributions (containing early vital records), and the first volume of Hartford Particular Court Records.

The Connecticut Historical Society published the French and Indian War Muster Rolls (2 vols.), and also two volumes of rolls of the Revolutionary War, the latter supplementing the state publication, *Connecticut Men in the Revolution*, which also includes soldiers of the War of 1812 and of the Mexican War. The soldiers of the Civil War are listed in a separate volume issued by the state.

There are printed family histories of many Connecticut families. Of collective genealogy, the most ambitious attempt was that of R. R. Hinman in *First Settlers of the Colony of Connecticut* (1846); (a more comprehensive second edition, begun in 1852, covers only "A" to "Danielson", plus the Hinman family, which, although badly arranged, is still useful). The most accurate work was that of Frank Farnsworth Starr in *Goodwin and Morgan Ancestral Lines* (1915), and other books. Other works dealing with many Connecticut families which are useful to consult are Nathaniel Goodwin's *Genealogical Notes* (1856), the second volume of *Dawes-Gates Ancestral Lines* (1932), by Mary Walton Ferris, *Ancestry of William F. J. Boardman* (1906), by himself, Ernest Flagg's

---

[14] Consult, for these, the subject index to the first fifty volumes of the *Register*, and *Index to Genealogical Periodicals*.

The Founding of New England (1926), and *Family Records* (1935), issued by the Connecticut Chapter, Founders and Patriots of America.[15]

Charles W. Manwaring's Digest of *Early Connecticut Probate Records, Hartford District,* is extremely useful because its three volumes cover a large territory to the year 1750.

Town histories not mentioned in our list, and the several county histories, while less important genealogically, often contain items which may be helpful to the searcher. *The Commemorative Biographical Record,* published by J. H. Beers & Co., for the individual counties of the state between 1901 and 1903, contains a wealth of data, although the early generations are not always correctly worked out, and that comment applies also to *Genealogical and Family History of the State of Connecticut* (4 vols., Lewis Historical Publishing Co., 1911).

Documentary Sources

TOWN VITAL RECORDS.—Vital statistics were fairly well kept by Connecticut towns in the 17th and 18th centuries, although some towns were more lax than others and some, such as Hartford and Fairfield, have few records for that period. The pre-Revolutionary records of Danbury were destroyed, and the records of New Fairfield were lost by fire. Most towns grew lax in keeping vital records during and following the Revolution, and from 1800, few records were entered until 1820, when by statute the entry of marriages was required. Birth and death records had to await another statute in 1848 to be resumed. Hence, while the early records are good, from 1780 or 1800 until 1848, there are few vital entries except marriage records from 1820 onward.

Through the generosity of Lucius B. Barbour, the vital statistics of the state prior to 1850 were completely copied, and these have been indexed at the State Library (the "Barbour Index").

---

[15] Perhaps the first volume of *The Waterman Family* (1939), and *The Granberry Family* (1945), and *Hale, House and Related Families* (1952), compiled by D. L. Jacobus for Edgar Francis Waterman, merit footnote mention with works of this class.

CHURCH RECORDS.—The deficiencies of the vital statistics are made good to some extent by church records when these exist. Since these records were kept by the individual churches and were in private hands, many have disappeared. Some early ministers used their own account books for the entry of baptisms, and they or their heirs retained these as their personal property. Nevertheless, a large number have survived, and many original church registers have been deposited at the State Library, which is gradually performing the service of indexing them—the majority are still unindexed. For church records on deposit, consult Bulletin No. 19 of the State Library (1951). The Connecticut Historical Society at Hartford has a fine collection of copies of church records made by the Colonial Dames and by others. Other historical societies have such copies pertaining to their own sections of the state.

GRAVESTONES AND NEWSPAPER RECORDS.—These are here considered together because, as a W. P. A. project, supervised by Charles R. Hale under the direction of the State Librarian, all the inscriptions in cemeteries in the state were copied to date, and also all death and marriage notices in the files of Connecticut newspapers to the Civil War period. These have been completely indexed and, known as the Hale Collection, are an adjunct of the State Library. They aid marvelously in supplying the defects of the public and parish records. It is a mistake, however, to use the index without consulting the actual copies of records which, naturally, often contain more information than can be included in the card index.

TOWNS AND PARISHES.—In Connecticut, the term for township is *town*. A place of settlement within a town is a village or, sometimes, a borough or city. The original towns comprised a large area. Each town had its ecclesiastical society but, with the development of several villages within the towns, for convenience, parishes were split so that one town might have from one to six or seven parishes. Later, as settlements grew in size, they were set off as separate towns, with bounds which often but not always coincided with the bounds of the parish which was already located in that village. The *Register and Manual* published by the state tells when each town was founded or incorporated, and if it was a "succession" town, from what previous town or towns it was set off. The parishes sometimes changed their names, as for example the North Society in New London became known as the Montville Society after that part of New London had been set off as the town of Montville. This also illustrates the fact that many parishes are older than the towns in which they are now located, for the present Montville Society goes back to 1720, while the town of Montville was not incorporated until 1786. An excellent and most helpful guide to this maze is *List of Congregational Ecclesiastical Societies established in Connecticut before October 1818* (1913), prepared by Albert C. Bates and published by the Connecticut Historical Society. Other helpful guides (not limited to Congregational Societies) are the *Reports of the Examiner of Public Records* for the years 1906 and 1924, issued by the state.

TOWN AND LAND RECORDS.—The early towns had several types of records. The original proprietors had a right to the outlying lands, not yet distributed, to which later inhabitants had no claim unless they bought out all rights of an original proprietor. Hence books were kept of Proprietors' Records, in which the later distributions to the proprietors or their heirs or assigns were entered. This applies only to the early towns, not to the later "succession" towns. Some towns have preserved their early records of town meetings, some have not. Some have the minutes kept by the selectmen. Records of these classes are retained by each town, except a few volumes which have been deposited at the State Library.

The most important town records, genealogically, are the land records. In most towns in the period before 1700, a book was started in which a page was assigned to each land owner with a list and brief description of his lands; a notation would be made in the margin when he sold a piece of land, while new purchases were entered with their dates below his original holdings. But shortly it was found necessary to copy the actual conveyances into the records; that began at a different date in different towns, in New Haven, for example, in 1679, over forty years after the town was founded. The very early land entries are hence less informative, genealogically, than the later ones. Throughout the 18th century, they are of the utmost importance. Often estates did not go through probate, one of the heirs merely bought out the others, and the family relationships are to be found specified in the land transactions.

Because Connecticut did not have the county system of land registration, one has to go to the land records in each town. This is particularly difficult when a family lived in a region which became a "succession" town. For example, one is tracing a family which in 1850 lived in Monroe. The Monroe deeds go back only to 1823, when that town was taken from Huntington; one then has to go to Shelton and search the Huntington deeds back to 1780, when that town was taken from Stratford and the deeds before that are at Stratford. Yet, the family may have resided on the same farm throughout that period. Enfield was annexed from Massachusetts in 1749, as were also Suffield and Woodstock; deeds of those towns before 1749 can be consulted at the proper county seats in Massachusetts, but after that in each town.

Useful information about town records and their consultation will be found in the *Reports of the Examiner of Public Records* for 1930 and 1940, issued by the state. However, thanks to the Latter-Day Saints, the State Library now has copies on microfilm of the land records of each town to at least 1850.

STATE RECORDS.—The State Library now has custody of some early books of colonial deeds, and of many documents which were preserved in the colonial files. The latter are kept in many volumes resembling scrapbooks, and have been completely indexed under several appropriate categories, such as Towns and Lands, Colonial Wars, Ecclesiastical Affairs, Private Controversies, Crimes and Misdemeanors (which, oddly enough, includes early divorces), Revolutionary War, and many others. Many Revolutionary documents, pay rolls, orderly books, and the like, formerly in private hands, have been given to the State Library, and there is a supplemental index for these.

COUNTY AND PROBATE COURTS.—In 1666, three years after the union of Connecticut and New Haven Colonies, four counties were set up: Hartford, New Haven, Fairfield and New London. These counties had judges appointed, who presided over a joint County and Probate Court. The early probate court orders (appointment of administrators and guardians, acceptance of wills and inventories, and court orders of distribution to the heirs) are therefore to be found in the County Court record volumes, along with the civil actions and trials for misdemeanors which customarily are heard by a Court of Common Pleas. The record books of the four counties have been deposited at the State Library, and are complete from 1666, except that the first volume for Fairfield County (1666-1700) appears to be lost, and the second volume (1700-1735) is still kept in the County Court House at Bridgeport. The files of the four counties, so far as preserved, are at the State Library. Record books of the four later counties, Litchfield, Windham, Middlesex, and Tolland, are genealogically less important, as they were set up after probate functions had been separated from the county courts.

The four original probate courts kept separate record volumes in which to enter wills and inventories, and these have been preserved since 1666, except that both the record volumes and the files of the New London Probate District prior to 1700 were burned; Hartford, New London and New Haven Districts retain all their own record volumes, as does Fairfield except for the first ten volumes which are deposited at the State Library. The files of all these districts, and of most of the probate districts which later were set off from them, are at the State Library, where the estates have been completely indexed. From time to time, for convenience, probate districts were split up, until today all the larger towns and some of the smaller ones have their own probate districts. A helpful list, both by district and by town, is printed in the front of the first volume of Manwaring's *Digest*, already mentioned under printed sources. See also the 1928 *Report of the Examiner of Public Records* for a list of the files deposited up to that date at the State Library.

Other early Probate Districts of importance are Guilford, Windham and Woodbury, established in 1719, Stamford in 1728, Litchfield in 1742, Danbury in 1744, Plainfield in 1747, Norwich in 1748, Middletown in 1752, and Sharon in 1755. The only old districts which still retain their files are Guilford and Stamford; these places have to be visited to examine the probate records, not only of the towns themselves, but of some neighboring towns which formerly belonged to those districts. However, it is always a wise precaution to examine both the files and the record volumes, for some files are incomplete and many court orders in the record books have no counterpart in the files; on the other hand, disapproved wills and sometimes receipts from heirs and other documents were placed in the files without being recorded.

SUPERIOR COURTS.—The original Superior Court was the Court of Assistants (the upper house of the legislature) which convened at stated intervals in the different counties to hear appeals from the lower court or the probate court and to try the more serious cases. One of its important functions was to act on petitions for divorce. The records of the Superior Court to 1796 are at the State Library, arranged by counties, and with dockets for each year, but unindexed. After 1796 each county had its own permanent Superior Court, and the records should be sought at the appropriate county seat, unless its files have been sent to the State Library.

Since, as each year passes, more and more records are deposited by the towns and counties and probate districts with the State Library, it is wise to ascertain first of all whether the records one desires to consult are there.

LIBRARY COLLECTIONS.—The State Library has the duplicate copy of every Connecticut Census from 1790 to 1870, inclusive. The schedules are unindexed, and have to be read through to locate desired items. It has also, in addition to the Hale Collection already described, copies of the inscriptions in many cemeteries (for a list see the 1930 Report of the State Librarian). Of manuscript compilations we mention only, as samples, Colonel Parkhurst's *New London Families,* and Olmstead's *East Hartford Families* and, most important, Barbour's *Hartford Families.*

The Connecticut Historical Society, in addition to church and cemetery records and manuscript genealogies, complete or partial, of many individual families, has several large collections made by professional genealogists, of which the most valuable is perhaps that of Mrs. Elisha E. Rogers, the able Norwich genealogist, who worked for years in New London and Windham Counties. There are also the Weaver manuscript of Windham families, the Gay collection of Farmington data, and the collection of Charles Camp of New Haven. Such collections are not public documents and doubtless contain errors, since genealogists in their work often copy data from all kinds of sources, knowing what to accept and what to discard, and all such collections, no matter how useful and valuable, the consultant must learn to use with reserve.

The Middlesex County Historical Society at Middletown owns the manuscript collection of Frank Farnsworth Starr, which contains copies of church and cemetery records made years ago, some of the cemeteries having disappeared since these copies were made.

There is space to refer but briefly to the Fairfield Historical Society, which has copies of many church and cemetery records of Fairfield County and the manuscripts of Orrando P. Dexter and Winthrop H. Perry; the New Haven Colony Historial Society, which owns Nathan G. Pond's and George Clarke Bryant's manuscripts of Milford families, Ralph D. Smith's early collection of Guilford data, Dr. Alvan Talcott's compilation of Guilford families (a copy of which is at the State Library), and Haven's East Haven families; and the New London Historical Society, which has valuable manuscript collections relating to that county.

E. RHODE ISLAND

The records of Rhode Island and Providence Plantations, both of Colony and State, are very different from those of any other state. The only county records are those of the Superior Court, all other records being in the custody of the town clerk in whose town the land sales and other business occurs. In order to understand fully the reasons for keeping the records in this manner, a short account of the history of Rhode Island is necessary.

Providence, the first town and now the capital of the state, was founded in 1636, Portsmouth in 1638, and Newport in 1639. Warwick was started in 1643, but no action was taken by the inhabitants as a town until 1647. In that year, the four towns united under the Earl of Warwick's charter, but each town had the same relationship to the central Colonial government as each state now has to the government in Washington. Each town kept its own land evidence, probate matters, and the vital records which were commenced very early. As new towns were formed, the same procedure was followed, and it has been continued ever since.

The early Land Evidence contains grants of land to the inhabitants. As the colony was purchased from the Indians by the first settlers, the lands were granted by the towns and not by the King as was usual in some of the Colonies. As the area of Rhode Island itself is small, these grants are almost neligible when compared with those of some of the southern states whose western borders seemed limitless. On the island of Rhode Island, after the farms were given out, the usual grant of land was 12 acres to each freeman. The Land Evidence also contains deeds, mortgages and leases, and fence agreements which sometimes give useful information about the owners not found elsewhere.

A closer relationship and personal knowledge of the deceased often gave to these local probate court records a more intimate touch than is found in the records made by a county probate court. Often, when a man died intestate a will was made by those neighbors of his who knew his family and circumstances. The probate records were kept separate from the regular town council business, and if they were written in the same book, they were generally placed in the back of the book.

The colony of Rhode Island always called the governing body of the town a Council except during the regime of Sir Edmund Andros as Governor of the New England Colonies, 1686-89. Andros ordered the governing body to be called Selectmen and dictated the method of electing them and their length of service, but as soon as Andros was deposed, the town returned to their "Councils".

The records of these councils as a governing body give a survey of the towns and their inhabitants which probably surpasses the early town records of any other colony. One of the duties of the council was to watch the strangers who came into the town and to see that they either bought real estate or gave a bond from their last legal place of abode. Otherwise, they were warned out of town. Often these warnings gave not only the name of the man but also the names of his family.

The town meeting records also give some information which may be useful to the genealogist. Besides the usual election of town officers, there was other business which was sometimes finished by the council. The names of new inhabitants and strangers often occur in these records as well as the poor of the town, among whom the transient school master may often be found.

The law for recording marriages, births and deaths was passed by Warwick in 1647 and the other towns soon followed but, as there was no penalty attached to this law, the records are by no means complete. These vital records up to 1850 were compiled by James N. Arnold and published by the state in 1883. Unfortunately, they contain some errors, those of Little Compton being copied from a book made by the town clerk who had added a number of items which are based on hearsay and guesswork. For this reason, any vital records of this town should be carefully checked by all means obtainable.

The various records in most of the towns are practically complete. North Kingstown had a fire which damaged nearly all the books, but they have since been repaired and a great deal can be found in them. Two of the books of Richmond were completely destroyed by fire. The earliest records of Providence were destroyed when the Indians burned part of the town in 1675. The records of Newport were carried to New York by the Tory town clerk when the British left Newport in 1779 and the vessel on which they were carried was sunk on the way. The ship was later raised and the records returned to Newport. The salt water had damaged some of the papers, and, although they have been cleaned and mounted on silk, some of them are almost blank.

The towns of Bristol, Little Compton, Tiverton and Warren were in Bristol County, Massachusetts, until 1747. All records of these towns before that date are to be found in Taunton, Massachusetts. The records of East Providence and part of Pawtucket prior to 1862 are also to be found in Taunton. Fall River, Rhode Island, which comprised the northern part of Tiverton was ceded to Massachusetts in 1862 and records after that date are either to be found in Fall River or Taunton, Massachusetts.

As time went on, the early towns were cut into smaller ones; the number of towns now in the state is 39. Of course, the old records stayed in the parent town, each new town starting a set of records of its own. This sometimes causes trouble for the searcher, especially if the date of the incorporation is not known. The *Report on the Archives of Rhode Island,* by Clarence S. Brigham, will, if the searcher can obtain a copy from some library, give these dates, explain the division and tell where these various records may be found.

Many of the inhabitants of Newport embraced the Quaker faith in 1657 and it soon spread over the whole colony. The Friends' records contain a vast amount of genealogical material, those of the southern part of the state being in the custody of the Newport Historical Society, while those of the northern part are to be found at the Moses Brown School in Providence.

The State House at Providence contains the archives of the

state and colony comprising the records of the governing body, some of the older court records and the first record book of the Island of Rhode Island. This book contains the Compact made and signed in Boston in 1683 before the signers left that town to found Portsmouth. Here, too, are some of the state census records, the rest being in the custody of the Rhode Island Historical Society of Providence. Another source of information is the index of thousands of names which appear on petitions to the legislature.

The Rhode Island Historical Society now has custody of a large collection of original papers of every conceivable kind, mounted and bound, which formerly were in the Providence City Hall. Although these are called The Providence Papers, all parts of the colony are represented and considerable miscellaneous information can be gained from them. The main trouble which occurs in searching this collection is deciding which classification applies to the person wanted. The papers are indexed by subject matter, and may be confusing to the inexperienced searcher.

Both the Newport and Rhode Island Historical Societies contain many original records of all kinds which are fully indexed. Each society has very full newspaper files and old account books as well as genealogical libraries, that of the Rhode Island Society being especially fine.

Although Rhode Island had many early "Counts of Inhabitants", the first census giving the names of the heads of families was taken in 1774; this has been published. A military census was taken in 1777 but, as part of the state was occupied by the British troops at that time, it is not complete. In 1782, another census was taken, this time of the entire state. Others, giving the names of all members of the families, were taken in 1865, 1875 and 1887.

Of the printed books on Rhode Island which will help the genealogist, Austin's *Genealogical Dictionary* is outstanding, especially if used with G. Andrews Moriarty's "Additions and Corrections" in the several volumes of *The American Genealogist*. The *Rhode Island Historical Quarterly* probably ranks next with the publications of the Newport Historical Society following. The *Narragansett Historical Register* gives considerable information about the people of Washington County. Smith's Lists and the *Rhode Island Colonial Records* also give considerable information. *The Providence Oath of Allegiance and its Signers,* and *Rhode Island Colonial Money and its Counterfeiting*, two books by Richard LeBaron Bowen, contain a wealth of genealogical data. The first books of Portsmouth and Warwick contain much genealogical material. Providence has printed many of its early records and many of the smaller towns have published their histories. In using the published biographical books and county histories, one must frequently use caution as some of the genealogical lines contained in them are unproven and merely hearsay.

CHAPTER II

NEW YORK

A. NEW YORK CITY *

New York City is a complex organism. Greater New York is composed of five boroughs, each constituting a county of New York State. The boroughs are: Manhattan (New York County), the Bronx (Bronx County), Brooklyn (Kings County), Queens (Queens County), and Richmond (Richmond County). For the purposes of the present section, the records of Manhattan only will be considered; the boroughs of Kings and Queens are considered in Section C, Long Island.

Genealogical Reference Works

As is to be expected from a city the size and importance of New York City, many printed works dealing with the genealogies of its families have been published. These are secondary works and, as emphasized in other chapters, they must be treated as such; whenever possible, original sources must be consulted. However, they provide much information on the city's old families, many of which can be traced to the period of Dutch rule.

The principal genealogical reference works for this area are: *Genealogical and Family History of Southern New York and the Hudson River Valley*, by Cuyler Reynolds (3 vols., 1914); the same author's *Hudson-Mohawk Genealogical and Family Memoirs* (4 vols., 1911); *Genealogical and Family History of Southern New York*, by William Richard Cutter;[1] *Famous Families of New York*, by Margherita Arlina Hamm (2 vols., 1902); and *Early Settlers of New York State, Their Ancestors and Descendants*, by T. J. Foley (1934-37).

---

* Grateful acknowledgement is made to Miss Rosalie Fellows Bailey, who critically reviewed this section and contributed many valuable suggestions for its improvement, and to Dr. Herbert F. Seversmith, for providing much information relating to the genealogical bibliography of New York City.

[1] Mr. Cutter also published works of similar nature for Central, Northern and Western New York.

We are inclined to think of early New York as being so distinctively Dutch that we occasionally forget there was a large Scandinavian population on Manhattan Island during the New Netherland regime. In fact, it has been recorded that in 1643 there were no fewer than 18 different languages spoken in the city—evidence of its cosmopolitan character over three centuries ago. In 1916, Dr. John O. Evjen published his *Scandinavian Immigrants in New York, 1630-1674;* not only does he give briefly the histories of the Norwegian, Danish and Swedish immigrants and their familes, but he also has appendices on the Scandinavians in Mexico and South America, 1532-1640; Scandinavians in Canada, 1619-20; Some Scandinavians in New York in the Eighteenth Century; and German Immigrants in New York, 1630-74.

The late William J. Hoffman, F. G. B. S., F. A. S. G., rendered an outstanding service to students of colonial genealogy when he published his "Armory of American Families of Dutch Descent" in *The New York Genealogical and Biographical Record* from 1933 to 1941. This periodical, the organ of the New York Genealogical and Biographical Society, was founded in 1870, and it has published hundreds of other family genealogies as well as a tremendous amount of source materials. Other works of general importance for the student of early New York genealogy are T. G. Bergen's *Register of the Early Settlers of Kings County; with Contributions to their Biographies and Genealogies* (1881), and James Riker's *Harlem, Its Origin and Early Annals, Notices of Its Founders Before Emigration; also Sketches of Numerous Families* (1904).

Printed Sources

The student of New York genealogy will find a wealth of published sources at his disposal. A basic work is Isaac Newton Stokes' great *Iconography of Manhattan;* it is particularly valuable for early land and ownership titles. The New York Historical Society's many volumes of *Collections* contain abstracts of wills from the earliest period to 1800; muster rolls of provincial troops, 1755-64; indentures of apprentices,

1718-27; tax lists, 1696-99; deeds 1672/3/75; Revolutionary War muster and pay rolls, 1775-83, etc.

The Colonial Dames of the State of New York have issued volumes entitled *Calendar of Wills on File and Recorded in the Offices of the Clerk of the Court of Appeals, of the County Clerk at Albany and of the State of New York, 1626-1836* (1896), and *Minutes of the Orphanmasters of New Amsterdam, 1665 to 1863*, by Berthold Fernow (2 vols., 1902-7). Especially valuable for the Dutch period is *The Record of New Amsterdam from 1653 to 1674*, edited by Berthold Fernow (7 vols., 1897); it contains, among other records, the minutes of the Court of Burgomasters and Schepens.

New York City church records have been published in abundance. In its *Collections* (as distinguished from its periodical, the *Record*) the New York Genealogical and Biographical Society has published Reformed Dutch Church registers of New Amsterdam, as well as other communities in the former province. Other Reformed Dutch Church records have been published by The Holland Society of New York, including the *Record of the Dominee Henricus Selyns, Minister of the Reformed Dutch Church at Nieuw Amsterdam*. (1916). The *Ecclesiastical Records, State of New York* (7 vols., 1901-16), covers the period 1621-1801, and is invaluable for historical, biographical and genealogical purposes.

Of importance for the student of New York City genealogy and history of the *Calendar of New York Historical Manuscripts Dutch* (especially valuable for 17th century settlers), and the 15-volume *Documents Relating to the Colonial History of the State of New York* (1853-87).

Indispensable for the student of New York City is the *Guide to Genealogical and Biographical Sources for New York City (Manhattan), 1783-1898*, by Rosalie Fellows Bailey, A. B., F. A. S. G., with introduction by John Ross Delafield, LL.B., D. S. M. (afterwards F. A. S. G.). In this 100-page work, Miss Bailey comprehensively discusses Probate and Related Records; Means of Identifying the Church of an Officiating Minister; Name Lists and Biographical Sketches by Occupation; other Name Lists; Education, Memberships, Wealth, etc.; the Non-Native New Yorker, State and Federal Census Records; Maps, Street, and Land Records; Burial Records and Cemeteries; Military Records; Vital Statistics; Church Records; and many other subjects. The *Guide* begins with the year 1783, because, as she observes, "the half century or so following the Revolution is often the most difficult period in America for which to find first-class proof of a lineage."

Public Records

PROBATE AND ESTATE RECORDS.[2]—The basic material relating to wills, administration records, etc., is on file at the Surrogate's Office, Hall of Records, Chambers Street, New York, N. Y. It contains wills, 1665-1927; administration bonds, 1742-1828, 1835-1926; letters of administration, 1743-1927; guardianship bond books, 1802-1927; Record of Dower, 1831-1927; letters testamentary, 1830-1927; renunciation of executors, 1831-1914, etc. The first 56 libers of wills, covering the period 1665-1823, were lithographed in 1870-71, and may be seen at the New York Historical Society, 77th Street and Central Park West, New York, N. Y. The New York Historical Society also has 610 original papers relating to inventories of estates in the Southern District of New York. The New York County Clerk's Office, Room 703, Hall of Records, Chambers Street, has 7 libers of wills recorded in the Supreme Court, 1787-1829, 1847-83, and in the Court of Common Pleas, 1805-29, 1886-92, with a card index.

LAND RECORDS.—The Office of the Register of New York County, Hall of Records, Chambers Street, has a complete set of conveyance libers for Manhattan since 1683,[3] of mortgage libers since 1754, and of power of attorney libers since 1825. Until 1811, many deeds were recorded with the Secretary of State, hence it is always well to consult the records of the Land Office at Albany, where there are good card indexes. All

---

[2] See Rosalie Fellows Bailey's article on probate records in the *New York Genealogical and Biographical Record*, vol. 81, in which she critically compares the official indexes with the abstracts published by the New York Historical Society.

[3] Deeds and mortgages of earlier dates are in the City Clerk's Office. See the Holland Society *Yearbooks* for 1900 and 1901.

readily identifiable land records are now grouped in a special series called "Re-Indexed Conveyances". Charles F. Grim's *An Essay Towards an Improved Register of Deeds, City and County of New York to Dec. 31, 1799, inclusive* (1832), contains an "Index of Deeds in the Office of the Secretary of State that relate to lands in the City and County of New York, as so lettered." The 51-volume *Index of Conveyances Recorded in the Office of the Register of the City and County of New York* (1857-58) should also be consulted.

VITAL STATISTICS.—New York State records of vital statistics were not kept until 1880, but they were maintained at earlier dates in New York City. The New York City records are on file in the Bureau of Records and Statistics, City Department of Health, 125 Worth St., New York 13, N. Y. The original records are not available to the general public, but, fortunately, they have been microfilmed and the films may be examined there free of charge by researchers. The Department of Health will make a search of the records for a fee. Microfilms of death records are at the New York Genealogical and Biographical Society for the use of members only. The law for registering births and marriages in the city was effective 1 July 1853, although some birth records go back to 1842 and some marriage records to as early as 1829, but they are very scanty. A city ordinance of 26 October 1801 required the registration of deaths; this was a means of studying possible health measures for controlling epidemics. Sextons and others in charge of burial places in the city were ordered to make weekly reports on burials to the municipal authorities. Even so, there are gaps in the records, but starting with 1866, the death records are rather complete. In 1958, records prior to 1866 were transferred to the Municipal Archives and Records Center, 238 William St., New York, N. Y.

NATURALIZATION RECORDS.—The naturalization records of the Supreme Court, the Superior Court, the Court of Common Pleas, and (before 1821) the Mayor's Court commence in 1792. They are under the jurisdiction of the New York County Clerk and are located (with card indexes) in Room 315, Supreme Court Building, 60 Centre Street, New York, N. Y. The United States District Court's records (1824-1906) are maintained, with a consolidated index for *all* New York Courts before 1906, by the Immigration and Naturalization Service, U. S. Department of Justice, New York, N. Y. Pre-1824 naturalization records are at The National Archives in Washington, D. C.

CENSUS RECORDS.—The 1855 State Census for Manhattan, at the County Clerk's Office, 31 Chambers Street, New York, N. Y., gives the number of years resident here, whether native-born or naturalized alien, county of birth, if in New York State, relationship to head of household, etc. The 1890 New York City police census for Manhattan and part of the Bronx, replaces the burned Federal Census of that year. The 1905, 1915, and 1925 State censuses for New York City are at the County Clerk's Office, 60 Centre Street, together with recently completed master indexes of street addresses. The only comprehensive census for the colonial period was in 1703; it has been printed.

MAPS.—Maps are important for all parts of the country, but for the complicated New York City they are absolutely essential. Early 19th century maps show the names and locations of many of the city's landowners, churches, cemeteries, and other institutions. The Office of the Register of New York County maintains a map room in Room 104, Hall of Records, Chambers St. The Register has custody of 5,200 filed maps, approximately 5,000 maps copied from conveyance libers, thousands of maps taken from various public offices of the city, and numerous maps reconstructed from descriptions in old conveyances or old maps platted on present street lines, etc. Other important repositories for maps in the city are the New York Public Library and the New York Historical Society.

Church Records

Records of the many churches that have existed in New York City for several centuries are extremely important, but we can only touch on them briefly in this section of the New

York chapter. The headquarters of the principal denominations are (all in New York City, unless otherwise stated) : *Baptist:* Baptist City Society, 152 Madison Ave.; *Roman Catholic:* Chancery of the Archdiocese of New York, 451 Madison Ave.; *Episcopal:* Registrar of the Diocese of New York, 1047 Amsterdam Ave.; *Methodist:* Methodist Historical Society Library, 150 Fifth Ave., and the New York Public Library (Manuscripts Division), where are all the Methodist records; *Presbyterian:* New York Presbytery Office, 156 Fifth Ave.; *Quaker:* Keeper of the Records, Friends Meeting House, 221 E. 15th St. (for Friends' records of the entire State of New York) ; and *Reformed Dutch:* Gardiner Sage Library, Theological Seminary, New Brunswick, N. J. For details of churches, records, and denominations, consult Bailey, *Guide to Genealogical and Biographical Sources* . . . (1954), pp. 59-65; and W. P. A. Historical Records Survey's *Guide to Vital Statistics in the City of New York; Borough of Manhattan— Churches* (1942), and *Inventory of the Church Archives in New York City* (unfinished).

The manuscript collections of the New York Genealogical and Biographical Society contain transcripts of virtually all New York City churches, except the German Reformed, which are at the New York Historical Society.

B. UPSTATE NEW YORK

General Information

Upstate New York in this section is Albany County of 1683 [1] within present limits of the State,[2] exclusive of the Hudson

---

[1] Map of "The Original Counties of 1683", the ten within the Province of New York and in insets its two dependencies, Cornwall Co., Maine, and Dukes Co., Mass., in *History of the State of New York*, ed. by A. C. Flick, State Historian, 10 vols. N. Y. 1933-1937. II, op. 112.

[2] *Report of the Regents of the University on the Boundaries of the State of N. Y.* 2 vols. Albany, 1874, 1884 (N. Y. Sen. doc. 1873, no. 108, and, 1877, no. 61 with a continuation by D. J. Pratt).

Valley, its expansion in 1763 into New France,³ its gradual extension into the Iroquois or Six Nations country⁴ and final annexation following the Revolution.

All white settlements, except part of Delaware Co. taken in 1797 from Ulster,⁵ were in Albany prior to its division in 1772 ⁶ when Tryon Co. was created of its western and Charlotte Co. of its northern frontier. It retained chiefly its Hudson Valley. In 1784, Tryon Co. was renamed Montgomery Co., and Charlotte Co., Washington Co. A map, based on the reorganization Act of 7 March 1788,⁷ shows all of the Six Nations lands annexed to Montgomery Co. The Act created Clinton Co. from the northern frontier of Washington. It gives the boundaries of Montgomery "E. by counties of Ulster, Albany, Washington and Clinton, S. by State of Pennsylvania, W. & N. by bounds of State." The then Tryon and Charlotte are now 42 counties.

For creation of subsequent counties, see "Data Relating to the Organization of Several Counties of New York State", in *New York Genealogical and Biographical Record, LIV*, Jan., 1923, pp. 18-19, giving County Seat, Date Organized, Original

---

³ *Atlas of American History*, by J. T. Adams. N. Y. 1943. Plate 38, "New Eng.—N. Y.—New France frontier 1690-1753." Plate 29, "New France to 1763".

⁴ At the coming of the white man, the Iroquois, then "Five Nations", possessed all lands south of the St. Lawrence and Lake Ontario between the Hudson and the Genesee Rivers. By 1653, they had extended their lands to New York's western boundaries. Indian deeds and treaties were recorded in the Secretary of State's Office. Thesis of R. S. Rose (see footnote 31) states Vol. I, 1692-1714 was lost in the State Library fire.

⁵ *N. Y. Statutes, 1832*, 426 states the legislature transferred some records from Ulster to Delaware, Greene and Sullivan Counties. Those sent to Sullivan Co. were probably lost in its court house fire, 13 Jan. 1844.

⁶ Disregarding Cumberland and Gloucester Counties because their areas are in Vermont.

⁷ "A map of the State of New York with its counties defined by Statute, 7 March 1788", is frontispiece to *Proceedings of the Commissioners of Indian Affairs appointed by law for the Extinguishment of Indian Titles in State of N. Y.*, an original manuscript in the Library of the Albany Institute with an Introduction by F. B. Hough, Albany, 1861.

or parent county;[8] years agree with legislative acts in all except Schuyler erected 17 April 1854, not 1859. (This is a common error; however, its county officers were elected Nov. 1854 and the County Clerk's office has its state census for 1855.)

In the "Introduction" to the summary of the New York State Census of 1855 and also of 1865, F. B. Hough gives under each county its towns, dates formed and from what. Those with a colonial origin are given as original towns beginning with the Reorganizaton Act of 1788, even though they may have had earlier records.

Obsolete towns with county, date organized, date changed and to what are given in *New York Civil List* for 1889. Self-governing units within the county consist of towns, incorporated villages and cities. A town may have one or more incorporated villages within its limits over which it has no jurisdiction. Adelaide R. Hasse cites a list of 1897 with dates of incorporation.[9]

A List of Books relating to the History of the State of New York, by School Library Division of the University (Albany, 1916), lists county histories for all counties except Hamilton, for which no separate history has been issued, and other local histories.[10] Unless a county history quotes public records, it is

---

[8] *History of St. Lawrence and Franklin Counties New York,* by F. B. Hough, Albany, 1853, 205, 238 and 329, gives the names of the ten townships of unappropriated lands of Montgomery Co., established 10 Sept. 1787 (Land Office Minutes I, 264 Secy. of State's Office). They were in Montgomery, Oneida and Herkimer counties when taken to form the Town of Lisbon and annexed to Clinton Co. 1801. It also gives the petition and petitioners for the county of St. Lawrence and also for the Town of Lisbon and its electors of 1801. These are valuable for names of early inhabitants.

[9] "Special Report of Commissioners of statutory revision re villages and date of incorporation. 1897, 20 pp. (Sen. doc. 27, 1897 v. 4)", under General Works, Part I, in *Index of Economic Material in Documents of the States of the United States. New York, 1789-1904.* By A. R. Hasse. Publ. by Carnegie Institution of Washington, 1907.

[10] It should be noted that *Bibliography of County Histories of 3111 Counties in the 48 States,* compiled by C. S. Peterson, 1946, is very incomplete for New York State. It omits 14 counties, of which 13 have published histories. It inserts Tolland Co., which is in Connecticut, and erroneously states that New York has 102 counties. It has 62.

apt to omit transitory families. Upper New York has had an unusual share of these. Mohawk Valley and beyond has always been the chief thoroughfare westward from eastern New York, and all of New England and the Susquehanna Valley from Pennsylvania and the South. Public records of county or town often reveal transients. Washington Co., not a general thoroughfare except from Canada, was more normally settled. There, wars depopulated the area, leaving few pre-Revolutionary public records.[11] Fire, neglect and permissions to destroy after five years, have depleted public records. There was no state supervision till 1911.

The British burned the court house at Buffalo in 1813, and at Plattsburgh, county seat of Clinton Co., in 1814 but not its records. At Buffalo the fire destroyed records of Niagara and Cattaraugus Counties, 1808 to 1813, and those of Chautauqua prior to 1811. When Erie Co. was formed from Niagara Co. in 1821, Buffalo, formerly county seat of Niagara, became the county seat of Erie; the records remained with Erie, which included Cattaraugus Co., until 1817. The records of Herkimer Co., formed in 1791, begin with 1804. (A clerk stated earlier records were burned.) French's *Gazateer*[12] says Oneida (formed in 1798) took Whitesboro, Herkimer's county seat, and kept the records. Cayuga, formed from Onondaga Co. in 1799, took Onondaga's records; Onondaga copied the deeds and mortgages but not the other records.[13]

There were two independent Historical Records Survey groups in New York, one for New York City and its five counties, and the other for the 57 remaining counties, called "upstate". Survey workers inventoried all counties except Hamilton and originally planned to issue inventories of all

---

[11] The Town Book of Willsborough (Essex Co.) commencing 10 June 1765, when in Albany Co., was published in *Pioneer History of the Champlain Valley*, by W. C. Watson. Albany 1863.

[12] *Gazetteer of the State of New York*, ed. by J. H. French, Albany 1860. (P. 458; footnote 9.) 2nd edition, ed. by F. B. Hough, 1872.

[13] The copies made may be only for the area remaining in Onondaga Co. The county has preserved many other records beginning with 1799. It is doubtful if Cayuga preserved all those for 1794-98 which she kept.

counties (57), towns (932) and municipalities (614).[14] The Historical Records Survey issued *Inventories of County Archives* for Albany, Broome, Cattaraugus, Chautauqua, Chemung, Ulster, Part II, and had five more counties nearly ready when the Survey ended 30 June 1942. The final report[15] states that it left at the State Library at Albany "files of notes, forms and data", and "there one may consult the material from which publications were planned". Each county has its own method of recording and varies greatly in what has been preserved. It would have been valuable if all inventories had been issued. Onondaga is probably the only upstate county which has a published inventory of its county, towns, villages and city.[16] It has given fuller details in its records or preserved more than most counties. Cortland and Montgomery Counties have copied the records of all of their towns.[17]

In 1844, 1881, 1907 and 1910, before the fire of 1911 which almost totally destroyed the State Library, the Legislature had transferred many specified state archives to it. The Library specializes in history and genealogy so the numerous unpublished manuscripts that perished were a tremendous loss to both professions. The *94th Annual Report of the New York State Library* and the *8th Annual Report of the Education Department,* both for 1911, give the official reports on the fire. The latter contains a list of the principal sets of manuscripts and the approximate salvage of each. Subsequently, officers of departments, political units, societies, etc., created by the state were given authority to transfer records,

---

[14] Based on statistics for 1934 in Flick's *History of the State of New York,* VII, 277.

[15] "Final Report: The Historical Records Survey in Upstate New York, 1936-1942", by G. W. Roach, in *New York History,* XXIV, April 1943, 39-55, bound as *Proceedings of New York State Historical Association,* XLI.

[16] "Public Records of Onondaga County", by Herbert L. Osgood in *Annual Report of American Historical Association* for 1900, Wash. 1901, II, 147-163. (See footnote 22.)

[17] Address "On historical activities in New York State", by Dr. A. C. Flick, State Historian, before New York State Historical Association, 2 Oct. 1935. *Proceedings* XXXIV, 1936, 54-58.

etc., not in general use to the State Library.[18] Its vast collection of unpublished manuscripts make it the chief place for Upper New York general genealogical research. It reports that it has public records of 38 New York counties; at least half and probably more are Upper New York counties. A few local libraries have more on their own localities than has the State Library. The American Library Directory, under New York, lists all places with libraries, gives size and special collections of each. From this can be learned nearly all which specialize in local history and genealogy. The finding lists of genealogy and local history of the Grosvenor Library of Buffalo and of the Syracuse Public Library, both published several decades ago, show they were then good research places.[19] The Syracuse Public Library has enhanced the value of its department by many supplied name indexes. Rochester Public Library's special collection is the Rochester Historical Society Library. For the old part of Upper New York, the Mohawk Valley, the best research place is the Montgomery County Department of History and Archives at Fonda. They have prepared many name indexes to their material. All interested in Mohawk families should read L. W. McFee's "Ancestral Trails Along the Mohawk", with the "Addenda" in *New York Genealogical and Biographical Record,* LXXII, April 1941, pp. 105-119.

Guide to Depositories of Manuscript Collections in New York State, issued by the Historical Records Survey which has an excellent index, describes 226 public and private depositories. Among the holdings in the State Library it lists 35 collections, 55 other holdings and 23 prized manuscripts. The

---

[18] *New York State Legislative Manual,* 1945, p. 243.

[19] *Grosvenor Library Bulletin* no. 1, 1900 and Sup. 1 March 1903; *Finding List of Genealogies and Local History.* Syracuse, n. d. (1902), & Supp. 1903.

New York State Historical Association, in 1944 published a supplement to the *Guide* covering seven depositories.[20]

Court Records

The state judiciary continued the colonial courts. The Legislature, in 1778, took from the Governor his power over wills, intestate estates and marriage licenses, vested them in the Court of Probates and, in 1782, transferred such records and papers from the Secretary of State to the judge of such court with instructions to make a list of wills to be seen by anyone. This court was absorbed by the Court of Chancery in 1823 and received its records. The Court of Chancery was abolished in 1846 and the records, except a few papers in the offices of various county clerks, were deposited in the Court of Appeals building in Albany.[21] Records can be consulted in its office. Some wills were transferred to Suffolk Co., but there remained 1,660 wills of all counties, 1671-1800, and of the older counties, other commonwealths and foreign countries, to 1825.[22] B. Fernow calendared the wills in the Court of Appeals, County Clerk of Albany, and Secretary of State offices, 1626-1836.[23]

Details as to organization of courts can be ascertained from references cited in the footnote.[24] In general, the County Clerk is custodian of records, except that in counties having

---

[20] A selection was published as "Guide to Ten Major Depositories of Manuscript Collections in New York State (exclusive of N. Y. City)" in *Proceedings of the Middle States Association of History and Social Science Teachers*, 1940-41, XXXVIII, pt. 2.

[21] *American Revolution in New York*, "4" on p. 279 (see footnote 29); *New York State Laws*, 26 March 1782, I, ch. 24, 5th sess., 439; *Statutes* 1829, p. 279; and *Introduction to Albany County Archives* (see footnote 24).

[22] *Inventory of State Archives*, p. 129, by Prof. H. L. Osgood in his "Report of the Public Archives of New York State" (67-250) as part of the "First Report of the Public Archives Commission," issued as v. II of the *Annual Report of the American Historical Association for 1900*. Wash. 1901.

[23] Published by the Colonial Dames of the State of New York 1896.

[24] *Introduction to Albany County Archives*, no. 1, of H. R. S. *Inventory of County Archives* (exclusive of N. Y. City), Oct. 1937. Session laws; and *The Courts of the State of New York*, by H. W. Scott. N. Y., 1909.

more than 40,000 inhabitants, a separate surrogate's office was established in 1846.

The Surrogate's office is usually at the county seat, but that for Washington Co. is at Salem and that for Warren Co. is at Glens Falls. "Surrogates Courts and Records in the Colony and State of New York, 1664-1847", by R. W. Vosburgh, with references and annotations, is in New York State Historical Association *Proceedings,* vol. XX (1922), pp. 105-116. Additional family data not in the wills, intestate and guardianship records may be found in the miscellaneous files not itemized in the indexes. Of special interest are the petitions for probate or administration in which are given date of death, where, and last residence of the deceased, whether survived by husband or wife and list of next of kin, whether legatees or not, with relationship to the deceased and their addresses. Abstracts of wills, letters of administration, and indexes prior to 1850 have been compiled for many upper New York counties and manuscript copies sold, many being purchased by the New York Genealogical and Biographical Society.

An Amendment to the Constitution of 1894 authorized the legislature to establish Childrens Courts. By 1930, the only upstate countries having separate judges were Albany, Erie, Jefferson, Montgomery and the City of Syracuse. In other counties the County Judge or Special County Judge conducts the Childrens Court and its records are filed with the County Clerk.[25] Before 1922, children cases would be in the court minutes, etc., with adult cases. Often, County Clerks filed separately infancy papers, indentures of apprentices and bonds appointing guardians. Other miscellaneous court files found sometimes in County Clerk's offices consist of naturalization, divorces, adoptions, judgment rolls of various kinds, including partitions of estates with much family data, lists of jurors qualified to serve from towns and municipalities and those disqualified to serve by age, removal or death, declarations concerning age, etc.[26] For a printed list of court reports,

---

[25] Cahill's *Consolidated Laws,* 1930, pp. 2698-2706, cited in *Albany County Archives.*

[26] Based on records found in the Onondaga County Clerk's office.

etc., consult *List of Official Court Reports of New York, latest Digests, Indexes, Citations and of Law, Journals, Documents of the Legislature*, by New York State Library.[27]

Description of Federal court records and their whereabouts in 1939 are found in *Inventories of Federal Archives of New York State: The Federal Courts and The Department of Justice*, issued by the Historical Records Survey.

Land Records

Land grants and patents issued since the colonial wars have been chiefly for land in Upper New York. The British in 1761 forbade purchasing directly from the Indians. The area in New York was defined as the Treaty of Stanwix line of 1768.[28] The Convention of Representatives of the State of New York, 10 July 1776, declared all grants and charters made by Great Britain after 14 October 1775 null and void and later purchases of land from the Indians invalid unless authorized by the State Legislature. Loyalists' property was confiscated and sold in 100-acre lots. Quit-rents formerly due Great Britain were appropriated. Unappropriated lands taken over from the Crown were offered in 1781 as bounties. Records of these are in the state archives. Primogeniture and entails were abolished 12 July 1782; this destroyed manorial rights.[29] The Act of 1 April 1785 created in the office a Board of Commissioners to buy land of Indians and sell to settlers. The Act of 15 May 1786 gave them the sale of unappropriated lands, power to direct the sale of any unpatented lands and to lay out bounty lands to be settled in seven years. The decision of the Hartford Convention on the Massachusetts claim resulted in the session by New York of 6,000,000 acres of land. (New York was able to retain jurisdiction over the land because of a treaty of the Iroquois in 1701 with the New York

---

[27] Cited by A. R. Hasse. (See footnote 9.)

[28] "Fort Stanwix Treaty of 1768", by R. A. Billington, with map op. p. 184, in *Proceedings of New York State Historical Association*, 1944, XLII, 182-194.

[29] The *American Revolution in New York: Its Political, Social and Economic Significance*, prepared by the Division of Archives and History, Albany, 1926, "5" on pp. 12, 81, "7" on 230.

Governor which placed their country for protection and defense under the English Crown.)

The Land Office of the Secretary of State recorded all original grants and patents, large and small, including military land bounties and Indian purchases.[30]

The military tract chosen for bounty lands was in Montgomery Co., in the area set off as Herkimer Co. in 1791. The entire military tract was taken to form Onondaga Co. in 1794. It was found to overlap the Boston Ten Town tract.[31] This was adjusted by adding two townships to the military tract, making 28. Lots drawn in each of the 28 townships, by whom, and to whom delivered, are given in *The Balloting Book*.[32]

The State Library has some military land records from the Adjutant General's office. The Attorney General's office has land suits in which the State is a party. Other courts also have land suits. The Comptroller's office kept records of land subject to quit-rents and their later disposition. In the case of estates, this included names of persons to whom subgrants

---

[30] "A Catalogue of Records in Secretary of State office on 1 Jan. 1820", New York Sen. Doc. 2, 1820, also Sen. Journ. 1820, 13-51, cited in Third Report of the Historical Manuscripts Commission in *American Historical Association Annual Report for 1898*, 577-581. F. G. Jewett compiled a later one, Albany, 1898.

[31] The bibliography in a M. A. thesis at Syracuse University, May, 1935, on "The Military Tract of Central N. Y.," by Robert S. Rose, lists manuscripts in the Land Office of the Secretary of State and in the State Library Manuscripts Division at its date. *Gazetteer of the State of New York*, ed. by J. H. French (1860), p. 180, states Boston Ten Towns were sold to 60 persons and that their names are found in Act of 3 March 1789 (*Laws of New York* Folio edition 12th sess. p. 76). The land was in Broome, Tioga and Cortland Counties.

[32] The 28 townships listed in *The Balloting Book and other documents relating to military bounty lands in the State of New York*, Albany, 1825, in Onondaga Co., in 1794 are now nos. 1, 5, 6, 7, 9, 10, 14 and 15 in Onondaga; nos. 3, 4, 8, 12, 13, 18, 28 and part of 17 in Cayuga; nos. 19, 20, 24 and 25 in Cortland; no. 2 in Oswego; no. 21 in Schuyler; nos. 11, 16, 26 in Seneca; nos. 22, 23 and part of 17 in Tompkins; no. 27 in Wayne. Names of some have been changed, but their areas are as given.

were issued. These were probably obtained from patents and deeds in the Secretary of State's office.[33]

Gazetteer of the State of New York, ed. by J. H. French, 1860, and by F. B. Hough, 1872,[12] contains tables of the principal patents in colony and state with name, date, chief patentees, size, and location in the state patents, including county. These are Massachusetts' 6,000,000 acres with subdivisions; Macomb's Great Purchase in Franklin, St. Lawrence, Jefferson, Lewis, Oswego and Herkimer Counties; Chenango, Twenty townships; principal tracts granted in small parcels by the State. The introductions, texts and footnotes contain much locality land information. Both editions give first settlers and those who followed shortly in the upstate localities. L. D. Scisco made a typed name index to French's edition, and gave one to the Syracuse Public Library and the other to New York Genealogical and Biographical Society.

Conquering the Wilderness, vol. V of *History of the State of New York*, ed. by A. C. Flick,[34] is chiefly on Upper New York. Chapter 4, "The Valleys of the Susquehanna and the Delaware", and Chapter 5, "The Frontier pushed Westward", give the principal land tracts of the Six Nations area. Chapter 6, "The Settlement of the North Country", the bibliography to each chapter, and the end-cover map of the state with 226 numbered tracts and key, should be familiar to researchers. "Map of the State of New York showing the location of the original Land Grants, Patents and Purchases", which is map 3 of J. R. Bien's *Atlas of the State of New York* (1895), gives the 226 tracts with key and greater detail. This atlas has also county and city land maps. *Inventory of Maps* (partial), issued by the Historical Records Survey (1942) lists maps in various state, county, municipal and other public offices. *Catalogue of Maps and Surveys in the Offices of Secretary of State, State Engineer and Surveyors*, the *Comptroller and the*

---

[33] Comptroller's land records from Osgood's survey 1900, 116-120 (see footnote 22). The State Library has land grants to soldiers 1817-18 from Office of Adjutant General.

[34] See footnote 1.

New York State Library, by D. E. Mix (Albany, 1859) is also useful.

The county clerk's office files for its county all real estate transactions, but grantee and grantor indexes do not contain all early deeds. Some were recorded long after purchase when property was sold outside the family. The indexes give date of filing, not date of instrument, except in Erie Co., which gives both. The Act of 3 December 1798 required Ontario Co. to record all deeds. It became a general law by Ch. 175 in 1810. Some missing deeds are found in state archives, land company records, among family papers and local history collections. Some ownerships are indicated by deeds of adjoining property.

L. C. Cooley published in 1946 name indexes to O. Turner's *Pioneer History of Holland Purchase of Western New York,* 1850, and his *History of the Pioneer Settlement of the Phelps and Gorham Purchase,* 1851. The latter has a *Supplement* (493-624) on the part of the Purchase in Monroe Co. and the northern part of the Morris Reserve. The *Supplement* (493-588) in the Rochester 1852 edition, covers the Purchase in Ontario, Wayne, Livingston, Yates and Alleghany counties and the southern part of the Morris Reserve. It is not in the Cooley Index. The tract known as the Phelps and Gorham Purchase is the part of their purchase lying between the Genesee River and Seneca Lake, which they divided into townships and lots and sold as parcels. The State Library has some of their papers, 1788-1895. East of Seneca Lake was the military tract, and west of the Genesee was the Holland Purchase (Massachusetts land). It included all except a strip of New York land a mile wide along the Niagara River and the Indian Reservations. The Buffalo Historical Society has a very large collection of Holland Land Co. papers, 1792-1850. Their *Publications* for 1910, 1924, 1937 and 1941 are on the Purchase. All of the state west of the Genesee was the town of Northampton, Ontario Co., between 1797 and 1802, when it was divided. Prof A. H. Wright's *Old Northampton of Western*

New York[35] gives its legislative history. It contains the first tax list, the Town Records, 1797-1825, the earmarks of its parent, the District of Genesee, and a name index. "Abstract on land and dwellings owned on 1 April 1815 in counties of Niagara and Erie in the State of New York" is found in *U. S. Executive Documents.*[36] Paul D. Evans wrote of a large tract purchased by three English gentlemen, "The Pulteney Purchase".[37] The original documents of the *Calendar of New York Colonial Manuscript Indorsed Land Papers in the Office of the Secretary of State of New York, 1643-1803* (3 vols. Albany, 1864), including later ones to 1892, are in the New York State Library.[38]

Tax Records

Direct property tax, real and personal, was primarily a local tax. When New York received insufficient funds from duties, excises, licenses, etc., and the counties from fees for recording and consultation of documents, etc., the Board of Supervisors apportioned the amount of the state and county levies to each of the self-governing units within the county to be added to its local tax. A poll tax of the tenant class was the origin of the personal tax. It became permanent by the establishment of the income tax after 1913. State and county levies on real property continued to be collected with local taxes. Assessors annually revise their taxpayers lists and assign to each the amount of the three levies each must pay within a specified time. In counties where the inhabited area was small the lists might be found among the Board of Supervisors records, but it is doubtful if any in Upper New York are found in their offices. The Board usually publishes the journal of its proceedings, but some do not have their earliest ones. The journals contain much about taxes and mention many contemporary in-

---

[35] Rochester Historical Society; Publication Fund Series, VII, 235-424. The binder's title of the author's edition is *Old Northampton and Northampton Records.*

[36] U. S. *Executive Documents*, no. 38, 18th Cong. 2d. Sess. II,4.

[37] *Proceedings* of the New York State Historical Association, XX, 1922, 83-100.

[38] Mentioned in the bibliography of R. S. Rose's thesis (see footnote 31).

habitants with residences. During early statehood period tax lists were filed with local clerks and the county treasurers received with the funds raised by the state and county levies a delinquent tax list of parcels and owners. Beginning between 1850 and 1870, varying in counties, tax lists have been filed both in local clerks' and county treasurers' offices which are usually at the county seat, but in Washington County at a former seat, Argyle. Prior to the Sheriff sale for taxes a list of parcels with names of owners is published in a local newspaper or posted in a public place. Sheriff deeds and certificates, redemption records, and an index of unpaid taxes are usually in the county clerk's office. They also may have excise papers on file. Surrogates' offices usually have some inheritance tax data of estates.

Researchers failing to find the person of their search in a town tax list should examine the lists of parent town and adjoining towns, villages, cities and county. Whole towns and parts of towns have been taken to form new counties and have been added to cities. Boundary lines have been changed when official surveys have been made and after a state census to equalize assembly districts.

Tax lists in small towns and villages can be seen only by appointment. The local clerk or historian might examine the records for a fee. The Act of 11 April 1919 requires a local historian to be appointed in each local unit. It did not include county historians and yet, by 1926, nine counties had them. The office was created by Article 46, Section 1198, of the Educational law effective 8 April 1939. Comparatively few of the thousand or more towns, villages and cities of Upper New York [39] have published histories. Only part of these contain any tax lists. Some local units have complete or nearly complete tax lists and others did not value the early ones sufficiently to give them storage space. The Historical Records Survey's *Guide to Depositories of Manuscripts Collections* locates some that have drifted into historical and other

---

[39] Flick's *History of the State of New York*, VII, 288, gives for the 62 counties (of which 5 are in New York City) for 1934 "60 cities, 932 towns and 555 villages" a total of 1647.

libraries. Chief place listed is in the large collecton of original public records now in the State Library at Albany, which also has transcriptions by the New York D. A. R. and others. In the material left in the Library by the Historical Records Survey are some completed but unpublished town surveys. These include tax lists now in town-record files.

In 1900, the State Comptroller's office had assessment rolls, tax books and strictly chronological tax diaries in large numbers and records of county treasurers tax sales bid in for the State in 1811 and every five years thereafter (evidently defaulted patents and land grants in their counties), comptroller's sales books since 1853 and records of the inheritance tax bureau.[40] For a long period the Comptroller's office assessed and collected all special taxes. In 1915, the New York State Tax Department was created. It took over from the Comptroller his function of direct state tax, the duties of his Land Tax Bureau, the State Board of Equalization established in 1859, and the State Board of Tax Commissioners established in 1896. The Tax Department was enlarged in 1927. Its Division of Finance took over the duties of State Treasurer. The succeeding offices or the State Library would have the records of the extinct offices.

Vital Records

Between 1778, when New York began to function as a state, and its first Registry Act of 1846 requiring the keeping of public vital records, the larger part of Upper New York was settled, organized into counties and towns and gradually into towns, incorporated villages, cities and various kinds of districts. The Registry Act provided no remuneration and no penalty. The clerk of each school district was to consult the records of physicians and others and report all the births, marriages and deaths of his district to the town clerk, who was to file annually with the county clerk.

The Historical Records Survey's *Guide to Public Vital Statistics Records in New York State,* including New York City (3 vols., 1942) contains a survey of village, town, city

---
[40] Osgood's *Inventory of State Archives,* 116-120. See footnote 22.

and county offices. It shows that most towns compiled records for a year or more, 1847-1849, and a few for 1850 and 1851, but many of the returns were found in local and not in county clerks' offices. It gives an account of those in Onondaga Co., 1847-1868. They include returns from some of the towns for 1847 to 1850, some odd marriage certificates and a list of marriages by one clergyman during 1867 and 1868.[41] The introduction to the *Guide* lists 42 of the 62 counties with no birth records. The text shows only two of the 42 have any death records. From 1908 to 1 April, 1915, original marriage licenses and records were filed in the county clerks' offices and copies sent to the State Bureau, but thereafter the State filed the originals and copies were kept by the county clerk till 1935, when his duty was transferred to the town and municipal offices. The *Guide* shows no result from the Registry Act of 1864, repealed in 1865. The state censuses for 1865 and for 1875 give for each enumeration district the marriages and deaths for the preceding year ending June 1, 1865 and 1 June, 1875.

In 1936, from correspondence with departments, H. C. Durrell compiled "Centralization of Vital Records in the States". He indicates the New York State Department of Health, Albany, has births, marriages and deaths "on file from 1895" with exceptions in the New York City area, Yonkers, Buffalo and Albany. These were filed only in the city registrars' offices till later specified dates.[42] The Department of Health was

---

[41] The Survey shows that a few localities antedate legislative action of 1846. In Chautauqua Co.: City of Jamestown b. 1822—Town of Ellery b. 7 d. 1843-44, Carroll b. 1825. In Erie Co.: Buffalo m. 1811-1897, early years not complete. In Niagara Co.: City of Niagara Falls licenses 1837-1877, Town of Royalton b. m. d. 1818—. In Ontario Co.: Canandaigua b. m. & d. 1821-62, Victor b. 1821. In Oswego Co.: Westford b. m. & d. 1835-1852. These are in local offices and not in County Clerks' offices. The Buffalo Historical Society *Publications*, vol. XIV, 1910, App. B. article "Rough List of MSS." in its library on p. 453 lists "Buffalo Obituary Records" with dates of death, etc., of adults, incl. vicinity, 1812-1895, when City Bureau was established. It lists "Old Settlers, residents prior to 1830". (Compiled by C. K. Remington; this gives hundreds of names arranged by years of arrival 1789-1829, etc.)

[42] *The New England Historical and Genealogical Register* Jan. 1936, XC, 9-31 (New York, on 21-23).

organized in 1880 and then began to receive some returns. Some city bureaus antedate by a few years the State Bureau.⁴³ It took several years to organize the offices in the numerous towns and municipalities, although in the smaller ones the clerk serves as custodian. The date when all existing towns and municipalities, with the few exceptions noted above, were organized and sending returns to the State office is evidently 1895. It became compulsory to file records in 1914. In the 75 unbound volumes of Certificates of Births (Delayed) "are 920 certificates scattered through the years 1834-1879", and under marriages, "A small number of records was filed previous to the organization of the Department of Health in 1880, the earliest 1861".

Church, cemetery and census records given below, together with newspapers, Bibles, family data and genealogies are the chief sources for supplying missing vital records. The largest collection of Bible transcriptions in the State is in the New York State Library at Albany. It has fifty-five or more manuscript volumes of *Bible Records* with some family data transcribed by Daughters of the American Revolution of New York State." The Colonial Dames of the State of New York published *Genealogical Records,* edited by J. F. J. Robinson and H. C. Bartlett (1917). It contains vital records taken from family Bibles, 1581-1917.

In Upper New York, far from colonial settlements and supplies, there were no newspapers in early pioneering days. French's *Gazetteer*" gives for various localities dates and names of first newspapers with their publishers. Hough's *Gazetteer* gives those of 1872. C. S. Brigham's *Union List* with continuation by W. Gregory and the annotated catalogue of newspapers filed in the Wisconsin State Historical Society Library probably locate most of the early ones that now exist, except some in historical societies, small libraries not inven-

---

⁴³ Among them are: Amsterdam 1877, Buffalo, b. in 1878, Elmira, b. 1876, Rochester 1876, Syracuse b. and d. 1873, and 1874, Utica, b. 1873. Often a local bureau publishes in a local newspaper all births.

toried and files in offices of newspapers with which an early paper merged.

Writings on American History,[45] listing publications appearing each year, prior to 1940 had divisions "Regional Genealogy — Vital Records", "Regional Local-History — New York", "Genealogy-Collected" and "Genealogy-Individual Families". Most of the books and many of the articles published during the period on Upper New York are listed. In volumes since 1940, the only genealogies listed under that heading are those containing documents or biographical sketches, but other genealogies and vital records are included under "Local History". Many records of the region giving vital records are transcribed in *Early Settlers of New York State,* edited by Mrs. Janet (Wethey) Foley (it has a general name index), and in the *New York Genealogical and Biographical Record.* Many are located by both name and place divisions in *Index to Genealogical Periodicals,* by D. L. Jacobus, and its supplements.

Church Records

The Constitution of 1777 separated church and state, and the Act of 6 April 1784 gave all religious societies the right to organize and manage their temporal affairs. This placed the decision requiring the keeping of records with their church authority. Prior to such action by it, the clergy considered the records as private and took them when they left. The Historical Records Survey's *Guide to the Vital Statistics of Churches in New York State* (exclusive of New York City) 2 vols. (1942), includes 93 denominations; those required to keep records are the Methodist Episcopal, Presbyterian, Protestant Episcopal, Reformed Church in America and Roman Catholic. It does not give the dates when each were first required to keep them. The inventory covers only those records in the possession of the church. It gives location, date

---

[44] See D. A. R. under "Cemetery Records and Inscriptions".

[45] The years 1906, 1907 and 1908 were published by McMillan Co., 1912 to 1917 by Yale Press (New Haven); 1918 to 1940, and 1948—were published in the *Annual Report* of the American Historical Association or as a Supplement to it.

of organization, sometimes changed name or parent church, kinds of records with inclusive dates, and indicates D. A. R. and New York Genealogical and Biographical Society transcriptions found in the State Library.⁴⁶ The New York State Library *One Hundreth Annual Report*, 1917 (Albany, 1918, pp. 31-35) gives a complete list of church records received to June 1917 with statement of contents and dates. Subsequent reports list those received since that time.

Pre-organization meeting and incorporation of church papers found in the county clerks' offices name the first members. The earliest churches are often in the parent county.

Some upstate denominational collections are: Baptist in Rochester at the Colgate Divinity School, and in Hamilton at Colgate University and at Samuel Colgate Baptist Historical Collection; Methodist Episcopal at Syracuse University and at Troy Conference Historical Society; Seventh Day Baptists in Alfred Center at Alfred University; Universalists in Canton at St. Lawrence University; Shakers in the State Library and in Buffalo at Grosvenor Library. Mrs. J. C. Frost's transcriptions of New York Quaker meeting records are found in many libraries. Her title of "Quaker Records from Duanesburg later called Butternuts, Otsego County" is misleading. Butternuts M. M. was set off from Duanesburg, Schenectady Co., in 1810.⁴⁷

---

⁴⁶ The D. A. R. transcriptions are in their series of "Cemetery, Church and Town Records". The New York Genealogical and Biographical Society transcriptions were a large collection transcribed 1913 to 1917 of early New York church records edited by R. W. Vosburgh. The Society, the Library of Congress and the New York State Library each have a set; other libraries have microfilm copies. The Montgomery Co. Department of History and Archives has many.

⁴⁷ "Quaker Records in New York", by John Cox, Jr., in *New York Genealogical and Biographical Record*, 1914, XLV, 263-269, 366-373. On p. 370, "Butternuts was set off 1810 from Duanesburgh, M. M.". Evidently, the Butternut Quakers carried off the Record Book of Duanesburg and copied Butternut records in it since it gives b. 1778-1861 and d. 1809-1869. The Duanesburg records prior to 1810 are missing. The *Utah Genealogical and Historical Magazine*, April and July 1913, IV, 64-74, 119-125, gives "The Duanesburg Friends Meeting", births, 1810-1904 and deaths 1811-1907. "The Scipio Monthly Meeting of Friends", 1808 to 1821, incl., in *Collections of Cayuga County Historical Society*. Auburn, 1882, 87-90, gives by years arrivals, and from where.

Cemetery Records and Inscriptions

The largest collection of grave inscriptions in New York State is the transcriptions by the New York state chapters of the Daughters of the American Revolution. These are copied from old graves on farms, in churches and churchyards, in abandoned cemeteries and in the older sections of existing ones. Several copies are made. One is always sent to the D. A. R. Library, in Washington, D. C., and another to the New York State Library at Albany. The State Library has many volumes of *Cemetery, Church and Town Records,* and *Graves of Revolutionary Soldiers* with family data. Some chapters kept copies of their contributions and deposited them in a local library or historical society collection. The State Library and other libraries also have cemetery inscriptions and records by other transcribers.

If any tombstones exist in Central and Western New York at graves of their early dead, it is rather conclusive that they were placed there a number of years later and the inscriptions were from memory or family data. Transportation difficulties combined with remoteness from previously settled communities and from quarries and carvers of stone were chief factors. If an itinerant preacher officiated, he may have recorded the burial in his private records. If the deceased was a town officer, the minutes of the town meeting might mention his death. Even if the town clerk had attempted to record all deaths, the town was too vast, in this period, for him to hear of all deaths in his town. Owing largely to scarcity of paper until many years later when paper mills were built or supplies from outside became more frequent, few, if any, diaries were kept. When churches were built and church and churchyard received interments each church kept burial records with location of its graves. When cemetery associations were formed, its office in cemetery or elsewhere kept charts of sections with owners' names entered on lots sold and burial records with name, date, lot and location of grave of each interment. If an association was dissolved, the local government became custodian of the cemetery and its records (which it filed in its clerk's office) unless there was a park division, then it would have, if the lot owners had paid for perpetual care or the neighborhood demanded it, records of burials and location of graves. Sometimes families have re-interred kin on their lots in churchyards and cemeteries. Sometimes all graves of an abandoned cemetery have been transferred to a section of a newer cemetery.

The Montgomery County Department of History and Archives has the Federal Writers Project manuscripts of *Sweetman and West Charlton* (Saratoga Co.) cemeteries (1 vol.), and *Private Burial Grounds of Schenectady County*. It has also cemetery records of its ten towns and some of those of Albany, Fulton, Hamilton, Herkimer, Rensselaer, Saratoga, Schenectady and Washington Counties.

The H. R. S. *Guide to Depositories of Manuscript Collections* has 43 references to cemetery records. The Grosvenor Library in Buffalo has inscriptions from Chemung, Erie, Monroe, Niagara, Orleans, Wyoming and Yates counties. The *Guide* did not include the cemetery records in the Syracuse Public Library. That library has many transcriptions of individual cemeteries in Onondaga Co., a collection from nine towns by Edith Hall, old cemetery records throughout the county transcribed many years ago by W. M. Beauchamp and a D. A. R. deposit of some records of Onondaga, Oswego and Wayne Counties. Records of an abandoned cemetery in Syracuse are partly in the city clerk's office and partly in the park division office.

A few of the published books are *Inscriptions and Graves in the Niagara Peninsula*, by the Niagara Historical Society (1903); *Cemetery Inscriptions, Town of Spencer, N. Y. (Tioga Co.), 1795-1906*, by Mary F. Hall, comp. (1906); *Fenimore Cooper's Grave and Christ Churchyard* (Cooperstown, Otsego Co.), comp. by Ralph Birdsall (1911).

Census Records

Federal and state censuses taken in New York colony and state are listed by F. B. Hough in his "Introduction" to the summary of the 1855 state census. The State took a census in 1776, 1782, 1786, 1795, 1801, 1807, 1814, 1821, 1825, 1835, 1845, 1855, 1865, 1875, 1880, 1892, 1905, 1915, and 1925, after which date the state census was abolished. The 1880 state census was not a copy of the Federal Census for 1880, but a mere enumeration of persons and ages arranged in each district by initial of surname. The summaries of the state censuses of 1825, 1835 and 1845 were prepared by the county clerks; they kept the original returns. Some Boards of Supervisors voted to distribute them and the Federal censuses enumeration of the county to their towns. Most of these, for lack of storage space, were not permanently kept. Of the then 56 New York counties, the Census of 1825 of only Broome, Herkimer, Lewis, Orange, Schoharie, Tompkins, Washington and Yates Counties were in their county clerks' offices in 1946. A copy of the 1825 census for the Town of Otsego, Otsego Co., which then included Cooperstown, is in the Syracuse Public Library, and that of the Town of Mina, Chautauqua Co., is in Minerva Free Library at Sherman. Beginning with the state census of 1855, the original returns were sent to the Secretary of State's office where the summaries were prepared and the county clerks had copies to file. Prior to the State Library fire of March 1911 the returns from the Secretary of State's office were transferred to the Library. A report on losses lists all the original returns of New York state censuses for the years 1795, 1801, 1807, 1814, 1821 and all the figures after 1851.

The New York State Library published in 1937 *An Inventory of New York State and Federal Census Records*, compiled by Edna L. Jacobsen, based on reports from county clerks' offices. The fourth revised issue in 1942 includes Essex Co. 1915 and 1925. In 1945, the Library had enumerations for 1850, 1860, 1870, 1875, part of 1880, 1892, 1905 and 1925. The State Library now has by transfer all the earlier Albany County censuses.

The State census of 1855 introduced some new features: "Relation to Head", Born in County of N. Y., state or country", "Married or widowed", "No. yrs. res. in town or city", "native, naturalized, alien". The 1865 gives "parent of how many children" and "No. X married". It omits "length of res." The Works Progress Administration indexed for Onondaga Co. clerk's office its 1915 and 1925 census records, but there are some name omissions. The Syracuse Public Library supplements their file by copies of the Federal censuses for Onondaga Co. 1810 to 1840 with name indexes of each; 1790 and 1800 have been published.

The Grosvenor Library at Buffalo has an index to Census of 1850 of Buffalo and also of the 1855 census of Niagara Co. The D. A. R. Irondequoit Chapter of Rochester has census records of Monroe Co. arranged alphabetically under towns and wards. The Rochester Public Library has some microfilms of censuses.

Beginning with the Federal census of 1850 and the state census of 1855, each inhabitant is named in the enumeration instead of only the head of families as hitherto.

The published U. S. Census for 1790 for New York State claims "A complete list of the heads of families". A careful comparison of index and text of place with some known inhabitants of same places reveal omissions not owing to misreading of manuscript. In 1790 with the exception of a section of Ulster Co. taken to form a part of Delaware Co. in 1797 all of the settlements of Upper New York were then in Albany, Clinton, Montgomery, Ontario and Washington counties. In 1800, there were 30 counties in New York. *The New York Genealogical and Biographical Record* has published the 1800 census of twelve. The National Archives has a complete set of the 1810 census for New York except Cortland Co., which was set off from Onondaga Co. in 1808 and may have been given with Onondaga, or lost.

Military and Naval Records

During the colonial wars the Mohawk Valley was the only settled part of Upper New York outside the Hudson Valley. Its soldiers were in the Albany Co. regiments and records. Following the wars, New York issued patents to the north and east of the Hudson Valley. Patents to colonial soldiers gave the regiment of each. These were recorded in a separate file in the Secretary of State's office to which were added the military patents of the Revolution. A list of patents was published in 1793[48]. A map, 1775-1783, showing the boundary lines of the "Six Nations", the ten original counties of the New York colony and the four taken from Albany Co., is the frontispiece of *New York in the Revolution as Colony and State*, vol. 1 (Office of State Comptroller, 1904).

During the Revolution there were two militia brigades in Upper New York, (1) Albany and Tryon or the Mohawk Valley militia and the other (2) Charlotte, Cumberland and Gloucester. The area of the latter brigade, except Charlotte Co. west of Lake Champlain and in the Lake George region, became the State of Vermont in 1791. (Vermont soldiers are found in New York, Vermont and New Hampshire records.)

The office of State Historian was created in 1895 for the compilation and publication of *official* documents, memoranda and data, military and naval of the various wars. In 1915, the Division of History with the State Historian as chief, was combined with the Division of Archives. The Division prepared an excellent handbook *The American Revolution in New York*[49] giving organization of militia, minutemen, levies, line and navy, short history of the five regiments from New York (Sept. 1776) in the Continental Line, names of ten additional regiments with commanders largely recruited in New York Dec. 1776, exemptions except in invasion, difference between land bounties given for service in line and levies, and "land bounty rights" given in the latter part of the war, which are lists of men in militia classes who furnished one fully equipped soldier in each class to serve and the class received a transferable right[50], campaigns, invasions, raids and massacres by

---

[48] New York State, Secretary of State; *List of Names of Persons to whom Military Patents have been issued out of the Sec'ys office and to whom delivered.* Printed by Francis Child & John Swaine, Printers to the state in 1793. One of 300 copies is in the Library of Congress. It has pp. 9-10 duplicated and pp. 8-9 missing. This book is now very rare.
[49] "VII. *New York on the Battlefield*", pp. 129-177. See footnote 29.
[50] Sometimes they were assigned to the one who served. Land speculators purchased many. The State Library has some charred assignments and pay-rolls salvaged from the fire.

bands of Loyalists and Indians on the frontiers. It states that militia records prior to 1778 are very incomplete (this includes 1777 when in the Battle of Saratoga a maximum number served), that the "State Archives"[51] compiled by B. Fernow list about 40,000 soldiers, that the second edi'ion of *New York in the Revolution as Colony and State* lists 43,645, and that many names of officers and enlisted men of the Navy have been preserved. (In Upper New York, the Navy operated on Lake Champlain in May 1775 and in 1776.) It includes "Works relating to the American Revolution in the State of New York" (287-304) compiled by Peter Nelson, which lists bibliographies, sources, rosters, etc. Among listed works, with genealogical value are: Rosters of Oriskany and the Mohawk Valley Militia in N. Greene's *History of the Mohawk Valley, 1614- 1925.* 4 vols. Chicago 1925 (303); "List of New York Loyalists", compiled by Wm. Kelby, in New York Historical Society *Collections,* Jones Fund series, N. Y. 1917 (298); the various series of the *Collections* published by that Society with a list of volumes on the Revolution (297); "The Minutes of the Council of Appointment of the State of New York April 2, 1778—May 3, 1779", in the *Collections,* Publication Fund series, vol. LVIII, N. Y. 1925 (296); The New York State Historical Association *Proceedings* and the volume numbers of the regions featured (298), etc. (The *Proceedings* have general indexes that cover Vols. I—XXXIII. A few of the military papers are: "List of New York Patriots at Walloomsac August 16, 1777", vol. V, p. 103; "The Black Watch at Ticonderoga", with military rolls, *Proceedings,* vol. X, pp. 367-464. "Soldiers of the Champlain Valley" from a card catalog by S. H. Paine (The Revolution and the War of 1812) *Proceedings,* vol. XVII, 1919, pp. 300,428).

Calendar of Historical Manuscripts Relating to the War of the Revolution in office of Secretary of State (2 vols., Albany, 1868) contains rolls of regiment and data of individual soldiers. *Calendar of New York Colonial Manuscript Indorsed*

---

[51] "State Archives" is Vol. XV of *Documents Relating to the Colonial History of the State of New York.* This is sometimes referred to as "Colonial Documents".

Land Papers[52] contains claims, assignments and affidavits concerning revolutionary service of individual soldiers. Some omissions from rosters can be found by intensive search in contemporary and local sources, and publications and manuscripts of patriotic societies, pension records, etc. "Some New York Veterans in the American Revolution", prepared for the Syracuse Public Library by J. E. Bowman in 1926 contains over 200 items from various newspapers. Onondaga County Clerk's office has "Pension Papers and Physician Diplomas, 1799-1845", and also the military tract, "Awards of Onondaga Commissioners", vol. 1, 1798-1802.[53]

During the War of 1812, Upper New York consisted of 29 counties. In its area the conflict within New York raged and on its borders the two decisive naval battles of Lake Erie and Lake Champlain were fought. Governor Daniel D. Tompkins was the U. S. Major General in charge of military movements and in regulations of the commissary and pay departments. The accounts of the United States and New York became entangled. In 1818, Jabez Hammond was appointed agent to settle the claim of New York against the United States. In 1826, he reported to the Legislature that he had presented to the Third Auditor of the U. S. Treasury, without making copies, all the documents in his possession together with the returns of the arsenal-keepers in New York State during the late war. The National Government in 1892 transferred them to the Record and Pension Bureau, Washington, D. C. They included all the muster-in and muster-out rolls of the State. In 1900, the New York Adjutant General's Office had orders from 1801 to date and some incomplete pay rolls of the War of 1812 copied from records in Washington, D. C. The Historical Records Survey's *Guide to Depositories* locates several muster-

---

[52] See footnote 38 and text.

[53] R. S. Rose's thesis (see footnote 31) lists a Book of Awards of Cayuga County in Cayuga County Clerk's Office. Cuyuga was taken from Onondaga in 1799. He states that the Minutes of the Onondaga Commissioners were almost totally destroyed in the fire of 1911. The New York Historical Society library has "Report from the Commissioners for Settling Titles to Land in the County of Onondaga, N. Y." Albany, Feb. 1800. See also *Land Records* herein for military tracts.

rolls, and states that 25 volumes of War of 1812 records were transferred from the Comptroller's Office to the State Library in 1910, that among those salvaged from the fire are some payments to American prisoners of war, Niagara sufferers and a number of enlistment papers in the sea fencibles.

Among works published are: "Garrison Orders and Proceedings of Ft. Niagara" in New York State Historical Association *Proceedings,* 1926, 62-80, 152-178; *Documentary History of the Campaign on the Niagara Frontier* in the years 1812, 1813, 1814, edited by E. Cruikshank, 8 pts. in 7 volumes (1899-1905); *The Military Minutes of the Council of Appointment, 1783-1821,* compiled by H. Hastings, 3 vols. & Index (1901-1902). (It covers War of 1812 and gives changes of residences of some militia officers.)

No extant records of appointments exist for 1822-1830, but those for 1831 to 1846 are in the Adjutant General's office. That office has many records of the Civil and later wars. Its Annual Reports are published. County and other local histories usually give for their locality rosters of regiments and companies of the Civil War. Numerous histories of individual regiments have been published. Onondaga County Clerk's office has "Enrollment of Persons Liable to Military Duty, 1862-1866"; 66 volumes. Town of Manlius has records of service of officers, soldiers and seamen April 1861-1865. Other County Clerk's and Town offices should have such records for their localities. The State Census for 1865 gives for each enumeration district as of June 1, 1865, all men in army and navy, data of services, rank, promotions, regiment and reference to page and line in family enumeration, also deaths of officers with rank. The Adjutant General's office has a complete file of muster-in and muster-out rolls of the Spanish American War and should have the same for World Wars I and II.

C. LONG ISLAND

General Bibliography

Two pertinent bibliographies have been published for Long Island history and genealogy: *Bibliography of Long Island*, by Henry Onderdonk, which is an appendix to the *Antiquities of Long Island* by Gabriel Furman (edited by Frank Moore, New York, Bouton, 1875); and the comprehensive *Long Island Bibliography*, by Richard B. Sealock and Pauline A. Seely, published in 1940 (Edwards Bros., Ann Arbor, Mich.). In the former written at a time when historical and genealogical publications on Long Island were scant, the scope and emphasis were largely literary. However, Mr. Sealock and Miss Seely have compiled a work indispensable to the Long Island genealogist, and the competent researcher must be familiar with it, particularly with the sections on biography, directories, documents, and history and description.

Supplementing the foregoing are *American and English Genealogies in the Library of Congress*, Second Edition (1919); *Catalogue of American Genealogies in the Library of the Long Island Historical Society*, prepared under the direction of the then librarian, Emma Toedteberg (1935); and *Long Island Genealogical Source Material*, by this writer and published as Genealogical Publication No. 9 of the National Genealogical Society in 1948. Indexes to genealogical periodicals, notably those initiated by Daniel S. Durrie and continued to a fifth edition in 1900 by Joel Munsell's Sons *(Index to American Genealogies)*, and those published by Donald L. Jacobus.

Libraries with whose source material the investigator should be familiar include:

The East Hampton, New York, Free Library.

The Huntington, New York, Historical Society, at Huntington, New York.

The Long Island Historical Society, Pierrepont and Clinton Streets, Brooklyn, New York.

The New York Genealogical and Biographical Society, 122 East 58th Street, New York, N. Y.

The New York Historical Society, 77th Street and Central Park West, New York, N. Y.

The New York Public Library, 42nd Street and Fifth Avenue, New York, N. Y.

The New York State Library (Manuscripts and History Section), Albany, New York.

Queensborough Public Library, Long Island Collection, 89-14 Parsons Blvd., Jamaica, New York.

For the researcher who wishes to extend his field, collections in the major libraries in Boston, Washington (D. C.), Chicago, Salt Lake City and Los Angeles should be examined also.

General Historical Works: The Background

Silas Wood of Huntington, Long Island wrote *A Sketch of the First Settlement of the Several Towns on Long Island*, which was published by Spooner in Brooklyn in 1824. This 66-page work was followed by a more complete account by Benjamin Franklin Thompson, whose first edition of his *History of Long Island* was issued in 1839. It is Mr. Thompson's second edition, published by Gould in New York in 1843, which contained as he says, "notices of numerous individuals and families." While this pioneer work is of great value, Thompson's accounts of, for example, the Brewster and Thompson families are in error; and the listing of the earliest settlers of Islip include people who came much later. Mr. Thompson's *History* was expanded in an edition published in 1918 and edited by Charles J. Werner; it suffers from an uncritical approach.

In 1845, Nathaniel Scudder Prime got out his *A History of Long Island . . . with special reference to its ecclesiastical concerns*. Descendants of Long Island ministers will find it of use; however, the book was merely a follow-up on Thompson's *History*.

Later works take one of two forms: First, the somewhat generalized popular approach, and second, the detailed, biographic and genealogical form. In the first category, there is *Early Long Island, a Colonial Study,* by Martha Bockee Flint (1896). Mrs. Flint also published *The Bockee Family,* which is an omnibus recording a considerable number of Long Island families. One of them, Oakley, requires serious correction. Following Mrs. Flint, and in the second category, was Peter Ross' *History of Long Island,* 3 vols., with the genealogical work done in large part by William Smith Pelletreau, one of Long Island's early and indefatigable, if not always correct, genealogists. Here, also, must be included *The Refugees from Long Island to Connecticut,* by Frederick Gregory Mather and published in 1913 (Lyon, Albany, N. Y.), an absolutely indispensable reference work, although the genealogical part was contributed very largely by not-too-skilled amateurs. It deals of course with the era of the American Revolution. At the present time, the histories of Long Island by Henry Isham Hazelton and Paul Bailey have contributed biographical material of present day family connections. Late popular works have little genealogical significance.

Official and Other Printed Record Sources

General printed works include among others, land and court records, wills, marriages and census records. Some of these are by groups of individual towns on Long Island, but as they are collected and compiled under general headings, they are more conveniently referred to here.

Basic records include vol. 14 of *Documents Relating to the Colonial History of the State of New York (. . . Principally on Long Island),* edited by Berthold Fernow; the four volumes of the *Documentary History of the State of New York,* by E. B. O'Callaghan, and the *Calendar of Dutch Manuscripts* from the largely burned collection of colonial manuscripts on file in the New York State Library at Albany, New York, together with the *Calendar of English Manuscripts* from the same source.

The wills and administrations for Long Island have been maintained in various places, and the earlier wills were filed principally in New York City, with notable exceptions. *Abstracts of Wills on File in the Surrogate's Office, City of New*

York, beginning in 1665 and through 1800, were published in the *Collections* of the New York Historical Society, beginning in 1892. The abstracter was William Smith Pelletreau, but his zeal was not matched by his accuracy, for two volumes of corrections had to be published in 1907 and 1908; and the exact researcher should go to the original records. Berthold Fernow edited *Calendar of Wills on File and Recorded at Albany, New York,* many of which are for Long Island during the same period. In Suffolk County, the earliest probates were filed in the Lester Will Book, which Mr. Pelletreau bowdlerized as *Early Long Island Wills of Suffolk County, 1691-1703,* in 1897. For records filed in New York City and which may refer to Long Islanders, see also *Guide to Genealogical and Biographical Sources for New York City (Manhattan) 1783-1898* (1954), by Rosalie Fellows Bailey.

The Office of the Secretary of State in New York has published the early marriage licenses issued before 1784 under *Names of Persons for whom Marriage Licenses were Issued by the Secretary of the Province;* a supplemental list was also published, many referring to 17th century unions. With these should be included *New York Marriage Licenses in the Archives of the New York Historical Society,* by Robert H. Kelby.

General Genealogical Works and Workers

Long Island's first publishing genealogist may well have been Jordan Seaman of Jericho, whose *Copy of an account Written by Jordan Seaman* was printed in 1800. However, this account was but slowly followed by others for at least sixty years. Studies on individual families actively began in the last two decades of the 19th century, stimulated by a group of early genealogists who had the pick-and-shovel work to do.

Teunis Huntting compiled his MS *Long Island Genealogies* during this period; a near contemporary of his, James Le Baron Willard, also compiled a manuscript of the same name. Both of these manuscripts are in the library of the Long Island Historical Society. The redoubtable Mary Powell Bunker published her well-known *Long Island Genealogies* in 1895 after many years of collection of materials, and reading proof with failing eyesight. In the 20th century, Charles J. Werner published his *Genealogies of Long Island Families*. All of these contain a certain amount of critical research work, family records, and hopeless mistakes. The pitfalls sometimes seem to be unavoidable, as the present writer knows from compiling his *Colonial Families of Long Island, New York and Connecticut*, which has reached its fourth volume. Other works covering not only Long Island but adjacent areas as well have been published by William S. Pelletreau, William Richard Cutter and Cuyler Reynolds. Individual genealogies and pedigree books recently published are too numerous to list; it may be mentioned that the late Mrs. Samuel K. (Josephine C.) Frost was an author or compiler of many.

Kings County and Borough

Ordinarily, modern local maps do not indicate the boundaries of the towns which comprised Kings County, and which were the original centers of civil and ecclesiastical records: Brooklyn (Breuckelen), Flatbush (Vlackebos), Bushwick (Boschwyck), Flatlands (Nieuw Amersfoort), New Utrecht and Gravesend. Later, the town of New Lots was separated from Flatbush. The settlers were predominantly Dutch, with French, Belgian, English, German and Scandinavian nationalities participating in the colonization.

Basic records include town and court records, wills, deeds, church registers, cemetery inscriptions and vital records, most of the last being of more recent date.

None of the town records have been published in any complete form. The early records of Brooklyn were reputedly taken by the British during the war of the American Revolution. The originals for the other towns are in the Commissioner of Records' Office in Brooklyn; they include town records for:

Bushwick, 1660-1825.

Flatbush, 1652-1818 (this includes wills, 1670-1708, court actions, 1659-1692, and deeds also).

Flatlands, 1655-1868 (including court records, 1661-1684, and deeds).

New Utrecht, 1659-1894 (including deeds).
Gravesend, 1645-1872 (including court records, 1661-1699 and deeds).

The late Henry Onderdonk transcribed some of these in his *Kings County Records, 1666-1775*, the manuscript of which is in the library of the Long Island Historical Society. The Society has also a typewritten copy of the early town records of Bushwick.

The *New York Genealogical and Biographical Record* has published "Abstracts of Kings County Wills" (vol. 47, pp. 161, 227; vol. 48, p. 79) and "Abstracts of Deeds" (vol. 48, pp. 110, 291, 355 and vol. 54, pp. 105, 241, 303). Printed early church records include those for the Reformed Dutch Churches in Brooklyn *(Holland Society Year Book, 1897)* and Flatbush *(ibid., 1898)*. Those for New Utrecht were published in the *New York Genealogical and Biographical Record*, vol. 73, p. 96; and vital records for Gravesend were published in the same, vol. 4, p. 199. Cemetery records have been published by the Kings County Genealogical Club and issued privately by William A. Eardeley, among others. For general accounts of the first settlers, *A History of the City of Brooklyn*, published in 1867-70 by Henry R. Stiles in three volumes, gives much information for Brooklyn and Bushwick. This has been augmented by the fine work of Andrew J. Provost, Jr., whose *Early Settlers of Bushwick*, in two volumes has been completed.

The mentor of all Kings County genealogists is the late Teunis G. Bergen, whose *Register in Alphabetical Order of Early Settlers of Kings County* was published in 1881. This work has provided many a Kings County family with clues to its Long Island ancestry; it includes the famous Sarah (Rapalje) Bergen, reputedly the first white female child born in the New Netherlands, and who crossed the East River in a large washtub.

Queens County and Borough, and Nassau County

These two present-day political units were originally included in the older Queens County, and contain six towns, at the present time three in each county. These are Newtown, Flushing and Jamaica in modern Queens, and North Hempstead, South Hempstead and Oyster Bay in Nassau County.

The earlier wills and deeds for this entire area, when not filed in the depositaries already mentioned, were recorded at Jamaica. These records have been transcribed for the Long Island Collection of the Queensboro Public Library at the latter place, and copies are also in the library of the Long Island Historical Society. Indexes and some abstracts for 1787-1835 were privately gotten out in two volumes in 1918 by William A. Eardeley.

The town records of Flushing have been burned, with but little saved except from other sources. Those of the other towns have been published in very considerable part; they include also deeds and some wills (Jamaica and Oyster Bay) and court records (Newtown). Those for North Hempstead and South Hempstead are together as the original town represented by them bore the single name; they include records in all the categories cited.

The towns are well represented by published church records. Those of the Reformed Churches for Newtown and Jamaica have been transcribed by Josephine C. Frost; those for Wolver Hollow (in Oyster Bay) appear in the *New York Genealogical and Biographical Record,* vol. 73, pp. 26, 121, 200, and 273. The last provided the basic record for Henry A. Stoutenburgh's *A documentary history of het (the) Nederduytsche Gemeente,* Dutch congregation of Oyster Bay, published in parts from 1902 to 1907. Those for Manhasset (Hempstead) have been transcribed by Henry Onderdonk, Jr., and Josephine C. Frost. Ladd's *History of Grace Church (Episcopal), Jamaica, New York,* includes records of the Episcopal churches of Jamaica and Newton. In this connection, it may be mentioned that Mrs. Samuel K. (Josephine C.) Frost's transcriptions of Long Island church records for a great number of Long Island communities, in all counties, are in the library of the *New York Genealogical and Biographical Society*, New York, N. Y.

The records of transactions of the Society of Friends have been published by William Wade Hinshaw in his *Encyclopaedia of American Quaker Genealogy*, vol. 3 (New York). This includes all meetings on Long Island and notably those of Flushing, Westbury and Jericho.

The Presbyterian church records of Newtown have been published as vol. 8 of *Collections of the New York Genealogical and Biographical Society;* and those for Hempstead in the *New York Genealogical and Biographical Record*, vol. 53, pp. 235, 381 and vol. 54, pp. 30, 138. Those of the oldest Episcopal church, St. George's at Hempstead, have also been published in the *Record* in vols. 9, 10, 11, 12, 13, 14, 15 and 24. The records of the Episcopal church at Jamaica have been transcribed by Henry Onderdonk and Josephine C. Frost.

Some of the towns have not been without well-known historians and genealogists; James Riker, who published on Newtown families in his *History of Newtown;* the well-known Henry Onderdonk of whom we have already spoken, whose publications include *Documents and Letters Intended to Illustrate the Revolutionary Incidents of Queens County*, and *The Annals of Hempstead;* and Mrs. Samuel K. (Josephine C.) Frost, whose transcripts of church and cemetery records have placed every Long Island genealogist in her debt.

Suffolk County

This large county contains the towns of Brookhaven, East Hampton, Huntington, Islip, Shelter Island, Smithtown, Southampton and Southold; and more recently Riverhead (from Southold) and Babylon (from Huntington). The records pertaining to this county are fairly complete and many of them have been published. The county records are filed at Riverhead, the county seat.

The wills and administrations of the county to 1850 have been abstracted and are on file in the library of the Long Island Historical Society, and in that of the D. A. R. at Washington, D. C. Indexes of the Surrogate's records with some abstracts of wills were issued by William A. Eardeley in 1905. Deeds on file at the county seat have not been published; a manuscript index of earlier grantors and grantees is in the library of the New York Genealogical and Biographical Society in New York City.

The town records, including deeds filed in town halls, have been published for Smithtown, Brookhaven, Southampton, and East Hampton, and are quite complete with respect to the earlier records. Likewise, the earliest town records of Southold have been published; and selected deeds, town records, assessment lists, vital records and Revolutionary papers have been published for Huntington and Babylon. The early records of Islip, rendered unavailable by a fire years ago, were only recently discovered, and are at the town clerk's office.

The early residents of the county were largely of the Presbyterian faith. Printed church records exist for Babylon (published by the church), East Hampton (in the back of volume 5 of the printed *Town Records*), Huntington (edited by Moses L. Scudder), Smithtown *(New York Genealogical and Biographical Record,* vol. 42, pp. 128, 272; vol. 44, pp, 279, 384; and vol. 45, p. 8), and Southold *(ibid.,* vol. 64, pp. 217, 322; vol. 65, pp. 47, 152, 261, 329; and vol. 66, pp. 51, 257, and 293). Early church records of Brookhaven are said to have been lost during the American Revolution; but the town historian Osborn Shaw has filed in the Town House at Patchogue all the known early gravestone inscriptions of the town, which compensates to a considerable extent for this loss. The *Salmon Records* of Southold comprise the vital statistics of this town for the pioneer days, and the Rev. Jacob Mallman has preserved the records of Shelter Island in his *Historical Papers of Shelter Island and Its Presbyterian Church.*

It remains to notice the works of some early historians: Henry P. Hedges *History of East Hampton* (with genealogies); George R. Howell's *The Early History of Southampton, L. I., with Genealogies* (second edition); and *Personal Index of the Town of Southold,* by Charles B. Moore. Of late, Mrs. J. E. Rattray has revised Hedges' work in her *East Hampton*

History and Genealogies, which should serve as an inspiration for other town historians.

Conclusion

In this chapter an endeavor has been made to summarize some of the basic and indispensable references for the genealogist interested in Long Island families. The reader doubtless knows of others which might have been mentioned. However, the genealogical reference works available grow while this is being written, and the research opportunities become ever more extensive. A development of the bibliography given herein, together with on-the-spot examination of the various classes of records cited, should provide the researcher with much information.

CHAPTER III

NEW JERSEY

The Colonial Settlements

The history of New Jersey properly begins on 23-24 June, 1664, when the territory now comprised within the boundaries of that State were granted by the Duke of York (afterwards King James II) to John, Lord Berkeley, and Sir George Carteret, Proprietors of Carolina. It was named *Nova Caesarea* after the Channel Island of Jersey, over which Carteret had formerly been governor.

New Jersey was a part of New Sweden from 1638 until it fell to the victorious Dutch troops in 1655. From the latter year until the English conquest of 1664 it belonged to New Netherland. There were some Swedish and Finnish families settled in Salem and Burlington Counties.

English Puritans from New Haven, Connecticut, had begun to make inroads into New Sweden in 1641, but after the English conquest 23 years later New Englanders and Long Islanders began to flock to the region, settling in Elizabeth, Shrewsbury and Middletown. Newcomers from Massachusetts Bay and New Hampshire founded Woodbridge in 1665, and in the next year Piscataway was established by settlers from Piscataqua, near Portsmouth, New Hampshire. Congregationalists from Connecticut showed up at Newark in the same year. Salem was founded by John Fenwick and a group of Quakers from England in 1675.

New Jersey was divided into two provinces in 1676, the present North Jersey being called East Jersey and governed first by Carteret and later by a board of 24 proprietors. The present South Jersey was known as West Jersey, and came under the rule of William Penn and other Quaker leaders who had acquired Lord Berkeley's share of the land. Beginning in 1677 and continuing for a number of years, Quakers came from England and settled at Burlington, Gloucester, Newton, Rancocas, Willingsborough, and Pyne Poynte (now Camden).

The twin provinces were united into the Royal Province of New Jersey in 1701/2, and placed under the rule of the Governor of New York. It shared its chief executive with New York from 1702 to 1738, when it acquired its own royal governor. The last Governor of New Jersey to be appointed by the Crown was William Franklin, son of the redoubtable patriot, Benjamin Franklin.

With this brief survey of the State's colonial history, we turn our attention now to the genealogical resources of New Jersey.

Printed Works

New Jersey has many publications which provide much information on genealogical subjects. Francis Bazley Lee's *Genealogical and Memorial History of the State of New Jersey* (4 vols., 1910) records the genealogies of a large number of the State's families, but many errors have been found in it and care must be exercised in its use.

The Lewis Historical Publishing Company (later the American Historical Publishing Society) published histories of South Jersey (5 vols., 1924), Northwestern New Jersey (5 vols., 1927) and New Jersey (6 vols., 1930-32) which contain a great deal of biographical and genealogical data, but, again, caution must be exercised in their use for the family records were contributed by the families themselves and are subject to error. A useful work which gives not only sketches of families but source materials is John Edwin Stillwell's 5-volume *Historical and Genealogical Miscellany: Data Relating to the Settlement and Settlers of New York and New Jersey.*

A work that is much used is Orra Eugene Monnette's *First Settlers of Ye Plantations of Piscataway and Woodbridge, Olde East New Jersey, 1664-1714.* It was issued in seven parts, beginning in 1930. So long as it relies on source-materials it may be considered as reasonably accurate. But Mr. Monnette frequently indulged in speculations and argumentation. His theories concerning the origins of East Jersey families should always be treated with caution. He was easily offended when criticized, and wasted much printer's ink denouncing his opponents. His real contribution lay in the compilation of source materials. A thoughtful evaluation of Monnette's work was published by Donald Lines Jacobus in *The American Genealogist*, vol. 34, October 1958, pp 213-215.

Theodore Frelinghuysen Chambers' book, *The Early Germans of New Jersey: Their History, Churches, and Genealogies* (1895) is another work that must be treated cautiously. In his enthusiasm, Mr. Chambers occasionally introduced families of English and French origin into his pages, so that one wonders what happened to the Germans in New Jersey. But he does provide us with much useful information.

New Jersey's contribution to our early wars is contained in William S. Stryker's *Official Register of Officers and Men of New Jersey in the Revolutionary War* (1872) ; *Records of Officers and Men of New Jersey in Wars, 1791-1815* (1909) ; and *Records of Officers and Men of New Jersey In The Civil War, 1861-1865* (2 vols., 1876).[1]

The most important periodicals relating to New Jersey history and genealogy are the *Proceedings of the New Jersey Historical Society*, which has been published regularly since 1845, and the *Genealogical Magazine of New Jersey*, which was started in 1925 by the Genealogical Society of New Jersey. The latter journal was edited for many years by the late Russell Bruce Rankin, F. A. S. G. It devotes itself chiefly to source-materials (church records, Friends' meeting records, etc.), but also has articles on individual families. For a number of years it carried a series of articles entitled, "Genealogical Dictionary of New Jersey", by Charles Carroll Gardner, F. A. S. G. Since 1953, a quarterly magazine devoted to the State's history and genealogy has been issued by Harold

---

[1] The New Jersey Department of Defense has an alphabetical record, on cards, of every name appearing on the Revolutionary pay rolls and vouchers, which gives many names not in any printed list. Microfilms of these cards are in the State Library at Trenton and the D. A. R. Library in Washington, D. C.

A. Sonn, of Springfield, New Jersey, under the title of *The New Jersey Genesis.*

New Jersey Archives

New Jersey is more fortunate than some states in having its ancient archives in published form. In 1880 was begun the publication of the long series of volumes known as the *Documents Relating to the Colonial History of New Jersey* but more popularly referred to as the *New Jersey Archives.* Many of the volumes deal with the acts and proceedings of the Provincial Legislature, but there are 13 volumes in the series which contain abstracts of wills from 1670 to 1817. Volume XXI is the *Calendar of Records in the Office of the Secretary of State,* covering the period 1664-1703. The documents included are East Jersey Patents and Deeds, Revel's Book of Surveys, West Jersey Records, Salem Surveys and Deeds, and Gloucester Deeds. The value of the deeds is that they reveal the homes in the British Isles of many of New Jersey's first settlers. Volume XXII of the *New Jersey Archives* contains marriage records, but it must be emphasized that these printed records are incomplete.

From 1901 to 1917 five volumes were published under the title, *Documents Relating to the Revolutionary History of New Jersey;* this work is known as the Second Series of the *New Jersey Archives.*

Societies and Libraries

The New Jersey Historical Society at 230 Broadway, Newark 4, New Jersey, possesses original records and transcripts that should not be overlooked by the genealogist of New Jersey families. There one can find two volumes of the East Jersey Quit Rent Books (1683 and 1685), the Mansfield Township (Burlington County) Record Book, 1697-1773, Burlington County Birth Records, 1770-85, maintained by a Quaker resident of the county; Benjamin Smith Docket Book, 1788-92 (records, including marriage records, of a Justice of the Peace for Hunterdon and Salem Counties) ; and many other records. It has also on microfilm the registers of the Swedish Evangelical Lutheran Church and its successor, Trinity Protestant Episcopal Church, which were published in 1938 as *The Records of the Swedish Lutheran Churches at Raccoon and Penns Neck, 1713-1786*. The Society owns splendid genealogical collections, family papers and portraits, including the magnificent collection of Charles Carroll Gardner, who assembled notes and papers on thousands of New Jersey families.

The Genealogical Society of New Jersey does not have a headquarters, but its address is P. O. Box 208, Newark. There are about 15 local historical societies which are doing a fine job of preserving the records of their counties and localities. Many of them publish very useful magazines and monographs. A list of such societies appears in Stevenson's *Search and Research* (Revised Edition, 1959), pp. 192-194.

The Division of the State Library, Archives and History Department of Education, at Trenton, New Jersey, has card indexes for births, marriages, and deaths in the 18th and 19th centuries, prepared by the WPA Historical Records Survey. Its microfilms include lists of ratables during the last quarter of the 18th and the first quarter of the 19th century for the following counties: Bergen, Burlington, Cape May, Cumberland, Essex, Gloucester, Hunterdon, Middlesex, Monmouth, Morris, Salem, Somerset and Sussex.

Among out-of-state societies which devote considerable shelf space to New Jersey are the Genealogical Society of Pennsylvania in Philadelphia, which has transcripts and photostats of records of 13 counties, with special emphasis on Burlington; and the D. A. R. Library at Washington which has transcripts of church registers, abstracts of wills, Bible records, military records, etc., for many New Jersey counties.

Official Records

New Jersey is divided into twenty-one counties, and at the respective court houses are located the usual types of genealogical records, such as wills, deeds, mortgages, etc.

Although New Jersey has not attempted to centralize all of

its records, it has assembled at Trenton, the State capital, a great many original records, and it is well to begin a search there.

The Secretary of State's Office has the ancient deed books from the earliest settlements in East and West New Jersey; a card index has been compiled for them. The abstracts for the period of 1665-1703 have been printed in vol. XXI of the *New Jersey Archives,* but these are the documents themselves covering a longer period of time. An important source of biographical information relating to colonial ancestors is Liber AAA of Commissions, 1703-74, of which abstracts for the period 1703-69 were printed in the *Publications of the Genealogical Society of Pennsylvania, vols. VI-X.* The Secretary of State also has custody of bound volumes of marriage bonds, 1711-95; there is a card index for them.

Wills were formerly available in the Office of the Secretary of State, but are now under the jurisdiction of the Clerk of the Superior Court, Room 327, State House Annex. Before visiting the Court, it would be well for the researcher to consult the printed *Index to Wills, Inventories, Etc., in the Office of the Secretary of State Prior to 1901* (3 vols., 1912-13). "Unrecorded Wills" are indexed in vol. III, pp. 1417-52. In order to facilitate the search at the Superior Court for the desired will, the researcher should first consult these index volumes and obtain the testator's name, the year of probate, and the number of the will.

Vital statistics were started at Woodbridge as early as 1671, and all through the colonial period, for both East and West Jersey, and the later Royal Province of New Jersey, legislation was enacted requiring the maintenance of such records. However, little attention was paid to the requirement. In 1799, the State Legislature passed a law stating that parents could, *if they desired,* have their children's births registered. It was also ordered that deaths must be registered, within three years of the occurrence. These laws also were largely ignored.

In 1848, the registration of births, marriages, and deaths

was made compulsory in New Jersey. The present custodian of all vital statistics since that year is the State Bureau of Vital Statistics, Department of Health, State House, Trenton, New Jersey. However, the cities sometimes maintained such records also, and there are instances in which no record was available at Trenton, but was found in the records of the city wherein the person lived.

CHAPTER IV

PENNSYLVANIA

Printed Reference Works

Pennsylvania has a large number of useful printed books on genealogy and local history. One of the early writers on genealogy in the Keystone State was John W. Jordan, whose *Colonial Families of Philadelphia* (3 vols., 1911) is a classic. Although nearly half a century has elapsed since its publication, it may still be regarded as an authoritative work on the history of old Philadelphia families. The successor work, *Colonial and Revolutionary Families of Pennsylvania*, is now in its 19th volume. Its value is impaired by the "sources" listed; they consist generally of more or less accurate printed books and "Family Records", a vague statement which proves nothing. The series are helpful for providing clues for further research, but it must be remembered that the editor has not checked the pedigrees contributed by members of the family included in the volumes and, where doubt exists, primary sources should be consulted.

Numerous histories of Pennsylvania counties have been published. Some of them are invaluable for their genealogical and biographical accounts, such as Battle's and Davis's works on Bucks County (1887 and 1905, respectively), Cope's history of Chester and Delaware Counties (2 vols., 1904), Bean's Montgomery County history (1884), Watson's celebrated *Annals of Philadelphia and Pennsylvania in the Olden Time* (final edition, 3 vols., 1898)—poorly arranged but invaluable for the historian, and, with a little patient digging, for the genealogist; Westcott and Scharf's *History of Philadelphia* (3 vols., 1884), and Dunkelberger's history of Snyder County (1949), a compendious work of 982 pages *which has no index*.

An important bibliographical reference work for the student of Pennsylvania is the *Bibliography of Pennsylvania History*, edited by Norman B. Wilkinson (2nd ed., 1957). It expands the 1946 *Writings on Pennsylvania History* and advances the date to 1952. It is very inclusive in its coverage.

Periodicals

The most important genealogical periodical for Pennsylvania is the *Publications of the Genealogical Society of Pennsylvania*, which was renamed more appropriately the *Pennsylvania Genealogical Magazine* when the late Dr. John Goodwin Herndon, F. A. S. G., became its editor in 1947. The first 15 volumes contain tombstone inscriptions, church records, abstracts of wills, vital statistics, Friends' meeting records, etc. The magazine since volume 15 continues to publish source materials, but in addition it presents important family studies contributed by such scholars as Dr. Herndon, Lewis D. Cook, Meredith B. Colket, Robert M. Torrence, Rosalie Fellows Bailey, George H. S. King, H. Minot Pitman, William J. Hoffman, Walter Lee Sheppard, George Valentine Massey II, and others.

The next most important periodical relating to Pennsylvania genealogy is, curiously enough, the *National Genealogical Society Quarterly*, published at Washington, D. C., since 1912. A review of its 47 volumes reveals an astonishing number of articles describing the location of sources and facilities for genealogical research in Pennsylvania, as well as innumerable Bible records, cemetery inscriptions, family data, etc. As examples, the *Quarterly* has published articles entitled "Sources for Genealogy and Local History of the Scotch-Irish of Central Pennsylvania", by Raymond M. Bell (1945); "Geographical Aspects of Pennsylvania German Genealogical Study", by Albert H. Gerberich (1946); "German Reformed Church Records in Pennsylvania", by William J. Hinke (1949); and "Schwenckfelder Genealogical Records", by Selina Gerhard Schultz (1951).

Printed Sources

The most-used printed source material (and the most valuable for the colonial, Revolutionary, and post-Revolutionary periods) are the *Colonial Records of Pennsylvania*

(16 vols., 1838-53), and the ten series of the *Pennsylvania Archives*, which commenced publication in 1852. The series of the *Archives* of special value for genealogists are the Second (militia rolls, church records), the Third (militia rolls, tax lists, lists of land warrantees), the Fifth (muster rolls, chiefly of the Provincial and Revolutionary periods), and the Sixth (muster rolls covering the period from the Revolution to the War of 1812, marriage and baptismal records, inventories of estates confiscated during the Revolution, etc.). The millions of names in these series are indexed. The Second and Third Series have their own indexes, but the Fifth Series is indexed in the two parts of vol. 15 of the Sixth Series, while the Seventh Series constitutes an index for the first 14 volumes of the Sixth Series.

In 1949, the Division of Public Records of Harrisburg Issued a *Guide to The Published Archives of Pennsylvania Covering the 138 Volumes of Colonial Records and Pennsylvania Archives, Series I-IX*, by Henry Howard Eddy, with an Alphabetical Finding List and Two Special Indexes, by Martha L. Simonetti. The *Guide* provides a quick reference to topics in the *Colonial Records* and the *Archives*.

The Division of Public Records has custody of the official passenger lists showing arrivals at the Port of Philadelphia during the period 1727-1808. Those lists which date before the American Revolution concern immigrants from the Continent of Europe only, and do not cover persons who were British subjects. Almost all of the individuals included in the early lists were German or Swiss in origin. These lists of immigrants have been published *completely* in Strassburger and Hinke's *Pennsylvania German Pioneers* (3 vols., 1954), copies of which can be found at most large libraries and historical societies. Volume II of the set carries facsimiles of all signatures occurring in the original lists. Most of the passengers were described vaguely as "Palatines" or "Foreigners", but a few ship lists contained the original home of the settlers, such as Hessen, Hanau, Württemberg, etc.

The Division of Public Records also has custody of official

lists of aliens naturalized by Pennsylvania Courts during the years 1740-73. All information contained in these lists is available in printed form, some in *Pennsylvania Archives*, Second Series, vol. II, and others in M. S. Giuseppi's *Naturalizations of Foreign Protestants in the American and West Indian Colonies (Pursuant to Statute 13 George II, c. 7) (Publications of the Huguenot Society of London*, vol. XXIV, 1921). By special act of Assembly, aliens were on occasion granted a type of naturalization more limited than that granted by the courts. The numerous special acts passed for the purpose of naturalizing citizens are contained in the *Statutes at Large of Pennsylvania*, vols. II-VII, inclusive.

In addition to the muster rolls for the French and Indian War, the Revolutionary War, and the War of 1812, published in the *Pennsylvania Archives*, a valuable record of Pennsylvania's soldiers in the Civil War is contained in Samuel P. Bates' *History of Pennsylvania Volunteers, 1861-65* (5 vols., 1869-71). These hefty volumes are important for their detailed regimental histories. They include complete rosters, but unfortunately only the names of commissioned officers are given in the long index in vol. 5.

Some colonial court records have been published, among them *The Record of the Court at Upland in Pennsylvania, 1676 to 1681* (Historical Society of Pennsylvania, 1860), and the *Record of the Courts of Chester County, Pennsylvania, 1681-1697* (The Colonial Society of Pennsylvania, 1910).

Genealogical and Historical Societies

Pennsylvania has a number of societies in which genealogists may find information of value for their researches.

One of the most important of these organizations is the Genealogical Society of Pennsylvania at 1300 Locust Street, Philadelphia. Unfortunately, the emphasis there is on Southeastern Pennsylvania; its holdings are weak in the western, central, and northern parts of the State. Its collections consist of abstracts or copies of wills, administrations, church registers, Orphans' Court records, newspaper obituaries and death notices, unpublished family genealogies, *original* 18th century Supreme Court records (in 45 *unindexed* volumes), transcripts of English Friends' records from the earliest period of Quaker history to 1725 (invaluable for identifying the English homes of Quaker settlers in the American colonies), etc. The Society also possesses many private genealogical collections of which the best known is that of Gilbert Cope, whose data on 2500 families in Chester and other Southeastern Pennsylvania and nearby New Jersey counties are arranged alphabetically in 90 volumes.

The Genealogical Society is housed in the building of the Historical Society of Pennsylvania. The latter organization's Manuscripts Department contains many items of genealogical interest which may be picked up in the excellent card index. One *unindexed* collection in the Manuscripts Department which is of extreme value for the family historian is that of Gilbert Cope. It must *not* be confused with his well-organized collection in the Genealogical Society. The Historical Society's Cope collection contains marriage records, notes on families, tax lists, petitions, etc. One can spend days with this vast accumulation of data and still not exhaust its possibilities for increasing one's genealogical knowledge.

Pennsylvania also has a number of county societies which are doing an excellent job of preserving the historical and genealogical records of their respective areas. In 1939, the Pennsylvania Historical Commission published as its Bulletin No. 774 a *Guide to Depositories of Manuscript Collections in Pennsylvania*, which briefly describes the holdings of libraries and societies throughout the State.

The State Library [1]

The Genealogical Section of the Pennsylvania State Library at Harrisburg possesses a wide collection of source material. It has more than 5000 printed genealogies and many county histories of Pennsylvania and other states. Graveyards and church records are listed under the state and county where they are located. Various chapters of the D. A. R. and in-

---

[1] The section on the State Library was contributed by Mrs. Ethel S. Davenport, State Genealogist, State Library.

dividuals throughout the State and Nation have contributed church and cemetery records and personal family Bible records.

The alphabetical card index, consisting of 360 drawers of 3x5 inch cards, is one of the best in Pennsylvania.

Copies of the Federal Census taken every ten years in Pennsylvania, from the year 1790 to 1880, inclusive, can be used by patrons; Index to Registrations of Deaths of the City of Philadelphia, 1803-60 (transcript, 33 vols.); Philadelphia City Directories from 1791 to 1806, and other directories of the early period as well as early county atlas books are used to locate families and their properties.

Official Records

The Division of Public Records, a branch of the Pennsylvania Historical and Museum Commission known prior to 1948 as the State Archives, at Harrisburg, has official records almost exclusively, especially records of military service by Pennsylvania during the 1775-1861 period. Many of these are too fragile for consultation by others than the staff, but certificates can be secured for a fee of $1.00. Free Information Leaflets are available and helpful.

At the Division of Public Records indexes remain partial, but progress continues. There are microfilms covering many of the pre-1850 records of thirteen of the older eastern counties and also films for the Federal censuses for Pennsylvania taken from 1830 through 1880. These can be consulted in readers at the Division. A list of the county films available appeared in the *National Genealogical Society Quarterly* for June 1954, but inadvertently Chester County was omitted from that list, and more recently Bucks County has been added.

Information as to enrollment or service with Pennslyvania military units during the period 1775-1861 can, in many cases, be furnished by the Division of Public Records. However, the older records are incomplete and, therefore, failure to find a record must not be taken as negative proof. The military records in the Division's custody consist of thousands of rolls and accounts, papers which for the most part remain without indexes. Military records of persons serving with Pennsylvania units *after* 1861 are maintained in the Old Records Section, Department of Military Affairs, 29 North Office Building, Harrisburg.

Unlike Connecticut, Delaware, Maryland, and certain other states, in Pennsylvania there has been no centralization of county records. The originals of wills, deeds, mortgages, and other official records of local origin remain in the 67 court houses of the Commonwealth. The records for the City and County of Philadelphia are merged in the City Hall at 13th and Market Streets, Philadelphia. The Department of Records of Philadelphia was created by the Charter of April 1951 which reorganized the City Government; it is, therefore, the first of the older American cities to establish a municipal archives. In 1957, Charles E. Hughes, Jr., City Archivist, and Allen Weinberg, Archival Examiner, published a *Guide to the Municipal Archives of the City and County of Philadelphia,* which describes briefly the documents preserved by the Department of Records, some of which one would not expect to find in municipal records, such as the 91 volumes of the Declaration of Aliens Docket, 1821-1911, and Index to Naturalization Declarations, 1811-1903 (71 boxes, indexed in 12 index volumes), both included in the records of the Court of Common Pleas.

While in 1682 legislation was passed requiring the registration of births, marriages, and burials, little attention was paid to this requirement. Records of marriages, births, and deaths were kept by the Registers of Wills from 1852 to 1854, and such records may be found in the various county court houses, historical societies, and (very incompletely) the Division of Public Records. For a few years, commencing in 1885, the various Boards of Health maintained vital statistics, which are on record in the court houses. For the period since 1 January 1906, all records of births, marriages and deaths have been kept by the Vital Statistics Section of the Department of Health. Divorce records are on file in the office of the Prothonotary at the court house in the county where the divorce was granted.

While private deeds transferring title are recorded at the Office of the Recorder of Deeds for the appropriate county, Pennsylvania land patents, including military grants, are on record at the Bureau of Land Records, Department of Internal Affairs, in the Capitol Building at Harrisburg. They are very well indexed.

Church Records

Pennsylvania is fortunate in having a number of church archives where are preserved registers, correspondence, etc. The Friends' Historical Library at Swarthmore College includes among its extensive holdings Quaker meeting records (minutes, birth, burial, marriage, removal and membership records). Presbyterian church registers are at the Presbyterian Historical Society, Philadelphia; Reformed registers at the Historical Society of the Reformed Church in the United States, Fackenthal Library at Franklin and Marshall College, Lancaster; Episcopal records at the Archives of the Protestant Episcopal Church, Diocese of Pennsylvania, Philadelphia; Moravian records at the Archives of the Unitas Fratrum or Moravian Church in the United States of America, Northern Province, Bethlehem; Lutheran records at the Lutheran Theological Seminary, Krauth Memorial Library, Philadelphia; etc. Many registers are, of course, still in the custody of the churches. A number of church registers and Friends' meeting records have been published, in whole or in part.

A Peculiar Problem

Pennsylvania presents a peculiar problem which is not always understood by the genealogists of its families. During the course of the 18th century what now constitutes the northern tier of counties was claimed by Connecticut, while a large segment of the southern part was once considered part of Maryland. Virginia laid claim to the southwestern portion of the State. As a result of these claims, settlers from Connecticut, Maryland and Virginia poured into Pennsylvania and took up land. Deeds to these properties are not necessarily recorded in Pennsylvania, but may be found in the states which occupied portions of the Commonwealth. For instance,

Virginia's southwestern portion of Pennsylvania (which extended as far as Pittsburgh, was known as the District of West Augusta, being considered a part of Augusta County. The Augusta County records at Staunton, Virginia, contain many deeds for lands presently in Pennsylvania. An excellent account of the conflicting claims of these three states is contained in Frances Strong Helman's article, "Trailing Ancestors Through Pennsylvania", *National Genealogical Society Quarterly*, vol. 39, March 1951. In 1936, the Department of Internal Affairs of the Commonwealth of Pennsylvania published a "Genealogical Map of the Counties" which illustrates this problem very well.

CHAPTER V

DELAWARE *

Most of the records of Delaware which can be of assistance to the genealogist are centralized in the Hall of Records, under the administration of the Public Archives Commission, in Dover. This Commission was established in 1905 and, at first, its scope was quite limited. Later, the law was modified, giving to it the custody of all State, county, and municipal records from the earliest time to 1850. That law has been further amended so that with a few exceptions the Public Archives Commission now has the custody of all of these records which are seventy-five or more years old. For example, the land records of the Recorder of Deeds for each county are still retained in the local offices, as transferring them to the Public Archives Commission would interfere with the tracing of land titles. On the other hand, the Proprietary warrants and surveys for the period 1682-1776, are to be found in the Hall of Records. Another exception to the law mentioned above is that records of any State, county, or municipal agency which ceases to exist, must be transferred to the Public Archives Commission. Thus, agencies of short duration, such as the Delaware-New Jersey Boundary Commission, The Delaware Tercentenary Commission, The New Castle County Temporary Emergency Relief Commission, and the State Council of Defense, which completed their assigned duties, have deposited their records in the State Archives.

Among the groups of official records of the State, there are those of the executive department, which for the Revolution and the early Federal period contained the correspondence of Congress and other Federal departments with the governor. There are also the registers containing lists of appointments and official acts of the governors, as well as a series of papers showing the administration of such state officers, as the State

---

* Reprinted from the *National Genealogical Society Quarterly*, XXXXV, March 1947, pp. 1-3.

Treasurer and Auditor, and other agencies which developed with the years. The *Governor's Register 1674-1851*, published by the Public Archives Commission in 1926, contains much valuable information regarding gubernatorial appointments during those years.

The military records of the State are, strictly speaking, a sub-division under the executive papers, inasmuch as the Adjutant General is an official deriving his authority from the Governor. Delaware military records for the Colonial Wars, the Revolution, and the War of 1812 have been published in the five volumes of the *Delaware Archives*. The first three volumes of the series comprise the records for the Colonial Wars and the Revolution. The few records extant for the Mexican War, the Civil War, the Spanish-American War, and World War I are also in the State Archives. In addition, an effort has been made to obtain a copy of the Separation Form of each Delawarean serving in World War II. These latter records, however, will not be available for public examination until a later date.

Other records under the State classification are the legislative and judicial records. There is practically nothing among the Colonial Legislative Papers except the early journals, and those which are in existence, namely, 1739, 1740-42, 1762 and 1765-70, have been published. The legislative papers from statehood on are fairly complete. They contain petitions, committee reports, communications, resolutions, bills not passed, messages of the Governor, and the approved or Enrolled Bills. There are also the published Journals of the House and the Senate. It should be pointed out, however, that the legislative papers and journals are much richer for historical research than for genealogical purposes.

The judicial records cover the Colonial period as well as the Revolutionary and early Federal periods. In some instances, the court records are as recent as 1860, but in many cases it was found expedient to leave the original court dockets in their office of origin. For example, the Orphans' Court dockets after the period of statehood are still in those offices, as transferring them to the State Archives was claimed to interfere with legal searches.

Among the county records, undoubtedly the richest source for genealogical purposes are the probate records. These original wills, administration accounts, settlement papers, distributions, inventories, and lists of sales have been transferred to the Hall of Records and can easily be consulted there. Card index files have been compiled summarizing all the essential genealogical information regarding the will or administration account, so that a quick examination discloses whether or not the records of a particular estate are extant. By this means the time of a visiting genealogist is conserved, and it is not necessary to page through volumes of 17th or 18th century writings unnecessarily. Furthermore, as an additional aid to genealogists and other research workers, the Public Archives Commission published in 1944 a *Calendar of Kent County, Delaware, Probate Records 1680-1800*, in which the names, dates, and other essential facts of each estate are listed.

Other county records of primary genealogical value are the guardian accounts and the vital statistics. The latter group of records includes birth, baptismal, marriage, and death records. The majority of these records were acquired from the office of the Clerk of the Peace of each county. Prior to 1913, that officer was charged with recording vital statistics in this State. Unfortunately, the law under which they functioned had little compulsion, with the result that vital statistics were not recorded, and it was not until 1914 that the Bureau of Vital Statistics was established under the State Board of Health. Since that time, vital statistics are complete and consecutive. In order to supplement the many gaps existing in the earlier file of vital statistics, copies of church records have been made, newspaper files have been consulted, and copies of family Bibles have been solicited in an effort to provide records to fill these hiatuses. Numerous records have been acquired by this means, and it is hoped that many others may still be acquired from family Bibles and similar records.

To supplement the files of vital statistics the State purchased in 1937 the large collection of "Delaware Tombstone Records" compiled by the late Walter G. Tatnall. Over a period of years Mr. Tatnall had collected and carefully compiled the names and dates appearing on tombstones in the cemeteries and graveyards throughout the State. These are an invaluable source for those attempting to prove ancestry.

Another group of private records, purchased to supplement the official state records, were the files of the late Rev. Joseph Brown Turner. Mr. Turner was a retired minister and a well-known genealogist, who had worked on the families of the Del-Mar-Va Peninsula for over forty years. He had not only examined the records of this region, but had traced a number of families to England, Ireland and Scotland. The files containing the results of his many years of research are listed by families and are available for public examination.

Other groups of county records that may probably be of more interest to the historian than the genealogist are the official administrative records of the counties. These contain the minutes of the Levy Courts, the County Treasurer's accounts, the County Auditor's records, the books and minutes of the Overseers of the Poor, Fence Viewers, Rangers, Flour Inspectors, Constables, Coroners Inquests, District School records, and those of other county offices.

The deeds and other land records are in the court houses of each of the three counties at Wilmington, Dover, and Georgetown. As already mentioned, the Orphans' Court records, and the original wills and administration accounts after 1860, are also in the court houses. At present, there is a rule in each county that these records may be used only by an attorney. Such a ruling is indeed regrettable as it interferes with serious research and has been very disturbing to genealogists and other research workers who have traveled from a distance to find that the records are not accessible to them. However, by making application to the resident judge of the particular county in which one desires to work, it is frequently possible to obtain permission from him to have access to the records desired.

The only large city in Delaware is Wilmington and, as it is

a rather old city, a considerable volume of records have been amassed through the years. The earlier records of Wilmington are in the custody of the Public Archives Commission, and the more recent ones are either in the vault of the Public Building in Wilmington or in their respective offices of origin. Among the records that would be particularly interesting for genealogical research are the early assessment lists, and for biographical purposes, the Borough Council minutes and accounts give glimpses into the life of each individual who may have been a member of the borough or the city council or may have transacted business with it. The vital statistics of Wilmington for recent years are in the office of the City Board of Health in Wilmington. After being retained there for a period of about a year, they are transferred to the Bureau of Vital Statistics, State Board of Health, in Dover. All vital statistics of this city prior to 1913 which are still extant are in the Hall of Records in Dover.

In addition to the state, county, and municipal records that have been mentioned, there are groups of unofficial records which may have interest for the genealogist. These are centered, for the most part, in the Historical Society of Delaware, Old Town Hall, Sixth and Market Streets, Wilmington. There are collections of family letters, deeds, surveys, Bible records, church records, some tombstone records, family and mercantile account books, manuscripts of private and official nature, as well as local histories and genealogical reference books. In undertaking research, a genealogist working on Delaware materials should not overlook this main source of private records.

Newspapers, which are often a rich source of genealogical and historical data, are in four main depositories: The Historical Society of Delaware, The Wilmington Institute Free Library, the News-Journal Company (all located in Wilmington), and The Memorial Library (University of Delaware at Newark).

CHAPTER VI

MARYLAND

From the time of the landing of the first colonists from the *Ark and Dove* at Saint Mary's in 1634, Maryland history falls into four periods, the proprietary government (1634-89), the royal administration (1690-1715), the second period of proprietary rule (1716-76) and statehood (1776-date).

The colony was founded partly as a Roman Catholic refuge but religious toleration was marked from the beginning. The Puritan element was strong, especially in Anne Arundel County, and a large number of Quakers also settled there and in Talbot County on the Eastern Shore. In later years, Dutch, Swedish, Scotch-Irish and French settlers came into the Cecil County area and there was a large German population in Western Maryland. After 1689 the Church of England was established as the state church.

In general there are four geographical sections of the State: Southern Maryland (between the Potomac River and Chesapeake Bay south of Washington, D. C.), the Eastern Shore, the Baltimore area, and Western Maryland (from Frederick (County west).

Among the more useful historical accounts which will provide the background material necessary for an understanding of the Maryland Records are Charles M. Andrews, *The Colonial Period of American History* (New Haven, Conn., 1936; vol. 2, pp. 274-379), John T. Scharf, *History of Maryland* (Baltimore, 1879), and Clayton C. Hall, *The Lords Baltimore and the Maryland Palatinate* (Baltimore, 1902). A recent "commercial" history is Matthew Page Andrews, *Tercentenary History of Maryland* (4 v.; Chicago and Baltimore, 1925) which has three volumes of biographies of present day Marylanders.

The first source to be consulted in undertaking a genealogical search in Maryland is Eleanor Phillips Passano, *Index of the Source Records of Maryland* (Baltimore, 1940), a comprehensive bibliography of printed and manuscript materials, with location symbols indicating the holdings of the Library of Congress, Maryland Historical Society, D. A. R. Library, Johns Hopkins University Library and the Library of the Diocese of Maryland in Baltimore, now consolidated with the Peabody Institute Library. The first 362 pages comprise an index of surnames giving the location of material about each family. The remaining 115 pages form the bibliography, which is broken down by such categories as State Records—General (with sub-headings for account books, deeds, land records, marriages, maps, rent rolls, wills, etc.), State Records—County (listing both original record books and published abstracts for each county), biography, genealogy (collections), magazines and newspapers, fiction, church records (by denomination, subdivided by county), tombstone inscriptions (by county) and war records.

Two magazines which have published Maryland genealogical data are the *Maryland Historical Magazine* (54 vols.; Baltimore, 1906-date) and the *Maryland Historical and Genealogical Bulletin* (20 vols.; Baltimore, 1930-49). The former is a publication of the Maryland Historical Society and has contained a wide variety of historical and genealogical materials. The present policy of the Society is to exclude genealogical information from the magazine, but among useful series published in the past are "Index to Chancery Depositions, 1668-1789" (vol. 22), "Maryland Gleanings in England" (vols. 1-5; notes from Prerogative Court of Canterbury Wills), "Vestry Proceedings of St. Anne's Parish, Annapolis" (vols. 7-10), and "Baltimore County Land Records" (vols. 24-36).

The *Maryland Historical and Genealogical Bulletin* was privately published by Robert F. Hayes, Jr. The contents were miscellaneous in character, consisting of Bible records, militia lists, county marriage records and the like. A most useful series was "Baltimore City's Dead Prior to 1806" which reprinted gravestone inscriptions from a rare volume, *Memoirs of the Dead & Tomb's Remembrancer* (Baltimore, 1806).

The *Archives of Maryland* (Baltimore, 1883-date), published by the Maryland Historical Society and now comprising 68 volumes, consists of several series of colonial and early state records including the Proceedings and Acts of the Assembly, 1637-1774 (32 vols.), the Proceedings of the Council, 1637-1770 (11 vols.), the Journals and Correspondence of the Council of Safety, 1775-77, and the State Council, 1777-84 (8 vols.), the Correspondence of Governor Horatio Sharpe, 1753-71 (4 vols.), the Proceedings of the Provincial Court, 1637-79 (9 vols.), and Proceedings of the Court of Chancery, 1669-79 (1 vol.). There are also three volumes containing Proceedings of the County Courts of Charles County (1658-74), Kent County (1648-76), Somerset County (1665-68) and Talbot County (1662-74) and of the Manor Court of St. Clement's Manor (1659-72) and one volume of muster rolls and other records of service of Maryland troops in the American Revolution.

The three major depositories of records in the state are the Maryland Historical Society, 201 West Monument Street, Baltimore 1, the Hall of Records, Annapolis, and the Land Office, now located in the New State Office Building, Annapolis.

The Maryland Historical Society is a private organization with a library rich in manuscript and printed material. Many collections of family papers have been donated to it through the years. A history and calendar of one of their most important collections, the Calvert Papers, appears in *The Calvert Papers, Number One* (Maryland Historical Society, *Fund Publication*, no. 28; Baltimore, 1889). Some holdings of the Society will be mentioned hereafter.

The Maryland Hall of Records at Annapolis is the custodian of all state and county records created prior to the ratification of the Federal Constitution in 1789, except for several categories of records which are in the custody of the Land Office. Many later records have also been transferred to the Hall of Records by state officials and county clerks and copies of others are available there on microfilm.

The Hall of Records has prepared card indexes for a number of the series of records most useful to the genealogist. These indexes and those available in original volumes and on microfilm are listed in *Index Holdings, 1956* (Maryland Hall of Records, Bulletin no. 10) with the inclusive dates of each.

The probate records prior to 1777 were recorded not only in the county courts but also in the central Prerogative Court. Since the Prerogative Court records have been preserved, the Maryland wills, inventories and estate accounts for all counties are in existence until 1777, even though the County Court House was destroyed by fire, as in the case of Anne Arundel (1704), Calvert (1882) and Saint Mary's (1831) counties. The volumes are described in Elizabeth Hartsook and Gust Skordas' *Land Office and Prerogative Court Records of Colonial Maryland* (*Hall of Records Commission, Publications*, no. 4; Annapolis, 1946).

James M. Magruder, *Index of Maryland Colonial Wills 1634-1777* (3 vols.; Annapolis, 1933) lists the name of the testator, year made, county, and book and page of all Prerogative Court wills. Jane Baldwin Cotton, *The Maryland Calendar of Wills* (8 vols; Baltimore, 1904-28) abstracts each of these wills through 1743 and James M. Magruder, *Magruder's Maryland Colonial Abstracts* (5 vols.; Annapolis, 1934-39) covers the years 1772-77.

The original wills and other estate papers from several counties have been preserved and can be located through the card index at the Hall of Records.

Maryland colonial inventories are unique in that they were signed by the two nearest of kin and two greatest creditors. The relatives frequently were brothers or brothers-in-law, rather than children, and it is sometimes possible to establish family connections through these signatures when other records fail to identify the family of the deceased.

The consolidated card index of wills, inventories, accounts, testamentary papers, balance books and other records contains entries only for the name of the deceased, except in the case of accounts when the executor or administrator is also indexed. The Testamentary Proceedings (minutes of the actions of the Prerogative Court) have been fully indexed on cards at the Hall of Records.

There is a series of seven volumes, 1751-77, containing

Balances of Final Distribution of Estates. In many instances, all of the heirs are named, although other entries state only that the heirs were unknown to the Proprietary Office.

The wills of most counties are available at the Hall of Records on microfilm until well into the 20th century. The terminal dates for microfilm copies of inventories, accounts, bonds, guardians' records, and sales of estates vary widely and some series of records have not yet been microfilmed. It would be well for the searcher to determine the holdings of the Hall of Records before visiting the county Court House, however, since the microfilming of the Maryland records is a continuing project.

The Maryland Land Office, which has created as a separate entity in 1680, has custody of land patents, surveys and grants, the Proprietary rent rolls, chancery papers and some other court records. The Land Office holdings are described in Hartsook and Skordas, *op. cit.*

Under the first Conditions of Plantation issued by Lord Baltimore land was granted for the transportation of settlers to the province. After 1683, however, title to land could be secured only on a cash purchase basis. The early books, which name the persons for whose transportation land was claimed, form a valuable census of Maryland immigrants. Some of these names are printed in the *Maryland Historical and Genealogical Bulletin, passim.*

An index of all persons to whom patents were issued or grants made has been prepared at the Land Office. Another index lists the tracts in each county by name and refers to the patent, survey or grant. The tract names are most helpful to the genealogist in tracing descent of land since they are not duplicated, although there may have been slight variations made upon a name when additional land was patented and there are frequent instances of such entries as "Addition to Whitley's Choice" and "Resurvey on Addition to Marsh Head."

Transfers of land subsequent to the original grant are contained in the county deed books which are available in the original volumes or on microfilm at the Hall of Records to

1850, and in some instances as late as the 20th century. Conveyances which were recorded in the Provincial Court (1637-1776) and the General Court of the Western Shore (1778-1805) are at the Land Office, however.

Since Maryland was governed by a Proprietor, to whom land rent was due, during most of the colonial period, the Rent Rolls and Debt Books serve to identify all land holders. These two are complementary series, the former listing the holdings in each county by name of tract (designating the acreage held by each person), while the latter are arranged by name of individual (designating the acreage and names of the tracts held by him).

Since they concerned rent due the Proprietor, the Rent Rolls were private papers rather than government documents. Many of the earlier books are missing and none until 1734 is preserved at the Land Office. A considerable number are in private collections, however, particularly in the Calvert Papers at the Maryland Historical Society. These are described in *Maryland Historical Magazine,* vol. 19, pp. 341-43, and several of the rolls are printed in vols. 19-26. The earliest roll in the Calvert Papers is that for St. Mary's, Calvert, Charles and Kent counties to 1659 and a photocopy is also available at the Land Office. After 1734, the Land Office has a continuous yearly series for the several Eastern Shore counties and a similar series (not yearly) for the counties on the Western Shore.

The Debt Books at the Land Office begin in 1733 for the Eastern Shore and 1753 for the Western Shore. Almost one-third of the books are missing, mostly of Eastern Shore counties. Only St. Mary's and Charles counties are complete. The Maryland Historical Society has a 1750 Debt Book for five Western Shore counties among the Calvert Papers.

Harry Wright Newman's *Seigniory in Early Maryland* (Washington, 1949), published by the Descendants of Lords of the Maryland Manors, contains a brief description of the manorial system in Maryland and lists of the manors and manor Lords.

Birth and death records were not kept throughout the state

until 1898. The Hall of Records has prepared a card index of the earlier births and deaths which have been preserved in county records. These consist of births 1804-77 and deaths 1865-80 of Anne Arundel County and some 17th century entries for Charles, Kent, Somerset and Talbot counties.

The extant registers of various churches are listed in detail in Passano, *op. cit.*, pp. 401-36, with indication of the location of the original records and of copies. Those records of the Episcopal Church which were described by Passano as being at the National Cathedral have since been transferred to the Hall of Records.

Marriages from the period of the American Revolution to the present for many of the counties are extant. The Hall of Records has a consolidated card index of some early colonial marriages from Charles, Kent and Somerset counties, of marriages from Anne Arundel, Caroline, Cecil, Dorchester and Prince George's counties from about 1777 to the mid-1800's, and of Frederick County from 1778 to 1798. There is a separate card index of Baltimore County marriages for 1777-1851.

Marriage and death notices from the *Maryland Gazette*, printed at Annapolis 1727-34, 1745-1821, have been published in the *Maryland Historical Magazine*, vols. 17-18, 42.[1]

Records of suits which were brought before the state Chancery Court are preserved at the Land Office. A card index has been prepared naming the plaintiffs and defendants. The early proceedings of the Provincial Court and Court of Chancery are a part of the Court Records series of the *Archives of Maryland*.

In 1776 and again in 1778, a census was taken in Maryland. The first was in pursuance to a resolution of the Continental Congress for ascertaining the population of the United Colonies and the second was to determine the free white males over 18, who had failed to take the oath of fidelity.

---

[1] An unexpected source of information concerning marriages of one Maryland county is the *New England Historical and Genealogical Register*, vol. 73 (1919), pp. 134-154, 217-232, 261-279, "Marriage Licenses in Prince George's County, Maryland, 1777-1824."

The extant lists cover only a small portion of the state. They have been indexed on cards at the Hall of Records and the lists for Prince George's, Frederick, Charles, Anne Arundel, Caroline, Dorchester, Harford, Queen Anne's and Talbot counties are published in G. M. Brumbaugh, *Maryland Records, Colonial, Revolutionary, County and Church* (2 vols.; Baltimore, 1915-28). The 1790 Federal census was published as a part of the series, *Heads of Families at the First Census* (Washington, 1907). Subsequent censuses are available at The National Archives and those from 1830 to 1880 can be purchased on microfilm. The 1830 census of Montgomery, Prince George's, Queen Anne's, Saint Mary's and Somerset counties is missing.

The Hall of Records has a small collection of muster and pay rolls for the colonial wars, 1732-72, for which a card index has been prepared. Revolutionary records were published in the *Archives of Maryland*, vol. 18, and other material is available at the Hall of Records in two series, Revolutionary Records and Revolutionary Papers, both of which are indexed on cards.

The oaths of fidelity taken in 1778 are available for most counties and a card index has been prepared at the Hall of Records for all preserved there. A number of the oath lists are printed in Brumbaugh, *op. cit.* vol. 2, in Margaret R. Hodges, "Unpublished Revolutionary Records of Maryland" (7 vols.; typewritten; n. p., 1939), in Brumbaugh and Hodges, *Revolutionary Records of Maryland* (Washington, 1924), and in *The National Genealogical Society Quarterly*, vol. 41.

Federal pensioners and recipients of bounty land are named in Harry Wright Newman, *Maryland Revolutionary Records* (Washington, 1938), which also contains a list of soldiers mentioned in applications for pensions at The National Archives. No record of service is shown, however, the compiler merely stating that the information can be supplied for a fee. A valuable section of the book gives marriages proved through statements in the pension applications.

The *Publications* of the Hall of Records Commission contain a sub-series, *Calendar of Maryland State Papers*. The volumes printed thus far cover The Black Books (Proprietary and royal papers, 1636-1785), The Bank Stock Papers (Maryland stock in the Bank of England), The Brown Books (government and military communications, 1747-1803), the Red Books (3 vols., state papers, 1773-1825) and Executive Miscellanea (1684-1821, but with two-thirds of the material in the period 1775-78).

A new genealogical publication, *The Maryland-Delaware Genealogist* (vol. 1, 1959/60), edited by Raymond B. Clark, Jr., promises to make available in print many more of the unpublished records of Maryland.

CHAPTER VII

VIRGINIA *

Assuming that a researcher wishes to trace a Virginia family to the immigrant ancestor, the following suggestions are offered.

The first step would be to learn if anything had been published on the family and for that one would consult the *Virginia Historical Index*, 2 volumes, compiled in 1934 and 1936 by Dr. E. G. Swem. This is the master index for: *Lower Norfolk County Antiquary*, vols. I-V, 1895-1906; *Tyler's Quarterly Historical and Genealogical Magazine*, vols. I-X, 1919-1929; *Virginia Historical Register and Literary Advertiser*, vols. I-VI, 1848-1853; *The Virginia Magazine of History and Biography*, vols. I-XXXVIII, 1893-1930; *William and Mary College Quarterly Historical Magazine*, First series, vols. I-XXVII, 1892-1919; *William and Mary College Quarterly Historical Magazine*, Second series, vols. I-X, 1921-1930; *Calendar of Virginia State Papers and Other Manuscripts, 1652-1869*, 11 vols., Richmond 1875-1930; *The Statutes at Large, Being a Collection of all the Laws of Virginia, 13 vols.*, Richmond, 1809-1823; William Waller Hening, compiler. Indexes of volumes of the magazines subsequent to 1930 must be consulted.

Tyler's Quarterly has not been published since 1952 and *The William and Mary Quarterly*, Third series, since 1944 has not published genealogical material. A new magazine, *The Virginia Genealogist*, begun in 1957, has taken their place in the genealogical field. *Index to Virginia Genealogies*, R. A. Stewart, 1930, is often helpful, too.

Another "must" in research is Clayton Torrence's *Virginia Wills and Administrations 1632-1800; an Index* (1930). This includes wills and administrations in those counties formed before 1800 which are now in West Virginia.

---

* Since Mrs. Hiden's death, this chapter has been brought up-to-date by John Frederick Dorman. ED.

Do not overlook *Adventurers of Purse and Person, Virginia, 1607-1625,* compiled and edited by Annie Lash Jester, in collaboration with Martha Woodroof Hiden and sponsored by the Order of First Families of Virginia (1956). This contains a complete transcription of the Muster of the Inhabitants of Virginia of January and February 1624/25 and accounts through four generations of the families of Virginia immigrants and members of the Virginia Company of London whose present-day descendants have been traced. John C. Hotten's *Original Lists of Persons of Quality Who Went From Great Britain to the American Plantations,* London (1874, reprint New York 1931) gives ship lists and also includes lists of the living and of the dead on the plantations in Virginia after the massacre of March 1622/23.

Mention should also be made of *Virginia Genealogies* by the Rev. H. E. Hayden (1891, reprint 1931). Mr. Hayden collected a great number of Bible and family records not found elsewhere. *Old Churches and Families of Virginia,* Rt. Rev. William Meade (2 vols., 1857), *Index,* J. C. Wise (1910), contains information about numerous families, but is not to be accepted unless corroborated elsewhere. *Encyclopedia of Virginia Biography,* under the editorial supervision of Lyon Gardiner Tyler, LL.D. (5 vols., 1915), often provides a good start for research.

The following books are noted with the localities to which they refer, since the titles afford no clue to the contents. *The Cabells and their Kin* (1895), by Alexander Brown, author of *The Genesis of the United States,* deals with families of Amherst, Nelson, Buckingham and adjacent counties. *Our Kin* (1930), by Mary D. Ackerly and Lula E. J. Parker, is concerned with Bedford and Campbell County people. *Over the Mountain Men* (1933), Anne Lowry Worrell, contains abstracts of county court records from Bedford, Botetourt, Carroll, Floyd, Grayson, Montgomery, Pulaski and Roanoke counties. *Virginia Frontier* (1938), F. B. Kegley, *Annals of Southwest Virginia* (1929), L. P. Summers, and *History of Southwest Virginia* (1903), also by Summers, have abstracts of numerous Botetourt and Washington County court records, biographies of citizens of the latter county, and an account of the development of the region. *The Edward Pleasants Valentine Papers* (4 vols., 1927), are abstracts of county court records, covering a wide range in time and space relative to some 33 families connected with the Valentines, and are invaluable. *Notes on Sunnyside Virginia,* by Walter A. Watson (Bulletin of the Virginia State Library, vol. XV, Nos. 2-4, Sept., 1925) has extracts from Amelia and Nottoway County court records as well as biographical sketches of some of the residents of these counties. *The Douglas Register,* edited 1928 by W. Mac Jones, is the record kept from 1750 to 1797 by the Rev. William Douglas, rector of Saint James Northam Parish, of births, deaths and marriages occurring in the counties of Spotsylvania, Orange, Goochland, Louisa and Fluvanna. *The County Court Note Book,* edited by the late Mrs. Milnor Ljungstedt (vols. I-X 1921-1931), consists of items from court records in Virginia as well as in other states. *Virginia Colonial Abstracts* (34 vols), are abstracts by Mr. Beverley Fleet from county court records of the following counties: Accomack, Charles City, Essex, Henrico, King and Queen, Lancaster, Lower Norfolk, Northumberland, Richmond, Washington, Westmoreland and York. Volume XXX of the series is a list of Virginia source material (1607-1850) in the Huntington Library, San Marino, Calif. This series is being continued by the Rev. Lindsay O. Duvall who has published four volumes relating to Lancaster, Northumberland, and James City Counties and to the members of the Virginia Company of London. *An Index to the Source Records of Maryland,* compiled by Mrs. Eleanor Phillips Passano (Baltimore 1940), lists on p. 474 many Virginia books helpful to researchers. *Massanutten, Page County, Virginia* (1924) by H. M. Strickler, contains early records of Mill Creek Church beginning in 1809 when Page was the southern part of Shenandoah County.

Mrs. H. A. Knorr has published the early marriages of eleven counties (Brunswick, Charlotte, Chesterfield, Culpeper, Greensville, Halifax, Pittsylvania, Powhatan, Prince Edward, Southampton and Sussex) and the city of Fredericksburg.

Data are often found in the report of cases determined in the

General Court of Virginia, and in the Supreme Court of Appeals of Virginia. The earliest of these are *Virginia Colonial Decisions*, the reports of Sir John Randolph and Edward Barradall of decisions of the General Court of Virginia, 1728-1741, edited with historical introduction by Robt. T. Barton (2 vols., 1909). Later reports in several series compiled by Thomas Jefferson, Peyton Randolph, William Waller Hening, William Munford and others cover later 18th century and much of the 19th. They are listed in detail in *Bulletin of Virginia State Library*, vol. X (1917). In 1792, as a step between county courts and the Supreme Court, the state was divided into eighteen districts with semi-annual courts at a central point in the district. These were abolished in 1809 and our present system of circuit courts substituted.

Records of the District Court at Staunton have been included in the *Records of Augusta County, Virginia, 1745-1800* (3 vols.), abstracted by Judge Lyman Chalkley and published 1912. Abstracts of the wills filed with the chancery suit papers in the district of which Williamsburg was the center were published 1906 by the Genealogical Association, W. A. Crozier, editor, as vol. III, *Williamsburg Wills*.

Abstracts of some of the papers in suits in the Fredericksburg District have been published by George H. S. King under the caption "Copies of Extant Wills from Counties Whose Records have been Destroyed", in *Tyler's Quarterly Historical and Genealogical Magazine, The Virginia Magazine of History and Biography* and *The Virginia Genealogist*. Little has been published from any other districts and many of the papers have been destroyed.

Published official records of importance are: *Journals of the House of Burgesses*, 1619-1776 (13 vols., Richmond 1905-1915); *Legislative Journals of the Council of Colonial Virginia 1680-1770* (3 vols., Richmond 1918-1919); *Minutes of the Council and General Court of Colonial Virginia, 1622-1632, 1670-1676* (1 vol., Richmond 1924); *Executive Journals of the Council of Colonial Virginia, 1680-1754* (5 vols., Richmond 1925-1945); *Journals of the Council of the State of Virginia 1776-1781* (2 vols., Richmond 1931); *Official Letters of the*

Governors of Virginia; vol. I, *Letters of Patrick Henry, 1 July 1776—1 June 1779;* vol. II; *Letters of Thomas Jefferson, 1 June 1779—3 June 1781;* vol. III; *Letters of Thomas Nelson and Benjamin Harrison, 7 June 1781-27 February 1783* (1926, 1928, 1929).

After this general discussion of books helpful to a genealogist, we come to two questions which the researcher must answer, the "when?" and the "where?". To learn when a certain man lived is more difficult in Virginia than to learn where he lived, for vital statistics do not begin until 1853. They are missing for some periods and incomplete until 1912, when the present system of recordation was established. Unpublished, they were housed in the Bureau of Vital Statistics in Richmond. As some compensation for the lack of early vital records, the Archives Division of the Virginia State Library has for the Colonial period parish registers and vestry books of the Church of England, which was the Established Church of Virginia. Some of the books have been published and their publication will be continued. The extant Church of England books are but a remnant of those once in existence, for the disrepute into which the Episcopal church fell after the Revolution, together with the loss of its glebes and church buildings, did not encourage preservation of its records. Also in the Archives Division are records of churches of other denominations containing lists of births and marriages. Virginia Quaker records were published in 1950 as Vol. VI of the series *Encyclopedia of American Quaker Genealogy.* Typescripts of some Virginia Quaker records are in the Valentine Museum, Richmond, and originals are in the Quaker libraries in Baltimore, that of Stony Run Meeting House being located at 5116 North Charles St., and of Homewood Meeting House at 3107 North Charles St. The Archives Division has typescripts of Obituaries and Marriages compiled from files of *The Religious Herald* (Baptist) 1828-1930, indexed and bound, also Marriages compiled from files of The Southern Churchman (Episcopal) 1835-1930. There are microfilms of the Census of 1830, 1850 and 1870 for Virginia in the Archives Division. The State Library published as *Bulletin of the Virginia*

State Library, vol. XIV No. 4, Oct. 1921 an *Index to Obituary Notices in the Richmond Enquirer from May 9, 1804 through 1828 and the Richmond Whig from January 1824 through 1838.*

The foregoing material should assist in finding the time in which the ancestor lived; to find where he lived is the next question.

Naturally, the first grants of land were made by the Virginia Company of London, chartered 1606, under whose rule the Colony was from 1607 until 1624 when the King dissolved the Company and assumed control. For background history, the *Records of the Virginia Company*, edited by Myra S. Kingsbury, published by the Library of Congress, vols. I and II, 1906; vol. III, 1933; vol. IV, 1935, are, of course, indispensable. The Land Patent Books available in the Archives Division of the Virginia State Library begin in 1623 and are invaluable. Abstracts of the patents for 1623-1666 were published in 1934 by Mrs. Nell M. Nugent of Virginia Land Office under the title, *Cavaliers and Pioneers*, vol. I.

Since Virginia was a Crown Colony, land owners paid a yearly rent per acre to the King and these lists arranged by counties with name and acreage of every land owner were sent to England annually. This did not apply to the land lying between the Potomac and the Rappahannock Rivers, known as the Northern Neck, which was a proprietary.

Of the rent rolls sent to England, only one complete list, that of 1704, has been found in the Public Records Office, London. Published in 1922 by Dr. Thomas J. Wertenbaker as an appendix to his book, *Planters of Colonial Virginia*, and more recently in Louis des Cognets' *English Duplicates of Lost Virginia Records* (1958), photostatic copy of this roll is in the library of the Virginia Historical Society. Scattered and incomplete rent rolls for various counties and lists of tithables from some counties are in the Archives Division. These help bridge the gap between the 1704 Quit Rent Roll and 1782, the year in which the real and personal tax books were set up for all the counties by the Commonwealth of Virginia. These books are also in the Archives Division. *Heads of Families* at the First Census . . . *State Enumerations: 1782 to 1785, Virginia*, published by the Census Bureau in 1908, and *Virginia Tax Payers, 1782-87*, compiled by Augusta B. Fothergill and John Mark Naugle, 1940, contain names from the tax records of all counties in the state.

The county is the unit of government in Virginia. Extant city records begin around the last quarter of the 18th century; the larger amount of research, therefore, must be done in county records housed in their respective county seats.

Through the generosity of The Genealogical Society in Salt Lake City, court record books from all the Virginia counties up to 1865 have been microfilmed, and a copy placed in the Archives Division of the Virginia State Library. The Library also has over one thousand photoduplicate volumes of records from sixty-five counties. Anyone planning research in Virginia would do well to learn first what is available in Richmond in the State Library and in the library of the Virginia Historical Society. If no solution of the problem is found, certainly future procedure is made clearer without loss of time.

County development is shown in the *Bulletin of the Virginia State Library,* vol. IX (1916), *Virginia Counties* by Morgan P. Robinson. This notes date of formation and bounds of every county, its parent county or counties, and any changes occurring in its boundaries. However, the most complete account of the formation and changes of the counties is in *How Justice Grew*, by Martha W. Hiden (1957), which describes in detail the successive boundaries of the counties, and includes a map of Virginia as of 1671, and charts indicating the gradual dividing of counties that took place. For information on sources by counties, the searcher is referred to "Guide to the Counties of Virginia", a listing of manuscript and printed materials relating to each county, which is being published serially in *The Virginia Genealogist*.

Records of civil service are found in *Colonial Virginia Register*, (1903), by W. G. and M. N. Stanard, in *Journals of the House of Burgesses* and Hening's *Statutes at Large for Virginia*, both mentioned previously, in *Justices of the Peace of Colonial Virginia, 1757-1775*, issued as *Bulletin of the Vir-*

ginia State Library, vol. XIV, Nos. 2, 3 (1921), in county court order books, in *A Register of the General Assembly of Virginia*, E. G. Swem and John W. Williams (1918), and *Bibliography of Virginia*, parts 1 and 2 (1916, 1918), *Indexes*, E. G. Swem. Military service is of record in *Gleanings of Virginia History*, (1903), by W. F. Boogher, *Virginia Colonial Militia* (1905) by W. A. Crozier, *List of Colonial Soldiers of Virginia (Special Report of Department of Archives and History, for 1913)* Richmond (1917), and in county court order books. Legislative petitions in the Archives Division, although dated much later, were sometimes put in to obtain the bounty land authorized, 1763, for services in the French and Indian Wars of the preceding decade.

Revolutionary service is found in county court order books in *List of Revolutionary Soldiers of Virginia* (2 vols.; *Special Report of the Department of Archives and History, 1911-12)*, compiled by H. J. Eckenrode, in John H. Gwathmey's *Historical Register of Virginians in the Revolution* (1938), in John Frederick Dorman's *Virginia Revolutionary Pension Applications* (a continuing series begun in 1958), in G. M. Brumbaugh's *Revolutionary War Records: Virginia*, in the Special Virginia Edition (1884) of Hardesty's *Historical and Geographical Encyclopedia*, in the unpublished service claims from the counties and in individual legislative petitions in the Archives Division. Mrs. Passano's *Index to the Source Records of Maryland*, previously mentioned, has on page 460 an excellent list of books on the Revolution of Virginia. *Old Kentucky Entries and Deeds*, W. R. Jillson (1926), and Brumbaugh's *Revolutionary War Records*, mentioned above, give military warrants and entries for Virginia Revolutionary soldiers.

The State Library published in 1851 *Pay Rolls of Militia Entitled to Land Bounty* under the Act of Congress of September 28, 1850, and in 1852 *Muster Rolls of the Virginia Militia in the War of 1812*, being a supplement to the Pay Rolls. There are other unpublished records of this war in the Archives Division but the records in the National Archives in Washington are more complete than those in Virginia.

The Confederate records of the Civil War in the Archives Division are extensive and excellent. The National Archives, Washington, also has these records.

Besides the collections of the State Library and the Virginia Historical Society, the Alderman Library of the University of Virginia has extensive collections of family papers, newspapers and business ledgers. The Library of the College of William and Mary also has a large amount of valuable manuscript material, family papers and records. There are several county historical societies of more or less vitality; two of them, Albemarle and Clark, issue publications from time to time.

There is no published collection of tombstone and cemetery inscriptions for the state. Probably the library of the National Society, Daughters of the American Revolution, has the largest collection of Virginia inscriptions that has been made.

The Virginia State Library has for years been photoduplicating Bible records and now has in the Archives Division a large collection of these available to researchers.

CHAPTER VIII

NORTH AND SOUTH CAROLINA

In both of these states it is essential that the researcher have adequate knowledge of the formation and prolifieration of the counties, in order to determine where to search. Sources of such information will be mentioned in the discussion of records of each state.

In both states, also, it is especially important to study (1) the settlement pattern of the various areas, and (2) the lines of migration into and out of the state. For the first, general state, county and local histories, selected from bibliographies mentioned below, will be helpful. For the second, the best account at present (1959) is Lewis' *Emigrant Trails East of the Mississippi*.[1] This work is in process of revision by Herman R. Friis, and when the new edition, with a new map, appears it should be substituted as a reference.

A. NORTH CAROLINA

In North Carolina, vital records as such were not kept.

The county is the governmental unit and, except for recent city records, the public records most useful to the genealogist are those of the county.

Church records are scarce. The established churches were few and only in rare instances have their colonial records survived.

For specific dates of births and deaths, one is dependent on private sources, such as tombstone and Bible records.

To do any research, a clear picture of the formation of counties is essential. For this purpose, use Corbitt's *Formation of North Carolina Counties, 1663-1943*.[2]

---

[1] Marcus W. Lewis; *The Development of Early Emigrant Trails East of the Mississippi River*, Genealogical Publication No. 3 of the National Genealogical Society. (1933)
[2] David L. Corbitt; *Formation of North Carolina Counties, 1663-1943*. (1950)

Settlement began along the Coast in the last quarter of the 17th century. Some of the records of these settlers are to be found in the record of contiguous Virginia counties. By 1700 there were four counties, by 1740 these had been extended and divided into thirteen, by 1760 to twenty-five, and so on. The maps in the back of the book show the counties in successive periods. It is not uncommon that in order to secure records of a single generation that never moved, one must examine records of as many as seven counties.

Census

Following the primary rule, to begin with the most recent generation for which there is adequate proof and trace backward, documenting each step, unless generations back to 1800 are supported by Bible or tombstone records or other sources of definite dates, it is well to check the Federal Census for the county in which the family was resident at each census period from 1880 back to 1790.

The 1790 Census is printed and indexed.[3] However, Caswell, Granville and Orange Counties are missing. The 1800 census is complete. Of the 1810, four and of the 1820 five of the most important counties are missing. The 1850 and 1880 are particularly important. Census schedules from 1800 to 1880 inclusive are not printed or indexed. The originals of all the census schedules from the beginning to 1870 and microfilms of the 1880 are in the National Archives. Microfilm copies of the 1850 to 1880 schedules inclusive are available at the North Carolina Department of Archives and History in Raleigh, the Daughters of the American Revolution Library in Washington, the Utah Genealogical Society Library in Salt Lake City, and probably in other libraries. Microfilm of the 1830 to 1880 schedules may be purchased from the National Archives at varying prices.[4]

---

[3] U. S. Bureau of the Census; *Heads of Families at the First Census of the United States taken in the year 1790 .. North Carolina.*

[4] Write the National Archives (Washington 25, D. C.) for *List of National Archives Microfilm Publications* (1953) and *Federal Population Censuses 1840-80* (furnished gratis on request) for counties covered by each reel and prices.

Bibliography

To begin research one needs to know (1) what records were originally created; (2) what records are still in existence, and where; (3) what records have been printed; (4) what genealogies or biographies on the family or members of it have been published; and (5) what county, local, or general histories have been published that may cover the area of interest.

From the standpoint of the genealogist, the best bibliography available at present is *North Carolina Genealogical Reference*.[5] While there are errors in titles and proper names, and the arrangement is poor, it nevertheless lists most of the material in print and is a good guide to publications on the local level or by families. (It must be remembered, however, that "recollections", general county histories, and all too many genealogies (especially those written prior to the last quarter of a century) must be used with caution.) This volume, in addition to listing many printed sources, lists the most important manuscript collections in the North Carolina State Library, the North Carolina Department of Archives and History, the University of North Carolina Library and other depositories.

The information on county records and church records is too abbreviated to be of much value but even so the book is a good guide for beginners and a convenient reference for the more experienced genealogist.

For publications not strictly genealogical but which may supply clues on activities of individuals or as to location of collections of papers which may contain desired records, there are two comprehensive reference works: *A Bibliography of North Carolina, 1589-1956*[6] and *Official Publications of the Colony and State of North Carolina, 1749-1939*.[7]

---

[5] W. R. Draughon; *North Carolina Genealogical Reference; a Research Guide.* (1956)

[6] Mary Lindsay Thornton; *A Bibliography of North Carolina, 1589-1956.* (University of North Carolina Press, 1958.)

[7] Mary Lindsay Thornton; *Official Publications of the Colony and State of North Carolina, 1749-1939.* (1954)

County Records

After the preliminary background reading, and checking of census records, research begins. It is always best, when feasible, to work first in the original source material, or abstracts therefrom, i. e., county, state, and federal records.

While the above mentioned bibliography gives some information about county records, it is far from complete. To determine records still in existence consult *The Historical Records of North Carolina,*[8] which lists such records in great detail. Since 1938, many of the older records indicated in these volumes as located in the county of origin have been transferred to the North Carolina Department of Archives and History in Raleigh. Such transfers are usually listed in the annual reports of that Department, which should be consulted. In the case of a specific record in which the researcher is interested, inquiry may be made by letter to the Department. Of course, additional records have been discovered since the survey was made, particularly of "loose papers". Those which have been transferred to the Department of Archives and History are listed in the annual reports. These papers or records are so few, however, that the possibility can be ignored until comprehensive search has been made through the listed official records.

The volumes just mentioned list the records in existence. To see the original books of record one must go to Raleigh or the county concerned. So it is of primary importance to know whether any of these records have been printed, either in full or in abstract form.

The usual sequence of examination is: Wills, administrations, settlement of estates, marriage records, deeds, land causes and surveys, court records of various types, and miscellaneous records and papers.

With respect to wills, the situation at first glance seems to be good. Grimes' *North Carolina Wills*[9], and *North Carolina*

---

[8] The North Carolina Historical Commission. *The Historical Records of North Carolina* (1938-39) 3 v.

[9] J. Bryan Grimes; *Abstract of North Carolina Wills.* (1910)

Wills and Inventories[10] contain abstracts of the majority of the wills prior to 1760 and are well indexed. Olds' *North Carolina Wills, 1760-1800*[11] gives brief abstracts; the volume is arranged by counties, but is not indexed. Wills of the earliest eastern counties are to be found in the *North Carolina Historical and Genealogical Register*,[12] generally known as "Hathaway". This is not indexed, but a partial index was issued by Worth S. Ray in 1945.[13] The D. A. R. Library has a typescript index.

However, none of these compilations of abstracts is wholly satisfactory. Grimes so abbreviated his notes, to lessen the bulk of the book, that there are important omissions; also, some wills found in the counties were not included and others have been discovered since publication. Olds' is full of errors and omissions. Much of it was based on notes made for Colonel Olds by the county clerks who hastily went through their will books, jotting down pertinent facts. Hathaway is probably more accurate than either of the others. But the fact remains that none of them can be considered as complete, either in the list of testators or the abstracts. However, if a will seems to pertain to the family or field of interest, a photostat of the original record can be readily secured from the Department of Archives and History or the county, as the case may be.

In addition to these general works, there have been published abstracts of wills of specific counties, many of which are listed in the bibliography mentioned above.

Much valuable information is to be found in the county court minutes. Until recent years it has been necessary to consult the original records in Raleigh or the county seat, but ab-

---

[10] J. Bryan Grimes; *North Carolina Wills and Inventories.* (1912)

[11] Fred A. Olds; *An Abstract of North Carolina Wills from about 1760 to about 1800.* (1925)

[12] J. R. B. Hathaway, ed.; *North Carolina Historical and Genealogical Register*, 3 v. (1900-3)

[13] Worth S. Ray; *Index and Digest to Hathaway's North Carolina Historical and Genealogical Register.* (1945)

stracts of some are now being published, such as that of New Hanover.[14]

As for marriage records: The original marriage bonds that have survived the vicissitudes of time are in the North Carolina Department of Archives and History in Raleigh. Nearly all, if not all, of the marriage records of various types which are still in existence have been copied by The Genealogical Society at Salt Lake City. Typed copies, indexed, are in the Library of that Society, the North Carolina Department of Archives and History and the D. A. R. Library in Washington. In most instances they cover the period from 1750 or from the Revolution down to 1850. Marriage records of some counties have been privately copied and in some instances published. Most of these are listed in the bibliography referred to above.

It must be remembered that these records do not cover all marriages. No record was made of many marriages by dissenting ministers in colonial days, by traveling ministers thereafter, by justices of the peace, or some other civil officers, and even where record was made, many such records have disappeared. Frequently the date of a marriage cannot be ascertained, but the fact of the marriage can be proved from a marriage settlement or the gift of a father or brother to the bride of a slave or land, that is, by documents found recorded in deed books or the miscellaneous records of a county.

Even when the originals of other county records are still in the court house concerned, microfilms of many (although not of all) of the county records are in the North Carolina Department of Archives and History at Raleigh. The D. A. R. Library in Washington has microfilms of Bladen, Sampson and other counties and is steadily expanding the collection.

State Records

The Colonial and State Records of North Carolina (happily with a consolidated index) contain much information for the genealogist and should always be consulted.

---

[14] Alexander McDonald Walker; *New Hanover County Court Minutes, 1738-1769.*

Land grants, other than those mentioned incidentally for one reason or another in the *Colonial and State Records,* have not been published. Originals are available for reference in Raleigh.

Church Records

The most complete printed church record is that of the Society of Friends (Quakers), in Hinshaw's Quaker Records.[15] Adelaide Fries' work on the Moravians [16] has much data on members of that church.

The Archives of the Presbyterian Church South at Montreat, N. C., contain much information which would be helpful in tracing Scotch-Irish and other Presbyterian families. There are few church records of births, deaths and marriages as such, but notes of marriages and burials occur in diaries and day books kept by ministers, if one has the time and patience to go through them. The session records, when preserved, often contain dismissal to other churches, and hence furnish evidence of migration and identity.

Periodicals

The only state-wide genealogical periodical on North Carolina being issued now is *The North Carolinian,*[17] a quarterly which began publication in 1955.

From time to time, North Carolina genealogical source material has appeared in the *National Genealogical Society Quarterly, North Carolina Historical Review,* and the *D. A. R. Magazine.* These articles may be located by using the indexes of the respective publications or the *Index to Writings on American History.*[18]

---

[15] Wm. Wade Hinshaw; *Encyclopedia of American Quaker Genealogy,* vol. 1 (North Carolina).

[16] Adelaide L. Fries; *Moravians in North Carolina (1752-1837).* (1922-1954)

[17] *The North Carolinian; A Quarterly Journal of Genealogy and History.* Wm. Perry Johnson and Russell E. Bidlack, eds. 1955-.

[18] American Historical Association; *Index to Writings on American History, 1902-1940.* (1956)

B. SOUTH CAROLINA

In South Carolina, vital records as such were not kept. Aside from church records (to be discussed later), specific dates of births and deaths must be secured from Bibles and tombstones, except in the rare cases where a death date is mentioned in some court record or in a newspaper notice.

A brief account of the principal sources of information, both printed and unpublished, is given in "Genealogical Source Material in South Carolina", by Roberta P. Wakefield, in the *National Genealogical Society Quarterly*, September 1952.

Evolution of Counties

The county is now the governmental unit, but it was not always so. In the beginning there was a centralized government and so a central record office in Charleston. When the counties were formed, the subsequent changes were not, as in North Carolina, a simple matter of expansion and division. Fortunately, there are two concise but fairly complete accounts of the evolution of and complex structure leading to the formation of the present counties, "Evolution of South Caroline Counties,"[19] by Roberta P. Wakefield, and *South Carolina Counties, Districts, Parishes and Townships*, by Janie Revill. There are slight differences in these, due to different interpretation of the records, but the basic information for the researcher is clearly set forth.

A brief summary will here be helpful. Settlement began at Charleston about 1672. All records were kept or filed there. Soon after, the Province was divided into four counties: Craven, between the Pee Dee and the Santee Rivers; Berkeley, from the Santee to the Ashley; Colleton, from the Ashley to the Combahee; and Granville, from the Combahee to the Savannah. Craven and Berkeley extended north to the North Carolina line, and Colleton and Granville north to the Indian lands. In 1706, they were divided into ten parishes for the purpose of electing representatives. These ten were later subdivided into quite a number more. Most men signed them-

---

[19] In *National Genealogical Society Quarterly*, June 1944.

selves as of the parish in which they lived, so the parish is important for identification purposes. In 1769, these counties were divided into districts for the purpose of holding circuit courts. These districts were: Charleston, Beaufort, Orangeburgh, Ninety Six, Camden and Cheraws. In 1785, the districts were divided into counties. Both of the references mentioned above list the counties in each district. In 1798, the state was divided into judicial districts once more. Miss Revill's pamphlet lists the counties under each judicial district and indicates those of which the records have been destroyed. Miss Wakefield's article gives the same information with respect to the counties in each district in slightly different form. These judicial districts were later changed to counties and further subdivisions made.

Miss Revill's pamphlet lists the 25 parishes, giving the date established and location of each and also the 14 townships. While no records were kept in the townships, the location is important for purposes of identification.

Usually names of both parish and district, county and district, or township and district or county, are used, but each may be used alone.

Bibliography

Fortunately for the researcher, there is available a very complete bibliography of printed materials on South Carolina in Dr. Easterby's *Guide to the Study and Reading of South Carolina History*.[20] This work includes both books and articles in periodicals. The more important classifications to be examined in order to select publications of interest are "Church of England", "marriage and death records", "epitaphs", "church records other than Church of England", "particular denominations" and "genealogy". However, "public records" (particularly "miscellaneous"), "lists of soldiers", "local histories", "bibliography", "diaries", and in fact every classification, should be read with care.

---

[20] J. H. Easterby; *Guide to the Study and Reading of South Carolina History; A Classified Bibliography*. (1950; with subsequent Supplements.)

As this publication was issued in 1950, examination of periodicals, and book reviews in them, since that date will in a short time give a fairly complete coverage of available printed sources, except material published in the *National Geneaogical Society Quarterly*, the latter publication not being available to Dr. Easterby when he was compiling his bibliography. As the *Quarterly* published considerable South Carolina material it should be examined also.

The South Carolina Archives Department has issued a list of its publications and of the microfilms available for purchase. Many of these contain source material of a genealogical nature.

It will be noticed that for South Carolina much has been published in the way of recollections, general, local and church history, and various secondary works, but little actual genealogical source material except in the publications of the South Carolina Historical and Genealogical Society, the South Carolina State Historical Association, and the South Carolina Huguenot Society, and in the *National Genealogical Society Quarterly* and the older issues of the *D. A. R. Magazine*. These should be carefully examined.

Census Records

The Federal Census for 1790 is printed and indexed. The remaining census schedules have not been printed. That for 1800 is complete except that Richland Co. is missing. Those for 1820 to 1880 inclusive are complete. The original schedules of 1800 to 1870 are in the National Archives in Washington. Microfilms of the 1830 to 1880 schedules may be purchased from the National Archives.[21] Microfilm copies of 1830 to 1880 inclusive are in the South Carolina Archives Department at Columbia, The Genealogical Society at Salt Lake City, from 1850 in the D. A. R. Library in Washington, and presumably other libraries.

Then there are the Mortality Schedules. In 1850, 1860, 1870 and 1880, census enumerators secured information as to deaths

---

[21] See footnote 4.

which had occurred in the twelve months preceding the taking of the Census. It has been estimated that 13 per cent of all deaths occurring in this 31-year period are listed in these schedules. These schedules are now in the South Carolina Archives Department in Columbia.

Public Records

Prior to 1785 all records were made in or sent to Charleston and there recorded. After the judicial districts began to function in 1772, cases were tried in the District but the records were sent to Charleston.

After 1785 wills and deeds as well as judicial records were recorded in the District court houses, which later became the county court houses. However, because of changes and consolidation of counties and sub-division of districts one sometimes finds records pertaining to an area in a court house of another county, one that apparently had little relation to the area.

When the court houses were established wills and deeds already recorded were not transferred to them. Such records prior to 1785 for all of South Carolina remained in Charleston and are still in the court house there. Microfilms of many of these records are now in the South Carolina Archives Department in Columbia.

In 1939, the Works Progress Administration completed the copying of all wills in all counties formed prior to 1853 up to approximately that date. A typed copy is in the Archives Department in Columbia. Microfilms of many of the county records from 1785 to 1865 have been made and are in the Archives Department. The originals are still in the counties.

Unfortunately for those tracing lines in South Carolina between 1785 and 1865, of the 27 counties established in 1798, records of six were destroyed during the Civil War or soon thereafter. These are Beaufort, Chesterfield, Colleton, Georgetown, Lexington, and Orangeburgh. Records of nine more have been damaged by fire at one time or another, with varying losses. These are Abbeville, Union, Lancaster, Kershaw, Darlington, Sumpter, Marion, Charleston, and Williamsburg.

While deeds and wills prior to 1785 are still in Charleston, the bulk of the other records have been transferred to the South Carolina Archives Department in Columbia. A brief description of the more important types is given in the article by Roberta P. Wakefield in the *National Genealogical Society Quarterly* for September 1952, referred to above.

These records vary in type but are tremendously valuable to the genealogist. The land records include more than 50,000 surveys between 1730 and 1780, which show where the land was located and gives the names of adjoining landowners. They are indexed. There are many land records, known as "Memorials", which give still more information about subsequent owners; some of these have been abstracted by Mrs. Jerome A. Esker and published under the title, *South Carolina Memorials (Registration of Land Grants)*.

Other records there marriages, settlements, five volumes containing these between 1785 and 1865. A number of such settlements are also in the 130 volumes of miscellaneous records (1770-1870), which also contain deeds other than of land, gifts, powers of attorney, claims, citizenship certificates, etc. There are 65 volumes of mortgages, some as early as 1711.

Those interested in the Revolution should not overlook the series of published "Stub Indents",[22] covering payments to former soldiers and those furnishing supplies. The Archives Department also has a splendid card index of every name, even of a witness, on the original petitions and claims with respect to Revolutionary services. Many of these bear signatures which are not only interesting but sometimes valuable in determining identity.

Church Records

Prior to the Revolution the Church of England was the Established Church. All Episcopal parish registers still in existence have been published, as have records of the Quakers in

---

[22] *Stub Entries to Indents issued in payment of claims against South Carolina growing out of the Revolution.* Published by the South Carolina Archives Dept.

Charleston and the Stoney Creek and Circular (Congregational) Churches. Specific references are given in Dr. Easterby's bibliography.

Marriage Records

Prior to 1911 marriage records were not kept regularly in South Carolina. Newspaper notices are an important source for specific marriage dates. Many of these, beginning with 1732, have been abstracted and published either separately or in various periodicals. These, too, are listed in Dr. Easterby's bibliography.

Manuscript Collections

The South Caroliniana Library of the University of South Carolina has an extensive manuscript collection which includes not only private papers but church session and minute books of considerable genealogical value.

Numerous collections of South Carolina unpublished materials are in the manuscript departments of the libraries of Duke University and the University of North Carolina. These are particularly valuable for the period from 1800 to 1850.

Summary

The genealogist beginning work in South Carolina should first get Dr. Easterby's bibliography (footnote 20) and examine it carefully for published materials on the family, the locality in which it lived, and all related families and persons. These books should then be consulted. After exhausting these references and any developed in the course of such examination, the next step will be to send to the South Carolina Archives Department for the list of its publications and also the list of microfilms available there.

Pertinent publications not heretofore seen should then be procured and studied. But, in all probability, sooner or later one must either go to South Carolina or employ competent research assistance there.

Time will be saved if the evolution of the counties has been clearly understood, and if the materials available in Columbia have been studied, from the references herein suggested and the list of microfilms and other records available which can be procured from the South Carolina Archives Department.

For work in original records, Columbia is the place to begin, followed by Charleston for the period prior to 1800, the county seat of the county concerned or the neighboring counties, and the manuscript collections of various colleges and universities, in that order.

In spite of the tremendous destruction of records in South Carolina, much remains but one must search for it. There is no easy way of doing genealogical research in South Carolina!

CHAPTER IX

GEORGIA *

Georgia, the thirteenth Colony, was founded by General James Edward Oglethorpe, in 1733. The charter, granted by George II of England, created a board of trustees, called "The Trustees for Establishing the Colony of Georgia in America", for a term of twenty-one years.

In 1741 the Province of Georgia was divided into two counties: Savannah and Frederica. The latter division never actually functioned as a separate government, its affairs being placed two years later under the jurisdiction of the Savannah officers. Thus, until the Revolution and the subsequent adoption of the first Constitution, the State had but one county. The trustees of the Colony surrendered their charter in 1752, and Georgia became a Royal Province. In 1758, a statute was enacted dividing the several districts and divisions of the Province into parishes. The first eight were: Christ Church, St. Matthew, St. George, St. Paul, St. Philip, St. John, St. Andrew, and St. James. In March 1765, four additional parishes were created: St. David, St. Patricks, St. Thomas, and St. Mary: Administration of the affairs of the Province thus assumed the mixed character of civil and ecclesiastical authority which lasted until the adoption of the first State Constitution in 1777. With the adoption of the Constitution of 1777, seven counties were created from the parishes. Wilkes, the eighth county, created in 1777, was made from original territory.

Savannah was the scene of much upheaval during the Revolutionary War, and many of the colonial records were scattered and destroyed; therefore, it became necessary for Georgia to have transcripts made of such of her records as are filed in the British Public Records Office in England. To learn the names of emigrants, grantees, persons receiving civil

---

* Reprinted from the article, "Genealogical Research in Georgia", which appeared in the *National Genealogical Society Quarterly*, June 1952, slightly condensed and brought up to date by Jean Stephenson with information furnished by Mrs. Bryan.

and military commissions, etc., it is necessary to consult *The Colonial Records of the State of Georgia*, Allen D. Candler, editor, published under the authority of the Georgia Legislature, vols. 1-19, 21-26. Vols. 27-39 have been transcribed, typed, and indexed, but not published. A general index to Candler's published *Colonial Records* was brought out as a typewritten manuscript in 1937 as *Official Project No. 165-34-6999, W. P. A.*, supervised by the Savannah Historical Research Association. Vol. 20 (1734-1735, original papers, correspondence to and from trustees, General Oglethorpe and others) has now been typed and indexed and is available in the Department of Archives. Duplicate copies of all typewritten manuscripts of Georgia's *Colonial Records*, vols. 20, 27-39, are filed with the Georgia Historical Society, 501 Whitaker Street, Savannah. A *List of the Early Settlers of Georgia*, edited by E. Merton Coulter and Albert B. Saye (University of Georgia Press, Athens, 1949), contains names of "Persons who went from Europe to Georgia at the Trustees' Charge and Persons Who Went from Europe to Georgia on their own Account."

Historical Collections of the Joseph Habersham Chapter, Georgia D. A. R., vol. III, published 1910, pp. 161-172, list approximately 402 of Georgia's Colonial Wills, 1734-1779, either in recorded or original form, on file at that time in the Office of the Secretary of State, State Capitol, Atlanta. These original wills and recorded wills (Books A and AA) are now on file in the Department of Archives. Colonel Telamon Cuyler abstracted many of these wills, and there are typewritten copies of his abstracts entitled "Georgia Colonial Wills" at the Georgia Historical Society, Savannah, and at the Savannah Public Library. The following original manuscript volumes on file in the Department of Archives also aid the genealogist in research of colonial records:

Bonds, Bills of Sale, Deeds of Gift, Powers of Attorney[1]

1755-1762—Book I	1772-1777—Book Y	1779-1780—
1761-1765—Book O	1777-1829—Book HH	1783-1792—Book O
1765-1772—Book R	1778-1782—	1792-1813—Book D

---

[1] This series contains some marriage contracts.

Conveyances

1751-1766—Book C [2]	1769-1771—Book V	1775-1798—Book DD
1766-1769—Book S	1771-1774—Book X [2]	1783-1802—Book BZ
1769-4/19—Book U	1774-1784—Book CC [2]	

Estates, Appraisement, and Administration

1755-1771—Book D [3]	1771-1775—Book Z [3]	1777-1778—Book G [4]

Estates, Inventories of

1754-1771—Book F	1776-1777—Book FF	1777-1778—Book D

Mortgages

1755-1763—Book E	1765-1770—Book Q	1775-1822—Book EE
1762-1765—Book G	1770-1785—Book W	

Letters of Guardianship
1757-1776—Book N

Entry of Claims
Ca. 1753 to Ca. 1757—Book U [5]

Marks and Brands
1775-1793 [6]

There were only six colonies of immigrants of any size that entered the Province of Georgia. First, under Oglethorpe, 1733; second, Salzburgers, 1734; third, Moravians, 1735; fourth, Scottish Highlanders, 1736; fifth, the second band of Salzburgers and Moravians, 1736; sixth, the Dorchester, S. C. people 1751. *The Colonial Records of Georgia*, vol. X (Candler), which includes the "Minutes and Proceedings of the Governor and Council, 1767-1769," relates on pp. 690-694, the origin of the Quaker settlement at Old Wrightsboro. The names of the Georgia Quakers appear also in *William Wade*

---

[2] In 2 volumes.

[3] Orders issued by the Provincial Governors for the appraisal and administration of estates.

[4] Includes orders of the Register of Probates for the appraisal and administration of estates in Chatham Co. Volume presented to the Georgia Historical Society, Savannah, 11 Feb. 1928.

[5] Entry of claims records, claimants' names, number of acres, situation of lands, and names of original grantees.

[6] Cattle brands recorded in the Secretary's Office and includes the names of persons having names recorded.

Hinshaw Index to Quaker Meeting Records, with the North Carolina group, on file in the Friends Historical Library of Swarthmore College, Swarthmore, Penna. The small Jewish Colony which arrived in Savannah in 1733 should not be overlooked, with such names as Sheftall, Minis, DeLyon and Nunis, who gave great strength to the young Colony of Georgia.

Among the most important colonial church records which survive are: (1) The original "Ebenezer Church Record," giving baptisms, marriages and burials of the Effingham County Salzburgers. The original manuscript written in German is on file in the Library of Congress, Washington. The manuscript was translated by A. G. Voigt, D.D., LL.D., and published 1929 under the title *Ebenezer Record Book;* (2) *"Register of Midway Congregational Church, 1754-1788,"* gives births, baptisms and marriages of the Dorchester people in Liberty County, original manuscript on file with the Georgia Historical Society, Savannah. A typewritten manuscript of this *Register* in 2 volumes has been presented to the Department of Archives by the Georgia Historical Society. Stacy's *History of Midway Church,* published 1899, is based on much of the material in the above mentioned manuscript.

An Act of the Colonial Legislature in 1763 established a press in the Colony, and the first issue of the *Georgia Gazette* appeared April 7, 1763. There is a *General Index to the Savannah, Georgia, Newspapers, 1763-1845,* in the Library of the Georgia Historical Society. Typewritten manuscripts of the *Index* are on file at the Georgia Historical Society, Savannah Public Library and the Department of Archives and History in Atlanta.

The greatest bibliography on Georgia is *A Catalogue of the Wimberley Jones de Renne Georgia Library,* 3 vols. (Wormsloe, Savannah, 1931). This library was purchased by the University of Georgia, Athens, and is now housed at the University. Two other bibliographies should be mentioned. Ella May Thornton, *Finding-List of Books and Pamphlets Relating to Georgia and Georgians* (Atlanta, 1928), and a chapter, "Select Bibliography-Note on Sources," in the revised and enlarged edition of E. Merton Coulter's *A Short History of Georgia* (Chapel Hill, University of North Carolina Press, 1947). As a general background of Georgia from her beginning, and before taking up a study of Georgia families and their migrations, Coulter's *History* is recommended. *The Georgia Historical Quarterly*, edited and published at the University of Georgia in Athens, by the Georgia Historical Society, has been appearing quarterly each year beginning with 1917. Particular mention should be given here to an article by W. S. Yenawine entitled "A Checklist of Source Materials for the Counties of Georgia", which appeared in the April 1948 issue of the *Georgia Historical Quarterly*. The genealogist will find this list invaluable as a guide. If available for circulation, some published county histories, publications of the Georgia D. A. R., and other books bearing on genealogy may be borrowed through inter-library loan from the Librarian, Library Extension Service, 92 Mitchell, S. W., Atlanta.

There are two kinds of land grants in Georgia, one known as Head-Rights, and the other as Lottery Grants. Head-Right, grants were first issued by the Trustees, under authority of the King, then by the royal governors, under authority of the same, then by the State. Thirty-five counties make up the Head-Right territory: Bryan, Bullock, Burke, Camden, Chatham, Clarke, Columbia, Effingham, Elbert, Emanuel, Franklin, Glascock, Glynn, Greene, Hancock, Hart, Jackson, Jefferson, Johnson, half of Laurens, Liberty, Lincoln, Madison, McDuffie, McIntosh, half of Montgomery, Oconee, Oglethorpe, Richmond, Screven, Taliaferro, Tattnall, Warren, Washington and Wilkes; also parts of the following lottery Counties are in Head-Right territory: Baldwin, Gwinnett, Habersham, Hall, Walton and Wayne. It was not until 1803 that the Lottery System came into being.

Under the Act of 11 May 1803, the first land lottery was held in 1805. Between 1805 and 1832 there were six lotteries, and the counties organized and distributed by the lottery method follow alphabetically, with the date of the Lottery Act in parenthesis: Appling (15 Dec. 1818); Baldwin, Districts 1 through 5 (11 May 1803), and Districts 6 through 20 (26 June 1806); Carroll (9 June 1825); Cherokee, land and gold (21 Dec. 1830); Coweta (9 June 1825); Dooly (15 May 1821); Early (15 Dec. 1818); Fayette (15 May 1821); Gwinnett (15 Dec. 1818); Habersham (15 Dec. 1818); Hall (15 Dec. 1818); Henry (15 May 1821); Houston (15 May 1821); Irwin (15 Dec. 1818); Lee (9 June 1825); Monroe (15 May 1821); Muscogee (9 June 1825); Rabun (15 Dec. 1818); Troup (9 June 1825); Walton (15 Dec. 1818); Wayne (11 May 1803); Wilkinson, Districts 1 through 5 (11 May 1803), and Districts 6 through 28 (26 June 1806). Twenty-two counties were organized and distributed by the Lottery system.

It will be noticed by the dates of the Acts, that not all lotteries were held the same year of the Act calling for same. The years held were namely: 1805, 1806, 1820, 1821, 1827 and 1832. In Cherokee County, one section was laid off in 160 acre land lots, and the other section was laid off in 40 acre gold lots; therefore, the first mentioned was called the Cherokee Land Lottery, while the other was called the Cherokee Gold Lottery, both were authorized by Act of 21 Dec. 1830, and both lotteries were held in 1832. By studying the Head-Right counties and land lottery counties, one quickly sees that all other counties have been made from those named above.

Hall's original county map of Georgia, showing present and original counties and land districts, is very useful to the genealogist; photostats of Hall's Map can be ordered for $1.00 from the Department of Archives and History. Also available from the Department of Archives is the pamphlet, *Authentic List of All Land Lottery Grants made to Veterans of the Revolutionary War by the State of Georgia* ($1.12).

If the searcher does not have access to Georgia Laws or Digests, the following publications quote pertinent sections from the Acts governing Head-Right and lottery grants: S. G. McLendon's *History of the Public Domain of Georgia*, 1924, and L. L. Knight's *Georgia Roster of the Revolution*, 1920. In Knight's book, attention is called to pages 193-197 which is an explanatory chapter on "Head-Rights and Lottery Land

Grants of Georgia." All manuscript records mentioned by McLendon and Knight as being in the Office of the Secretary of State are no longer in that office, but are filed in the Department of Archives and History, which is under the jurisdiction of the Secretary of State. There is an index of approximately 43,660 cards to head-right and bounty grants, arranged alphabetically, in the name of the grantee. Example of entry: *Alexander, Samuel,* St. George's (Parish) (Book) E (p.) 13, 48 (acres), 1764. Therefore, by consulting this general name-index to head-right and bounty grants, the location of the land, in which book the land is recorded, the page number in the original book, the number of acres the grantee received, and the year granted, can be found. This index is particularly useful when the searcher does not know in which parish or county his or her ancestor received a grant.

Bear in mind, however, that the grants very seldom list heirs or give genealogical data, but are helpful by showing where the land was granted and the date of the grant.

The appendix to Smith's *Story of Georgia and the Georgia People* (1900), under the caption "Headrights granted by the Colonial and State Governments from 1754 to 1800" lists names of many persons receiving grants, grouped roughly by counties. While there are numerous errors and it is not complete, it is helpful to those unable to work in the records in Georgia.

Unfortunately, the census records of Georgia prior to 1820 were destroyed. Census records from 1820 to 1880, inclusive, are available at the National Archives in the original or on microfilm, and at the Georgia Department of Archives and History on microfilm. Copies of those from 1830 to 1880 may be purchased from the National Archives.

Another useful tool is the Department's General Catalog of approximately 100,000 names, arranged alphabetically, giving colonial service; all state and federal officers 1777-1952; military officers 1777-1860; county officers 1777-1800, including sheriffs and justices of the peace through 1815. Dates of commission for many of the justices of the inferior court are also included, but are not complete. The service records have been

taken from source materials on file in the Georgia Department
of Archives and History, but vital dates and names of wives
have been secured from members of families.

Early Tax Digests of Georgia, Ruth Blair, 1926, fills to a
large extent the loss of the 1790, 1800 and 1810 federal census
reports. This volume was indexed, and a typewritten manuscript of the index is on file in the Department of Archives and
History. The original tax digest 1790-1818, also some for
later years, are on file in the Department of Archives and History. A copy of *Early Tax Digests of Georgia,* with index,
has been presented to The National Archives for use in the
general Search Room.

For the names of North and South Carolinians and Virginians coming into Georgia between 1773 and 1775, the most
valuable record from the genealogist's standpoint is the "Land
Court Journal to ceded Lands, 1773-1775". This manuscript
was formerly in the Greene County, Georgia, courthouse, but
is now deposited in the Department of Archives and History.
The manuscript had fallen to pieces and was beyond repair before it reached the Department. Fortunately, it was copied
and published in *Early Records of Georgia, Wilkes County,*
Davidson (2 vols., 1932). The *Journal* appears in vol. I, pp.
4-29.

At the time of the Revolution, Georgia's population did not
number twenty thousand. It was not until 1781 that the State
began to provide land for those who had rendered service in
the Revolution. "Bounty" grants were given only to those
who had rendered service during the Revolutionary War.
Franklin and Washington Counties were almost entirely settled by Revolutionary veterans. The original grant was 250
acres of land, with tax, 1781, and by the Act of 1784, this was
increased to 287½ acres with no tax exemption. These
counties were head-right territory; therefore, it is very necessary that the word "bounty" appear in connection with the
land. An Act of 1777 had provided that: "Every free white
person, or head of a family, shall be entitled to, allotted and
granted him, 200 acres of land, and for every other white person of the said family, fifty acres of land . . ." Therefore, it

is easy to see that a man, not a soldier, with wife would receive 250 acres of land, and could be confused with the Revolutionary Grant for 250 acres. "Bounty" is proof of Revolutionary service.

Revolutionary Soldiers' Receipts for Georgia Bounty Grants (lithogravure reproduction of original record on file in the Department of Archives and History) shows approximately 1,040 names of refugees, citizens, and soldiers of the Georgia Line, officers and men of the Georgia State Galleys, etc. This is a supplemental record which should be consulted along with Knight's *Revolutionary Records of Georgia or Roster of the Revolution*, 1920. Although not of great genealogical value, it is well to call attention to *The Revolutionary Records of the State of Georgia*, A. D. Candler, ed. (3 vols., Atlanta, 1908).

Hero of Hornet's Nest, A Biography of Elijah Clark, Louise Frederick Hays (Stratford House, Inc., New York, 1946), has 60 pages of footnotes and a bibliography dealing with Revolutionary source material in the Department of Archives and History, as well as data in other depositories and in private collections. The footnotes and bibliography would aid the genealogist.

The Department of Archives is now listing on cards 23,983 names which appear in four manuscript volumes entitled *A List of Names of Those Entitled to Draw Under the Act of May 11, 1803*. This is a most important list as it gives the county in which the person was residing at the time he was entitled to draw. It also serves as a census record for 1802 as the person must have resided in the state twelve months prior to the passage of the Act, in order to be entitled to draw.

The volume of *Passports, 1785-1820,* issued to citizens, many from the Carolinas, traveling through Georgia to the "Louisiana Territory", "Mississippi Territory", etc., is valuable material for the genealogist. This typewritten volume is from original manuscripts in the Department of Archives and History. There are approximately 2,617 entries in the index. Many of these *Passports* have been published in *Passports Issued by Governors of Georgia, 1785-1809*, by Mary G. Bryan

(Special Publication No. 21, of the National Genealogical Society, 1959).

Patriotic societies in Georgia, mainly the D. A. R. Chapters, are depositing with the Department of Archives and History valuable typewritten, notarized copies of Bible records, abstracts of marriages, cemetery inscriptions, church records, wills, estate papers, deeds, genealogical charts, and similar records. This source must not be overlooked by the genealogist.

Georgia records after 1777 are, for the most part, on file in the individual counties except where they have been destroyed by fire, neglect, and carelessness. By visiting the county seat, in the Office of Ordinary, wills, marriages, administration of estates, etc., may be found. In the office of Clerk of Superior Court, are tax digests, deeds, minutes of the Superior Court, etc. The Secretary of State prepares and publishes each year *Georgia's Official Directory of State and County Officers*. This is distributed free, and is a useful tool to genealogists who need to know the names of officials whose records they desire to examine.

The Georgia Department of Archives and History has, since 1951, been microfilming the records of the oldest counties. These include deeds, wills, returns on estates, marriages, court minutes, etc. Among those already on file in Atlanta are: Camden, Chatham, Liberty, Richmond (all 1777), Franklin (1784); Montgomery, Oglethorpe, Screven and Warren (1793); Jackson (1786); Tattnall (1801); Telfair (1807); Emanuel (1812); Newton (1821); Stewart (1830); Webster (1853).

County histories have been published covering a number of the 159 counties, and many of these have included some source materials, such as marriage records, cemetery records, or abstracts of wills. Publications of local historical societies likewise contain such records. Examples are: "DeKalb County Marriages 1840-1853" in vols. 2, 3 and 4 of *Atlanta Historical Society Bulletin*, and *Abstracts of Wills, Chatham County, Georgia 1773-1817*, by Mabel Freeman LaFar and Caroline

Price Wilson (Publication No. 6 of the National Genealogical Society).

The Georgia Historical Society in Savannah was organized in 1839 for the purpose of preserving history of Georgia and Savannah in particular. It has published eleven volumes of *Collections of the Georgia Historical Society*, the first in 1840. It also publishes *The Georgia Historical Quarterly*. While devoted primarily to historical articles the documents, diaries, etc., appearing from time to time often provide information to the genealogist. The Society has extensive collections, both of old books and manuscripts, which are open to the public, except its files of rare newspapers, these being available to members only.

Births and deaths were not recorded by the State of Georgia prior to Jan. 1, 1919. However, Atlanta (Fulton County) began recording births in 1887 and deaths in 1896. Savannah (Chatham Co.) has births recorded from 1890 and deaths from 1803. The Mortuary Records (deaths), 1803-1832, were published in *Annals of Georgia; Mortuary Records*, vol. 3, by Caroline Price Wilson (1933).

CHAPTER X

THE WESTWARD EXPANSION

The Trails West

Before the American Revolution, adventurers and Indian fighters from the thirteen English colonies found their way through the mountain barrier that stretches from New England to Georgia. These were the trail breakers and they followed the natural paths to Tennessee, Kentucky and Ohio. In moving toward the interior, explorer and hunter were followed by Indian trader and then by speculator, settler and merchant. This movement of settlement matched the spread south to Georgia and the spread north in New England and New York. Beyond the river valleys of the seaboard and piedmont, geography mainly determined the areas to be settled first. In tracing the origins of the first migrations, it is helpful to identify the paths or trails through the gaps in the mountain barrier to any particular valley or area. Important factors were buffalo and animal trails, Indian trade routes, the locations of salt licks, so indispensable to settlement, springs and abundant game. In some areas belligerent Indian groups, such as the Six Nations of New York, constituted a formidable barrier against the westward movement around which the trails must lead. Generally speaking, however, migrations followed the parallels of longitude to the West.

Kentucky and Tennessee

The first settlers of Kentucky arrived at Boonesborough from North Carolina in 1775 and at Harrodsburg that same year from Virginia. Later, settlers followed the Ohio from western Pennsylvania and in the valleys of the Kentucky, Ohio and Cumberland there was a merging of families that originated along the seaboard from New Jersey to the Carolinas. Many families were restless and would not stay in Kentucky or Tennessee. They were to make a major contribution to the rest of the settlement of the West, moving into southern Ohio, Indiana and Illinois, and on into Iowa and Missouri. Eventually, they were in the vanguard of migration to Oregon and California and later to the mountain states. Others went south to help settle all the area from Alabama west to Texas. Those who went across the Ohio River quickly began to mingle with a great stream of New Englanders which had first migrated north into New Hampshire and Vermont and then west by the Mohawk in New York to Ohio. Those who went south were joined by those who migrated from Carolina into Georgia. It is this great divide in the migration to Kentucky and Tennessee that makes most western Americans of Revolutionary origin related to every other part of America. This path through Ohio, Kentucky or Tennessee is a major key which all students of genealogy must remember in tracing the movements of any particular family.

The French

To most rules in relation to patterns of settlement and migration there are exceptions. Such is the migration pattern of the French from Louisiana and Canada. Since they followed the great rivers and their goal was trade with the Indians, their centers of settlement were isolated posts like Kaskaskia and St. Louis. As fur traders, they knew no bounds and traveled freely across the lands of the Indian. Naturally, therefore, they led in the settlement of most of the north and far west. Since they were beyond the edge of family settlement, some took as wives women of Indian origin, without benefit of clergy. Years later, such unions were often formalized by a Christian marriage when the first minister or priest visited the remote area of settlement. At this time, the children would be baptized and all of these sacraments would be recorded, an essential document for the use and interpretation of later generations. Another group of French settlers were the Acadians scattered by the British in 1755-56 among their colonies to the south of Canada. Received as enemies, they naturally tended to gather together in the face of hostility, and with the aid of the French and Spanish to concentrate in Louisiana.

Spanish and Russian

Outside of the main stream of migration were the Spanish settlers of the Southwest who were in the Rio Grande Valley of New Mexico in 1598. It was the culmination of a century of exploration, conquest and settlement north from the lands of the Aztecs. The desert mountains had been overcome by one discovery of silver and other minerals after another. From Zacatecas to Durango, San Luis Potosi, Saltillo and Moncolva, the occupation had led very nearly to the present bounds of Mexico by 1590. Every step was planned, directed and financed by men of wealth who employed armies of Indian and half-breed workers and caravans of animals. The following century witnessed bloody revolts by enslaved Indians and racial outcasts, struggles between land owners and missionaries over Indian labor, and consolidation of settlement in agricultural lands, but no real advance. It was 1769 before Portola and the Franciscans marched up the West Coast to found San Diego and the other missions and presidios of California. The white population in all of this development tended to mingle with Indian and Negro elements, since many more men than women migrated from Spain. Nevertheless, Spanish families throughout South America and in California still send their sons to be educated in Europe where they tend to marry. Numerically, however, the actual Spanish population in the southwest was insignificant in comparison with the modern Mexican migrations witnessed in this century. Similarly, the Russians who migrated from Siberia to Alaska and Northern California brought few permanent settlers with families, and they are completely overshadowed by the concentration of White Russians which came to Northern California following World War I.

The Tory Pattern

Most Tories who left the colonies at the end of the Revolution were settled by the British in Nova Scotia, New Brunswick and Ontario. They often represented wealthy and professional classes in the original colonies and, because of the common bond of loyalty to the Crown, many have migrated within Canada as a group. Others returned to their original homes within a decade or so after the Revolution or tended to cross back over the border following the Great Lakes and the water routes into the northern tier of states.

Asylum

Many groups who settled in the west were refugees, some even from American persecutions. There were those who came from Europe for economic reasons, like the Swiss whom Lord Selkirk brought to the Red River colony. Confronted with a bleak world and armed hostility they fled to Minnesota and a group of them went east to found Vevay, Indiana. There were those who were wrenched from their homes by political events. The Revolution of 1848 brought the Germans to St. Louis, the potato famines brought Irish to many of the major cities of America, while the political prisoners of France were shipped by their government to San Francisco. Instinctively, each element of a common experience tended to join forces. Thus, there was a cultural and religious bond between Irish and French in California. It was natural that new citizens adopted old economic occupations and that French, Italian and Hungarian revolutionaries moved into those parts of California where wine culture was possible. The very presence of these linguistic groups in the west led to migrations of later refugees from the homeland to California, of French upon the fall of Napoleon III, of Hungarians from the revolutions of 1918 and of Mexicans from the Revolution of 1910 to join the older Spanish-American population. Each group, when it became part of America, tended to follow the migration patterns of those around them. Thus, it was logical that French merchants followed the gold rushes from California to Oregon, Idaho, Montana, British Columbia and Alaska. In the middle west, the foreign settler also followed the established geographic patterns of the area of settlement. Such was the numerically significant migration of the Scandinavians who first came to Minnesota, Wisconsin and then spread west to the Dakotas and more recently to the Pacific Northwest and Alaska. In the coast seaport areas they were to join Scandinavians who had come as seafarers and fishermen as early as 1860.

Motives

Except for immigrant Scotch Irish and Germans, much of the original western movement up through 1820 originated with the older populations of the 13 original states. A family might move once a generation and, although one life could have witnessed the migration across the Continent, the moves tended to match a time-scale that was slightly longer. Thus, a great-great-great-grandmother moved from New Jersey to the mountains of North Carolina by 1771, to Kentucky by 1799, to Illinois in 1824. Her grandson, born in Kentucky, completed the trip across the Continent to Oregon in 1852, and his daughter and family migrated east to Idaho in 1886. Some of the motives behind this urge to move westward are significant and explain the importance of certain records commonly used to trace families. They may be defined as follows:

(1) The predominance of large families, too many heirs for a single farm.

(2) Soil exhaustion within a generation after the first settlement and the consequent decrease in crop yield which made new lands most attractive.

(3) Rises in land values, the establishment of large land holdings and the economic dominance of a few so that only those with capital could see a future in their own state.

(4) The development of many small urban centers which failed to obtain necessary economic activity to insure their continued life. As transportation changed from river and turnpike to canal, to railroad, to modern highway, first one type of town after another has been supplanted by rivals. The extent of short-lived ghost towns across the American map is illustrated in the birth and death rate of post offices and platted subdivisions. Many towns were stillborn, purely speculative in character and had no real populations. The citizens of the other towns that really died moved on to new livelihoods not necessarily in the successful neighboring settlement, but in the towns of the area to which their farm neighbors were migrating.

(5) Failures to establish land titles drove many groups west. In

search of land which they had not owned in Europe, they were hungry for acres of basic wealth. Often these people were victims of legal battles over titles, the mismanagement of land speculators and land companies. Naturally, they kept moving until they obtained their goal of landed wealth, and speculation was their meat and drink.

(6) The migrations were inspired and directed by propaganda, conscious and unconscious. Letters from those who had migrated served as a major source of such inspiration. Newspapers, pamphlets, guides, all fed this dream of a land where the grass was greener and taller.

(7) The partially settled areas sought, and their representatives in Congress obtained, laws which opened the public domain. The first group to benefit were major speculators, the second, officers and soldiers in the Revolutionary and succeeding wars, the next those with meager capital, and lastly, just those who would come. Extreme were the donation land claims of the Oregon Territory which provided a man and wife with one square mile and an unmarried man with a half square mile.

(8) The frontiers were restless places and there were many who came but did not fit into the pattern of society as it became organized. As a result, they fled from their own acts, from acts of others, or because of personal characteristics which were unacceptable to others. If there was a school and a church within five miles, it was time for such people to move on to more remote areas.

(9) Divorce was not socially acceptable, and where it occurred, the migration of both parties frequently resulted, the man disappearing so far as the woman's family is concerned.

Unmarried Men

The unmarried man has always been free to follow opportunity as it beckons and his migrations conform to no set pattern. One brother might go east to the great cities, or to school and never return, while another might go west to the newest frontier in search of gold, work or land. The greatest influencing factors in their migration and their choices are the migration of their friends and of members of their own families. Thus, when the unmarried paternal grandfather came to Oregon in 1850, he came with his married sisters. Similarly, the unmarried maternal grandfather came to California in the gold rush of 1849 with a group of men from his own community who had organized themselves into a company to go to the gold fields. As a result, when one examines the first Oregon census of 1850 and the second census of 1860, one finds groups of men from the same place living together, whether they be from Missouri, Scotland or Finland. Later, census records show that they married locally or if they were foreign, sent or went back for wives, and that others had come to the area who undoubtedly were relations of their wives.

Women and the Family

The clue to the migration of women is bound up with the institution of the family, for women migrated usually in family groups. Thus, a great-grandmother and four sisters came to Oregon in 1852 with their husbands and near grown children, of which the paternal grandmother was one. This pattern of migration had been repeated for at least three generations in more than one branch of the family, when sisters and their families had moved from New Jersey and Virginia, to Pennsylvania and North Carolina, to Kentucky and from Kentucky to Illinois. Usually, a few members of the family went ahead to blaze the trail.

Those Who Stayed Behind

When a migration took place, often older married children left parents behind with the youngest brother or sister. If a farm was involved, there may be a deed at the court house, in which all brothers and sisters relinquish their right in their father's farm to that younger brother. If only men migrated, then there may be descendants in the area by the female line. Marriage records of daughters will be valuable in helping to identify modern cousins. They are likely to have letters from the west. If the family is no longer in the community, they may still be in neighboring communities, and even more likely in the nearest city. There is still a steady move from country to city going on all over America.

Mysteries of the Family

The tracing of a lineage may stop with a person whose origin is shielded in mystery. People who migrate alone often migrate for reasons. Youths who run away may have been appalled by some simple deed. One of the Far West's early literary figures turned out to have fled his mountain home and changed his name when he rolled a stone down a hill and killed his neighbor's cow. Women in particular may be attempting to rise in social class. One such mysterious great grandmother who refused to talk about her origin was the daughter of a jailer, an occupation that was despised in colonial times. In both cases, the general area from which they might have come was obvious and the identity was established through a study of records of probate in court houses.

Crimes

Those who assume aliases or migrate for more serious reasons are very difficult to trace and it may be years before anyone knowing of the search recognizes the key which unlocks the door to their past. A study of the history of the area where they are known to have lived may help, and in particular a study of their friends. Identify the men and women who witness documents for them. See if there is correspondence of famous and near famous individuals preserved in special collections relating to the area where they lived. Some of the crimes from which men fled are not crimes today. More than one man fled the threat of the debtors prison while many married women fled from the blot of divorce. Treason drove many of our ancestors to this country and their modern counterparts we know as political refugees. In the light of time, treason becomes acceptable. Yet, because of the fear of reprisal, such persons often hide their identity. Within America, both Tory and Confederate went west as well as the remnants of families broken by divided loyalties of the wars.

Church and Migration

One of the strongest influences on the course of migration was the inspiration of a religious leader. The Mormons are only one of many groups that gathered together under inspired leadership and went out into the wilderness to seek the promised land. Most, if not all, states in the West boast of at least one such colony. As sincere believers in the right they also often disagreed and there were major schisms, many of which their descendants would deny. In tracing lost families the records of a particular church may therefore be the key you seek. Often churches record the movements of their members. Even if people lived in a missionary district, their religious experiences from baptism to death may be recorded in a missionary or circuit record book covering a wide area. The custody of such records may remain with the church or be in the hands of some regional or national church archives. Helpful in locating records are two bibliographies, "Church Archives in the United States and Canada . . .", by Edmund L. Binsfeld, published in the *American Archivist* for July 1958, vol. 21, no. 3, pp. 311-332, and *A Survey of American Church Records*, by E. Kay Kirkham (Salt Lake City, 1958).

Professions

Early settlers may basically be hunters who migrated from some other fringe of settlement, and the key to their migration will be buried in the records of the fur companies. There are the Astor papers at the Baker Library, Harvard University, and the American Fur Company papers in the New York Historical Society, New York City, for which the American Historical Society published a Calendar as part of its *Annual Report 1944*, vols. 2 and 3. If they served the Hudson's Bay Company, its records are in the company archives, Beaver House, Great Trinity Lane, London, E. C. 2, England. Later immigrants would be farmers and are likely to have come from areas where the initial virgin fertility of the soil is exhausted. Persons connected with economic developments, road building, canals, inns, lumber, newspapers, mining, tend to follow those developments across America. The men in the mining camps knew each other from some place else and similarly the men in lumber industry tended to follow the same pattern from Maine to Michigan to Minnesota and west. In each area, new elements were introduced like the Scandinavians in Minnesota; nevertheless, the same families are still following the timber in Oregon, California and British Columbia. Similarly, men went from California's gold fields to Nevada, Oregon, Idaho, Montana, Colorado, British Columbia and the Yukon.

Tracing Back

To summarize the sources for tracing migrations, here is a check list:

(1) Biographical sources available in large libraries, including encyclopedias, *Who's Who*, and local histories.

(2) Family papers and memoirs, your own, and your relatives, often in the hands of descendants of the youngest son.

(3) Land records, local in court houses, federal in The National Archives.

(4) Powers of attorney recorded in court houses.

(5) Tax rolls and census records of the counties where families lived, in court houses, state archives and the federal census (to 1880) in The National Archives.

(6) Probate records in local court houses, and if wills were challenged, the records of higher state courts. There are often a number of probate series in each county.

(7) Court records, both criminal and civil. Again, where cases exist, it pays to see if an appeal was made to a higher court.

(8) The papers of family friends, and even enemies, in historical societies and libraries, including diaries.

(9) Pension records in The National Archives from the Revolution to the Spanish-American War, or in each southern state, for Confederates.

(10) Church records, in the custody of the church, some denominational archives, or some historical society, or a library, often connected with the church. Other records will be peculiar to the area in which you are searching. Outside of the published guides to help the genealogical worker, the State Archives or the State Historical Society will have to direct your attention to tools in their area, such as newspaper indexes, D. A. R. cemetery indexes, etc.

Tracing Forward

Part of genealogy is not only to find ancestors, but also to locate descendants. Those who work on such a project compile genealogies that are all inclusive. A grand tour of the United States may be necessary if the account goes back beyond the Civil War, but first it would be wise to exhaust some of the published sources available in major libraries. These would include not only the biographical accounts in standard biographies, but the collection of current city directories and telephone books. For unusual names it may also be possible to obtain lists of licensed drivers from Motor Vehicle Departments. Once these sources have been exhausted and initial contact made by mail or in person, with all members of the family, then a trip to Washington, D. C., is in order. Here, one should check the following obvious sources:

(1) All pension and military bounty claim files in The National Archives for individuals of the same name from the area in which you are sure you are concerned. A spot check of other files may reveal an interrelationship and the files for ex-slaves are invaluable for the data which is contained therein on former masters.

(2) Once you have these names and the data their files reveal, turn to the U. S. Census and check the record of each family census by census from 1790 to 1880.

(3) Check the publications at the Library of Congress, and D. A. R. Library for and from each county in the nation where the family was known to live for further data. These include directories as well as local histories and other publications of a local character.

With this information in hand, one is then ready to plot a tour of the areas where the family lived. En route, one will visit the persons with whom one corresponded as a result of the directory search and, certainly, one will check the indexes in the court house for the surname in the following records: (1) Deed records: (2) marriage records; (3) probate records and wills which may be separately recorded; (4) miscellaneous records or powers of attorney; (5) court cases, and (6) tax rolls. (In the case of a key family, it may pay to skim the records for the names of witnesses. For many records where two parties are involved, there may be two indexes.)

In each community there may be relatives with papers, cemeteries, and perhaps church records of value. The department of vital records is often in the capital city, but searches cost fees, and in many western states the records do not begin until this century. At the state archives in the capitol, one should find more census, tax, veterans and state land records, all of which may help, as well as special indexes to pioneers and their biographies, and to newspapers in state libraries and historical societies. The nature of the record will vary from place to place, but the searcher will be dependent upon the staff and facilities of the institutions which he visits for guidance and help.

The Great Blank Wall

Sometimes genealogical research is up against a great blank wall and whole families disappear. This event can only be explained in terms of the events of that day which made history. A student faced with such a problem must look for possible trails of migration in terms of the condition of affairs when the wall appears. First, there are local newspapers that often record national or regional events; second, the publications of historical societies and local histories; and third, annual yearbooks through which the general conditions of the times can be followed, such as *Niles Register, 1811-1849*, and Appleton's *Annual Cyclopaedia,, 1861-1903*. Of these sources, the newspapers may be the hardest to find. Each state has major collections, but there are always gaps and *American Newspapers, 1821-1936*, a union list edited by Winifred Gregory, is a basic tool. Major events have widespread results. The unrest in Missouri which formed such a vivid part in the background of the Civil War led to the great migration from that state to Oregon. The actual trails of migration inspired those who lived along the road to follow the endless stream of wagons that rolled by on the way West. If there was excitement over gold, the family may have caught the fever. If there was some area being opened up for settlement, the land rush was the magnet. On the other hand, Indian Wars drove people out of the fringes of the frontier back to more settled areas. This return to civilization is unexpected but, nevertheless, part of the pattern. It will pay to read widely the reminiscences of those who witnessed life in the general area where the family lived. They may suddenly open up a vista leading to the origin or the destination of a missing family. The student who looks for clues in the published sources suggested above should be particularly careful to examine advertisements in newspapers and to watch for significant economic data which will explain the direction in which the people of the area were migrating.

Libraries on the West

General libraries on the history of the United States and on the history of the West are natural keys wherein may be found the information one seeks. Remember that without travel, through the use of microfilm for study in a library or home, the treasures of many can be obtained.

The Library of Congress Local History and Manuscripts Divisions are particularly important to all searchers for their wealth of information on the national as well as the local scene. Its Union Catalog will locate rare publications in libraries throughout the country, when no example can be found in a nearby library. Its newspaper collection is one of the best.

The New York Public Library American History and Manuscripts collections are equally as rich as those of the Library of Congress.

Several historical societies bearing the names of their states are really devoted to the history of all America. They were founded long before the others and the wealth of original sources is outstanding, Massachusetts, New York, Pennsylvania and Wisconsin being pre-eminent. At the last named are the Draper manuscripts, one of the best sources relating to the settlement and development of the Kentucky-Tennessee key area.

Several libraries have specialized in original sources for all the Far West. The Newberry in Chicago also has a genealogical collection, but the Coe Collection at Yale University, the Ellison Collection at Indiana University at Bloomington, the Bancroft Library at the University of California at Berkeley, the Clarke Collection (important for Montana) at the University of California at Los Angeles, and the Henry E. Huntington Library at San Marino, California, are principally historical libraries serving the historian and trained social scientist. Nevertheless, here may be found the answers to many genealogical questions.

Many state, public and university libraries maintain local history if not genealogical collections. A list would be long, but should include the Tennessee, Indiana, Oregon and California State Libraries, the Sutro Library in San Francisco (a state institution), the Los Angeles, and Seattle Public Libraries, and the Wyoming, Washington, Cornell, Duke and Oregon University libraries. *The American Library Directory* will guide genealogical inquiries to the right source. The larger the local history collection the more likely help is available to the searcher.

Pre-eminent for genealogical research is the Genealogical Society at Salt Lake City, where may be found basic records not only for the Mormon Church and its members but for many eastern states and some western, as well as many foreign countries.

Historical Societies

State and local historical societies in many instances maintain important collections. The degree to which they assist the genealogist depends upon the value and interest they see in such research. The *Directory of Historical Societies and Agencies in the United States and Canada,* published by the American Association for State and Local History (1959) will furnish addresses and the 1944 edition will furnish data on the character of each society and its work.

Archival Establishments

The growth of state archival agencies in the United States has been slow, but is important to the student of genealogy. In the south, many state departments of archives date back to the beginning of the century and they recognize the value of family research. In the Middle West, Illinois and Indiana are well established and most helpful. The others are new, as are most of those in the West and their helpfulness will vary according to the available staff and the emphasis placed on family history by their directors. The "Annuaire International des Archives", published as Volume 5 of *Archivum* in 1955 is a basic tool for all genealogical workers who wish to consult archives all over the world. For the United States, the *Report of the Committee on State Records* of the Society of American Archivists for 1957 best summarizes the activities of the state archival agencies and will further guide the genealogist who wishes to know what to expect.

Local Records

The local records of the States of the United States were to have been inventoried by the W. P. A. Historical Records Survey. In representative counties across the nation their contents were described and the inventories published. One is indeed fortunate to be able to walk into a court house with such a publication at hand, for many custodians have no concept of the older records in their custody or where they may be stored. The published "inventory" usually provides some sort of location guide and with this it is possible to locate essential records forgotten or unknown to those who work in the court house. In the states where there are active archival programs, county records as described in the inventory may now be in the state archives. In many states county record destruction laws have been passed and older records may no longer exist. Some were undoubtedly useless, but unless the destruction has been directed by an archival agency, essential records that should have been saved may be gone. Meanwhile, the Mormon church is recording on microfilm for their use and for the use of the state archives, the most valuable county records in each state. In time, we can expect to use such materials for all the states, either in the state archives or in Salt Lake City at the Genealogical Society headquarters. This library is already becoming the answer to the prayer of the genealogist who cannot afford the luxury of general travel but can visit and use a single source.

CHAPTER XI

CANADA

A. BIBLIOGRAPHY

In the preface to Mlle. Jeanne Grégoire's helpful little work on genealogical research in Canada, *Á la Recherche de Nos Ancêtres:Guide du Généalogiste* (1957), Father Lionel Groulx has written: "La généalogie au Canada Français n'est pas seulement une science; pour le grande nombre, c'est une passion."

He is quite correct. Genealogy among the French Canadians is a passion. Alone among all the ten provinces of the Dominion, Québec has developed genealogy to an exact science. This is reflected in their numerous publications. The Abbé Cyprien Tanguay's *Dictionnaire Généalogique des Familles Canadiennes* (7 vols., 1871-96) is a classic, in spite of the fact that many errors have been found in it. Tanguay was a pioneer in the field, as was François Daniel, whose two works, *Nos Gloires Nationales, ou Histoire des Principales Familles du Canada* (2 vols., 1867) and *Histoire des Grandes Familles Françaises du Canada, ou Aperçu sur le Chevalier Benoist et Quelques Familles Contemporains* (1 vol., 1867) told in considerable detail the story of Canada's "national glories", the great families of Longueuil (LeMoyne), Lotbinière, Eschambault, Salaberry, and many others.

In his time, Benjamin Sulte was the leading French-Canadian historian. His *Histoire des Canadiens-Français, 1608-1880* was published in eight impressive volumes (1882-84). In this work he gave several complete censuses that were taken in the 17th century. The first census in North America was that of 1666, printed by Sulte in Volume 4, pp. 52-63. It is interesting to note the data included in the enumeration; the following example was chosen at random: Jacques Cochon (which means "pig"), 31, habitant (resident); Barbe-Delphine Le Tardif, 17, sa femme (wife); Marie-Magdelaine, 2;

Jacques, 3; Charles le Tardif, 15, et Guillaume Le Tardif, 11, pensionnaires (boarders).

Other scholars who have made important contributions to French-Canadian genealogy are: Abbé Charles Beaumont, *Archives Canadiennes, Généalogie des Familles de la Côte de Beaupré* (1912); Rev. Father Archange Godbout, *Origine des Familles Canadiennes-Françaises* (1925); and Brother Eloi-Gérard, *Recueil de Généalogies des Comtés de Beauce-Dorchester-Frontenac, 1625-1946* (11 vols., 1949-55). In 1909, the "Committee of Ancient Families" published *Le Livre d' Or de la Noblesse Rurale Canadienne-Française,* in which they listed (pp. 59-124) the families of the Province of Québec which were living in 1908 on the same land their ancestors had occupied 200 or more years earlier.

In 1943, the Société Généalogique Canadienne-Française (French-Canadian Genealogical Society) was founded, and in January 1944 appeared the first issue of its *Mémoires.* Since then, there has been poured into the pages of this quarterly periodical a constant stream of genealogical studies, source materials, articles describing methods of research, etc.

The Province of Ontario has many ties with the United States, through the steady immigration in the late 18th and early 19th centuries of Loyalists, Quakers, Mennonites, and others. From time to time efforts have been made to do justice to its families, but many attempts appear to have been abortive. Edward Marion Chadwick issued *Ontarian Families. Genealogies of United Empire Loyalist and other Pioneer Families of Upper Canada* (2 vols., 1898). For a time a periodical known as *The Ontarian Genealogist and Family Historian* seemed to hold the spotlight, but it lasted only from July 1898 to April 1901. In 1956, George T. Heath founded *Pedigree: A Genealogical Quarterly,* in which he publishes articles, source-materials, queries, etc. Its address is P. O. Box 456, Hamilton, Ontario. Some years ago an Upper Canada Genealogical Society was formed, but it seems to have become inactive.

A truly monumental work, *Pioneer Life on the Bay of Quinté, Including Genealogies of Old Families and Biographi-*

cal Sketches of Representative Citizens, the author and date of which are alike unknown (but published early in the 20th century), portrayed (sometimes in romantic language) the history of over 280 families on the shores of this bay in Prince Edward County, Ontario.

Nova Scotia and New Brunswick are other provinces that have ties with the United States since before the Revolutionary War. The story of our associations with the former province is told by Edward H. West, F. A. S. G., in "Pre-Revolutionary Migration to Nova Scotia", *National Genealogical Society Quarterly,* vol. 30, March 1944, and Jean Stephenson, F. A. S. G., "The Connecticut Settlement of Nova Scotia Prior to the Revolution", in *Special Aids to Genealogical Research in Northeastern and Central States* (Special Publication No. 16 of the National Genealogical Society, 1957). Other works dealing with Nova Scotia that have some genealogical interest are Howard Trueman's *The Chignecto Isthmus and Its First Settlers,* and David Allison's *History of Nova Scotia* (1916), vol. III (Biographical Volume).

For New Brunswick, we have the excellent work by Lilian M. Beckwith Maxwell, *An Outline of the History of Central New Brunswick to the Time of Confederation* (1937). The compiler gives sketches of early settlers and public officials, military lists, lists of grantees of land, etc. It has several indexes, including one of persons. Genealogically, it is important. Other works of value are James Hannay's *History of New Brunswick* (2 vols., 1909) and the *Collections of New Brunswick Historical Society* (3 vols., 1894-1909).

Newfoundland, England's oldest colony, is Canada's youngest province, having been admitted to the Dominion in 1948. D. W. Prowse's *A History of Newfoundland, from the English, Colonial, and Foreign Records* (1895; 2nd edition, 1896) is a hefty volume, replete with names; the descendants of Newfoundland families will find much of value in it.

Prince Edward Island has two books that contain much information on its families, namely, *Past and Present of Prince Edward Island,* published under the advisory editorship of Hon. D. A. MacKinnon and Hon. A. B. Warburton, which contains a vast amount of information on individuals and families; and *Hebridean Pioneers,* by Malcolm A. Macqueen (1957), who tells very well the story of the settlers in Prince Edward Island from the Highlands and Western Isles of Scotland.

The Province of Manitoba has a wealth of printed material. F. H. Schofield's *The Story of Manitoba* (1913) tells the story of its leading citizens in volumes II and III. Another important work is Dr. George Bryce's *A History of Manitoba, Its Resources and People* (1906), pages 309-692 being biographical. The story of Lord Selkirk's famous Red River Settlement, which included Manitoba, Minnesota, and North Dakota, will be found in John Perry Pritchard's *The Red River Valley, 1811-1849* (1942), Dr. George Bryce's *The Romantic Settlement of Lord Selkirk's Colonists (The Pioneers of Manitoba)* (1909), and Chester Martin's *Red River Settlement, Papers in the Canadian Archives Relating to the Pioneers* (1910).

The western provinces are represented by *History of Saskatchewan and the Old North West* (2nd ed., 1913); *The Story of Saskatchewan and Its People,* by John Hawkes (3 vols., 1924; vols. II-III biographical); *History of the Province of Alberta,* by Dr. Archibald Oswald MacRae (2 vols., 1912, vol I, pp. 475-598, and vol. II biographical); *History of British Columbia, 1792-1887,* by Hubert Howe Bancroft (1890), containing many names and a good index; and *British Columbia from the Earliest Times to the Present,* by E. O. S. Scholefield and F. W. Howay (4 vols., 1914; vols. III-IV biographical).

It will be noticed that the farther west we go, the fewer become the strictly genealogical publications. All of the provinces have historical societies, both on the provincial and the county level, which have published periodicals containing much genealogical information, such as church registers, family sketches, biographies, etc.

One of the important migrations to Canada from the United States was that of the Pennsylvania Germans; their story is told very thoroughly and with thousands of names mentioned in Dr. G. Elmore Reaman's *The Trail of the Black Walnut* (1957). The Loyalist claims were published in two volumes in 1904 by the Ontario Bureau of Archives. Gérard Malchelosse, F. A. S. G., published an article entitled "Généalogie et Généalogistes au Canada", in *Les Cahiers des Dix* (1948), which describes in considerable detail the progress of genealogical research in the Dominion, both in French and in British Canada.

The sections which follow deal with Quebec, Ontario, and Nova Scotia. For a succinct account of repositories of vital records, probate records, etc., in the other Canadian provinces, the North West Territories, and Yukon Territory, see Noel C. Stevenson's *Search and Research* (2nd ed., 1959), pp 313-323.

B. QUEBEC

Origins of the Civil State [1]

The institution of the civil state dates from modern times. The ancients, even the Greeks and Romans, were hardly concerned with it. No one ascertained marriages and deaths, although they inscribed the birth of the children of free citizens. In the course of the Christian Middle Ages, nothing subsisted of this custom and nothing had filled its place. About 1400 appeared the parish registers of the Catholic clergy. They took the place of the civil state, in France, until the Revolution. But still, it was only a matter of baptismal registers, the Church having need of them in order to apply the canonical laws which prohibited marriages among relatives.

A short time after appeared registers of marriages and deaths, but rather in the form of account books of the parish priests. It is only later, under Francis I, that the royal ordinance of Villers-Cotteret stipulated, in 1539, the keeping of registers of death and birth, and only in 1579, under Henry III, following the recommendations of the Council of Trent,

---

[1] *Cf.* Hervé Roch, *Actes et registres de l'État civil et rectification* (Montréal, 1949); Mgr. Olivier Maurault, "Le premier registre de l'État civil de Montréal", in *Les Cahiers des Dix*, no. 23, 1958.

the ordinance of Blois demanded the careful maintenance of marriage registers.

Other ordinances followed: First, that of a Paris synod in 1627, prescribing the signatures of priests, godfathers and godmothers and prohibiting erasures and excessive charges; then, in 1667, that of Louis XIV requiring the mention, in burial records, of the date of death and, in baptismal records, of the date of birth, and recommending the maintenance in duplicate of the registers; finally, the judgment of Chancellor d'Aguesseau, under Louis XV, in 1736, rigorously imposing this time the transcription of the records in two original or identical registers initialed by the royal judge, of which one remained in the church and the other was to be deposited each year in the registrar's office of the community.

The Registers of the Civil State in New France

New France and Acadia were submitted to these prescriptions. This system was continued, among the Roman Catholics, after the cession of Canada to England, the French civil laws having moreover been guaranteed by the Treaty of Paris of 1763.

The arrival of the English and other immigrants necessitated the application of new arrangements, in a manner to benefit the Protestant churches. Thus, in 1795, a first organic law imposed on all Protestant churches or congregations of the Province of Quebec the obligation to maintain two registers, as was the practice among the Roman Catholics. Codified in 1861 in the Revised Statutes of Lower Canada, that law has become, with certain modifications, the second Title of the First Book of the Civil Code of the Province of Quebec, and it presently embraces all of the congregations of the United Church of England, Scotland, and Ireland, as well as of all other religious societies or cults.

Quebec, founded by Samuel Champlain in 1608, should have had its registers of baptisms, marriages and burials from that epoch. But, on 15 June 1640, a fire destroyed the Chapel of Nôtre-Dame-de-Recouvrance, and the registers of the civil state were burned in that catastrophe.

Trois-Rivières (Three Rivers), founded in 1634, still possesses, of its first registers, those of burials since 1634; of baptisms since 1635; and of marriages from 1654.

On 17 May 1642, Paul de Chomedey, Sieur de Maisonneuve, debarked at Montreal with fifty colonists. Immediately, the first register of the civil state for births was begun; it covers the years 1642-1668. That of marriages began in 1647 and continued until 1670. And the first register of burials extended without interruption for every year from 1643 to 1680.

Formerly the inhabited part of the country was divided into three distinct governments, that of Quebec having at its head, the governor general, and those of Trois-Rivières and Montreal having respectively their own governors, appointed by the King of France. Until the conquest of 1760, the duplicates of the parish registers of the colony were preserved in the three governments, except those of the upper country— Detroit, Michillimackinac, Fort de Chartres, the outposts of St. Joseph, St. Philippe, Vincennes, Kaskaskia, etc. Since then, here and there floods, humidity, fires, even rats and mice have destroyed the registers. Thus, the genealogist is sometimes halted in his researches by the gaps in the church or the registrar's office, often in both places at the same time. As to the registers of Acadia,[2] today known as Nova Scotia, they disappeared since the expulsion of the Acadians, in 1755, and that is why it is so difficult to trace the lines of deported Acadian families, which we pick up again in the Provinces of Quebec and New Brunswick, in Louisiana and in Maine and on the Coasts of New England. It is an arduous task and one which leads to feeble results.

Today, the Province of Quebec is divided into 28 judicial districts, each with a chief town where are deposited the copies of the parish registers of all the churches—Catholic, Protestant, and others—and it is there that genealogists should

---

[2] An abstract of the parish registers and of the civil state relative to the dispossessed Acadians in the Archives of Canada, at Ottawa, has been made by Roger Comeau and published in the *Mémoires de la Société généalogique canadienne-française*, vol. 7, pp. 185-189.

attempt their first researches, later completing them in the parishes where are preserved the original registers in the registrar's offices.

Following is a list of these judicial districts which correspond to the Bureaus of Vital Statistics in the United States and in the other Provinces of the Dominion of Canada:[3]

Names	Chief Towns	Electoral Districts
Abitibi	Amos	Abitibi-Est and territories.
Arthabaska	Arthabaska	Part of Arthabaska, Megantic, Drummond.
Beauce	St. Joseph-de-Beauce	Beauce, Dorchester, part of Frontenac.
Beauharnois	Valleyfield	Beauharnois, Châteauguay, Huntingdon
Bedford	Sweetsburg	Missisquoi, Shefford.
Bonaventure	New Carlisle	Bonaventure.
Chicoutimi	Chicoutimi	Chicoutimi and the territory of Mistassini.
Gaspé	Percé	Gaspé, Îles-de-la-Madeleine.
Hull	Hull	Hull (except the north), Papineau (except the northwest).
Iberville	St. Jean	Iberville, St. Jean, Napierville.
Joliette	Joliette	Berthier, L'Assomption, Joliette, part of Montcalm, part of Maskinongé.
Kamouraska	Rivière-du-Loup	Kamouraska, Témiscouata.
Labelle or Montcalm	Mont-Laurier	Labelle, part of Papineau, part of Hull, and the non-organized territories.
Montmagny	Montmagny	Bellechasse, L'Islet, Montmagny.

[3] *Revised Statutes of the Province of Quebec*, 1941, Chapter XV.

Names	Chief Towns	Electoral Districts
Montréal	Montréal	Chambly, Hochelaga, Jacques-Cartier, La Prairie, Laval, Soulanges, Vaudreuil, part of Verchères and the city of Montréal.
Nicolet	Nicolet	Part of Nicolet.
Pontiac	Campbell's Bay	Pontiac.
Québec	Québec	Québec-Est Québec-Centre, Québec-Ouest, Saint-Sauveur, Lévis, Lotbinière, Montmorency, Portneuf, Beaumont-village, St. Octave-de-Dosquet.
Richelieu	Sorel	Richelieu, Yamaska, part of Verchères.
Rimouski	Rimouski	Rimouski, Matane, Matapédia.
Roberval	Roberval	Lac-Saint-Jean.
Rouyn Noranda	Rouyn	Abitibi-Ouest and territories.
Saguenay	La Malbaie (Murray Bay)	Charlevoix, Saguenay.
St. François	Sherbrooke	Compton, Richmond, Stanstead, Wolfe, Sherbrooke, part of Frontenac, part of Arthabaska.
St. Hyacinthe	St. Hyacinthe	Bagot, Rouville, St. Hyacinthe.
Terrebonne	St. Jérôme	Argenteuil, Terrebonne, Deux-Montagnes.
Trois-Rivières	Trois-Rivières	Champlain, St. Maurice, Trois-Rivières, part of Maskinonge.
Témiscamingue	Ville-Marie	Témiscamingue and territories.

As a complement to this list, one may consult with profit the *Dictionnaire historique et géographique des paroisses, missions et municipalités de la Province de Québec,* by Hormisdas Magnan (1925), the work of C.-E. Deschamps entitled *Municipalités et paroisses dans la Province de Québec* (1896), and *Canada ecclésiastique* which gives the date of the canonical erection of each parish.

The Judicial Archives of the District of Montreal [4]

The old *Palais de Justice* (Palace of Justice), where are deposited the judicial archives of the District of Montreal, shelters the most important, the most considerable, and the richest storehouse of notarial acts and parish registers of the Province of Quebec. There are heaped up in the basement, in the vaults, in files and on shelves filled with documents, registers, dossiers, and maps of all sorts.

Preserved almost since the foundation of Montreal, these archives represent extremely precious assets for the genealogist. They comprise registers and dossiers of tribunals, registers of the civil state, notarial files, lawsuits, and land surveys for Montreal, Île Jésus, and the surrounding parishes.

In the City of Montreal there are now 175 Catholic parishes, of which the registers of the oldest, Nôtre-Dame, began in 1642. The establishment of parishes or religious denominations around Montreal followed: Boucherville, Contrecoeur, Sault-Saint-Louis, vulgo Caughnawaga, all founded in 1667-68. In 1864, when Nôtre-Dame Parish was divided, additional parishes in the City of Montreal appeared: St. Vincent-de-Paul, Ste. Brigide, St. Pierre, etc. and from 33 parishes existing in 1874 the Diocese of Montreal now has in the City nearly 175 parishes or churches, and about 60 others on Isle Jesus and vicinity.

A detailed inventory of the registers of the Civil State preserved in the files of the Judicial Archives of the District of Quebec was published by Pierre-Georges Roy in 1921.

---

[4] For the Judicial Archives of Montreal, see E.-Z. Massicotte, *Bulletin des recherches historiques,* vol. 32, 1926; Maréchal Nantel, *La Revue du Barreau,* Montreal, Feb. 1946.

Research Permits and Fees

Any person of Canadian or American origin wishing to consult the registers of the civil state in the Province of Quebec must first fulfill a formality. A permit for research purposes will be accorded him if he requests it in writing to the Department of the Procuror General (Département du Procureur Général), at the Hôtel du Gouvernement, Quebec, specifying the type of researches he desires to make and at what judicial office these researches will be made. Once in possession of this permit, which will serve as a pass for him, the researcher can present himself at the registrar's office where the deputy prothonotary or the archivist or his assistant will be pleased to assist him in the mazes of his archives.

If it is a matter of making researches in the registers of a parish church, the researcher must solicit authorization from the priest *(curé)*. For those who desire to obtain by correspondence copies of acts of baptisms, marriages or burials, the fees are ordinarily $1.00 per act (record), whether in the archives of the tribunals or in the churches. A document is authenticated by the seal of the parish or the tribunal.

Manuscript Sources

Sources of genealogical and historical documentation may be classified in two distinct divisions: (1) Manuscript sources, and (2), printed sources, i. e., books and brochures.

The manuscript sources are further subdivided into six categories, as follows:

(1) Registers of baptisms, marriages and burials of the civil state; registers of confirmation. It is noted that the registers of adjuration, if they really existed under the French regime, have disappeared from the archives.

(2) The notarial files: Marriage contracts, donations, wills, concessions, sales, inventories, engagements of servants, etc. The files of deceased notaries or those who no longer practice are generally deposited in the office of the judicial district.[5]

---

[5] A compilation concerning practicing notaries and notaries whose files have been deposited in the vaults of the different judicial districts of the Province of Quebec was published under the title, *Tableau de l'Ordre des notaires de la Province de Quebec* (Montreal, 1942).

(3) Administrative dossiers deposited in the Provincial Archives at Quebec.

(4) Documents deposited in the Archives of Canada at Ottawa.

(5) French records: National Archives at Paris; the d' Hozier collection; the archives of the Colonies and of the departments of War and the Navy; departmental or communal archives; notarial minutes at La Rochelle and other towns. (See the chapter on France.)

(6) Private manuscripts: Archives of communities, hospitals, archbishoprics, bishoprics, parishes, seminaries; archives of historical and other societies; archives of libraries and museums; family archives.

The Archives of the Province of Quebec.[6]—The principal series of documents of the French regime preserved in the Provincial Archives of Quebec are: The judgments and deliberations of the Sovereign Council, 1663-1760; the insinuations of the Sovereign Council; the papers of various governmental departments of the Province (such as the Admiralty); an important collection of judical, notarial, etc., pieces, collected by Philéas Gagnon and comprising 6,000 pieces; registers of permits to travel to the West;[7] judicial dossiers; military documents; and many others.

Registers and Marriage Records in the Archives of Canada. —The Archives of the Dominion of Canada at Ottawa contain, in addition to a great series of public documents, original parish registers and transcripts of registers, including those of Pontchartrain de Détroit, 1703-1818 (2 vols.); the Illinois and Arkansas country—Nôtre-Dame de l'Immaculée-Conception, Chartres, Kaskaskia, St. Philippe, St. Joseph (Michigan), 1695-1834 (2 vols.); St. Ignace de Michillimackinac, 1695-

---

[6] Cf. Pierre-Georges Roy, *Les Archives de la Province de Québec et nos inventaires*, Montreal, 1926; Fernand Ouellet, *L'Histoire des Archives du Gouvernement en Nouvelle-France*, Quebec, 1958.

[7] A list of these permits to travel in the West for the years 1670-1821 will be found in the *Rapports de l'Archiviste de la Province de Québec*, 1921-22, 1929-30, 1930-31, 1942-43, 1943-44, 1944-45, 1945-46.

1790; and three Louisiana parishes, of which the earliest, that of Mobile, covers the years 1704-64.

The Dominion Archives has indexes of marriages for a large number of Roman Catholic and some Anglican and Presbyterian churches, as well as the Indian mission at St. Régis. The oldest marriage record index is that of the Boucherville church, 1677-1739. The Archives also possesses indexes of marriage records of the old families of Detroit for the period 1710-83.

Printed Sources

The printed sources can be divided into numerous categories, such as the publications of the Archives of Canada and of the Provincial Archives of Quebec; the censuses; genealogical dictionaries; family genealogies; parish monographs, etc.

Publications of the Archives of Canada.—The first reviews of the activities of the Archives of Canada appeared in the Sessional Papers, from 1872 to 1881. Beginning in 1882, they were the subject of the more important *Annual Reports,* printed in French and English. With the new Archivist, Mr. Kaye Lamb, the formula was modified in 1950. About twenty provisional inventories of the different classes of manuscripts have been published and have proved to be very useful.

The *Annual Reports,* published almost without interruption from 1882 to 1949, form about 50 volumes; those from 1884 to 1896 are devoted to the famous Haldimand collection of documents; the two volumes of 1905 contain Placide Gaudet's *Généalogies acadiennes, the Généalogies des familles de l'Île d' Orléans,* by Abbé Forgues, and *Généalogies de la Beauce,* by Abbé Beaumont.

Publications of the Provincial Archives of Quebec.—The principal publications of the Archives of the Province of Quebec include the Archivist's *Rapports* (Reports) in 39 annual volumes, published since 1920 by Pierre-Georges Roy and continued by his son, Antoine Roy, who succeeded him as Archivist in 1947; *Inventaire d'une collection de pièces judicaires, notariales,* etc. (2 vols., 1917); *Lettres de noblesse, généalogies, erections de comtés et baronnies insinuées par le*

Conseil souverain de la Nouvelle-France (2 vols., 1920); *Inventaire des Testaments, Donations, et Inventaires du régime français* (3 vols., 1941); *Inventaire des Greffes des notaires du régime français* (18 vols., 1942-57); and *Inventaire des Contrats de Mariages du régime français* (6 vols., 1937-38).

Before the establishment of the Bureau of Archives by Pierre-Georges Roy in 1920, the government of Lower Canada (1791-1840), then that of the Union (1841-1867), and finally that of the present Province of Quebec, published a number of important works, including: *Edits, ordonnances royaux, déclarations et arrêts du conseil d'Etat du Roi concernant le Canada* (2 vols., 1803-6); *Jugements et Délibérations du Conseil Souverain de la Nouvelle-France* (6 vols., 1885); and *Lists of Lands granted by the Crown in the Province of Quebec, from 1763 to 1890* (1891).

The Censuses

The censuses are of extreme importance in genealogical research in French Canada, because they complete the gaps in many cases, enable one to discover new figures in the ancestral line, and finally, often swarm with very useful information.

The first enumeration was made in New France in 1666. It was followed by those of 1667 and 1681. They were printed in Benjamin Sulte's *Histoire des Canadiens français*, vols. IV-V. The census of 1666 is also found in the *Rapport de l'Archiviste de la Province de Québec* for 1935-36.

The census of the town of Quebec for 1716, street for street, house for house, was published by Abbé L. Beaudet in 1887. Other census records, for the towns of Quebec, Montreal, and Trois-Rivières were published in the *Rapports de l'Archiviste de la Province de Québec* for 1925-26, 1936-37, 1939-40, 1946-47, and 1948-49. An unedited census of Montreal of 1741, found in the Judicial Archives there, was published with commentary by E.-Z. Massicotte in the *Mémoires de la Société royale du Canada*, in 1921.

Mgr. Tanguay's Genealogical Dictionary

In French Canada, as in the United States, genealogical

studies have developed considerably during the last half century. The reason for this is undoubtedly that the Province of Quebec is the only part of America where almost every family can retrace its ascendance, from sons to father, to the first ancestor who came from Europe.

This colossal work was undertaken in 1865 by Abbé (later Monsignor) Cyprien Tanguay (1819-1902). His *Dictionnaire généalogique des familles canadiennes* (7 vols., 1871-90) gives us today the results of the formidable inquiry which he pursued for more than 20 years among the innumerable registers of the Quebec parishes. It is one of the greatest works in this particular field of historical study. Although there were others before him who were interested in the study of family histories, it is correct to say that Mgr. Tanguay was the incontestable father of genealogical studies in French Canada. He gave the tone and the impetus to this dry science an extreme importance for history.

While thus bestowing upon Mgr. Tanguay's fine work a well-merited commendation, it must be stated at the same time that the *Dictionnaire*, for long accepted everywhere with confidence, contains errors, gaps, defects of arrangement as numerous as its genealogical accounts. Mgr. Tanguay failed to notice, in whole or in part, registers of several parishes, especially in the Montreal region. In his calculation of missing birth dates, he utilized the censuses of 1666 and 1681, but not that of 1667, which is considered much more exact. He very frequently installs in a family people who were by no means related. He gives as the first generation in Canada some couples who never came here. The date which he assigns to the burial is often that of the death. The *Dictionnaire's* alphabetical principle rests on the men's names. Thus, in order to find the names of women, it is necessary to consult all of the volumes, page by page.

Because of the typographical errors and multiple mistakes in the *Dictionnaire*, especially in the early period down to 1700, a number of persons and organizations since 1935 have attempted to revise the work, but the several projects, for one reason or another, have been abandoned. One of these,

Père Archange Godbout, attempted a resumption of the first volume of the *Dictionnaire*, but on a plan totally different from the old one, under the title of *Nos Ancêtres au XVIIe siècle* (Our Ancestors in the 17th Century). But he succeeded in publishing only the letters A and B.

Mgr. Tanguay's Continuators

The gigantic work inaugurated by Mgr. Tanguay has been completed up to a certain point by later researchers. Important contributions in the field of French-Canadian genealogy have been made by the Sulpician, François Daniel, author of the *Histoire des grandes familles françaises au Canada* (1867); Pierre-Georges Roy, who published no fewer than 50 family studies from 1901 to 1941; Pascal Poirier and Placide Gaudet, who specialized in Acadian genealogy; the indefatigable Frère Eloi-Gérard Talbot, compiler of marriage records of Beauce, Dorchester and Frontenac Counties (11 vols., 1949-55); and others far too numerous to name in the present chapter.

Specialized periodicals devoted solely to Canadian genealogy are rather rare. At Montreal is published the excellent *Mémoires de la Société généalogique canadienne-française*, which has appeared since January 1944. In 1934, Alfréd Cambray founded at Cap-de-la-Madeleine the *Revue d'histoire et de généalogie*, but it has had an ephemeral existence.

* * * * *

We have sketched briefly the genealogical resources and named some of the principal genealogists in the Province of Quebec. The richness and fullness of the archives, at Quebec as well as at Ottawa, the records of the judicial archives at Montreal, Quebec, and Trois-Rivières, are invaluable, especially those of the French regime. By their notarial files, their registers of the courts of justice and the civil state, the different classes of archives of the Province of Quebec constitute an inexhaustible mine for the historian, the genealogist, the economist, and the writer of every kind.

C. ONTARIO *

The present Province of Ontario was the western part of Quebec until the passing of the Canada (called Constitutional) Act of 1791. From 1791 to 1841 the Province was called Upper Canada. From 1841 to 1867, the Province was called Canada West, being the western half of the Province of Canada. The name of Ontario has been used since 1867.

The earliest personal records available for genealogical research in Ontario are those which have to do with land. When settlement first began in the present Province, land boards were set up to review applications. At first, the land board at Montreal carried on but when the Loyalist immigration, beginning in 1783, created a demand for more machinery, four land boards were set up in the present southern Ontario in 1788. It may be said that generally speaking the land board records have not come down to us, except in the case of those of the district of Hesse which comprised the region on the Detroit River. These records have been published in the 1905 *Report of the Public Archives of Ontario*.

After the creation of Upper Canada the land boards were superseded by the land committee of the Executive Council, which in reality was the Executive Council sitting as a committee. An immigrant who came to the Province seeking land (and practically all immigrants wanted land) might claim on three grounds: (1) as a loyalist; (2) as a settler, and (3) as a military claimant. His application took the form of a petition to be read to the committee. For genealogical purposes the petitions of Loyalists are the most useful as in their case alone was there any point in showing family relationships. The reason for this was that sons and daughters of Loyalists could claim. Therefore, if an applicant

---

* This section was prepared in 1947, when it was planned to bring out the book. Due to the pressures under which we are presently operating to publish the volume this year (1959), we were unable to submit the section to the author for a complete revision. At the time he wrote the section, the author received advice and information from Miss Helen McClung, then Provincial Archivist of Ontario, and Norman Fee, formerly Assistant Dominion Archivist. ED.

could prove his relationship to an accredited Loyalist his path was easy. When the applicant was a settler or a military claimant indication of relationship to another person served no useful purpose. The petitions for land are preserved in the Public Archives of Canada, at Ottawa.

The petition having been read, and approved, the claimant was given an Order-in-Council. This he or his agent took to the surveyor-general's office in York (now Toronto). Here the applicant received a location ticket which described the land on which he was to settle. With a copy of his Order-in-Council and his location ticket the would-be settler went to the land agent nearest to his location and found out where to go. Once settled on his land the settler set out to fulfill his settlement duties. These consisted of clearing and fencing a certain number of acres, building a log house, and clearing a certain length of road. With his settlement duties performed the settler reported to a nearby justice of the peace who inspected the improvements and gave a certificate.

Armed with his Order-in-Council, his location ticket, and certificate of settlement duties performed, the settler or his agent returned to the Crown Lands Department where a patent was issued. This patent, or deed, in the early years was made of vellum, to which a large seal of wax was attached by a piece of tape.

When the patent was issued, three copies were made, one went to the settler, one went to the local registry office, and one remained with the Crown Lands Department, where it was given a number and was bound in the Domesday Book. The date of the patent had little if any relationship to the date of original settlement. A settler might perform his settlement duties in a few months or several years.

Now, the question may be asked, "Where are all the records covering the transactions described?" The petitions, as already stated, are in the Public Archives of Canada in Ottawa, but the key to these is to be found in the minutes of the land committee of the Executive Council. These minutes are called Land Books and are designated by letter: Land Book C or Land Book D, etc. The originals are in the Public Archives of Canada and clear photostatic copies are preserved in the Archives of Ontario. Each volume has all names indexed to the first letter. Consequently, searches through these volumes are tedious but feasible. The minutes give the date of the Order-in-Council, the kind of claimant, whether U. E. (United Empire, i. e. Loyalist), Military, or Settler. If a son or daughter of a Loyalist, the relationship will be given. Since the petitions for land are filed in date order in Ottawa, the date of the Order-in-Council, sent to the Public Archives of Canada, should produce a copy of the petition, which may or may not contain important information. Usually, the petition was a formal document, but some of the early loyalist petitions give much detail of activity in the royal cause. Incidentally, even if the petition was refused, the fact was recorded and the petition was filed as above.

The patents or deeds give little information but they do prove that a certain person lived on a certain parcel of land long enough to perform the settlement duties. The patents are listed in the Register of Patents preserved in the Crown Lands Office, Parliament Buildings, Toronto. All entries are made under township, concession, and lot; and the volumes are not indexed. Consequently, if a researcher does not know the township in which the person in whom he is interested lived, his chances of finding anything in the Register of Patents is slim. At the end of each entry in the Register is a number. This leads to the office copy of the patent preserved in the Domesday Book.

Manifestly, an index of patents would be invaluable for tracing the existence of persons, especially when, in the early days of the Province, almost every resident was a land holder. It is not generally known, but there are preserved in the office of the Provincial Secretary, Parliament Buildings, Toronto, indexes to all patents issued, whether for land or other purposes. The use of these indexes is restricted, but researchers who find themselves in Toronto can inquire about them. These indexes serve as a key to the area in which a person settled and thus limit the region of the search which, as will be shown below, must, in Ontario, generally be continued in local registry offices.

When once the crown had alienated land by issuing a patent its interest was gone. Subsequent transfers are recorded in the local registry offices. Furthermore, any search for persons who bought land from individual owners obviously must begin in a local registry office. A list of local registrars is to be found in the *Canadian Almanac* for any year. It is indexed under "Registrars of Deeds, Ontario".

Parenthetically, it might be added that there are three areas in Ontario where the crown lands records are barren. In 1826 the Canada Company was incorporated to sell one million acres of land, largely in the present county of Huron. Consequently, the first entry on any lot in this region is the original transfer from the Crown to the Canada Company. Any personal information must be taken from the first transfer from the Company to an individual. The records of the Canada Company have been transferred in recent years from the offices of the Company and the Canadian Archives to a single repository, the Provincial Archives of Ontario.

Likewise, when Great Britain acquired Canada by the treaty of Paris, 1763, individual French titles were protected. There were two seigneuries in the present Ontario, one in the neighborhood of Windsor and the other on the Ottawa River, the seigneuries of Baby and L'Orignal, respectively. Consequently, these parcels of land were never British crown land and so the first personal entry will be in the local registry office.

The clergy reserves also complicate the picture. In 1791 under the terms of the Canada Act, when a parcel of land was granted, an area equal to one-seventh of the land granted was set aside for the support of a Protestant clergy. However, these lands seem to have been leased and sold through the

Crown Lands Department and so can be treated as other crown lands.[1]

In 1805, an act was passed by the legislature of Upper Canada "to afford relief" to those persons who might be entitled to claim lands in the Province as "Heirs or Devisees of the Nominees of the Crown" in cases where no patent had been issued (45 Geo. III, chap. II). The Act was renewed several times. Manifestly, the records of the Heir and Devisee Commission set up under the Act would be of inestimable value in genealogical research for, in many cases, extensive genealogical information must have been received and passed on. But, unfortunately, the records do not seem to have been preserved.

Following the Loyalist immigration, which technically ended in 1798, and to a certain extent contemporary with it, many Americans entered Upper Canada as settlers. One colorful group was to be found in the German speaking settlers who opened up Waterloo County. Many Quakers also immigrated. Following the War of 1812, various settlements of disbanded British soldiers were set up. In the 1830's and 1840's, there was an extensive Irish immigration. In the 1850's, a second German immigration developed around the original settlement of fifty years before. These various groups fitted into the land grant picture just as did the earliest settlers and no special records were created by their presence. One exception is to be found in the records of Quaker meetings, which are preserved in the library of the University of Western Ontario. Dr. A. G. Dorland, head of the Department of History, is the official curator but manifestly cannot undertake research. Permission to use these records must be obtained from Professor Dorland.

Searches in local registry offices require a small fee for each docket. However, if the location of a person's land is known the fee is negligible as in some cases much genealogi-

---

[1] In a recent letter the author informed the editor: "Since I wrote the manuscript, a great deal of work has been done on the clergy reserves. I believe that today a student could achieve some success in looking up clergy reserve records in the Ontario Archives".

cal information may be obtained, such as death of owner, transfer to sons, and so on.

Wills have the same value in genealogical research in Ontario as they have in other places. With the exception of some early wills preserved in Osgoode Hall, Toronto, all wills are filed with the surrogate registrar in the county town. The *Canadian Almanac* lists surrogate registrars. The index under "Registrars, Surrogate, Ontario" shows where to look.

Assessment rolls are invaluable for genealogical research but, unfortunately, relatively few have been preserved. The Public Archives of Ontario possesses rolls for many of the townships of Eastern Ontario, the Hamilton Public Library has some rolls for certain townships in Wentworth County, and the library of the University of Western Ontario has some of the rolls of the townships of Huron County. These rolls give much information such as acres cleared and uncleared, cattle, horses, type of house and best of all, children under 16 and over 16, with the sex. In some cases, Christian names are given.

The Public Archives of Canada has the early census up to and including the year 1871. They are retained in the same condition in which they were originally filed, i. e., by provinces, counties, townships and localities. It is not very difficult to make a search provided you know the name of the person and the locality in which that person lived.[2]

Parish registers containing records of births, marriages and deaths are few and far between. Some are preserved in the Public Archives of Ontario, or the synod offices of various Church of England dioceses and churches. Several have been printed in the *Papers and Records* of the Ontario Historical Society.

When a search for an individual has narrowed down to a region, frequently the researcher is forced to work through

---

[2] The Public Archives of Canada has microfilmed the early census records which they possess, and consequently students now can consult them with very little difficulty. The Church of Jesus Christ of Latter Day Saints has microfilmed a great mass of genealogical records in Ontario.

miscellaneous material. Publications of local historical societies cannot be ignored. The Niagara Historical Society, particularly, in its series of publications, has printed biographical material and has two series of records copied from gravestones. As in other regions, various municipal, county, and provincial directories, historical atlases, etc., give names. The appendices to the *Journals of Upper Canada* have some lists of patents granted in the 1830's.

Newspaper files are extremely broken but if an early newspaper file is available a researcher can expect to find the same kind of records as he would find in, say, a file of a newspaper in northern New York of the corresponding period.

Official registration of births, marriages, and deaths did not begin in Ontario until 1869 (with the exception of some official lists of marriages in the 1850's) a fact which forces persons interested in genealogical research to turn to all kinds of sources to find what they want. Request for information subsequent to 1869 should be addressed to the Registrar General, Parliament Buildings, Toronto, Canada. Here are such of the marriage lists referred to above as have been preserved; they are indexed.

D. NOVA SCOTIA AND NEW BRUNSWICK

These two Canadian Provinces were formerly one—Nova Scotia, which had the distinction of being settled by the people of two nationalities, the French and the British. The French made their first settlement as early as 1605 but it was not until 1675 that they made permanent settlements which flourished until 1755 when the Acadians were driven or carried out of the Province. At that time, it is estimated that there were at least 10,000 inhabitants and most of them were deported, but some who hid in the forest survived and their descendants are still to be found in both Provinces.

In 1758, a proclamation was issued from Halifax by Gov. Lawrence inviting New Englanders to come and settle on the abandoned farms. One year later another proclamation was issued giving all Protestants the right to worship as they pleased. This proclamation which was sent all over New England and to many of the other colonies, started a migration from many points, and by 1775 there were nearly 18,000 inhabitants, some from as far south as Virginia. At the time of the War of the Revolution a large number of these people sided with the United States and returned, but many remained although they generally took a very small part in the war.

After the war, the Loyalists were brought here, about 10,000 arriving at Saint John, many others being scattered all over the Province. Owing to the difficulties in communicating with Halifax, it was decided in 1784 to found a new province, New Brunswick, with the dividing line running through the Chignecto Isthmus.

The genealogical searcher will have to use great care as there are many duplicates of names, for there were more migrations than the ones mentioned. In 1773/4 a large number of families from Yorkshire came here and besides these there were smaller migrations of Scottish, Irish and Scotch-Irish.

If the searcher knows that the ancestor was one of the first settlers, it is advisable to start with the Land Office at Halifax where there are many lists of men who were granted land. The list of grantees of the town of Horton comprises 133 names while that of Yarmouth on the other hand is divided into groups. This list contains the names of 96 New Englanders, 16 from Halifax, 10 from Philadelphia, and 4 from London. A great many of the towns were platted and with the list and plat it is easy to find the location of the original land of the grantee. To be sure, many of these men did not stay or else, not complying with the regulations of the Land Office about clearing a certain amount of land each year, their land was escheated.

After completing the search at the Land Office it is best to visit the Nova Scotia Archives situated on the campus of Dalhousie University at Halifax. Here is to be found not only the government archives but also a great deal of material for the genealogist. Many of the church records

NOVA SCOTIA AND NEW BRUNSWICK

have been deposited here, some of them as old as the settlement in which the church was situated. There are county and family histories in the library as well as a number of papers written by the staff. On file is what is left of the census records taken in 1770, four towns being included. Some of the other records of towns are there, in varying dates, up to 1800. Later census records are very scarce. There is also a large file of Nova Scotia newspapers in this building.

The Board of Vital Statistics is also in Halifax. The marriage records begin as early as 1763 but are incomplete up to 1864. The birth and death records began in 1864 but were discontinued from 1876 to 1908. The approximate date and the name of the county are necessary for a search.

The Land Office of New Brunswick is at Fredericton, where there are petitions for land and a large number of plats. There are also some deeds on file here.

The Archives of New Brunswick are at Saint John, but it is probable that the great fire of 1877 destroyed many of the early papers.

The Vital Records of New Brunswick do not commence until 1920. Although marriage records were made much earlier they are unfiled and unindexed, being stored away in different parts of the Province. The marriage records of Saint John which were not destroyed by the fire of 1877 are in the custody of B. L. Gerrow, Attorney, Saint John.

The land and probate records of both provinces are to be found in the county seats and differ very little from those of this country. There is a difference which any one from the United States will notice and that is the charge for searching the records. This varies with the different counties, sometimes it is a fixed charge and sometimes a slight charge by the hour.

Most of the churches have their marriage records, some of them stored in the vault of the county clerk.

Cemeteries are everywhere and the stones are generally in good condition. In some of the farm and small cemeteries where there has been little care the stones are down and one must search in the deep grass for them.

Anyone who has occasion to search around the Chignecto Isthmus should visit Fort Beausejour as the museum of that place has many family records and papers as well as the printed genealogies of many of the families of that district.

In searching through these two provinces do not be afraid to ask questions of the people. The name of the man to whom the question is put may be the same; though he descends from another ancestor the chances are that he can set you on the right track. He may even bring out his family Bible or history and show just where you are right or wrong. Most of the people in both provinces are anxious to accommodate and help the stranger.

For the benefit of those interested in Nova Scotia families who are unable to go to Nova Scotia to work in the original records, the following references to sources available in the United States covering the period prior to the Revolution will be of interest.

The most valuable source is the series of *Reports* of the Public Archives of Nova Scotia. *Nova Scotia Archives*, vol. I (1860), lists the original settlers of Halifax, giving name, "quality", children and servants, and regiment or ship if the settler was a former soldier or sailor. It also contains a list of those who settled in the vicinity of Halifax between 1749 and 1752.

For the French families that remained after the deportation, either because they had taken the oath of allegiance to the English Crown, or were absent or "escaped" when the deportation was made, the first reference to consult is "Acadian Genealogy and Notes", in the *Report of the Dominion Archives, 1905,* vol. II.

Good short historical accounts of the New England settlements and those financed by Philadelphia merchants are "Acadia: The Pre-Loyalist Migration and the Philadelphia Plantation", by W. O. Sawtelle, in the *Pennsylvania Magazine of History and Biography*, vol. 51; "The Rhode Island Emigration to Nova Scotia", by R. G. Huling, in the *Narra-*

gansett Historical Register, vol. 7, and "Rhode Island Settlers on French Lands in Nova Scotia in 1760 and 1761", by A.W.H. Eaton, in *Americana,* Vol. X. In addition to the areas indicated in the titles, these articles give many names of the settlers of the "New England Townships" of Horton and Cornwallis.

Census reports for many of the counties during the 1770-1775 period are printed in the *Report of the Board of Trustees of the Public Archives of Nova Scotia for the year 1934.* The same *Report* for 1935 gives the German settlers at Lunenburg.

The *Collections of the Nova Scotia Historical Society* contain much of interest, for example: vol. 9 tells of the Irish at Onslow, vol. 13 the Yorkshire migration at Chignecto, vol. 15 the English in Cumberland, etc.

The New England Townships in Nova Scotia kept vital records which, though not wholly complete, are of first importance. Either originals or transcripts are in Halifax, but also originals or transcripts are in the Dominion Archives at Ottawa, and transcripts, more or less complete, of those of Horton, Cornwallis, Falmouth, Windsor, and Newport are in the Eaton Collection in the New England Historic Genealogical Society in Boston.

Parish records of Annapolis Royal and copies of many tombstones are in William Inglis Morse's *Gravestones of Acadie.*

During the Revolution, many of the New England settlers sided with the Colonies and returned, leaving all their possessions behind them. After the close of the war, those who applied were granted lands in Maine and Ohio as compensation for their losses. For lists of these, see the *Bangor Historical Magazine,* vol. 9, and *American State Papers; Public Lands,* Vol. I.

The Crowell Collection in the New England Historic Genealogical Society in Boston contains many complete pedigrees and sketches of New England families that went to Nova

Scotia, many of which were printed a half century ago in various Nova Scotia newspapers.

A comprehensive bibliography of Nova Scotia prior to 1783, divided according to unpublished materials, published primary records, and secondary sources, is that in John Bartlet Brebner's *The Neutral Yankees of Nova Scotia*. Many of the historical and biographical articles listed contain much genealogical information.

Additional printed materials may be located by reference to the *Index to the Writings on American History, 1902-1940*, under "Nova Scotia", "New Brunswick", and "Loyalists". With respect to the latter, do not overlook the Loyalist Claims in the *Second Report of the Bureau of Archives of the Province of Ontario, 1904*. (Also of interest will be the description of "Records of the American Loyalist Claims in the Public Record Office", by Roger H. Ellis, in *The Genealogists' Magazine*, September and December 1957 and March 1958.)

Part 4

PRE-AMERICAN ANCESTRY

CHAPTER I

FEUDAL GENEALOGY

Feudal Genealogy Defined

Feudal Genealogy deals with the genealogy of those families which held their lands by frank tenure, that is by knights' service, sergeanty, thanage, cornage, etc., between 1086, when the Domesday Book was compiled, as only a few English pedigrees can be traced back of this date, and the great Subsidy of 15 Henry VIII (1523/4), which has been happily described as the "Domesday Book of the Middle Classes". It is further to be observed that in feudal genealogy it is seldom possible to obtain, save in the case of a few of the greatest families, a complete list of the younger sons and of the daughters, as a result of the law of primogeniture. While it is true that a great many of these can be placed, and descents from cadets who, as was common, received fees which their mother had inherited, or who had made a marriage with an heiress or obtained eminence in the law or as great merchants, can in many instances be fully proved, yet, as a rule, it is only the line of the eldest son and heir which can be traced. Consequently all descents from younger sons should be carefully scrutinized to determine the adequacy of the proof offered. Although in some cases, when manor court rolls (which are private records) exist, pedigrees of the lower social classes may be compiled for a few generations (cf. also *The Genealogists' Magazine,* Vol. VI, p. 306 sq.), nevertheless continuous pedigrees down to today can seldom be compiled. Owing to the constant intermixture of the classes, a peculiar feature of English mediaeval society, the blood of the feudal families is now widely diffused among all classes in England and among Americans of English descent.

Record Sources

The outstanding feature of feudal genealogy is that, while the records upon which it is based are most voluminous, they are of an entirely different sort from those employed for the construction of pedigrees from the sixteenth century onwards. As in all genealogical work, the descent of land is the fundamental base, but while the genealogist of later periods relies largely upon wills, deeds, parish registers, and records of chancery suits as his principal sources, the mediaeval genealogist finds these of little use, with the exception of deeds or charters. Parish registers do not exist prior to 1538, and while the regular series of wills commence at the end of the fourteenth century, these are meagre in number and content, except in a few counties, such as Kent and Suffolk, prior to the time of Henry VIII. The chancery suits, which commence about the same time, are valuable for the fifteenth century, but they are not as numerous as they become later.

The records relied upon in the feudal period vary in value and volume in the different centuries. The twelfth century, roughly the period from Domesday to the loss of Normandy (1204), is the most difficult period to bridge in feudal work, owing to the paucity of the public records prior to the end of the century. Many pedigrees, which can be traced to this time, end in the return of 1166. With the latter part of the reign of Richard I and the commencement of the reign of King John (about 1197-1205), the great mass of public records preserved in the Public Record Office at London commences. These are greatly superior to similar records on the Continent and render the thirteenth and fourteenth centuries the best for record searching in our period. The fifteenth century is marked by a decrease in the volume and value of these records, because of the national decline which attended the loss of the French provinces, the Wars of the Roses, and the social confusion which accompanied the end of the feudal period. In this century, the chancery cases and wills begin to be of use as do the valuable but little known Pardon Rolls.

The Twelfth Century

England has the unique good fortune to possess in the Domesday Book an almost complete list of the landowners, both tenants in chief and undertenants, arranged geographically, rather than feudally. This great inquest, compiled for taxation purposes, is the starting point of English feudal genealogy. This has been printed by the British Record Commission. As already stated, from Domesday down to the close of the 12th century, the public records are meagre. Surviving are partial inquests for Leicestershire, Northamptonshire, and Lincolnshire, made in the reign of Henry I, but there is no general return until the return of 12 Henry II (1166); this is arranged feudally by the cartae of the tenants in chief and their undertenants, rather than geographically. This return exists in the *Liber Niger* printed in the 18th century by Hearne and in the Great Red Book of the Exchequer, which contains this and later inquisitions, such as that of 1212. It has been printed in the Rolls Series and was edited by the late Hubert Hall. As this edition is not wholly accurate, it should be used in conjunction with Dr. J. Horace Round's criticism of it. The other great series of public records which commence in this period, are the Pipe Rolls which record, year by year, the money due the Royal Exchequer. These commence in 1154, with one previous roll, that of 31 Henry I (1130). Both these and the inquisitions above noted are indispensable to the genealogist of this period.

The most important source of genealogical information for this period in England, as on the Continent, are the Monastic Cartularies or private registries of deeds, compiled by the various monastic houses, and such original deeds or charters as have come down to us. These give considerable genealogical information as to the families of the donors and are usually followed by later confirmations by the donor's heirs. The list of witnesses in these charters are of great value as they usually are witnessed by the relatives and tenants of the donor or by his overlord. Although usually undated, their date can generally be approximated from internal evidence, a process which requires considerable skill. As these cartularies fell into private hands in the 16th century many have been lost in the succeeding centuries, but a vast number of them still survive. The great collection of copies made in the 17th century by Garter Dugdale and Roger Dodsworth were printed by Dugdale in 1682 in his *Monasticon Anglicanum,* a new and larger edition of which was printed in the last century. The Public Record Office contains a tremendous number of original charters for the entire feudal period and has printed eight or nine volumes of abstracts of these, but of course the series is as yet incomplete. A great many of the monastic cartularies have been printed by the various local antiquarian societies and others, but the majority of them are not as yet in print. Many of them are in the great collections of mediaeval manuscripts and records at the British Museum, such as the Cottonian Library and the Harleian Collections. The cartularies are the great source for feudal genealogy for the 12th century and are of great use in the 13th, after which their value to the genealogist decreases as the period of donations to the religious houses ended, generally speaking, toward the close of the latter century. With these and other records, pedigrees can be carried back to the tenant in Domesday, but such pedigrees are the exception rather than the rule. A great number of pedigrees can be traced only into the 12th century.

The Succeeding Centuries

With the commencement of the 13th century, the great mass of the public records preserved in the Public Record Office commences. Adequate abstracts of many of these are in print for the 13th and part of the 14th centuries, as the Record Commission and, after them, the Public Record Office, have been engaged in their publication for well over one hundred years. To list all classes of these records would be impossible in a short sketch like the present one, and notice will be confined to a few of the more important records, genealogically speaking.

THE FEET OF FINES.—These concern the transfer of lands. They commence in 1197.

THE PATENT ROLLS.—Relating to public acts of the Crown. These are printed down to 1485.

FEUDAL GENEALOGY

THE CLOSE ROLLS.—Relating to private acts of the Crown. These are in print down to about 1440 and their publication still continues.

THE FINE ROLLS (not to be confused with the Feet of Fines).—These contain records of the fines and feudal dues owing to the Crown and are of especial use to the genealogist, as they contain records of the reliefs due from the heir upon the death of a tenant. These are published down to the latter part of the 14th century and are·still continuing.

THE CHARTER ROLLS.—These contain royal charters and Crown confirmations of previous charters, etc. These *inspeximuses* of old charters are of the utmost value, as they often set out 12th Century and other charters, which have not survived otherwise. These are printed well into the 14th century and are still continuing.

CURIA REGIS ROLLS AND ASSIZE ROLLS. These are the records of court cases. The *Curia Regis Rolls* commence with King John; in the time of Edward I, they were divided into the *Coram Rege Rolls* (i.e., criminal matters) and the Common Pleas *(De Banco Rolls)*. The suits over land are of the greatest genealogical value as the pleadings often contain pedigrees of a number of generations, sometimes as many as eight or nine. It must be remembered that these are *ex parte* statements and when they set out remote descents must be checked carefully by other contemporary records. Owing to their great volume, this valuable series of records remains uncalendared and their volume makes the cost of searching them prohibitive. To search a given period, clubs are formed and the searcher is given the names desired. The late General Wrottlesley printed a great number of pedigrees from them in *The Genealogist*, under the title "Pedigrees from the Plea Rolls". Manuscript abstracts of many of these suits made by the late eccentric antiquary, Plantagenet Harrison, are in the Legal Room at the Public Record Office. The Assize and Eyre Rolls are of like nature and a few have been printed by local societies.

THE HUNDRED ROLLS, which have been printed, commence in the time of Edward I and should be consulted.

THE QUO WARRANTO ROLLS.—These consist of inquests into various rights claimed by land owners. They commence in the reign of Edward I and often contain most valuable data. These have been printed.

THE INQUISITIONS POST MORTEM.— These are one of the most important series to a genealogist. They contain a list of fees held by a tenant in chief at his death, show how they were held, and give the name and *approximate* age of the heir. They commence in the reign of Henry III and so far have been printed down to the middle of the reign of Edward III.

INQUISITIONS.—The general inquisitions into the lands held all over the kingdom, such as Domesday, the return of 1166 and the return of 1212, were continued from time to time, and the various inquisitions, including the great one made in 1242, are contained in the Testa de Nevill, compiled in the reign of Edward I. This was printed over one hundred years ago by the Record Commission, and recently the Public Record Office has brought out a new and more accurate edition under the title of *Book of Fees*. The latter inquests have been published under the title of "Feudal Aids." These return the feudal incidents (taxes) owed at certain times. They include the return of 1284, of 1302, another of 1316, known as the *Nomina Villarum*, the one taken in 20 Edward III, as the Knighting of the Black Prince (especially good and containing the names of the predecessors in title of the tenant), and one for 1428 which, as was to be expected, is somewhat meagre.

SUBSIDY ROLLS.—These are the lists of those taxed to pay the subsidies voted by the Parliament. Commencing with the great subsidies of Edward I and ending with the poll tax of Richard II, these are useful lists of names. After the poll tax above noted no names are given, merely the amounts collected, until we reach the subsidy of 1524 referred to at the commencement of this article.

This is only a very small and imperfect list of some of the more important series of public records vital to a genealogist. The student in this field can make himself familiar with the source record material in our greater libraries, such as the Library of Congress, the Newberry Library of Chicago, the New York Public Library, the Widener Library at Harvard, the Yale University Library, and the Peabody Library in Baltimore.

Private Records

Besides the public records above noted, there are enormous collections of charters and other mediaeval documents in the private muniment rooms of various families. Abstracts of a great many of these will be found in the *Reports* of the Deputy Keeper and in the Historical Manuscripts Commission's series.

Chronicles

Besides the public and private records, the Chronicles compiled in the various monastic houses are an important source of genealogical and biographical information. The value of these, of course, varies with the writer. They can usually be relied upon for contemporary and local events. Among the outstanding chronicles may be noted Orderic Vitalis, for

England and Normandy in the 11th and early 12th centuries; Simeon of Durham, for the same period in the North of England; William of Malmesbury and Henry of Huntingdon; and for the 13th century, Matthew Paris. Many of the chronicles have been printed in the Rolls Series and the student learns to appraise them at their proper value.

Mediaeval Genealogical Compilations

The Genealogia Fundatoris, which usually appear in the cartularies of the various monastic houses must be used with *great caution* and their statements should not be relied upon, unless confirmed from other sources, as they are often quite careless compilations; of course, some are superior to others. On the other hand, the genealogies, unfortunately few in number, compiled in the mediaeval period for certain families by monastic antiquaries are usually of a high grade and were based on record evidence. The pedigrees compiled in the 15th century in Northern monastaries for the Nevills and Fitz-Hughs are especially noteworthy. The collection of pedigrees for Northern England compiled between 1480 and 1500 and printed by the Surtees Society under the title of *Visitation of the North* are of an especially high degree of accuracy and are most valuable as they cover an otherwise difficult period, the fifteenth century. On the other hand, the Visitation Pedigrees compiled by the Tudor and Stuart Heralds, with a few exceptions *must not be relied upon back of the third or fourth generation* of the person entering the descent, as the work of almost all of the antiquarians of this period was uncritical and often downright dishonest. However, the work of such men as Robert Glover, Roger Dodsworth, Camden, and Dugdale is not open to this stricture; they were antiquaries of the first rank.

Modern Sources

Much excellent work in printing record material and in compiling feudal genealogies has been done in the last hundred years with critical ability by the various local societies and by scholars of the highest standing. The works of J. Horace Round lead the way in mediaeval genealogical research and his *Peerage and Family History* and *Peerage and Pedigree* should be handbooks for the beginner in this field. His *Calendar of Documents Preserved in France,* his *Feudal England,* and his *Geoffrey de Mandeville* are especially useful. Dr. Farrer's *Early Yorkshire Charters* and his *Honors and Knights Fees* are indispensable books of reference.

The articles in *The Genealogist,* the *Miscellanea Genealogica et Heraldica,* the *Herald and Genealogist,* and *The Ancestor* are of the highest quality. The Victoria County Histories, *The Complete Peerage,* and the monumental *New Complete Peerage* are especially to be noted. Among the earlier works one should note the various county histories, which of course vary in merit, and Dugdale's *Baronage,* which is still, after three centuries, a valuable book of reference.

This account of feudal genealogy, very sketchily restricted, and condensed, touches only too briefly upon some of the most important phases of the work, but it should serve the beginner in the field as a guide to some of the more important points. It is not intended to do more. In closing, it should be noted that an ability to read mediaeval Latin, and, to some extent, Norman French, is essential to anyone who wishes to engage seriously in the construction of a feudal pedigree.

CHAPTER II

ROYAL AND NOBLE GENEALOGY

American genealogists often find it amusing to trace their ancestry beyond the settler who came from Europe and, if they are so fortunate as to find an immigrant ancestor who belonged or whose forebears belonged to the gentry, it may be possible to follow the filiation back through the ranks of the nobility to a royal family. Beginners in this field of research would do well to read an excellent article by Donald Lines Jacobus, "Royal Ancestry", in *The American Genealogist*, vol. 9. Mr. Jacobus points out that all of us have an appalling number of ancestors if we go back thirty generations, or roughly a thousand years, and that it is not unlikely that the vast majority of persons of European descent have lines from Charlemagne, but for every line of this sort they must possess thousands of lines from the freemen and serfs who were contemporary with Charlemagne. It is, of course, impossible to trace an ancestral line for a thousand years unless we do connect with royalty or the baronage, because in the earlier centuries no genealogical records were kept of the common people.

In this chapter, we shall, therefore, consider first the problems of the American genealogist who wishes to find a royal or noble ancestry, and then we shall take up the more general topic of royal and noble genealogies, especially in Europe.

It is regrettable that a good deal of nonsense has in the past been written concerning the royal and noble ancestry of a number of families, not only American but also British and continental European. As Milton Rubincam has pointed out, the Hungarian house of Esterházy used to assert that it was descended from the grandfather of Adam, the first man. Pedigrees only slightly less fabulous appear in lists of Irish, Scottish, and Welsh kings, tracing them from Biblical characters, Greek mythological figures, or both. The Tolomei family of Siena, Italy, used to claim descent from the Ptolemies of Egypt, and the Roman family of Massimo from Fabius Maximus Cunctator, who died in 203 B. C. Happily, these claims are no longer maintained. In England, it was common practice for the heralds in the 16th and 17th centuries to furnish newly created peers and others with pedigrees stretching back to 1066, which had little or no basis in fact, but which were devoutly believed to be true by members of the families concerned. A number of these utterly erroneous pedigrees appeared in early issues of the peerages by Collins, Playfair, Burke and others, and some of these claims have persisted till quite recent times. The United States also had its share of foolishness in this regard, and here we need only mention Browning's *Americans of Royal Descent*, and David Starr Jordan's *Your Family Tree*, as examples of books to be avoided because of their complete lack of critical analysis. There are, regrettably, a number of books which belong in the same category.

Sir William Dugdale (1605-1686), the great British antiquary who wrote the *Monasticon Anglicanum, Antiquities of Warwickshire,* and *Baronage of England,* deserves a tribute for possessing a critical point of view and for being the first English author of genealogies to use modern scholarly research methods. But the amount of information which Dugdale had was, of course, much less than is now available. No other British author of comparable critical abilities interested himself in the problems of royal and noble genealogy until the second half of the 19th century, when a trio appeared whose works should be known to all searchers in the field, George Edward Cokayne, J. Horace Round, and Oswald Barron. Cokayne wrote the *Complete Baronetage* and the first edition of the *Complete Peerage,* then, with the help of Vicary Gibbs and others, he commenced the splendid second edition of the *Complete Peerage,* the first volume of which was published in 1910, and the publication of which is not yet complete. Round, a great mediaevalist with mordant wit, was the author of *Geoffrey de Mandeville* (1892), *Feudal England* (1895), *Studies in Peerage and Family History* (1901),

Peerage and Pedigree (1910), and many other books and articles, in which he demolished numbers of fanciful pedigrees stretching back to 1066, which had little or no basis in fact. Oswald Barron is known chiefly as the editor of *The Ancestor*, a quarterly review published from 1902 to 1905, containing many violent though entertaining attacks on the fabulous, the fabricated, and the fraudulent genealogies of British peers and gentry. Due to the work of Cokayne, Round, Barron and their followers, recent British genealogical work, particularly on the Middle Ages, is far more careful and accurate than the work of earlier days.

Similarly, in the United States we find a group of contemporary genealogists who know how to utilize, and do utilize, all of the available source material as well as their own critical faculties in establishing a pedigree from a mediaeval royal or noble family. The most noteworthy of these genealogists are George Andrews Moriarty, Jr., Walter Goodwin Davis, and Donald Lines Jacobus. An American who wishes to see just how one should go about tracing the descent of a colonial New England settler from the great folk of mediaeval England, proving every step of the way, would do well to peruse Mr. Moriarty's "The Royal Descent of a New England Settler", in the *New England Historical and Genealogical Register*, vol. 79. Mr. Davis' chapters on "Lewis, of Shrewsbury," "Marshall, of Shrewsbury," "Mitton, of Weston-Under-Lizard," and "Beaumont, of Wednesbury," in his *Ancestry of Nicholas Davis* (1956), which show conclusively the line of descent from King Henry III of England to Elizabeth Marshall, wife of Thomas Lewis, who settled in what is now Maine in 1631; finally, Mr. Jacobus' *Bulkeley Genealogy* (1933) contains fully documented lines of ancestry going back from Rev. Peter Bulkeley, founder of Concord, Mass., and his two wives, to a number of royal and noble families. There are a number of other works, by the three cited authors and by other American writers, which also prove lines of descent from European royal and noble families to American settlers, but these are listed as samples of excellence.

Two authors frequently consulted by Americans wishing

to establish a royal or noble ancestral line are Marcellus D. R. von Redlich and Rev. Frederick Lewis Weis. The former wrote *Pedigrees of Some of the Emperor Charlemagne's Descendants* (1941) which, though containing some correct lines, is unsatisfactory since no references are cited for statements. There is a bibliography at the end of the book, containing good, middling, and bad works, with no indication of which books pertain to which pedigrees. Dr. Weis is the author of *Ancestral Roots of Sixty New England Colonists* (1950), a *Supplement* thereto (1952), and *The Magna Charta Sureties* (1955). These are far better than von Redlich's work, and Dr. Weis has made an attempt to cite authorities for his statements. Yet, there are in these books too many errors for comfort, and the interested searcher should study the reviews in *The American Genealogist,* vols. 28, 31, and 32, and in the *National Genealogical Society Quarterly,* vol. 44, p. 36.

In the foregoing paragraphs, an attempt is made to point out to American seekers for royal and noble lines the chief models to be followed and some of the pitfalls to be avoided. Now come the questions of where and how the constructive searches should be made. First of all, the seeker should plan to spend time in one or more of the great American libraries. There are a number of libraries in the United States which are rich in material on British genealogy, but there are fewer that have a wealth of books pertaining to continental European genealogy. The searcher must remember that even though his sought-for line of noble ancestry may begin in Britain, it will very soon lead to the continent of Europe, and thus to books in languages other than English.

The first category of works to consult are the various encyclopedias and biographical dictionaries. The *Dictionary of National Biography* contains excellent articles on all important British royal and noble personages; the *Allgemeine Deutsche Biographie* performs the same function for personages who lived in the area comprised in pre-1918 Germany and Austria. For France, there are two 19th century biographical dictionaries, those of Didot and Michaud, as well as a new *Dictionnaire de biographie française,* begun in 1933, but which, by 1959, has only reached the letter "C". For Italy, there is the *Enciclopedia Italiana,* containing biographic sketches of all important Italians, and, in vol. 30, the best genealogical, historical and biographical account of the House of Savoy. Similar works are in existence for nearly every European country and race, though the rarer ones may only be found in the larger libraries. Most of these works contain some account of the family of each individual mentioned, as well as bibliographies after each sketch.

Next, we come to the category of Ancestor Tables. Here, continental Europeans, and above all Germans, far surpass the British in expertness and fecundity. Beginning with Eyzinger's *Thesaurus principum* (1591), more and more accurate Ancestor Tables of European and usually central European royal and noble personages were constantly published. We cite here only a few: Philipp Jakob Spener, a noted theologian who was also an excellent genealogist, compiled his *Theatrum nobilitatis europaeae* between 1668 and 1678. J. Seifert's *Ahnentafeln* in 5 volumes appeared 1715-1722. L. Le Blond's *Quartiers généalogiques,* 2d ed., was printed in 1773. Stephen Kekule von Stradonitz's *Ahnentafel-Atlas* was published in Berlin, 1898-1904, and contained seven generations of the ancestors of each sovereign and consort of a sovereign living in Europe in 1898, together with full information on birth, marriage and death of each individual, as far as such information could be ascertained. In this work, furthermore, the author established the numbering system for Ancestor Tables that has since become standard, the *probans* or subject being numbered 1, his father 2, his mother 3, and so on. Baron Otto von Dungern published his *Ahnen deutscher Fürsten: Hohenzollern* in 1906, containing Ancestor Tables of ruling members of the Hohenzollern family. This special topic was expanded by Prince Wilhelm Karl von Isenburg, who, in 1931, published *Die Ahnen der Deutschen Kaiser, Könige, und ihrer Gemahlinnen* (Ancestor Tables of the German Emperors, Kings, and their wives), and, in 1938, he followed this with *Ahnentafeln der*

Regenten Europas und ihrer Gemahlinnen (Ancestor Tables of the Rulers of Europe and their wives). Baron M. de Troostenbergh compiled a *Recueil des quartiers de noblesse des familles belges*, 2 vols. (1912-1914). In Germany, there was a spate of Ancestor Tables in the period 1925-1944. Collections called *Ahnentafeln der EDDA*, or Ancestor Tables of contemporary German nobles, appeared in 4 volumes, 1925-39, and the *Ahnentafeln berühmter Deutscher*, or Ancestor Tables of famous Germans, was printed in 6 volumes, 1929-44. In Switzerland, J. A. Zwicky von Gauen published two series, *Sammlung schweizer Ahnentafeln* (1939), and *Ahnentafeln berühmter Schweizer* (1942).

In addition to the foregoing collections of Ancestor Tables, there are volumes devoted to the ancestry of a single individual. Here again continental, and especially German, works predominate. Baron A. A. von Malzahn wrote *4096 Ahnen Kaiser Wilhelms II* (1911); Dr. W. H. Hammann compiled a book in 1913 on the Ancestor Tables of Prince Wilhelm Karl von Isenburg to the number of 4096, and, in 1925, Prince von Isenburg himself published a great work, *Meine Ahnen* (My Ancestors), an enlargement of Hammann's book to the number of 16,383 ancestors. The celebrated Dr. Erich Brandenburg compiled extensive Ancestor Tables of Frederick the Great of Prussia (1934), the Empress Maria Theresa (1937), Augustus the Strong of Saxony (1937), and of Goethe's patron, Karl August of Sachsen-Weimar (1943). Even more remarkable than all these is the *Ahnentafel Rübel-Blass* by E. Rübel and W. H. Ruoff (2 vols., 1939), tracing all discoverable ancestors of a Swiss family, some members of which live in Brookline, Mass. Though neither the Rübel nor the Blass families are noble, they had noble and royal ancestors, all of whom are traced with the greatest care and by citation of evidence to the early Middle Ages. Somewhat briefer in compass are Otto Forst-Battaglia, *Ahnentafel des Erzherzogs Franz Ferdinand* (1910), an Ancestor Table to the number 1024 of the Archduke who was murdered at Sarajevo in 1914, and Père Cherubin de Renaix; *Tableau des 1024 quartiers du*

Duc de Croy (1924), and *Tableau des 1024 quartiers du Duc d'Arenberg* (1931).

Royal Ancestor Tables have not heretofore been quite as popular in the English-speaking world as on the continent of Europe. To be sure, G. R. French published *The Ancestors of Queen Victoria and Prince Albert* (1841), which traces these ancestors to the number 1024. The best-known printed work of this sort in English is Lt. Col. W. H. Turton, *Plantagenet Ancestry* (1928), an attempt to trace all the known ancestors of Elizabeth of York (1465-1503), wife of King Henry VII of England. Turton was moderately successful with the generations of ancestors closest to Elizabeth of York (although even here he had trouble with the rather obscure Wydeville ancestors), but he went far astray with the early mediaeval lines and committed many errors. Fortunately, George Andrews Moriarty, Jr., has revised that part of Turton's work which deals with the ancestry of King Edward III of England and his wife, Philippa, of Hainaut; this revision, though still in manuscript, has been microfilmed by the Harvard University Library, and copies of the microfilm are available from that library. It is reported that Sir R. I. K. Moncreiffe, Bt., Unicorn Pursuivant-at-Arms, is working on a complete Ancestor Table of Charles, Prince of Wales and Duke of Cornwall, son of Queen Elizabeth II and Prince Philip. Should this work be published, it will be the most stupendous of its kind.

The third category to consider is that of general Genealogical Tables of European royal and noble families. Early works of this sort appeared in the 16th century, but they were inaccurate and have been completely superseded by later works. The first important opus of this type is Johannes Hübner, *Genealogische Tabellen . . zur Erläuterung der politischen Historie*, 3 vols., Leipzig, 1725-28. The first volume contains 333 tables, beginning with Adam and the Biblical patriarchs, continuing through the kings and leaders of the Jews, the monarchs of the Ancient Near East, Roman Emperors and barbarian rulers, Merovingians, Carolingians, and dynasts of all Europe in the Middle Ages. In all these tables, Hübner's work is quite incomplete and, in some places, incorrect. But, beginning about 1400, Hübner's information is very accurate, especially for German families, and it so continues down to the date of publication. The second and third volumes of Hübner's series are devoted to German counts, and here also the information from 1400 to 1725 is very good. Shortly after Hübner's work there appeared the first book of this type in English, James Anderson, *Royal Genealogies* (2nd ed., 1736). Like Hübner, Anderson is poor for early pedigrees, and he includes the fabulous ancestries of the early Irish and Welsh kings (which Hübner does not). But Anderson himself points out that the early pedigrees of the Irish monarchs are fabulous (see discussion by Donald Lines Jacobus, "Kings of Ireland," *The American Genealogist*, vol. 9). Anderson is rather better than Hübner on Spanish, Portuguese and Italian families; both Hübner and Anderson are poor on Russian, Polish and other eastern European dynasties.

Later important manuals of royal genealogy include Antonio Chiusole, *La genealogia moderna delle case più illustri di tutto il mondo* (Venice, 1746), which, while stressing Italian families actually does contain noble pedigrees from all Europe, including the British peerage; T. G. Voigtel, *Stammtafeln zur Geschichte der europäischen Staaten* (1811), with 2nd enlarged edition by Ludwig A. Cohn (1871). Fr. Brömmel, *Genealogische Tabellen zur Geschichte des Mittelalters* (1846) is of special use for the Middle Ages. Kamill von Behr, *Genealogie der in Europa regierenden Fürstenhäuser* (2nd ed., 1870, with supplement, 1890) is wonderfully accurate, but stresses genealogies of the families actually regnant in 1870, though there is an appendix on the House of Capet, which in 1870 was not reigning anywhere. Twenty years ago, the indefatigable genealogist Prince Wilhelm Karl von Isenburg published the first edition of his excellent *Stammtafeln zur Geschichte der europäischen Staaten* (2 vols., 1936-37), the first volume on German, the second on non-German dynasties. Prince von Isenburg followed the same sequence of families that had been used 200 years earlier by Hübner. Since World War II, Prince von Isenburg and his collaborator, Baron Frank von Freytag-Loringhoven, have brought out another edition of this work, much enlarged, which contains not only ruling and formerly ruling dynasties, but also eminent houses of non-German nobility such as the Churchill and Spencer-Churchill family, so that the reader may easily see the great Sir Winston and his paternal ancestors and relatives.

A remarkable work which belongs in the category of general Genealogical Tables is A. M. H. J. Stokvis, *Manuel d'histoire, de généalogie et de chronologie de tous les états du globe* (3 vols., 1888-1893.) The result of incredible labor and erudition, the first volume is devoted to the non-European world (Asia, Africa, North and South America, and Polynesia). Stokvis's second volume is devoted to Europe outside the bounds of the old Holy Roman Empire; his third volume contains pedigrees and lists pertaining to the area once covered by that empire; Germany, Austria, the Benelux countries, Switzerland and Italy. Genealogists should remember that Stokvis's work is a historian's genealogy rather than a genealogist's genealogy. Wives are omitted in most of the tables unless they are heiresses; only important children are given instead of all children; years only instead of complete dates appear. Nevertheless, it is a great work, the only one in which dynasties and lists of rulers and governors of the whole world can be found all together.

Our fourth category deals with works on descendants of a single ancestor or ancestral pair, in all lines, male and female. Pre-eminent in this category is the great book by Dr. Erich Brandenburg, *Die Nachkommen Karls des Grossen* (1935), which traces all the descendants of Charlemagne for fourteen generations, contains a special section on "probable but unproved" descendants, and has full references for each family. Other examples of this category are Père Cherubin de Renaix, *Descendance du Prince Charles de Ligne, Duc d'Arenberg* (2 vols., 1921-31), a series of tables containing the complete descendants in every line of a man who married in 1587. The

Marquis de Ruvigny (an Englishman despite his French title) began in 1903 a series called *The Plantagenet Roll of the Blood Royal of England*, in which he intended to trace all the descendants of King Edward III. Five volumes appeared which, though incomplete, are useful.

A fifth category deals with books which present a certain number of ancestors of a given individual as well as all their descendants, thus including uncles, aunts, and cousins of many degrees as well as closer relatives. Interesting samples of this type are Comte Henri Frotier de La Messelière, *Les alliances des familles composant les 64 quartiers généalogiques du Comte de La Messelière* (2 vols., 1904); Roman Freiherr von Procházka, *Meine zweiunddreissig Ahnen and ihre Sippenkreise* (1928), and Albert Fabritius, *Hans Majestaet Kong Christian X og hans Slaetninge* (1937), which presents (in Danish) the 16 great-great-grandparents of King Christian X and all their descendants.

Our sixth category should be called national or regional genealogies of royal and noble families. Here we come to the books of this type most familiar to the average American reader, the various British Peerage works. Despite their familiarity, a word should be said about them. The greatest is the *Complete Peerage,* new edition, already cited in this chapter. Though this is a work of vast scholarship, and the most authoritative of its kind, readers must remember that it contains information only on peers, their wives, and their eldest sons. Information on other children is almost never included. Special attention should be drawn to the Appendices in each volume. Some of these, such as Appendix A of vol. X, "Norse Predecessors of the Earls of Orkney", are works of outstanding erudition. The weaknesses of the early editions of Collins', Lodge's, Playfair's and Burke's *Peerages* in giving credence to fabulous ancestries have already been mentioned. These have been largely eliminated in recent editions of Burke's *Peerage* and *Landed Gentry,* while Debrett's *Peerage* lists only the holders of titles and their living relatives, and makes no attempt to trace ancestral lines. Of special interest is Sir James Balfour Paul, *The Scots Peerage*

(9 vols., 1904-14, fully indexed), an excellent and careful work. Mention should also be made of John W. Clay, *Extinct and Dormant Peerages of the Northern Counties of England* (1913), a fine example of regional genealogy. Readers of British peerage works will note some differences in usage between them and continental European works of similar nature. The British seldom mention places of birth, marriage and death, while modern continental authors nearly always give places as well as dates. The British Peerages which list children (that is, all except the *Complete Peerage*, which omits most children) always list all sons first, then all daughters. Continental European genealogists follow the more sensible system of listing children in order of seniority.

In France, there is no modern work comparable to the British Peerages which include articles on all the noble families. There were, however, excellent works of this type in the past, and there are fine recent monographs which cover the field partially. Père Anselme, *Histoire généalogique de la maison de France et des grands officiers de la couronne* (3rd ed., in 8 vols., 1726-33; reissued in 9 vols., 1879-82; partial revision by Potier de Courcy, 1953) is the primary work. Louis Moréri, *Grand dictionnaire historique* (1739 ed.) contains excellent genealogical articles on French and some other noble families by Chasot de Nantigny. François de La Chesnaye des Bois, *Dictionnaire de la noblesse*, published in several editions in the 18th century, and reprinted without additions in 19 volumes in 1861, is very good for noble families of the 16th, 17th and 18th centuries, not so good on earlier periods. J. B. P. de Courcelles, *Histoire généalogique des pairs de France* (12 vols., 1822-33) and his *Dictionnaire de la noblesse de France* (5 vols., 1820-21) are good for the families they treat, but they do not include the whole nobility. The same criticism can be made of Viton de Saint-Allais, *Nobiliaire de France*, issued 1814-43 and 1872-95. Edouard Garnier, *Tableaux généalogiques des souverains de la France et de leurs grands féodataires* (1861) is excellent for the many branches of the House of Capet and for the great mediaeval families such as the Dukes of Brittany and Counts of Armagnac. One must not forget P. d'Hozier, *Armorial général* (several editions) and H. Jougla de Morénas, *Grand armorial de France* (4 vols., 1934-39), which contain genealogical as well as heraldic data. Vicomte A. Révérend, *Armorial du premier empire* (4 vols., 1894-97), *Armorial de la restauration* (6 vols., 1901-6), and *Titres et confirmations de titres, 1830-1908* (2 vols., 1909), are indispensable works for the modern period. Révérend often gives the genealogical background of the families he treats from the early 18th century. Baron Woelmont de Brumagne, *La noblesse française* (4 vols., 1929-35) contains superb articles on many noble families, but does not cover all the noblesse of France. The same author's *Notices généalogiques* (9 vols., 1923-36) are equally good. Since World War II, a new genealogical scholar has arisen in France, all of whose books are good, and each better than the preceding one. He is Joseph Valynseele, author of *Le sang des Bonaparte* (1954), *Les maréchaux du premier empire* (1957) and *Les princes et ducs du premier empire non maréchaux* (1959). Having covered the Bonapartes and the Napoleonic peerage, M. Valynseele intends to continue with families ennobled at the Restauration, especially the maréchaux de France. In connection with M. Valynseele's first book, one should point out that it supplements but does not entirely supersede Léonce de Brotonne, *Les Bonapartes et leurs alliances* (1893), which includes sections on the Ramolino, Fesch, Arrighi, Ornano, Beauharnais, Tascher de La Pagerie, Clary, Léon, Walewski, Boyer, Jouberthon, Montenuovo, and Morny families, all connected with the Bonapartes in one way or another.

In addition to the works dealing with all France, there is a large collection of books on the various provinces. We cite here only Comte E. de Foras, *Armorial et nobiliaire de Savoie* (6 vols., 1863-1938), Comte Henri Frotier de La Messelière, *Filiations bretonnes* (5 vols., 1912-26). There is a bibliography of these provincial genealogies in Otto Forst-Battaglia, *Traité de généalogie* (1949), p. 124.

For Italy, we have first of all the magnificent work of Conte Pompeo Litta, *Famiglie celebri italiane,* 11 vols. (1818-63), all hand-illuminated and decorated with coats of arms and portraits in colour of various members of the celebrated families. This is the most sumptuous of all genealogical publications, and contains an immense amount of information, even on minor branches of the great families. There is a supplement of 4 volumes (1902-12) dealing chiefly with families from Naples, such as the Caracciolo and Carafa. Other general works on Italian families are G. Crollalanza, *Dizionario delle famiglie italiane* (3 vols., 1886-90), S. Manucci, *Nobiliario del Regno d'Italia* (4 vols., 1925-29) and Vittorio Spreti, *Enciclopedia storico-nobiliaria italiana* (8 vols., 1928-36). There are also many regional works which are listed in Forst-Battaglia, *Traité de généalogie*, 126-7.

For Germany, mention should be made of Ernst Heinrich Kneschke, *Deutsche Grafenhäuser* (3 vols., 1852-4), the series of *Stammtafeln mediatisierter Häuser*, containing tables of all the mediatized princely and comital families of Germany, the various *Adelslexika* printed in the 18th and 19th centuries, the old works of Johann Seifert, *Genealogische Beschreibung aller Grafen und Herren* (4 vols., 1702-5) and *Genealogie hochadelicher Eltern und Kinder* (2 vols., 1716-24), as well as regional works such as Baron Otto Dungern, *Genealogisches Handbuch zur bayrisch-oesterreichischen Geschichte* (1931), J. Kindler von Knobloch, *Oberbadisches Geschlechterbuch* (3 vols., 1894-1919) and W. Moeller, *Stammtafeln westdeutscher Adelsgeschlechter* (3 vols., 1922-36). In addition, vast amounts of information on German noble families will be found in the works of Hübner, von Behr and Prince von Isenburg already mentioned, and in the almanachs and monographs which will be mentioned below in the seventh and eighth categories.

For Austria, the same works of Hübner and Prince von Isenburg are of primary importance; so are the almanachs and monographs. In addition, one should consult Karl von Wurzbach, *Biographisches Lexikon des Kaiserstaats Oesterreich* (60 vols., 1851-91), containing genealogies of the principal Austrian families.

In Switzerland, there is great interest in both heraldry and genealogy. The relatively few Swiss families among the titled nobility generally bear Austrian, Prussian, French, or Papal titles, and are treated in the works on Austrian, German and French nobility. There is an interesting bibliography of works on Swiss genealogy in Forst-Battaglia, *Traité de généalogie*, 119-22.

For Belgium, the Netherlands, and Luxembourg, the most important works are F. G. Goethals, *Dictionnaire des familles nobles de Belgique* (4 vols., 1849-52, and the same author's *Miroir des notabilités nobiliaires* (2 vols., 1857-62); C. Poplimont, *La noblesse belge* (1856-58) and *La Belgique héraldique* (11 vols., 1863-67). For the mediaeval period, an indispensable work is L. Vanderkindere, *La formation territoriale des principautés belges* (2d. ed.,; 2 vols., 1902). Also important are A. Ferwerda, *Adelijk Wapenboek van de zeven Provincien* (3 vols., 1760-81), A. Vorsterman van Oijen, *Stam- en Wapenboek van aanzienlijke Nederlandsche Familien* (3 vols., 1885-90) and F. B. Wittert van Hoogland, *De Nederlandsche Adel* (1913).

Considering the well-known Spanish quality of pride, it is not surprising that there are many works on Spanish noble families. Seventeenth century nobiliaries by López de Haro, Rivarola, Salazar y Castro and Villadermoros still have a certain value. The German genealogist Jakob Wilhelm Imhof wrote two works in Latin, dealing with Spanish and Italian noble houses, *Corpus historiae genealogicae Italiae et Hispaniae* (Nürnberg, 1702) and *Genealogia viginti illustrium in Hispania familiorum* (Leipzig, 1712), and, according to Professor Garrett Mattingly (to whom grateful acknowledgment is made for this information), the latter contains pedigrees of the family of Alvárez de Toledo, Dukes of Medina Sidonia, to which house belonged the admiral of the Spanish Armada who is the hero of Professor Mattingly's forthcoming book, *The Armada* (1959). Special mention must be made of Francisco Fernández de Bethencourt, *Historia genealógica de la monarquía española* (9 vols., 1897-1912), a splendidly detailed work which, however, treats of relatively few families, though these include the important ones of Acuña, Borja, and Fernández de Cordoba. F. Pifferer, *Nobiliario de España* (6 vols., 1857-60) is worth consultation, but the most extensive work is A. García Caraffa, *Enciclopedia heráldica y genealógica hispano-americana* (in progress since 1919; this work reached vol. 79 in 1958).

For Portugal and its former colony, Brazil, we should cite A. C. de Souza, *Historia genealogica da Casa Real Portugueza* (12 vols., 1735-48), which lists all descendants in male and female lines, legitimate and illegitimate, of the dynasties which have ruled Portugal. The same author's *Memorias dos grandes de Portugal* (1754) is also noteworthy. A. da Silveira Pinto, *Resenha das familias titulares e grandes de Portugal* (2 vols., 1877-91), P. Ferreira, *Livro de ouro da nobleza de Portugal* (1902 sq.), and M. J. Costa Felguieiras Gayo, *Nobiliario da familias de Portugal* (1938) are all useful for the modern period. The Brazilian J. S. de Vasconcellos, *Archivo nobiliarchico brasileiro* (1916) contains excellent accounts of the Brazilian nobility created by Emperors Dom Pedro I and II, as well as of Portuguese nobles who settled in Brazil.

Turning to Scandinavia, we find in Sweden the work of G. Anrep, *Svenska Adelns-Ättar-taflor* (4 vols., 1858-64), with continuation by F. N. Wrangel (3 vols., 1897-1902); Gustaf Elgenstjerna, *Svenska Adelns Ättar-taflor*, (9 vols., 1925-36) is a revision and enlargement of the work of Anrep and Wrangel. In Denmark and Norway, there are: *Leksikon over adelige Familier i Danmark, Norge og Hertugdommere* (3 vols., 1787); A Thiset and P. L. Wittrup, *Nyt dansk Adelslexikon* (1904); S. O. Brenner, *Leksikon over danske Familier* (1927 sq.); W. Lassen, *Norske Stamtavler* (1868), and H. Krog-Steffens, *Norske Slaegter* (1915). More work needs to be done on Scandinavian families of the early mediaeval period.

In the Baltic area, the aristocracy was nearly all German or Swedish in origin. This area is covered genealogically by a set of volumes, *Genealogisches Handbuch der baltischen Ritterschaften*, divided into three sections, Estland, Kurland and Livland, according to provinces in the former Russian empire which, after 1918, became the republics of Esthonia and Latvia. These volumes were published in Germany, 1929 sq. It is surprising to find in the part on Livland, pp. 793-800, a fine account of the La Trobe family, descended from a brother of the American architect and engineer, Benjamin Henry Latrobe (1764-1820).

In Finland, also, the aristocracy was mostly of non-Finnish origin. The single Finnish genealogical author interested in royal and noble lineage was Osmo Durcham, who published a number of articles in both Swedish and Finnish in the Helsinki magazine *Genos* in the 1930s.

The Hungarian and Czechish princely, comital and baronial families all appeared in the almanachs to be discussed later, as did also the Polish princes and some Polish Counts.[1]

For imperial Russia, the earliest good work is Prince Peter Dolgoruki, *Rossiiskaia rodoslovnaia kniga* (4 vols., 1855-57), with 2d. ed. by Prince A. B. Lobanov-Rostovsky (1895); P. N. Petrov, *Istoriia rodov russkogo dvorianstva* (1886); V. V. Rummel and V. V. Golubtsov, *Rodoslovnii sbornik russkich dvorianskich familii* (2 vols., 1886-87); L. M. Savelov, *Lekcii po russkoi genealogii* (2 vols., 1908). Mention must also be made of the most useful collections of death records edited by Grand Duke Nicholas Mikhailovich of Russia, the *Petersburgskii Nekropol, Moskovskii Nekropol,* and *Provincialnii Nekropol.* Since the Russian Revolution, exiled nobles and gentry have attempted by labors of love to keep alive the traditions of their ancestors through genealogical publications, and they have succeeded to a remarkable degree. Nicolas Ikonnikov published a first edition of *La noblesse de Russie* (2 vols., 1937-38), and a new and much larger edition (1957 sq.). In New York, exiled Russians published a periodical, *Novik* (1936 sq.), containing genealogical articles, obituaries, etc.

Separate notice must be given to the work of an eminent Russian genealogist whose chief concern was mediaeval Rus-

---

[1] There are a number of genealogical works in Magyar, Czechoslovakian and Polish which will be useful to the genealogists who can read those languages.

sia. Nicholas de Baumgarten began his work in Moscow: *Rodoslovnie Otryvki* (1909); *K'proiskhozhdeniu Kniazei Viazemskich* (1915); after the Revolution, he fled to Rome, and there achieved his most productive work: "Généalogies et mariages occidentaux des Rurikides russes du Xe au XIIIe siècle," *Orientalia Christiana*, May, 1927; "Le dernier mariage de Saint Vladimir," *ibid.*, May, 1930; "Pribyslava de Russie et Cunegonde d'Orlamunde," *ibid.*, Dec., 1930; "Généalogies des branches regnantes des Rurikides du XIIIe au XVIe siècle," *ibid.*, June, 1934; "Origine de Michel Wisniewiecki roi de Pologne," *ibid.*, 1935; "Polotzk et Lithuanie," *ibid.*, 1936; "Halitch et Ostrog," *ibid.*, 1937. These are by far the best works on the descendants of Rurik and on mediaeval genealogical connections between Russia and her neighbors.

Proceeding to southeastern Europe, we next consider the Byzantine Empire. The chief work is Charles du Fresne Du Cange, *Familiae byzantinae* (1680), on all the dynasties and magnates of the empire. Charles Hopf, *Chroniques grécoromanes* (1873) contains marvelous pedigrees of the later Byzantine families, the Latin crusading families who settled in Greece and the Aegean archipelago, and Serbian and Albanian families who intermarried with them. For the Palaeologus dynasty, students should examine Archimandrit Averkios Th. Papadopulos, *Versuch einer Genealogie der Palaiologen* (1938) and "Ferdinand Paleologus", in *The Journal of the Barbados Museum and Historical Society*, 7 (1940). A perfectly fascinating series of mediaeval genealogical and financial problems was presented by Professor Robert Lee Wolff, "Mortgage and redemption of an emperor's son: Castile and the Latin Empire of Constantinople," *Speculum*, 29: 45-84.

Prince Eugène Rizo-Rangabé, *Livre d'or de la noblesse phanariote* (Athens, 1904) covers the princely families, descendants of the Greeks of the Phanar quarter in Constantinople, who were appointed rulers of Wallachia and Moldavia by the Sultans of Turkey, and became ancestors of the 20th century Romanian and Greek aristocracy. Philip P. Argenti, *Libro d'oro de la noblesse de Chio* (2 vols., 1955) is a splendid and complete work on Greek families originally from the Island of Chios, who have made their way to many other parts of the world. The Ralli family, perhaps the most intercontinental of all families, is treated here in all its many branches.

Crusading European families are best treated in Du Cange, *Familles d'outre-mer* (ed. Rey, 1869). Of the kings of Armenia, there are pedigrees in R. Grousset, *Histoire de l'Arménie* (1947), and of the kings of Georgia in M. F. Brosset, *Histoire de Géorgie*, while F. Justi, *Iranisches Namenbuch* (1895) contains genealogies of the rulers and chieftains of Armenia, Georgia, Iran and adjoining regions. The leading contemporary specialist on Georgian families is Prince Cyril Toumanoff, author of "On the relationship between the Founder of the Empire of Trebizond and the Georgian Queen Thamar," *Speculum*, 15:299; "Christian Caucasia between Byzantium and Iran," *Traditio*, 10:109; "Chronology of the Kings of Abasgia," *Le Muséon*, 69:73; "La noblesse géorgienne," *Rivista Araldica*, 54:260, as well as the article on the former reigning family of Georgia (Bagration) in *Novik*.

The seventh category concerns almanachs and periodicals. Pre-eminent among these is the *Almanach de Gotha* (German edition called *Gothäisches Hofkalender*) published continuously from 1763 to 1944, inclusive, by Justus Perthes Verlag at Gotha. An amazingly accurate work, the *Almanach* was divided into two parts, the "Annuaire généalogique", and the "Annuaire diplomatique et statistique," while the first part was again divided into three divisions. These concerned, first, the ruling families of Europe; secondly, the mediatized German and Austrian princes and counts, whose families had been sovereign prior to the dissolution of the Holy Roman Empire; thirdly, princely and ducal families of Europe. In addition to the *Almanach de Gotha*, Justus Perthes published the *Taschenbuch der gräflichen Häuser* (1828 sq.), containing the families of the non-mediatized German counts, as well as Austrian, Hungarian and some Polish counts; the *Taschenbuch der freiherrlichen Häuser* (1848 sq.) which performed the same function for barons; the *Taschenbuch der uradeligen Häuser* (1900 sq.) and *Taschenbuch der briefadeligen Häuser* (1927 sq.) which covered the noble but untitled German and Austrian families. All these publications came to an end in World War II, when Gotha was bombed and finally handed over to the "German Democratic Republic" under Soviet auspices. Happily for the genealogist, however, the C. A. Starke-Verlag began in 1951 a series of publications designed to replace those of Perthes. These are called the *Genealogisches Handbuch des Adels*, and have about the same coverage as the former Perthes publications. The work that is the equivalent of the *Almanach de Gotha* is entitled *Fürstliche Häuser*, and is divided, as was the *Almanach*, into sections dealing with reigning and recently reigning families, mediatized families, and the princely and ducal families of Europe. Starke-Verlag's other publications are called *Gräfliche Häuser, Freiherrliche Häuser* and *Adelige Häuser*. An advantage of the Starke-Verlag over the Perthes publications is that each volume contains a complete surname index and, as an added attraction, the Starke-Verlag editors have included in each volume a few Ancestor Tables of specially fascinating individuals.

A number of publications, more or less modelled on the *Almanach de Gotha,* began to appear in various countries in the 19th century. One of the most interesting of these was H. R. Hiort-Lorenzen, *Livre d'or des souverains* (several editions, last and best 1908), which surpassed the *Almanach* by listing *all* members, living and deceased, of the sovereign and mediatized and former sovereign families of Europe from about 1750 to the time of publication. We should perhaps also cite the *Almanach de Bruxelles,* published for a few years in World War I days as a protest against the German origin of the *Almanach de Gotha.*

As for the national serials and periodicals pertaining to the nobility, there are many. In Spain: Juan Moreno de Guerra, *Guía de la grandeza* (1917 sq.) ; Roberto Moreno Morrison, *Guía nobiliaria de España* (many editions), *Revista de historia y genealogía española* (1912 sq.) ; in France, the *Annuaire de la noblesse de France* (1844 sq.) and *Rex* (1909-

14); in Belgium, the *Annuaire de la noblesse belge* (1847 sq.); in the Netherlands, the *Nederlands Adelsboek* (1903 sq.); in Denmark, *Danmarks Adels Aarbog* (1884 sq.); in Sweden, *Sveriges Adelskalender* (1900 sq.); in Italy, *Annuario della nobiltà italiana* (1878-1905), followed by the *Libro d'oro della nobiltà italiana* (1910 sq.), and *Rivista araldica* (1903 sq.); in Austria, the *Jahrbuch der heraldischen Gesellschaft Adler* (1873), the *Monatsblatt des Adler* (1881 sq.), the *Jahrbuch des oesterreichischen Instituts für Genealogie, Familienrecht* and *Wappenkunde* (1928 sq.), and Karl Friedrich von Frank's *Senftenegger Monatsblatt* (1951 sq.); in southern Italy, *L'Araldo, almanacco nobiliare napoletano* (1880-1913), and in Bavaria, Prince Franz Joseph zu Hohenlohe-Schillingsfürst's *Der in Bayern immatrikulierter Adel* (1950 sq.).

The eighth category pertains to monographs on individual families, and here the amount of publication is truly immense. We must content ourselves with the citation of a few outstanding examples. There are works on each of the German dynasties, but the best is perhaps Carl Knetsch, *Das Haus Brabant* (1931), a most careful study of the Dukes of Brabant and of the Landgraves, Electors and Grand Dukes of Hessen. Other fine examples of discriminating genealogical work are J. M. van de Venne and others, *Geslachts-Register van het Vorstenhuis Nassau* (1937), and Alexander A. M. Stols, *Geslachts-Register van het Vorstenhuis Lippe* (1938), published in commemoration of the marriage of the present Queen Juliana of the Netherlands and her consort, Prince Bernhard. An Italian example is Gaetano Pieraccini, *La Stirpe de' Medici di Cafaggiolo* (3 vols., 1924-27), a fine account of the celebrated Florentine family.

It should be remembered that memoirs, especially German or Austrian memoirs, often contain a genealogical appendix. Such is the case with Gräfin Lulu Thürheim, *Mein Leben* (4 vols., 1923-4), in the last volume of which there is both a pedigree of the Thürheim family and an Ancester Table of the authoress.

Our ninth and last category consists of a list of some miscellaneous books which may be interesting or thought-provoking. No one interested in mediaeval genealogical problems can overlook Comte J. M. J. L. de Mas-Latrie, *Trésor de chronologie et de géographie pour l'étude et l'emploi des documents du moyen-âge* (1889) or *L'art de vérifier les dates des faits historiques* (2nd. ed., 42 vols., 1818-44). Everyone interested in aspects of heredity will wish to consult Auguste Brachet, *La pathologie mentale des rois de France* (1903), and W. Strohmayer, *Psychiatrisch-genealogische Untersuchung der Abstammung König Ludwigs II und Ottos I von Bayern* (1912), Stephan Kekule von Stradonitz, *Ausgewählte Aufsätze aus dem Gebiete des Staatsrecht und der Genealogie* (1905) contains remarkable genealogical and legal-genealogical essays. Baron Otto von Dungern, *Mutterstämme* (1924) is an extremely interesting study of matrilineal lines of descent. One learns with some surprise that the most remote known ancestress of Queen Victoria in the matrilineal line was Iñez, illegitimate daughter of King Theobald of Navarre in the 13th century. Otto Forst-Battaglia, *Das Geheimnis des Blutes* (1932) is an entertaining series of essays, all genealogical, which show the mixture of blood and genes that takes place over many generations. It contains a number of Ancestor Tables. The same author's *Traité de généalogie* (1949) contains a superb series of bibliographies, of which much use has been made in this chapter, as well as interesting folding genealogical tables.

CHAPTER III

ENGLAND AND WALES

The bulk and complexity of those English and Welsh records from which the American genealogist might possibly derive assistance is so great that only a small number of the existing classes can be even mentioned here. The documents in the Public Record Office alone have recently been estimated to number more than fifty million. Furthermore, an explanation of why the existing documents are what they are and where they are would amount almost to an administrative history of the English Church and State. The following small selection has, therefore, been made with an eye almost exclusively to the needs of the American genealogist seeking the origins of an American settler. The use of some classes of record is an art in itself, their nature having to be understood before their evidential value can be appreciated. Often one series may be used as a key or index to another.

The following general guides will be found useful:[1]

Origines Genealogicae, by Stacey Grimaldi, 1828;

Manual for the Genealogist, by Richard Sims, 1856;

Records and Record Searching, by Walter Rye, 1897;

How to Write the History of a Family, by W. P. W. Phillimore, 2nd edition 1900;

Genealogical Research in England, Scotland and Ireland, by J. H. Lea, 1906;

Guide to the Victoria County History, 1912;

Pedigree Work, by W. P. W. Phillimore, 3rd edition, 1936;

A Select Bibliography of English Genealogy, by H. G. Harrison, 1937.

English Genealogy, by Anthony R. Wagner, 1959. (See p. 327)

---

[1] Also helpful may be *The Genealogist's Handbook*, published by The Society of Genealogists, London; and *Genealogical Research in England and Wales,* by David E. Gardner and Frank Smith (Vol. I, 1950, Vol. II, 1959). ED.

A. ARCHIVES

The following are the principal depositories of original records. Several of these also contain collections of extraneous matter which the genealogist will find useful, which have from time to time been added to the archives as of kindred interest. A valuable general guide is Hubert Hall's *Repertory of British Archives, Part I, England,* 1920, published by the Royal Historical Society.

The Public Record Office, Chancery Lane, London, W. C. 2

The Public Record Office Act of 1838 provided for bringing together under one control and making available for consultation, records belonging to the Crown which had previously been scattered among a large number of separate offices and depositories. An account of the process is given in the *Guide to the Public Records, Part I, Introductory,* 1949. The large number of different classes of records now deposited in the Public Record Office are briefly described and listed in *A Guide to the Manuscripts Preserved in the Public Record Office,* by M. S. Giuseppi, 2 vols. 1923-4. A new *Guide to the Public Records* is to appear in parts. Part I, *Introductory,* was published by H. M. Stationery Office in 1949. A long series of lists, indexes, and calendars of particular classes of documents have been produced by the Office over a period of years and are constantly being added to. The list of those available can be obtained from H. M. Stationery Office, York House, Kingsway, London, W. C. 2.

Probate Registries

Down to 1858, the testamentary jurisdiction belonged to the Church, but was exercised by a patchwork of special authorities, large and small, each with its own jurisdiction sometimes extending over a diocese or a province, sometimes only over a parish or two. The general ecclesiastical division of the country on which the Probate divisions were based is best understood from the *Liber Regis vel Thesaurus Rerum Ecclesiasticarum,* by John Bacon 1786. Particulars of the Probate jurisdictions and their records are given in full in a series of Parliamentary Returns of Courts empowered to grant Probate of Wills of 1828, 1829, and 1932. Their contents are briefly summarized in *A Handbook to the Ancient Courts of Probate and Depositories of Wills*, by Ceorge W. Marshall, 1895, and in *Wills and their Whereabouts*, by B. G. Bouwens. The probate jurisdiction was transferred in 1858 to the Probate Division of the High Court and the ancient records are at present divided between Somerset House, Strand, London, W. C. 2, and certain Provincial Probate Registries and approved depositories. Bouwens gave a list of these as existing in 1939, the Second edition brings it up to 1951.[2] Some of the documents have been moved from provincial Probate Registries to other places of deposit, for example, the Rochester Wills are now in the County Record Office, Maidstone, Kent, the Lancashire Wills from Chester are at the County Record Office, Preston, and the wills for all the Welsh Probate Courts are at the National Library of Wales, Aberystwyth. Calendars and Indexes of Wills and Administrations in a number of the Courts have been made and printed by the British Record Society and a few by other persons and Bodies, but for many of the courts there are only manuscript lists or indexes available, and these are not always complete or reliable.

General Register Office, Somerset House, Strand, London, W. C.

General Civil Registration of Births, Deaths and Marriages in England and Wales was made compulsory from the 1st of July 1837, but for the first few years it is not safe to assume that registration was in fact complete. The quarterly indexes of the registers are available for public consultation at Somerset House. Births and Deaths at Sea since the 1st of July 1837 are also registered.

In addition, the Register General has in his custody a large number of non-parochial registers of baptisms or births, burials or deaths and, in a few instances, of marriages kept

---

[2] The Second Edition of *Wills and Their Whereabouts* was published in 1951, after Mr. Bouwens' death. The changes in the locations of wills since the publication of the first edition in 1951 were made in the Second Edition by Miss Helen Thacker.

by various non-conformist bodies and congregations. A *Report of the Non-Parochial Registers and Records in the Custody of the Registrar General at Somerset House*, 1859, gives a list.

The Registrar General's records also comprise Registers of Births, Baptisms, Marriages, Deaths and Burials of British subjects abroad, kept by British consuls and similar records for military stations abroad, kept by Army chaplains.

Churches and Chapels

CATHEDRALS.—In or attached to each ancient cathedral is a Diocesan Registry in which are preserved, among other documents:

BISHOPS' REGISTERS, often going back to the Middle Ages, recording presentations of clergy and many other matters. Some of these have been edited and printed by the Canterbury and York Society and a few by other bodies.

RECORDS OF MARRIAGE LICENSES and connected documents beginning at different dates in different dioceses.

THE BISHOPS' TRANSCRIPTS OF PARISH REGISTERS, copies which the clergy were ordered in 1597 to send in annually, which in fact were not always made and are much more completely preserved in some dioceses than others. There is an account of them in *The History of Parish Registers in England*, by J. S. Burn, 2nd edition, 1862, chapter 9.

PARISH CHURCHES.—

PARISH REGISTERS: The keeping of these was first ordered by Thomas Cromwell in 1538, but few of them go that far back. A full account is given in Burn's *History* above mentioned, and a full list in the Parliamentary *Parish Register Abstract*, printed 1834. The contents of this are briefly indexed in A. M. Burke's *Key to the Ancient Parish Registers of England and Wales*, 1908. Most parish registers are kept in the churches, though some have, with the Bishop's approval, been deposited elsewhere. Many have been copied, printed and indexed. The Society of Genealogists printed in 1937 a *Catalogue of the Parish Registers in the Possession of the Society of Genealogists,* 2nd edition, and in 1939 a *National Index of Parish Register Copies,* compiled by Kathleen Blomfield and H. K. Percy-Smith.

RATE BOOKS: Among other parish documents, the Rate Books of some city parishes exist and are of importance, but have usually been deposited elsewhere.

CHURCH AND CHURCHYARD INSCRIPTIONS on monuments can scarcely perhaps be claimed as archives, but are of great genealogical importance. Many manuscripts and printed copies exist.

NONCONFORMIST CHURCHES, CHAPELS AND INSTITUTIONS: The majority of the old non-parochial records are in the custody of the Registrar-General at Somerset House as noted above, but some early and many later non-parochial registers are preserved in the churches and chapels. Many registers of the Society of Friends are at Friends' House, Euston Road, N. W. 1, together with extensive and valuable collections and indexes relating to the Quakers. A number of Roman Catholic Registers have been printed and indexed by the Catholic Record Society and a number of French Protestant Registers by the Huguenot Society. The Society of Genealogists' printed catalogues, mentioned above, cover many of these.

The College of Arms, Queen Victoria Street, London, E. C. 4

The Kings, Heralds and Pursuivants of Arms existed from a much earlier date, but were first incorporated into a College in 1484 and again in 1555, when they acquired the site of the present building. They kept Records of Armorial Bearings from the 14th, if not from the 13th, century, but their responsibility for the official record, correction and control of arms appears to date from the 15th century. Before the end of that century the need to record title to arms had led them to keep records of pedigrees also. The Heralds' Visitations under Royal Commission began in 1530 and about a hundred Visitation books preserved in the college record arms and pedigrees by counties. The last Visitation Commission was issued in 1686, but the registration of pedigrees

on voluntary application has continued from before that date
to the present time; each pedigree having to be submitted with
evidence and passed by examiners before registration. The
college also has the Records of Grants of Arms from the 15th
century. The Funeral Certificates record funerals of the
nobility and gentry conducted by the Heralds in the 15th,
16th and 17th centuries with particulars of their deaths,
families and arms. The college also has the records of state
ceremonials conducted by the Heralds. The extensive genealogical collections at the college are described below. A
general account of the Heralds and their records is given in
the article on "Heraldry" in Chambers' Encyclopaedia 1950
edition, and an account of the college records and collections
was published by the Burke's Peerage Ltd.[3] The records are
not available for direct consultation by the public, but inquiries may be addressed to the Secretary of the College or
to any individual Herald by name.

*Commonwealth Relations Office, King Charles Street, London,
S. W. 1.*

In that part of the Commonwealth Relations Office which
was formerly the India Office are preserved the Records of
the East India Company, which comprise remarkably full
records of the Company's Civil and Military Servants in the
18th and 19th centuries. A good account of the India Office
Records by Major V. C. P. Hodgson will be found in *The
Genealogists' Magazine,* vol. 6, 1932, pp. 198-208.

Local Records

A general account of these is given in Hall's *Repertory of
British Archives* above mentioned. Additional information
on the accessibility of these records as well as of diocesan and
probate records will be found in the *Bulletin of the Institute
of Historical Research, Special Supplement No. 1,* 1932. The
reports of the Historical Manuscripts Commission, whose
headquarters are at the Public Record Office, give details of

---

[3] Anthony Richard Wagner, Richmond Herald; *The Records and Collection of the College of Arms* (1952) obtainable from the author.

many municipal records as well as of records in private hands. The National Register of Archives, whose headquarters are also at the Public Record Office, is compiling a general list of local and private archives. The chief depositories are:

COUNTY RECORD OFFICES.—A number of County Councils, beginning with Bedfordshire in 1914, have set up County Record Offices, primarily to preserve the Quarter Sessions Records and their own modern records, with those of superseded authorities whose functions they have taken over, and secondly, to receive deposits of private and other records of local interest, of which many have been deposited in the last few years.

MUNICIPAL RECORDS.—These, especially in the ancient boroughs, comprise records of great genealogical value, such as records of freedoms and apprenticeships.

OTHER LOCAL REPOSITORIES APPROVED BY THE MASTER OF THE ROLLS.—An Act of Parliament of 1924 placed Manorial Court Rolls under the care and superintendence of the Master of the Rolls, who thereupon approved a large number of local repositories as suitable places for their reception. These repositories, which include the County Record Offices above mentioned and comprise a number of institutions of the most varied kind, such as archaeological and historical societies, museums and libraries, have since become places of deposit for other types of local records also.

Registries of Deeds

By Acts of Parliament of the Reigns of Queen Anne and George II, Registries of Deeds were set up for four districts of England:

FOR THE WEST RIDING OF YORKSHIRE. Beginning in 1704. Registry at Wakefield, Yorkshire.

FOR THE EAST RIDING OF YORKSHIRE AND HULL. Beginning in 1708. Registry at Beverley, Yorkshire.

FOR MIDDLESEX. Beginning in 1709. Records at the Land Registry, Lincoln's Inn Fields, London, W. C.

FOR THE NORTH RIDING OF YORKSHIRE. Beginning in 1736. Registry at Northallerton, Yorkshire.

Private and Institutional Archives

A number of private landowners still retain in their muniment rooms archives of great genealogical value, though many of these have in recent years been transferred to public, national or local repositories.

Many colleges, schools, charities and other institutions possess archives of great value relating to their properties, and some of them have also important archives relating to their special activities. For example, the universities, the Inns of Court, colleges, schools and professional bodies have records of the admission and careers of their members. Many of these are listed in the *Institute of Historical Research Special Supplements 1 and 2*, 1932-4.

B. COLLECTIONS OF SECONDARY MATERIALS

Genealogists have been at work in England and Wales for several centuries and before embarking upon a voyage in the vast sea of original archives, it is merely common sense to inquire first whether any of them has provided a chart of the particular territory which concerns us. As is well known, the work of pedigree makers presents many pitfalls, and should always be looked at in a critical spirit, but the more scholarly genealogists give references to the original sources of their information, and it is as a guide to these that it is here suggested that their work should be used. Printed genealogies are indexed in *The Genealogists' Guide,* by George W. Marshall, York Herald, last edition 1903, continued by *A Genealogical Guide,* by J. B. Whitmore, 1947. The following are the principal depositories of manuscript genealogical material:

The College of Arms, London, E.C.4

In addition to the official records, the College possesses extensive genealogical collections, including the working papers of many former Heralds which have been bequeathed or purchased, very large collections of abstracts of wills and other documents made in the course of research, and copies of parish registers specially made or purchased. Like the records, these are not available for direct consultation by the public, but inquiries may be addressed to the Secretary of the College, or any individual Herald by name.

The Department of Manuscripts, British Museum, London, W. C.

Among the vast manuscript collections in the British Museum are genealogical collections of the first importance both national and local. A *Catalogue of the Heralds Visitations, with references to many other valuable genealogical and topographical manuscripts in the British Museum,* 2nd edition 1825, and *An Index to the pedigrees and Arms contained in the Heralds Visitations and other genealogical manuscripts in the British Museum,* by R. Sims, 1849, contain valuable references to manuscripts acquired down to those dates, but many most important collections have been acquired subsequently and for these the indexes to the successive volumes of printed catalogues of the *Additional* and other manuscripts must be consulted. The *Index to the Charters and Rolls of the Department of Manuscripts, British Museum,* 2 vols., 1900 and 1912, is an invaluable topographical guide. Some of the most important local collections are noted in Gatfield's *Guide to Heraldry and Genealogy (supra).*

The Society of Genealogists, 37 Harrington Gardens, London, S. W. 7

Besides a valuable library available to members and, on payment of a fee, to non-members, the Society has a collection of manuscript, genealogical and topographical material and a large and ever-growing card index of genealogical material of very many kinds, which it is always worth while to consult in a difficulty. A series of *Marriage Indexes* for a number of English counties and an *Index of Apprenticeships* are of special value.

The National Library of Wales, Aberystwyth

Besides being, as already mentioned, the place of deposit

of the Welsh Probate Records and of the Welsh Ecclesiastical Records other than the parish registers, this library contains a most important collection of Welsh genealogical material generally.

Bodleian Library, Oxford

Some of the manuscript collections contain important genealogical material, notably the Dodsworth, Tanner, Dugdale, Ashmole and Gough Collections. Catalogues of these and others are printed, but differ considerably in the amount of detail given.

Local Collections

Some of the Public Libraries in the principal cities and some of the local archaeological societies possess important local genealogical collections. Special mention may be made of the Public Libraries at Newcastle-on-Tyne, Birmingham, and Manchester, the John Rylands Library at Manchester, and the Libraries of the William Salt Society at Stafford, the Yorkshire Archaeological Society at Leeds, and the Wiltshire Archaeological Society at Devizes.

C. RECORD SOURCES

The following very brief selection comprises only those records likely to be most useful in tracing the English origin of American settlers. The first step is to make sure that the settler's origin has not been discovered already by another genealogist, first by searching the American and English indexes to the printed sources and then by examining the most likely of the genealogical collections listed above. The next step depends on whether or not the American evidence gives a clue to the settler's place of origin. If the date of his birth is also known, the *General Register* at Somerset House will then be searched, if he were born after the 1st of July 1837, or the baptismal register of the parish, if he were born earlier. Unfortunately, the case is seldom as simple as this. If the settler came to America after 1851 and his English place of residence in that year is known or can be discovered, his place of birth may then be ascertained by consulting the records of the *1851 Census* in the Public Record Office. But, since this is arranged by localities and streets, it is necessary to know the exact address. This may often be ascertained from printed directories if not otherwise known. The *1841 Census*, the earliest which gives personal details, gives the age only to the nearest five years and states only whether the birth was in or outside the county of present residence.

For a 17th century settler, if there is no direct clue to the place of English origin, the history of the settlement in which he took part will often give one.

In the last resort, however, the first step will be to ascertain the general distribution of the name in England. When the name is a common occupational surname, this may be a hopeless task, but very many surnames, especially those of local origin, belong mainly or primarily to particular localities and are rare or unknown elsewhere. A good starting point for mapping the distribution of a name is to make lists from the printed calendars for the Prerogative Probate Courts of Canterbury and York. The clues thus given can then be further refined upon by making similar lists from the calendars of the local probate courts for those parts in which the name occurs. By this means alone, it has sometimes proved possible to pin a name down to a limited number of parishes.

The next step will usually be to make abstracts of all wills and administrations of persons of the name for the possible period. These will give a closer view of the status, occupation, and genealogy of the family. For the post-mediaeval period, it may indeed be said that wills are the backbone of genealogy. They have the great advantage over parish registers, and indeed most other classes of record, that a single will often specifies a number of relationships and so by comparison with others give a far firmer basis for identification of persons than the single statement in, *e.g.*, a baptismal entry that A was the son of B. The American searcher who finds the man he is pursuing mentioned in a will as "my nephew Thomas now dwelling in New England", or even "overseas" must count himself exceptionally fortunate, yet there are many such mentions in 17th century wills. For families with too little property to leave wills, reliance must mainly be placed on parish registers.

For families whose members were high enough in the social scale to describe themselves as "gentlemen" and to be accepted as such by the Heralds, the records of the College of Arms, and particularly the Heralds' Visitations are invaluable. A warning must here be given that a large proportion of the collections of pedigrees for different counties, which have been printed under the title of "Visitations", are in fact not Visitation Books at all, but compilations of greater or less accuracy, more or less directly derived from them. Because this has not been understood, the originals in the College have often been blamed for the inaccuracies of the copies.

There is in England no general central record of inheritance or conveyance of land, but from the 12th century down to 1834 many conveyances were made by Fine and are recorded in the Feet of Fines in the Public Record Office. Calendars of these for certain dates and certain counties have been printed and others exist in manuscript. From the 27th year of Henry VIII, deeds of Conveyance of Freehold are enrolled in the Close Rolls in the Record Office. The County Record Offices and private muniment rooms contain vast numbers of private charters and deeds conveying land, as well as leases, rent books and the like. The local Land Registries set up by Act of Parliament for certain localities in the early 18th century have already been mentioned.

The Lay Subsidy and Hearth Tax Rolls are Returns of Assessments for Taxation arranged by parishes and are invaluable as a Directory of Householders with an indication of their standing in the world.

Light upon the origins of men engaged in those trades which were subject to Guild control in the towns may often be had from the apprenticeship and other records, both of the Guilds or Companies and of the municipalities, and in some few cases, calendars or indexes have been printed.

Of the records of the Courts of Law, after the mediaeval period, those with the greatest genealogical value are the

Records of the Court of Chancery preserved in the Public Record Office. Calendars of these are printed from the reign of Richard II, when they begin, to the reign of Charles I, and a beginning has been made in the printing of later calendars. The Records of the membership of the Professions, the Army, the Navy, the Church, the Law and Medicine, are each a study in themselves, and references will be found in the general bibliographies mentioned above.

D. WELSH RECORDS

The Documentary nature of Welsh Records is not in general very different from that of English Records. The problems of Welsh genealogy are, however, in many ways different from those of English and call for some separate explanation. For a detailed account the reader may be referred to an article by Major Francis Jones, "The Background of Welsh Genealogy", Y Cymmrodor, 1948, pp. 303-466.

The first point of difference that will be noted is that surnames were not introduced into Wales until the 16th century and did not become universal until the 17th century and were then almost all patronymics and very few, comparatively speaking, in total number. The result is almost as if in England everyone were to have a surname of the relative frequency of Smith, while in the Probate Calendars one commonly finds entries calendared under the Christian names instead of the surnames. On the other hand, down to the end of the 17th century and even later, the Welsh were remarkably tenacious of family tradition. Until Henry VIIII abolished the Welsh tenures, estates had been divided equally among all the sons, and if the male descendants of one should become extinct, the descendants of others would have a reversionary claim. To keep record of one's descent was, therefore, a matter of serious practical importance. The recital of several generations of ancestry is constantly found in Wales in legal documents, and comparison with earlier record evidence has now shown that the traditional genealogies committed to writing in the 16th and 17th centuries rested to a great extent on firm foundations.

Particular value attaches to the great corpus of Welsh genealogies, accumulated and added to, over a long period, which is now in the College of Arms. As Major Jones has made clear, however, these genealogies have their own special weaknesses for which full allowance must be made. There comes a point in working backwards where the first known ancestor of a family had to be linked to an older body of princely pedigrees, which in turn are joined at an earlier point to the British Kings, the Kings of Troy and the Biblical Patriarchs. To the practiced eye, these sutures betray themselves readily enough.

From the reign of Henry VIII a mass of Welsh genealogical material exists in the Great Sessions Records of the several counties, but, unfortunately, this is uncalendared and unindexed, so that to make use of it is a matter of great labour.

* * * *

(Note: *English Genealogy*, by Anthony R. Wagner, Richmond Herald, published by the Clarendon Press, Oxford, will probably be available in October, 1959. In some 400 pages (well indexed and documented) the author discusses the oldest lines from which persons of English origin can trace descent (Royal pedigrees of Anglo-Saxons and Vikings, Irish, Scots and Welsh, Charlemagne, etc.); descents claimed or proved from pre-conquest English and Normans of the century of the Conquest; the class structure of English Society as it affects the genealogist (Barons, gentlemen, franklins and yeomen, country labourers, trades, merchants, craftsmen, clergy, arts, recusants, dissenters, etc.); the rise and fall of families, social movements and effect of rules of inheritance; settlers in England from abroad; settlers overseas (Ireland, 17th century settlements in the American mainland and islands, colonies of the old Empire, and 19th century migrations); the records of Church and State and private records, and their genealogical content and use; and, finally, the study and literature of English genealogy from early times to the present and the practical approach to the subject and some of the problems encountered. It will provide those interested in English genealogy with much information which could not be furnished within the space limitations of this Chapter. ED.)

CHAPTER IV

SCOTLAND

Scottish records may be divided into four classes, viz. National, Local, Ecclesiastical and Private.

THE NATIONAL RECORDS are preserved in the General Register House at Edinburgh and a complete and detailed list of same will be found in *A Guide to the Public Records of Scotland, deposited in H. M. General Register House, Edinburgh,* by Matthew Livingstone, Deputy Keeper of the Records, published in 1905, and also in *An Introductory Survey of the Sources and Literature of Scots Law,* published by the Stair Society, Edinburgh, 1936. It is impossible, in a limited work like this, to give all this information but those which are chiefly valuable to the genealogical searcher will be listed at the end of this chapter.

THE LOCAL RECORDS are preserved in the Sheriff Courts and Town Clerks' offices throughout the country. In the Sheriff Clerk's possession are the Registers of Proceedings in various legal actions before the Sheriffs, who are the County Court Judges. There are also Registers of Deeds, of Services of Heirs and the proceedings in Executrics of persons dying within their jurisdictions after 1830, including copies of wills and inventories of estates confirmed to executors. The Property Registers in the Royal Burghs (Registers of Sasines) are now being transferred to the General Register House, Edinburgh.

THE ECCLESIASTICAL RECORDS are those of the Church of Scotland and are in possession of the church authorities. Those of the General Assembly, Synods, Presbyteries and Kirk Sessions are deposited to a certain extent in the Strong Room at the General Assembly Hall, Edinburgh, though many of the Presbytery and Session Registers are still in the hands of their Clerks in the different localities.

The Registers of Baptisms, Marriages and Deaths from

1560 down to the year 1855 when compulsory registration came into force, were then brought to the Registrar General's Office, New Register House, Edinburgh, where they can be consulted under their different parishes. Very few of these records go back before 1600, many begin about 1689, and in some cases, after 1800.

The Census returns for the years 1841, 1851, 1861 and 1871 also can be consulted at the Registrar General's Office. These returns will give a detailed list of all households and the persons residing therein.

The Registers of Dissenting Churches, the Free Church and United Free Church, Scottish Episcopal and Roman Catholic, are still in the hands of the local churches, but those of the Secession and the United Presbyterian Church are now deposited in the Church of Scotland Offices, 121 George Street, Edinburgh.

Fasti Ecclesiae Scoticanae, 7 volumes, published 1914-26, volume VIII in the press, contains detailed information regarding all ministers of the Church of Scotland from 1560-1929 with particulars of their families.

In making a genealogical search for the ancestry of Americans of Scottish descent, all possible information regarding the ancestor who left Scotland should be supplied, such as any indication of the locality he is understood to have come from and the names of any known ancestor or of any relatives who remained behind. Unless such information is known, any search is impossible.

The Registers of Births, Deaths and Marriages of the parish from which he came are the first source of information that should be consulted. After that the Commissariat Registers of Testaments (Probates) for the district should be examined for any relating to the family. If the family owned any land or houses, a search on the appropriate Register of Sasines should be made.

The Records of the Court of the Lord Lyon, H. M. Register House, Edinburgh, should be consulted, not only the official ones but the immense collections of pedigrees and notes on various families on the unofficial file, to which there is a card index.

Scottish Family History: A Guide to Works of Reference on the History and Genealogy of Scottish Families, by Margaret Stuart, to which is prefixed *An Essay on How to Write the History of a Family*, by Sir James Balfour Paul, K. C. V. O., Lord Lyon King of Arms, published by Oliver and Boyd, Edinburgh, 1920, gives references to more printed sources where pedigrees will be found. The preface will also assist the searcher where to look for information and also contains a valuable list and details of the various records which should be searched.

The Scottish Ancestry Research Society, 4 North St. David Street, Edinburgh, was instituted during the late war, chiefly for the purpose of assisting Commonwealth and American soldiers to trace their ancestors who were Scottish. This Society undertakes to make searches in the General Register of Births, Deaths and Marriages for 150 years and inquiries should be addressed to the Secretary.

There are also private persons who undertake the work of searching all public and local records. The names of such reliable persons can be obtained by writing the Lord Lyon King of Arms, H. M. Register House, Edinburgh. As it is impossible to say what the cost of such a search may be, it is advisable for the inquirer to make arrangement with the searcher as to a sum beyond which he may not go without further instruction.

As most of the earlier records are in Latin and written in a handwriting which requires an expert to read it, it will be found more convenient and economical for the inquirer to employ such a private searcher who has knowledge of such registers and which should be consulted.

SOURCES OF INFORMATION

NATIONAL RECORDS.—

Acts of Parliament, 12 volumes, 1446-1706, printed.

Exchequer Rolls, 1264-1708, printed in 1600.

Returns & Services of Heirs, 1550 to date; printed indices.

Register of the Great Seal, 1306 to date, printed to 1608.

Calendar of Documents relating to Scotland in Public Record Office, London, 1105-1509, printed.

Register of the Privy Council, 1545-1706, printed to 1689.

Accounts of the Lord High Treasurer, 1473-1625, printed to 1566.

Register of the Privy Seal, 1488-1810, printed to 1548.

BOOKS OF COUNCIL AND SESSION OR REGISTER OF DEEDS, 1554 to date. This is the largest collection of deeds relating to all subjects. It is unfortunately only partially indexed and as sometimes only three days registrations are given in a volume, a search is one of great labour.

REGISTER OF ACTS & DECRIETS OF THE COURT OF SESSION 1542 to date. The papers in connection with many of the litigations will be found in the National and in libraries of the legal societies in Edinburgh.

REGISTER OF HEARINGS, INHIBITIONS AND ADJUDICATIONS, viz., GENERAL REGISTER OF HEARINGS 1610-1902. GENERAL REGISTER OF INHIBITIONS 1602-1924. There are also local registers for each county.

COMMISSARIAT REGISTERS OF TESTAMENTS in the various Courts, viz., Edinburgh 1567-1829. Aberdeen 1721-1824. Argyll 1674-1819. Brechin 1576-1823. Caithness 1661-79, 1790-1824. Dumfries 1624-1827. Dunblane 1529-1825. Dunkeld 1687-1820. Glasgow 1547-1823. Hamilton and Campsie 1564-1823. Inverness 1630-1820. Isles 1661-1824. Kirkcudbright 1663-1823. Lanark 1595-1823. Lauder 1561-1822. Moray 1684-1827. Orkney and Shetland 1611-1684. Peebles 1681-1699. Ross 1802-1824. St. Andrews 1549-1823. Stirling 1607-1823. Wigtown 1700-1823. Argyllshire Inventories 1693-1702. List of Consistorial Processes & Decriets in the Commissariat of Edinburgh 1658-1800. *Indices* to the above have been printed to 1800 by the Scottish Record Society.

REGISTER OF SASINES (PROPERTY REGISTERS).—
The General Register from 19 August 1617 to 31 December 1868.

The Particular Register for each county for similar period.

New General Register kept in County Divisions since 1868.

Royal Burgh Registers of Sasines.

These registers contain all deeds relating to the transfer, sale or mortgaging of land and of the succession of heirs in same.

REGISTER OF TAILZIERS, or Entails of Landed Estates from 1688 to date.

This gives information as to the various series of heirs who are called to the succession by the entailer.

NATIONAL PROTOCOL BOOKS.—Preserved in the General Register House and contain a record of all deeds executed by the Notary Public in his profession. Abstracts of the following have been printed by the Scottish Record Society, viz:

Gavin Ros 1512-32. Sir Alexander Gaw 1540-58.
Sir William Corbet 1529-55. Sir Gilbert Grote 1552-73
Sir Thomas Johnson 1528-78.
James Foulis 1546-53. Nicol Mounis 1559-64.
John Cristison 1518-51. Sir Robert Relloch 1526-52.
John Foular, town clerk of Edinburgh 1503-28.
James Young 1485-1815.

THE SCOTTISH RECORD SOCIETY has published many records. These form a most valuable source of information and should also be consulted.

COURT OF THE LORD LYON.—

Public Register of all Arms & Bearings in Scotland 1672 to date. Public Register of all Genealogies and Birth Brieves 1727 to date. Birth Brieves, Funeral Entries and Escutcheons from 1672. (*Index* printed by Scottish Record Society.)

Register of Arms of Sir Robert Forman, Lord Lyon 1554.

Acts and Decriets of Lyon Court 1629 to date.

Admission of Messengers at Arms 1630 to date.

Admission of Heralds & Pursuivants 1660 to date.

Lyons' Register of Processions, Letters of Precedency, Testificatis and Forfeitures 1679.

Funeral processions and ceremonies, first half of 17th century. Petitions for grants and matriculations of Arms 1819 to date. Unofficial file of pedigrees, searches and notes on families, including collections made by Charles Cleland Harvey, A. W. Gray Buchanan, Miss Mae Gilchrist-Gilchrist and R. R. Stodart.

List of H. M. Officers of Arms and Other Officials 1218-1945, with genealogical notes. (Printed by Scottish Record Society.)

Ordinary of Arms Contained in the Public Register of all Arms & Bearings in Scotland, by Sir James Balfour Paul, Lyon. (Printed 2nd edition 1903.)

ECCLESIASTICAL RECORDS.—

General Assembly Records of the Church of Scotland, Acts and Proceedings, 1560-1618. (Printed by Bannatyne and Maitland Clubs.)

Acts 1638-42 (Church Law Society)

Abridgement of Acts 1638-1810.

Commissions of Assembly 1647-52. (Scottish History Society.)

Synod Records for 16 Synods.

Presbytery Records for 93 Presbyteries.

Kirk Session Records. See list printed in Rev. Thomas Burns' *The Benefee Lectures*, 1905.

The following Session Registers date from before 1600, viz: Crail 1561; Galston 1568; Middle Kirk Perth 1577; Elgin 1584; Dunbarny 1594; St. Machar, Aberdeen 1596; Prestonpans 1596; St. Monans 1597; South Leith 1597; High Kirk, Glasgow.

A considerable number of books of Court History have been published giving abstracts or portions of these records. (See *Sources & Literature of Scots Law*, published by the Stair Society, 1936.)

GENERAL REGISTER OF BIRTHS, DEATHS AND MARRIAGES, 1560 to date.

The following Registers have been printed by the Scottish Record Society:

Holyrood Burial Register 1706-1908.

Greyfriars, Edinburgh, Burial Register 1656-1700.

Edinburgh Marriage Register, 2 vols. 1595-1800.

Canongate Marriage Register 1566-1800.

Chapel of Birnie and Tillydesk (Episcopal) 1763-1801.

Torpchichen Parish 1673-1714.

Restalrig Burials 1728-1854.

Durness Parish 1764-1814.

Kilbarchan Parish 1649-1772.

Dunfermline Parish 1561-1685.

Melrose Parish 1642-1820.

Canisbay Parish 1652-1666.

St. Andrews (Episcopal) 1722-1787.

Old St. Paul's Edinburgh (Episcopal) 1735-65 (*Scottish Antiquary* IV, V, VI).

St. Paul's Aberdeen (Episcopal) 1720-93 (*New Spalding Club Miscellany* II).

Stirling Parish 1585-92 (*Scottish Antiquary* VI, 159 et seq.).

Leith (Episcopal) 1738-75 (*Scottish Antiquary* VIII, 125, et seq.).

Brechin (Episcopal) 1796-1819 (*Scottish Antiquary* XIV, 96, et seq.).

Shetland. Register of Rev. John Hunter, Episcopal Minister 1736-1745 (*Scottish Antiquary*, VI).

Muthill (Episcopal) 1697-1847 (Printed by Rev. A. W. C. Wallon (1897)).

LOCAL RECORDS.—

SHERIFF COURT RECORDS: These are in the custody of Sheriff Clerks in the various Sheriffdoms. The following have been printed, viz:

The Records of the Sheriffdom of Aberdeen 1503-1660 (*New Spalding Club* 1904-7).

Kirkcudbright; Register of Deeds 1623-75. (Printed by Marquess of Bute.) Details of these records will be found in *Sources & Literature of Scots Law*, published by Stair Society.

REGALITY COURTS AND BARON COURTS.—The heritable jurisdictions were practically abolished in 1748, when the present Sheriff Courts were instituted. Their records are to a certain extent in the possession of the families who held them, but some are in the General Register House. Details will be found in the *Sources & Literature of Scots Law*, published by the Stair Society.

BURGH RECORDS: These are in the possession of various Town Clerks throughout the country. They include among other registers those of apprentices and Burgess Rolls. The Scottish Burgh Record Society has published twenty-two volumes dealing with the records of the following Burghs, viz: Edinburgh, Glasgow, Aberdeen, Peebles, Dundee, Stirling, Lanark, etc.

The Scottish Record Society has printed the following registers, viz:

Edinburgh Apprentice Register 1583-1666, 1666-1755.
Edinburgh Burgess Roll 1406-1846.

Glasgow Burgess Rolls 1573-1841.

Dumbarton Burgess Rolls 1600-1846.

The New Spalding Club, Aberdeen, has printed the Aberdeen Burgess Roll, 1399-1702 (Miscellany I & II).

The Marquess of Bute has printed the Rothesay Burgh Records 1653-1776, and Stirling Protocol Book 1469-1486 is given in *Scottish Antiquary* X, 55, et seq. The Protocol Books of the town clerks of Glasgow 1547-1600 and the Dunfermline Burgh Records 1488-1584 have also been printed.

MILITARY RECORDS.—

Charles Dalton's Scots Army (1909) 1661-1688.

Papers relating to Army, including Muster Rolls of different Regiments 1660-1688, in General Register House.

The Scots Brigade in Holland 1572-1782. (Scottish History Society.)

UNIVERSITY RECORDS.—Matriculations and rolls of graduates of the Universities of Aberdeen (Kings College from 1495), Edinburgh (from 1583), Glasgow (from 1728), and St. Andrews (from 1747) have been printed and may be readily located under the name of the university in many large libraries. *Scots Colleges, Douay, Rome, Madrid, Valladolid, and Ratisbon 1581-1900,* published by the New Spalding Club gives information on the institutions named.

PRIVATE RECORDS

Many valuable records are privately owned. The Historical Manuscripts Commission has issued *Reports* (Vols. I to XVI) on the Charter Chests of over a hundred families and institutions. Others have been published by the Scottish Record Society and similar organizations.

CHAPTER V

IRELAND

The immediate problem of Americans with regard to their Irish ancestors is that few know the parentage of the immigrant. It is of the utmost importance that the genealogist, for purposes of identification, shall locate with as much detail as possible the geographical origin of an Irish ancestor. A thorough preliminary search should be made in the United States for records of all classes pertaining to the immigrant ancestor, from the time he arrived in the first place of his settlement in America until his death. The time and expense devoted to an exhaustive preliminary search may save far more time and expense in the search of records in Ireland, or by correspondence with officials in the repositories of genealogical records in Ireland. For information about his Irish origin, a search must be made of family Bibles, church registers, Quaker meeting records (if the ancestor was a member of the Society of Friends), local histories, family records preserved in the historical society of the county where the immigrant lived, probate and land records, pension records, and passenger lists which are among the sources that may throw light on the ancestral home in Ireland. Once that is established, the researcher is then in a position to have the records of the Irish locality searched.

Traditions in families of Irish descent often state that a man came from one of the seaport cities such as Londonderry, Belfast, Larne, Coleraine, Dublin, Cork, etc., and may state further that he was employed in one of these seaport cities before sailing. Actually, he may have lived many miles from the seaport, to which he traveled only for the purpose of sailing from Ireland. Tradition may be even more confusing when it relates that the immigrant ancestor was Irish, but emigrated from Liverpool. As early as 1650, it was common practice for Irish to travel on small ships from Irish ports to Liverpool and then transfer to larger vessels for the long trip to America. In this English port city, the Irish might seek employment of any kind while awaiting a ship which would sail to the American port of choice. An American genealogist, unfamiliar with Irish history and customs of transportation, might accept the specific Liverpool sailing tradition but throw out the family tradition of Irish ancestry, being unable to relate the seemingly conflicting facts, particularly if the immigrant was employed in Liverpool before sailing.

The exact geographical origin of the Irish ancestor, when established, aids not only as an identifying factor, but determines the choice of Irish records to be searched. The geographical and ecclesiastical structure of Ireland must be understood by the genealogist before he attempts original Irish genealogical research.

Locations are indexed and described in the records by province, county, barony, diocese, parish, city, town, and townland. The names of baronies, dioceses, parishes and townlands are not to be found on a modern map of Ireland, but are shown in 19th century and earlier maps. Church records, whether they be Catholic or Protestant, are indexed by diocese and parish. As the established Church of Ireland (Episcopalian) until 1857 had ecclesiastical jurisdiction over testamentary matters, wills are also indexed by diocese, unless the testator owned property of more than five pounds sterling in value, in two or more dioceses, in which case the will was proved in the Prerogative Court of Ireland under the jurisdiction of the Archbishop of Armagh. Land records are described by county, barony, and city, town, or townland. Land outside of cities and towns (acreage), is divided and defined by the names of townlands.

PROVINCE: Ireland was in ancient times divided into five provinces, or "Fifths". These gradually passed to the several divisions which were organized into the present counties. *Munster*, the southernmost province, embraces the counties of Cork, Limerick, Kerry, Tipperary, Waterford, and Clare. *Leinster*, the middle and southeastern portion of Eire, includes Longford, Westmeath, Meath, Louth, Offaly (Kings County), Leix (Queens County), Kildare, Dublin, Carlow,

Wicklow, Kilkenny, and Wexford. *Meath*, the modern county of which is included in Leinster, was formerly the name of a separate province. *Connaught*, the western province, includes the counties of Mayo, Sligo, Leitrim, Galway, and Roscommon. *Ulster*, the northern province of Ireland, originally embraced the nine counties of Donegal, Londonderry, Antrim, Fermanagh, Tyrone, Cavan, Monaghan, Armagh, and Down.

COUNTY: The 32 counties are listed above. By the Government of Ireland Act of 1920, 6 of the 9 counties of Ulster, namely Antrim, Armagh, Down, Fermanagh, Londonderry and Tyrone, remained under the dominion of Great Britain, while the 26 remaining counties are now included in the Republic of Ireland. The names of 2 of the counties were changed at this time, and the old names appear above in brackets.

DIOCESE: There are 28 dioceses or ecclesiastical divisions of Ireland, dating from early Catholic jurisdiction. The boundaries were little changed as the Established Church became the State Church (Episcopal). The boundary of a diocese has little or no relation to that of a county, each diocese embracing parts of from one to six counties and, conversely, each county falling in from one to several dioceses.

THE COUNTIES OF IRELAND AND THEIR DIOCESAN JURISDICTIONS

County includes parts of	Diocese
Antrim	Connor, Derry, Down, Dromore
Armagh	Armagh, Dromore
Carlow	Leighlin
Cavan	Ardagh, Meath, Kilmore
Clare	Killaloe and Kilfenora, Limerick
Cork	Cork and Ross, Cloyne, Ardfert
Donegal	Clogher, Derry, Raphoe
Down	Connor, Down, Dromore, Newry and Mourne
Dublin	Dublin
Fermanagh	Clogher, Kilmore
Galway	Clonfert, Elphin, Killaloe, Tuam
Kerry	Ardfert
Kildare	Dublin, Kildare
Kilkenny	Leighlin, Ossory
Kings (now Offaly)	Clonfert, Kildare, Killaloe, Meath, Ossory
Leitrim	Ardagh, Kilmore
Limerick	Cashel, and Emly, Killaloe, Limerick
Londonderry	Armagh, Connor, Derry
Longford	Armagh, Meath

County	includes parts of	Diocese
Louth		Armagh, Clogher, Drogheda
Mayo		Killala and Achrony, Tuam
Meath		Armagh, Kildare, Kilmore, Meath
Monaghan		Clogher
Queens (now Leix)		Dublin, Kildare, Leighlin, Ossory
Roscommon		Ardagh, Clonfert, Elphin, Tuam
Sligo		Ardagh, Elphin, Killala
Tipperary		Cashel, Killaloe, Waterford and Lismore
Tyrone		Armagh, Clogher, Derry
Waterford		Waterford and Lismore
West Meath		Ardagh, Meath
Wexford		Dublin, Ferns
Wicklow		Dublin, Ferns

BARONY: This is an ancient division of land representing, roughly, the past holding of an Irish chieftain. The name of the barony was used in land and tax matters as descriptive of a district or section of the county. The *Down Survey Maps*, made by Sir William Petty, 1655-59, covering all of Ireland, showed it divided into 216 baronies.

PARISH: This is a subdivision of the diocese, under the ecclesiastical jurisdiction of the bishop of the diocese and the local incumbent of the parish church. Petty illustrated his *Down Survey* with 2,000 parish maps.

CITY AND TOWN: The names of these have changed little in the last two hundred years, and are to be found on detailed modern maps of Ireland.

TOWNLAND: The *Down Survey* shows, entered on the *Barony Maps*, some 25,000 place-names, mostly names of townlands, which were in fact small subdivisions of the barony; being acreage, farms, or family holdings. A place-name, said to be the name of the place of birth of the immigrant ancestor, or the location of the family residence, if not to be found on a modern map, is probably that of a townland, if not that of a barony, diocese, or parish in which the family resided.

The following publications which may be found in most of the larger American genealogical libraries and in the American Irish Historical Society Library, New York City, will aid in establishing the complete description of the family location, if the name of the county and some unfamiliar place-name are known.

Philips' Handy Atlas of the Counties of Ireland, by Bartholomew and Joyce, with consulting index, London, 1884. County maps show baronies by color; also parishes, and country seats (larger townlands), as well as cities, towns, villages, etc.

Lewis's Atlas of the Counties of Ireland, London, 1837. This has engraved county maps showing the baronies and parishes, etc.

Maps showing the relation between the counties and dioceses are to be found in the *Report of Her Majesty's Commissioners on the Revenues and Condition of the Established Church (Ireland)*, 1868, *and Appendix*, published as a separate volume.

A Topographical Index of Parishes and Townlands of Ireland in Sir William Petty's Manuscript Barony Maps (c. 1655-1659), collected and edited by Y. M. Goblet, Dublin, 1932. This book has a listing of every townland and parish in Ireland at the time the *Down Survey Maps* were made. Few names have changed. Townlands are listed alphabetically, giving the parish and county in which they are located. Parishes are listed alphabetically, by barony and county.

The General Alphabetical Index of Townlands and Towns, Parishes and Baronies of Ireland, Published with the Census of Ireland, by Alexander Thom, Dublin, 1861.

The Parliamentary Gazetteer of Ireland, 3 vols., Dublin, London, Edinburgh, 1841. This gives a brief description of cities, towns, villages and churches, placing them as to parish, diocese, barony and county.

Topographical Dictionary of Ireland, Its Several Counties, Cities, Boroughs, Corporate Market and Post Towns, Parishes and Villages, 2 vols., by Samuel Lewis, London, 1839.

Publication of the Census of Ireland, 1761-1872, 2 vols., by the Registrar General.

The Census of Population of Northern Ireland, 1926, Topographical Index. (Her Majesty's Stationary Office, Belfast. Reprinted, 1947.) The value of this to the genealogist is in the list of counties, baronies, parishes, towns and townlands, with cross indexes which make it possible to place any townland within its embracing barony, county, parish or town boundary, as well as electoral division, registrars district, etc.

Irish Names of Places, 3 vols., by P. W. Joyce, LL.D., Dublin, 1869, 1873, 1913.

Varieties of Synonymes of Sur-names and Christian Names in Ireland, by Robert E. Matheson, Dublin, 1890. This was compiled for the use of persons working with legal or government records, to show the variations in spelling of each surname, appearing in various legal and public records or documents. Some surnames are spelled in from two to a dozen ways, all referring to a single individual. When beginning work on a family, it is wise to consult this book and note all spellings of the surname to make sure no reference will be missed in examining indexes. The spelling of the surname, Dickson, for example, is interchangeably varied for the same family as Dixon, Dixson, Dikeson, Dixsone, etc.

Before enumerating and describing the more important classes of records and the extent and whereabouts of these records, a brief review will be made of the repositories which have the records most needed by the genealogist.

The Public Record Office of Ireland, Dublin

No understanding of the classes, the extent, and the availability of genealogical documents in Ireland can be had without some knowledge of the history and contents of the Public Record Offices in Dublin and in Belfast.

The Public Record Office of Ireland, located in the Four Courts, Dublin, was established in 1867. A search by correspondence will be given attention if accompanied with an initial search fee of $3.00 which can be sent by a post office money order. The charge will be at the rate of $1.00 per hour for genealogical research, record search, and correspondence, and an extra charge for photostating, certification, mailing, etc. (These charges are fairly general throughout Ireland and so will not be quoted for other repositories.) The initial fee may all be used for an estimate of what further work will cost and a report on what specific records are available.

The Deputy Keeper of the Records, under the provisions of the Public Records (Ireland) Act, 12 August 1867, was required to publish an annual *Report* regarding the work of classifying and arranging the records, the nature of the accessions, and an index to the documents by name of the principal, date, classification, and location, which were not included in the larger collections, carrying their own indexes. These *Reports of the Deputy Keeper of the Public Records of*

Ireland, published annually from 1869-1921, comprise 52 volumes with appendices, including extensive indexes. These made the public aware of the enormous collections of wills, administrations, deeds (earlier than 1708), leases, marriage records, parish records, chancery court records, census records, tithe lists, hearthmoney rolls, subsidy rolls, fiants, Commonwealth records, Catholic Qualification rolls, and numerous other classes of records. In 1895 and 1899, there were published as appendices, the *Indexes to the Act and Grant Books and to the Original Wills of the Diocese of Dublin,* circa 1635-1800; 1800-1858. In over 100,000 entries, the wills, administrations, marriage license bonds, chancery court records and about 30 other classes of records were indexed. The wills and intestacies were listed by name, place, occupation, and year of probate. The marriage license bonds give the name of the groom, bride, year of marriage, residence and occupation of the groom.

In 1922, the Public Record Office in Dublin was burned and almost all of the Prerogative and Diocesan Wills, marriage records, census records and other classes of records of genealogical interest were destroyed or badly injured. Some valuable collections of records in the fireproof strongroom were saved. These included the Lodge Manuscripts, which consist of a series of volumes from the Patent Rolls of Henry VII, James I, Charles I and Charles II, abstracts of the Catholic Convert Rolls, being alphabetical lists of Catholics who renounced their church (usually temporarily) to avoid persecution, save their property, or to hold office, etc. There are two lists of converts, c. 1703-1772, 1709-1773; and one list, 1662-1737, of Protestants who, upon coming to Ireland, took the Oath of Allegiance. Further details of the Lodge Manuscripts are in the *Fifty-Fifth Report,* pp. 116-122.

After the fire, appeals were made throughout Ireland, England, Scotland, and America, for all who had copied the records during the past 53 years, to send their copies or transcripts, abstracts, or notes, to replace the burned records. It was known that a large number of original records (wills, marriage records, parish registers, etc.) had never been sent to this office and these or copies were requested. The appeals brought tremendous response. Legal (solicitors') offices, governmental, historical and genealogical repositories in Ireland and abroad sent original records, transcripts, abstracts, and notes from the burned records, as gifts or on loan for copying. Genealogical collections representing the life work of great genealogists such as Betham, Crossle, Groves, Sadleir, etc., were given or sold to this office. Individuals by the hundreds sent collections of family documents covering several generations. Several hundred parish registers of baptism, marriage and burial, either original or transcripts, were in local custody at the time of the fire, and so were available.

One of the most valuable collections acquired, which for the genealogist, repaired the loss of the Prerogative Wills, is the great collection of 241 volumes of the Betham Genealogical Abstracts. Sir William Betham, Ulster King of Arms, filled 80 volumes of this collection with abstracts of about 37,000 Prerogative Wills, 1595-1800, which represented all that were proved in the Prerogative Court of Armagh during this period. The other volumes were: Two of Kildare Wills, 1661-1826; 16 of Prerogative marriage licenses, 1629-1801; 56 of Prerogative administrations, 1595-1800; 4 of Prerogative marriage licenses, 1629-1800. The last 29 volumes are miscellaneous extracts from court records, pedigrees and memoranda. An indexed catalogue of the collection is in the Public Record Office. Besides these Betham Manuscripts, there are 8 volumes of his letters dealing with his genealogical researches and memoranda and extracts on genealogical subjects and other important collections of manuscripts which are listed in the *Fifty-Eighth Report of the Deputy Keeper of the Records,* pp. 26, 27.

As these great collections were being accumulated, indexed, and made available to the public, additional *Reports* were published which furnished this information to all who were interested. In 1926, *The Fifty-Third Report of the Deputy Keeper of the Public Records,* which had been prepared in 1922, was published. Between 1928-1936, with the publication of the *Fifty-Fifth, Fifty-Sixth, and Fifty-Seventh Reports,* and in 1951, the publication of the *Fifty-Eighth Report,* these *Reports* have served as immensely valuable catalogues for the genealogist, of the records now in the Public Record Office, Dublin. These may be found in most of the larger genealogical libraries of the United States.

There are also card catalogues, in the public search room, and typed indexes to various collections. The card index of testamentary documents is very extensive; it indexes many thousands of wills, duplicates and official plain copies of wills, grants of administrations, and original unproved wills never lodged for probate, which became too numerous after 1936 any longer to index in the *Reports.*

The Crossle Family Index, a very large collection, is the index to the Philip Crossle Manuscripts, consisting of family records, pedigrees, family notes, compiled genealogy, extracts from historical magazines, original miscellaneous records, abstracts of Chancery bills and Equity Exchequer bills and answers setting out family relationships, etc.

The Deeds index is a topographical card index to the deeds prior to the establishment of the Registry of Deeds in 1708. The enormous number of deeds received among family documents, running into thousands, also are indexed.

The Betham Manuscripts and many others, such as the Tenison Groves collection; the Swanzy genealogical abstracts of wills, administrations and marriage licenses for Prerogative Court, 1681-1846; the Monk Mason Manuscripts, being abstracts of inquisitions, Counties Dublin and Wicklow, Henry IV to Charles II, also the Chichester House Claims (with notes on decisions), or before 10 August 1700; the Stewart Kennedy notebooks, which contain abstracts of Prerogative and Diocesan Wills; the Greene Manuscripts, being extracts from the Prerogative and Diocesan Wills, Grant Books, Parish Registers, and the Prim collection; are all indexed by the collection. Besides this, such collections as the Diocesan Marriage License Bonds are preserved for the 26 dioceses in index form and are in the public search room.

The Public Record Office of Northern Ireland, Belfast

The most complete collection of genealogical, legal, and historical records in the Province of Ulster is deposited in this great repository of records, located in the Law Courts Building, May Street, Belfast, Northern Ireland. Inspection of the indexes and records is permitted for genealogical, historical, or antiquarian research, upon application to the Deputy Keeper of the Records. A nominal fee is charged, depending upon the number of documents, collections of records, and books searched, and the time spent in the office. An initial fee of $3.00 (P. O. money order) is charged for a brief preliminary survey and written communication. This is not refunded. The fee for a more extended search may range from $10.00 to $30.00 or more, depending upon the time devoted to the search and the report. This is exclusive of abstracts, copies, and photostats of any documents which may be desired. Certification will be an additional expense. A table of fees will be provided upon request.

At the time of the destruction of the Public Record Office, Dublin, in June 1922, almost all of the documents relating to Ulster from ancient times, were as yet in that repository and were lost in the fire. By the Government Act of 1923, the Northern Government set up its own Public Record Office in Belfast, which was opened in March 1924. D. A. Chart, M. A. LL.D., the first Deputy Keeper of the Public Records of Northern Ireland, 1924-1948, a trained archivist, assumed the heroic task of trying to make good the loss of the Public Records, so far as it affected Northern Ireland. For half a century, historians, genealogists, solicitors, and representatives from other repositories had been copying, making abstracts or taking notes from the records. Duplicates of many 17th and 18th century collections which were burned in 1922 existed in other repositories or in private hands, and much material had been published. Consequently, when Mr. Chart and his staff made the same appeal as that made by the Dublin Record Office, throughout Ireland, England, Scotland, and America, for transcripts, abstracts, manuscript collections, printed records, original records, all forms of compiled genealogical manuscripts, church records, and in fact any copy of any record ever lodged in the old Dublin Record Office, the response, judging from the *Reports of the Deputy Keeper of the Public Records of Northern Ireland*, and the size of the card index files, catalogue indexes, etc.—has been tremendous beyond belief. These *Reports* are indexed catalogues of collections, and all classes of legal records, etc., make the most fascinating reading to anyone interested in Ulster genealogy. The many records, other than normal increments, are listed and indexed in the *Reports of the Deputy Keeper of the Public Records of Northern Ireland*, beginning with the *First Annual Report of 1924*. These are available in the larger libraries.

The Sir Bernard Burke collection of 42 volumes of pedigree charts is here. These were not the original work of Burke, but were copied by or for Sir Bernard Burke for his personal use while Ulster King of Arms, following Betham, from the 39 volumes of Sir William Betham's pedigree charts, which are in the Genealogical Office, Dublin Castle, Dublin. Burke's *Copies* of Betham's charts do not have his valuable notations, which appear to be additional information which he gathered from other sources. These pedigree charts are easily available to anyone who wishes to send for a photostat of one or more, for a published index to every Prerogative Will which has been charted is available. This is the *Index to the Prerogative Wills of Ireland, 1536-1810*, edited by Sir Arthur Vicars, when Ulster King of Arms. Dublin: 1897. It is in all large genealogical libraries in the United States.

In December 1956, the Ulster-Scot Historical Society was organized and largely sponsored by the Government of Northern Ireland, with a President and Council, of which Kenneth Darwin, Deputy Keeper of the Public Records of Northern Ireland, is a member and Honorary Director. The stated purpose of the society is to assist persons of Ulster ancestry to trace facts about their Ulster ancestors. This is in effect a new and better organized way of taking care of genealogical research among the records of the Public Record Office of Northern Ireland.

The Ulster-Scot Historical Society is located in the Law Courts Building, Chichester Street, Belfast, Northern Ireland. A registration fee of $3.00 for an initial search is not returnable. The Society states that no guarantee of success can be made and that the average search and report should not exceed $9.00 and a more difficult search should not normally exceed $30.00. Failure to produce a proven line of Irish ancestry through this Society must not dissappoint the searcher to the point of stopping the work, for it does not establish the fact that there are no records of the family in the Public Record Office in Belfast. The failure would more probably be due to the fact that the connecting links between the emigrant ancestor and his family are not in this office. There may be numerous records of various classes or a pedigree or history of the family of his surname who lived in the right locality but these records do not identify the emigrant. However, these seemingly unrelated records may be used as a clue or guide to further research in other repositories of records such as the Registry of Deeds in Dublin.

Registry of Deeds, Dublin

The Registry of Deeds, Henrietta Street, Dublin, is open to the public. The records here are complete from 1708. These include memorials of deeds, leases of over three years, mortgages, foreclosures, marriage settlements, partitions, assignments, and memorials of wills presented at the time of estate settlements where property is involved. In many respects, these records offer the most certain way of identifying an emigrant and in general, where genealogical work has not been done for a family, offer the most rewarding results of any original research in Ireland. Land in Ireland, as in England, was largely owned in estates of several hundred or several thousand acres, and from the early days was leased to tenants on long or short term leases, many holding leases which were assigned from father to son over a period of "61 years, or three lives, whichever period was longer." Some leases were in perpetuity. The genealogical value in the leases is that each time a transfer of the property was made from one person to another by assignment, a fee was paid to the landlord and a recital was recorded, as to each person who had held the lease and his right to hold it within the term of the lease. Relationships, often for three or more generations are stated. The shorter term leases are to be found in the Estate offices of the landlords who owned the property. Many of the early estate records have been gathered in to the Public Record Offices. As marriage settlements were common in Ireland among the people of even modest means, these often yield information on the parentage of the bride or groom and the brothers and sisters whose portion may be mentioned.

The records are indexed in two ways: *The Name Index* of grantors, is arranged alphabetically in periods of from about 20 years from 1708, to lesser periods of about 10 years each when there were more records registered per year. The name of the grantee appears in the index opposite that of the grantor but with no given name shown. Instruments are listed by number. Locations are not included in this index until 1833. Thus, if the leases or other records are wanted for the period 1708-1729, for the Dickson family, the work begins with examining all of the records under given names known in the family. *The Lands (or Place) Index,* under counties, provides an index to all transactions, by date and geographical location. This facilitates the tracing of the history of tenure or ownership of any given piece of property.

The Genealogical Society, Salt Lake City, has microfilmed 122 reels of the *Names Index,* 1708-1904, and 283 reels of the *Placc Index* or *Lands Index,* 1708-1904. By securing from this Index in Salt Lake City the reference to identify desired records, copies may be ordered from Dublin. Using the above *Names Index* microfilm, the author ordered copies of records, thus: "Taken from film No. 2004. Records 1708-1729. Dickson, William, to Coates. Vol. 38, p. 282. No. 24244." This last number is the number of the instrument and must be given if a copy is ordered. Certified copies may be ordered at about $1.00 per page plus mailing charges. An estimate will be given upon request.

Office of the Registrar General, Customs House, Dublin

The registration of births, marriages and deaths, has been compulsory in Ireland since January 1864. These records may be found in this Office. Also on deposit are the records of all Protestant marriages since 1845.

The Genealogical Office, Dublin Castle, Dublin

The Genealogical Office, Dublin Castle, now a department of the National Library of Ireland, is not open to the public for genealogical work. This office, formerly the Office of Arms, under Ulster King of Arms, was created by Edward VI in 1553. In 1943, the office of Ulster King of Arms was transferred from Dublin to London where it was united with that of Norroy. At this time the original records making up the great collections in this office, were retained at the Genealogical Office, Dublin Castle, but photographic copies of the records of the Ulster Office were made for the College of Arms, London.

Mr. Gerard Slevin, per pro Chief Herald and Genealogical Officer, is the present director of the Office. A first inquiry should be accompanied with a P. O. money order for $3.00, in response to which pedigree blanks will be sent to fill out for two or three generations for a start on Irish records.

Space does not permit to a list of the records here, but among them are: The pedigree charts made by Sir William Betham which fill 39 large volumes; these were made by Betham from his abstracts of the Prerogative wills of Ireland, 1536-1800, in the Public Record Office, Dublin. The manuscript collections are represented by such men as Bewley, Cavenagh, Crossle, Davis, Donovan, Drought, Fisher, Irwin, Kelly, Molony, Sadleir, Swanzy, and Welply. In these collections are will and administration abstracts, numbering about 7,500, which are indexed alphabetically by name, with place of residence, county (or diocese) and year. This printed index was published in *Analecta Hibernica,* by the Irish Manuscript Commission, No. 17, Dublin, 1949. There are 701 volumes of manuscripts, 300-600 pages, and 23 legal size boxes containing collections of original documents and family records. Some of the early records are: "Visitations", for Dublin, 1568, 1607, and Wexford, 1618; 8 volumes of Ulster grants of Arms; 4 volumes of Knights' Arms; 27 volumes of Record Pedigrees; 10 volumes of Peers' Pedigrees and other entries; 2 volumes of Baronets' Pedigrees; 13 volumes of Warrants; Funeral Certificates, 1588-1698, which contain the name of the deceased, their Arms, place of burial, marriage and issue; Inquisitions Post Mortem commence with the reign of Elizabeth I (a few in time of Henry VIII, and later), and come down to Charles II, 1550-1690. These set out the property of which the deceased died seized, naming descendants and rights to inheritance. Ulster and Leinster Inquisitions were printed in 1826. The Munster and Connaught Inquisitions are here in transcript. Freeholders' Lists show parentage and some marriages. The Fermanagh Poll Book, 1788, gives the abodes of some 3,500 voters. The Dublin Consistorial Marriage Licenses up to 1820 (copy imperfect), and copies of Prerogative Marriage licenses up to 1811 are here, also Prerogative Grants of Administration to 1802 for Ulster. Other collections are: Abstracts of Grants under the Acts of Settlement and Explanation, 1666-1684; Index to the Inrolments for Adventurers Soldiers, etc., 1666; transcripts of the Hearth-money Rolls, c. 1666, for various counties; John Lodge's abstracts from Patent Rolls, also abstracts from Chancery Rolls; the Carew manuscripts, covering the Commonwealth period, etc. This office has copies of the Religious Census of Ireland, 1766, for scattered parts of Ireland. Transcripts of the destroyed Census Records of Ireland have been gathered whenever possible.

Libraries, Ireland

THE NATIONAL LIBRARY OF IRELAND.—This great library located on Kildare Street, Dublin, has the largest and most complete collection of regional, county and town histories, parish histories, also the publications of the Royal Society of Antiquaries of Ireland and the Journals of the Cork, Galway, Kerry, Kildare, Louth, Ulster, and Waterford Historical and Archaeological Societies, and the Limerick Field Club. All of these publications are rich in genealogical material, family history, printed pedigrees and biography. The Tithe Allotment Books of over 200 parishes in Northern Ireland and a large collection for other counties, c. 1820-1830 and 1834-1837, constitute in effect a census of property owners and occupiers for the period. Griffith's *Valuation of Ireland, 1844-1856*, is a survey of property in Ireland, by Poor Law Unions within the counties, listing occupants and holdings. The collection of old newspapers here contains notices of births, marriages, deaths, emigrations, sailings, business matters. The especially valuable *Freeman's Journal* is being indexed.

This library has been very active in acquiring microfilms of all records of interest to the library, from manuscripts in libraries and archives in Ireland and abroad. *The Report of the Council of Trustees, National Library of Ireland,* for 1950-1951, is the third consecutive report on accessions of microfilmed material, 123 pp. An appendix contains 90 pages, listing microfilms in the year ending June 1952. Among these are 127 films of the collections of the Genealogical Office; 4 films of all the records of the Dublin Society of Friends; 120 films of the Parish Registers of 12 of the Catholic dioceses. Indexes for the Historical and Archaelogical Society journals, containing much genealogy, which have not had a master index, have been so indexed and the cards microfilmed. The two extensive indexes to the records in the Registry of Deeds are microfilmed and copies deposited here. Many other microfilms listed in the above *Report* are of genealogical interest. The collection of town and city directories for all of Ireland is most complete. A good collection of published genealogies is also in this library.

TRINITY COLLEGE LIBRARY.—This very old library has many special manuscript collections of genealogical interest. Various catalogues of the records have been printed. Robert H. Murray published *A Short Guide to Some Manuscripts in the Library of Trinity College,* Dublin, 1920. An earlier guide was published in 1854. Some of the collections are: One of the most complete collections of old newspapers in the country;

the Stewart Kennedy Notebooks, being a collection of extracts from 500 wills of Ulster testators, made at the Public Record Office, Dublin, before the fire; a collection of early wills, 1457-1483; a manuscript collection of 16th and 17th century pedigrees, bound in several volumes; a detailed list of people who fled to Chester, England, 1688, with records of the number in each family and value of estates; depositions of those who suffered losses in the 1641 Rebellion, also depositions of County Cork (for losses), 1653-1654, 6 vols.; *Alumni Dublinenses,* by Burtchaell and Sadlier, London, 1924, published from manuscripts; lists students, graduates, professors, and provosts of Trinity College, 1593-1846; alphabetically listed, the father, place of birth, earlier tutor, age upon entry, degree and date granted, and section of the college attended, are given for each student enrolled.

THE ROYAL IRISH ACADEMY.—This library, rich in old manuscript collections, at 19 Dawson Street, Dublin, is open to the public. Its holdings are described in *A Catalogue of Irish Manuscripts in the Royal Irish Academy,* by Elizabeth Fitzpatrick and Dr. Kathleen Mulchrone, assisted by A. I. Pearson, Dublin, 1948, pp. 586. This is another old library, rich in records for compiling genealogy. Some of its special records are: Ordinance Survey Records, 1833-1834; 1835-1837, etc., dealing with the parishes of Ulster, describing places and giving miscellaneous information, such as names of people who emigrated to America (name, age, religion (R. C. or P.), townland on which they lived, year of emigration, and city in United States or Canada where each intended to settle); many 17th and 18th century pedigrees in manuscript; Books of Survey and Distribution compiled in 1677, by Thomas Taylor (this survey was ordered to have records of names of the proprietors of property in Ireland before the Rebellion of 1640, and record of new proprietors to whom the estates were granted by the Commonwealth); a large collection of lists of Freeholders; the Wendele manuscripts, being 190 volumes containing pedigrees of Leinster and Munster families; and a large collection of newspapers. (*The Freemans'*

Journal, also called *The Public Monitor,* 1772-1773, a rare weekly paper, gave much personal news and is full of genealogical notes.)

LIBRARY OF THE REPRESENTATIVE CHURCH BODY.—This library, located at 52, St. Stephen's Green, Dublin, has a mass of documents, original and transcribed, relating to every diocese in Ireland. Transcribed Parish Registers, made by Tenison Groves in the Public Record Office before the fire, are here, as is a catalogue of the manuscripts (24 pages), published in Dublin in 1938, by the Rev. J. B. Leslie.

PUBLIC LIBRARIES.—These are too numerous to list. Especially good ones, having fine genealogical collections, are in some of the larger cities such as Cork, Limerick, etc. The County libraries vary. The County Library of Cork has a fine collection. Mr. J. P. Madden, Director, is most interested in genealogical records. The University Library, Cork (Mr. Cahill, Librarian), also has a fine genealogy section. A *Catalogue of the Irish Library, University College, Cork,* 1914, lists the older collections of this library. In the vault are kept the manuscript collection *Apprentice Indentures Enrolling Book,* 17 Jan. 1756—4 Dec. 1801, transcribed alphabetically by Richard Caulfield.

Some Libraries of Northern Ireland

PRESBYTERIAN HISTORICAL SOCIETY LIBRARY.—This Library, located on Fisherwick Place, Belfast, has gathered a large collection of published, original and transcribed church records. Many of these records are also in other repositories but this is a focal center for the study of Presbyterian Church Registers and records. Based on a questionnaire sent to all Presbyterian Ministers, a card file has been created cataloguing the condition and extent of church Registers. This records the inclusive dates of baptism and marriage Registers in 357 such Registers; there are no records of burials in the Registers. Some original manuscripts copied in the Public Record Office before the fire for the Presbyterian Historical Society are:

Petitions As To Dissenters, to the Irish Parliament or Lord Lieutenant, 1704-1782; Copied from the Parliamentary Papers, Bundle 28, Nos. 1-42; 50-100; 195-211. This list includes the names of Protestant householders, dissenters from the Church of Ireland, who signed petitions. The most complete Roll was taken in October and November, 1775. The enrollment was by borough, town, parish and county.

Parliamentary Returns Concerning Religion, The Protestant Householders in Antrim, Londonderry and Donegal, 1740, copied from No. 647, bundle 75. This lists the householders by county, barony, and town or borough, each householder being numbered. This constitutes a census of the Protestants of the locations included.

Parliamentary Returns Concerning Religion, No. 650, or the Religious Census of 1766. This manuscript concerns Ulster; it is incomplete.

Publications of some value in tracing the family of a Presbyterian minister are: *Fasti of the Irish Presbyterian Church,* 1613-1840, compiled by the Rev. James McConnell, revised by the Rev. S. G. McConnell, Belfast, 1951. Arranged in seven periods, with final chapter regarding *"Ministers of Irish Origin Who Labored in America During the Eighteenth Century",* it gives some biographical and vital records and, in some cases, the parentage of the ministers. *Records of the General Synod of Ulster,* 1601-1820, (3 vols., Belfast, 1890, 1897, 1898), contains information regarding the church sessions, the appointments, etc., of the ministers, and the representative elders.

The *Manuscript Church Sessions Books* are records of the minutes of the meetings of the various local governing bodies of the congregations. Problems of business and discipline were recorded, providing information about members. Many of these original Sessions books are in the library of the Presbyterian Historical Society; others are in Magee College Library, Londonderry.

LINEN HALL LIBRARY on Donegall Square, Belfast, has many genealogies, published mostly for families of Northern Ireland. A catalogue was published in 1917.

THE ARMAGH PUBLIC LIBRARY—A catalogue of the manuscripts was published in 1928. Situated in the Cathedral City of Armagh, its collections have become of great value to the genealogist.

COUNTY MUSEUM, ARMAGH—Original records have been deposited here in the past, such as pedigrees, leases, grants, probates, intestacies, rentals, also Prerogatives and Dromore wills, 1685-1896.

MAGEE UNIVERSITY COLLEGE LIBRARY situated on the campus of Magee University College, Londonderry, has extensive records of interest to the genealogist. The librarian, T. McC. Walker, is also a member of the Committee of the Cathedral of St. Columbs, Londonderry.

Parish Records, Established Church of Ireland

The records of baptism, marriage, and burial were kept in registers by the local rectors. According to Acts of Parliament of 1875 and 1876, all parish registers of baptism and burial prior to 30 December 1870, and marriages prior to 31 March 1845, of the Church of Ireland, were constituted Public Records and were to be deposited in the Public Record Office, Dublin. By Amendment of the Act, the clergy of all parishes who could show evidence of a safe place of local custody for their parish registers, were allowed to retain their records in their respective parishes, under retention orders. Of 1,643 parishes with parish registers, those of 1,006 parishes were sent to the Public Record Office from all parts of Ireland. However, transcripts of many registers were made by the local rectors before sending in the original records. In 1922, the burning of the Public Record Office in Dublin destroyed all but four of the parish registers. The problem of tracing the records still in existence was undertaken for the 26 counties of Southern Ireland, by the Public Record Office, Dublin, while those in the 6 counties of Northern Ireland were traced by that Record Office in Belfast. The various *Reports* of both Record Offices show, up to 1952-1953, what has happened to the records and also list the inclusive dates of baptisms, marriages and burials in each existing register. The Public Record Office, Belfast, has been photostating or microfilming the registers called in for temporary inspection or repair, before they are returned to local custody. As of the Report of the Dublin Office, 1951-2, the existing records are: Original Parish Records still in local custody, 457; those deposited in the Public Record Office, Dublin, 12; transcripts of original records in local custody, 104 parishes; transcripts in the Public Record Office, 30 parishes; extensive extracts of parish records in the Public Record Office, 75 parishes; printed registers for 29 parishes. A list of these with name of the parish, diocese, county, inclusive dates of the records, has been prepared. In Northern Ireland, there are 236 parishes with original registers in local custòdy; 116 parishes have allowed their registers to be copied by the Public Record Office, Belfast; 4 parishes have printed registers. The *Reports* of both Public Record offices, published since 1922, will show what registers are available, where they are and the inclusive dates.

The Memorials of the Dead, 13 vols., Dublin (1888-1921), published by the Association for Preservation of the Memorials of the Dead in Ireland, was continued by its successor organization as the Irish Memorials Association, from 1921-1932. This work contains information regarding parishes, churches, burial grounds, mural tablets, and many thousands of inscriptions on tombstones, lists of births, deaths, and marriages, and in some cases genealogical records for several generations of one family. Accompanying the above volumes are: *A Consolidated Index of Surnames and Place-Names,* for volumes I-VII, compiled by Vigors and Mahony, Dublin, 1914; *An Index of the Churchyards and Buildings,* Dublin, 1909; *Index of Personal and Place-Names in Vol. XI; Index to the Parish Register Section of Vol. XI; Coats of Arms from The Funeral Entries, Vols. VII and VIII.* The latter volume of 270 pages, with a good index, continues the publication of Coats of Arms taken from tombstones and funeral entries, begun in the Irish Memorials Association journals. Some 817 funeral entries are copied from various sources, including the British Museum, the legal survivors given. No genealogical work with Irish records is complete without an examination of the above publications.

The Parish Register Society of Dublin became active at about the turn of the century. The purpose of this Society, approved by the Master of the Rolls in Ireland, was to publish the more important and older surviving registers, beginning with those of Dublin, more especially those not deposited in the Record Office. The registers of the City of Dublin, besides containing the records of many of the old city families, are of great importance to those investigating scattered branches of the English families as well as origins of American and Colonial settlers. The early works published by the Society numbered 11 volumes, containing baptism, marriage and burial records. In 1921, this Society became incorporated with The Irish Memorials Association. Between 1921 and 1932, a section of each of The Irish Memorials Association publications was devoted to the printing of Dublin Parish registers.

The Indexes to the Marriage License Bonds which were filed in the Public Record Office, Dublin, were fortunately saved from the fire and are almost as valuable as the original records, as the names of the contracting parties, their place of residence, and the year of marriage, appear in alphabetical order for both bride and groom. The following indexes, copied from those in the Public Record Office have been published:

The Index to the Marriage License Bonds of the Diocese of Cork and Ross, Ireland, 1623-1750, edited by Herbert W. Gillman, Cork 1896-7. This contains the listing of about 11,840 presumptive evidence of marriages.

The Index to the Marriage License Bonds of the Diocese of Cloyne, Ireland, 1630-1800, edited by T. George H. Green, Cork, 1899-1900. This contains the listing of about 8,686 records as above. It also contains *The Table of Parochial Records—Diocese of Cloyne*. These were copied from *The Twenty-Eighth Report of the Deputy Keeper of the Public Records, Dublin*. One hundred and twenty parishes were listed, with the inclusive dates of the baptism, marriage and burial records, in each parish.

Irish Marriages, Being an Index to the Marriages in Walker's Hibernian Magazine, 1771-1812, 2 vols., by Henry

Farrar, London, 1897. Some nine thousand marriages indexed, give name of groom, bride, place, date, and in some cases, parentage.

Roman Catholic Parish Registers

Catholic parish registers are now being microfilmed in the National Library of Ireland. The work began in July 1950, with the plan of filming every Catholic Register of Ireland. There is at present no complete list of all registers. The library lists them as they are brought in for filming, and the list will be published at the end of the filming. The films are not available to the public, but the Genealogical Office, Dublin Castle, may use them. The dates of the registers vary greatly. The records tend to extend to earlier dates in the good farmland areas, like Tipperary, than in the poorer districts such as Galway. They are also of earlier dates in the towns than in the purely agricultural areas. The larger towns of 5,000 population and on up, have records beginning about 1790. In larger cities of about 25,000 population and upwards, the records begin about 1750. In good agricultural areas, they begin about 1820, and in the poorer areas, about 1835-40. These are average figures, given with the above information by Dr. Richard J. Hayes, Director of the National Library of Ireland.

The parish registers of Northern Ireland, presently in local custody, are only 68 in number, the records of baptism, marriage and dates of missing periods being recorded. The Public Record Office of Northern Ireland, Belfast, has made copies. The earliest dates appear to be 1744; most begin about 1835.

Records of the Society of Friends

The Dublin Society of Friends (Quakers) at Dublin Friends House, 6 Eustace Street, has records of births, marriages, and deaths, to 1859 for Carlow, Cork, Dublin, Edebderry, Grange, Lisburn, Limerick, Lurgan. Moate, Mountmellick, Richhill, Youghal (city), and Counties Tipperary, Waterford, Wexford, Wicklow; also throughout Ireland of births 1859-1949;

marriages 1859-1887, 1893-1947; and deaths 1859-1900, 1909-1949.

The Friends Records of Northern Ireland, housed in Friends House, Lisburn, are extensive. They have been copied by the Public Record Office, Belfast, and an account of the nature of the records, inclusive dates, and an extensive index to the personal records, are printed in the *Report of the Deputy Keeper*, 1951-1953.

Records of the Huguenot Church

The published Huguenot Registers are: *Registers of the French Conformed Churches of St. Patrick and St. Mary, Dublin*, 1668/9-1830; edited by J. J. Digges La Touche, for The Huguenot Society of London (vol. 7). *Registers of the French Non-Conformist Churches of Lucy Lane and Peter Street, Dublin*, 1701-31; 1771-1831; edited by T. P. Le Fanu, for the Huguenot Society of London. *Registers of the French Church of Portarlington*, 1694-1816; edited by T. P. Le Fanu, for the Huguenot Society of London.

Some Huguenot histories which contain genealogical and historical notes and biography of Huguenot families and their settlements in Ireland: *The History of the Huguenot Settlers in Ireland and Other Literary Remains*, by Thomas Gimlette, with maps and plates, 1888. *The Huguenots*, by Samuel Smiles, 1889. *The Huguenots in Ulster*, by R. A. McCall, 1915. *The Huguenot Settlements in Ireland*, by Grace L. Lee, London, 1936.

Records of the Methodist Church

Methodist vital records are practically non-existent in Ireland before 1850, except as they appear in the registers of the Church of Ireland. For the same reason as for all dissenters, in order to conform to the law, the rites of baptism, marriage and burial were performed or recorded by the rector of the Established Church of Ireland in his parish. In the early days, the Methodists had neither churches nor consecrated ground for the burial of their dead; consequently, a search for their records and earlier family vital records must be made in the church registers of the parish in which they lived. See *Parish Records of the Established Church of Ireland.*

Town and City *Directories* are valuable in locating individuals. The directories of Belfast began in 1812. *The Gentleman's and Citizens Almanac, Dublin,* for John Watson. 1736, 1759, 1760, 1765, 1771, and thereafter every year or so. *A Brief Directory of Cork,* 1758. Also for 1769-1770. Lucas' *Directory of Some of the South East Ireland Towns,* 1821. *Piggott's Directory,* 1824, lists men in the towns by profession. *Thom's Directory,* 1848-1864, *A Directory to the Market Towns, Villages, Gentleman's Seats and Other Noted Places in Ireland,* 2nd ed. by Ambrose Leet, 1814.

Tax Rolls

HEARTH-MONEY ROLLS.—These list all householders in Ireland, by barony, parish, town or corporation, with the number of hearths or other places used for fires within each householder's premises, each hearth being taxed at the legal rate of two shillings sterling. The taxes were levied between 1663-1669 and are valuable for locating a family. These rolls were burned in the Public Record Office fire in 1922; however, they had been copied extensively in the half century before the fire. Many county histories published such rolls. Those for County Tipperary were published by Thomas Laffan, Dublin, 1911. Many manuscript transcripts for various counties are in the Public Record Office, Dublin, and in the Public Record Office, Belfast.

SUBSIDY ROLLS.—These were the tax records which relate to the more prosperous class of people and the Rolls, taken by county, indicate its taxable wealth. These Rolls provide names of persons who possessed enough property to be liable to the tax, which constituted the chief manner of direct taxation in the late 17th century. The Rolls for County Down, 1663, are all that exist for Northern Ireland, except for partial lists which appear in various publications. The Down Rolls are in manuscript in the Public Record Office and the Presbyterian Historical Society, Belfast.

THE TITHE LISTS, for the Church of Ireland tax, have been mentioned.

"Census" Records

The Census of Ireland, 1659, edited by Seamus Pender, published by the Irish Manuscripts Commission. There is some evidence to indicate that this census of individuals in Ireland was, in fact, an abstract of the Poll Tax. The fact that no ministers are mentioned (ministers being exempt from the tax); also, all under 15 being excluded, supports this conclusion.

The Civil Survey of 1654-1656, published by the Dublin Stationery Office, for the Irish Manuscripts Commission, 1937. The entire survey covered 27 of the 32 counties, listing landlords, tenants and lands, with a particular account of Irish and English tenures of 1640. A certified copy of the original is in the Royal Irish Academy.

NATURALIZATION: The *Scots in Ulster, Their Denization and Naturalization*, 1605-1634, parts 1 and 2, by the Rev. David Stewart, D.D., 1952-53. This is a list of the early Scottish settlers in Ulster, both landlords and tenants, with the name, residence, and date of naturalization of each. The list, extracted from the *Ulster Inquisitions*, and other sources, appears to be far from complete. Another extract giving information on Londonderry is *A Particular of the Howses and Famylyes of Londonderry, May 15, 1628*, published 1936. It contains the list of householders with acreage and rent charged.

The Cromwellian Settlement of Ireland, by John Prendergast, 2nd ed., Dublin, 1875, names the Irish landlords, with occupants, who were forced to abandon their lands to the English Adventurers, and those of Cromwell's Army who were to receive land in payment for service. Adventurers, numbering 1,360 classified by rank, occupation, residence and price of land, are listed.

MUSTER ROLLS, 1631.—One of the conditions of the Plantation of Ulster was that the undertakers should muster their tenants periodically and parade them before the government muster master, who set down the names and arms of each person. The lists of 1631 are extant and the Presbyterian Historical Society possesses a copy. The persons enrolled were between 16 and 60 years of age, being capable of bearing arms. All were Protestants, and for 9 counties numbered 13,092. (See Stafford's *Letters and Despatches*, vol. 1, p. 199.) There was also a yeomanry of about 2,600, enrolled from all the counties of Ulster and a permanent garrison at Carrickfergus, just above Belfast. (See Pynner's "Survey of the Plantations", made in 1618-1619, published in Harris' *Hibernica*.)

ARMY LISTS, 1642.—Ten years after the aforementioned muster, the men were mustered for active service in the suppression of the Rebellion begun in October 1641. The Rolls of each regiment are extant, giving the companies, officers, and men, and thus forms a sequel to the muster of 1631. The Presbyterian Historical Society has a copy.

GOVERNMENT CENSUS OF IRELAND.—One of the worst losses of the fire in the Public Record Office, Dublin, was the destruction of almost all of the Census Returns of 1813, 1821, 1831, 1841 and 1851; also for each 10-year period from then to 1922. However, great numbers of transcripts have come to light. The Reports of the Public Record Offices of Dublin and Belfast, have listed all collections of the records which have been found.

Wills

Irish wills, 1536-1858, fall into two classes: Prerogative wills and diocesan wills. Prerogative wills were those proved in the Prerogative Court, owing to the deceased having died possessed of property above the value of five pounds sterling in each of two or more dioceses. The Prerogative Court was presided over by the Archbishop of Armagh, Primate of all Ireland. The courts of the 28 dioceses were called Consistorial Courts, each being under the jurisdiction of the Bishop of the Diocese. Before 1857, the wills which disposed of property in but one diocese were proved in its Consistorial

Court, and were termed Diocesan Wills. In 1857, the ecclesiastical jurisdiction over testamentary matters was abolished and a Court of Probate established. From this time on, wills, administrations, and all testamentary records were automatically deposited in the care of the Master of the Rolls, in the Public Record Office, Dublin. All of the above Prerogative and Diocesan Wills were also gathered there.

All will books and original wills, housed in the Public Record Office, Dublin, were burned in 1922, except those books containing copies of Prerogative Wills for the years 1664-1684, 1706-1708, 1726-1729, and portions of 1777, 1813 and 1834, which are still there. However, the loss of the Prerogative Wills prior to 1800 was largely repaired for the genealogist due to the fact that, as previously stated, Sir William Betham had compiled from the Prerogative Wills of Ireland what he termed his "Genealogical Analysis" of all Prerogative Wills of Ireland, 1536-1800. Also, about 5,000 Grants of Administration Intestate were abstracted by Betham. All abstracts were used for constructing his pedigree charts. As these charts were made for genealogical purposes, dates and geographical locations were included when the information was mentioned in the will. In the case of the Burke transcripts (see p. 354), vols. 1 and 2 are arranged somewhat haphazardly; vols. 3 and 4 show a planned system, dealing with the wills of dates earlier than 1700, arranged in alphabetical order. Each of Burke's volumes is indexed. The charts from the wills earlier than 1700 are not in perfect alphabetical sequence. The later volumes, 5 through 42, contain the charts of the wills, 1700-1800, being arranged in alphabetical order. Each volume is indexed, both as to names of testators and alliances recorded in the wills. An additional index volume of names of testators and persons whose property was subject to Grants of Administration, for the same period to 1800, has been compiled. The wills indexed in Vicars' *Index* named above, are thought to be all represented in the Betham and Burke collections, up to 1800. This makes it possible for anyone to consult Vicars' *Index*, and write for copies of charted wills.

The Diocesan Will books, which escaped the fire are those for Connor, 1818-1820, 1853-1858, and for Down, 1850-1858. Otherwise, aside from the Diocesan Wills which have been discovered in private collections or in other repositories, only the Indexes remain. However, as previously stated, the recovery of thousands of legal or plain copies, abstracts, and notes from these Diocesan Wills, has rebuilt the destroyed Diocesan Wills to a considerable extent. Thus, the Indexes to the Diocesan Wills are valuable, both for the information provided in the Indexes and as a guide to what wills may be sought in collections of transcribed wills or abstracts. The Indexes show the name of the testator, the year of the probate, and the location. These Indexes also furnish clues for checking land records for an estate partition, a transfer of a lease from testator to heir, etc.

The published Diocesan Indexes are as follows: *A Calendar of Wills in the Dioceses of Ossory, Ferns, Leighlin and Kildare, 1536-1800*, vol 1, edited by W. P. W. Phillimore, M. A., B. C. L., London, 1909; *Indexes to the Irish Wills in the Dioceses of Cork and Ross, Cloyne, 1548-1800*, vol. 2, edited by Phillimore, London, 1910; *Indexes to the Irish Wills in the Dioceses of Cashel and Emly, Waterford and Lismore, Killaloe and Kilfenora, Limerick, Ardfert and Aghadoe, 1615-1800*, vol. 3, edited by Gertrude Thrift, London, 1913; *Indexes to the Irish Wills in the Dioceses of Dromore, Newry and Mourne, 1678-1858*, vol. 4, edited by Gertrude Thrift, London, 1918; *Indexes to the Irish Wills in the Dioceses of Derry and Raphoe, 1612-1858*, vol. 5, edited by Gertrude Thrift, London, 1920.

While the original wills probated in Northern Ireland after 1858 were lost in the Public Record Office fire in 1922, a copy of each will proved in Northern Ireland after 1858 had been entered in a Will Book in one of the District Registries, in Belfast or Londonderry. For the period 1858-1900, one hundred and two Will Books are now in the Public Record Office, Belfast.

The Fifty-Fifth Report of the Deputy Keeper of the Public

Records, Dublin, 1928, Appendix II, and The Fifty-Sixth Report, 1931, Appendices I-VIII, contain the indexes to some 15,900 documents presented to the Public Record Office, 1923-1928. These include Wills, Letters of Administration, Marriage License Grants, official copies of Wills, Grants and Chancery documents. *The Fifty-Seventh Report*, 1936, indexes 16,000 documents of like kind, presented 1929-1930. These records are approximately half of dates 1630-1850, the remainder bearing later dates.

The Index of Will Abstracts in the Genealogical Office, Dublin, published in the Irish Manuscripts Commission's *Analecta Hibernica, No. 17*, Dublin Stationery Office, 1947, provides an index to about 7,500 will abstracts which vary in length from a few words to complete copies of wills. These abstracts have come to the Genealogical Office in the manuscript collections of men of great names in the field of genealogy. These include men whose works are in the Public Record Offices of Dublin and Belfast. Among these abstracts are those from the wills of persons who made charitable bequests and were included in the Report of the Commissioners, 1805 and 1814. Fisher contributed over 2,000 abstracts (surnames A-E) of 16th, 17th and early 18th century Dublin Diocesan Wills. In Volume F., the majority of the abstracts are from Cork and Cloyne Diocesan Wills. Swanzy contributed 863 abstracts, mainly from Down, Connor and Dromore Wills. Abstracts of the Welply collection of wills which went to the Society of Genealogists, London, is also here.

Every genealogist wishing to know about the existence of individual wills, etc., must read the indexes to the *Reports of the Deputy Keeper of the Records of Northern Ireland*, from 1925, as well as the *Reports* for the Dublin Office already named.

A Guide to Copies and Abstracts of Irish Wills, by the Rev. Wallace Clare, 1930, lists about 4,000 wills, transcripts, abstracts, etc., which, since the fire of 1922, are preserved. They have been located and indexed from repositories, publications, etc., from both England and Ireland.

The Index to the Dublin Diocesan Wills was printed in the Appendix, 1895, and 1899, of the *Report of the Deputy Keeper of the Records* in Ireland.

The Registry of Deeds, Dublin Abstracts of Wills, vol. I, 1708-1745; vol. II, 1746-1785; edited by P. Beryl Eustace, Dublin Stationery Office, 1956, sets forth the abstracts of over 2,000 wills, the memorials of which were lodged in the Registry of Deeds due to property involved.

The Quaker Records, Dublin, Abstracts of Wills, edited by P. Beryl Eustace and Olive C. Goodbody, Dublin, 1957; Appendix I: List of Quaker Wills at Lisburn; Appendix II: List of Miscel. Quaker Wills in the Historical Library, Eustace Street, Dublin. Abstracts of 224 wills are given.

* * *

As this chapter is written for those primarily interested in the past five hundred years, no attempt has been made to list any reference books for the genealogies of the ancient Irish families.

(NOTE: *Searching For Your Ancestors in Ireland.* By Margaret Dickson Falley, B. S., F. A. S. G., will probably be available in the fall of 1960. In some 550 pages, well documented and indexed, information is furnished for those who must write for records, as well as for those who can go to Ireland. Detailed information is given as to records in each repository, each class of records, and the use of existing collections of original documents, transcripts, etc. Lists of Church of Ireland (Episcopal), Presbyterian, Quaker, Huguenot, and Catholic registers or indexes are included. There is an extensive bibliography of published genealogies, periodical sources, pedigrees, etc.; also of collections of family documents and their locations, and of published American sources of Irish and Scotch Irish origins. It will provide those interested in Irish genealogy with much information which could not be furnished within the space limitations of this chapter. ED.)

CHAPTER VI

GERMANY *

Printed Works.—

Publications on genealogical research and families in Germany are voluminous. The most important series of collected genealogies is the *Deutsches Geschlechterbuch (Genealogisches Handbuch der Bürgerlicher Familien)*, which title is translated as *German Lineage Book (Genealogical Handbook of Middle-Class Families)*. Now in its 124th volume, the *Geschlechterbuch* has published since 1889 the pedigrees of thousands of families. Some of these families have American connections. Many of the volumes are devoted to certain German states, such as Hessen, the Palatinate, Bavaria, Baden, Württemberg, Brandenburg, etc.; others deal with families in all parts of Germany. This work is published by C. A. Starke-Verlag at Glücksburg/Ostsee (Baltic Sea).

In the 1930's, many compilations on the genealogy of famous Germans were issued. Subjects of these ancestor-tables included statesmen such as Count von Hertling and Prince von Bülow, rulers such as Emperor Maximilian I (died 1519) and Frederick the Great; soldiers such as Hindenburg; and writers such as Goethe and Schiller. These compilations were all included in the series of *Stamm- und Ahnentafelwerke* (Pedigree and Ancestor Table Works), published by the Zentralstelle für

---

* This chapter is based, in part, on *Genealogical Research in German-Speaking Lands: A Symposium* (Special Publication No. 19, National Genealogical Society, Washington, D. C.), by Dr. Ralph Dornfeld Owen, F. A. S. G., Karl Friedrich von Frank, F. A. S. G., Dr. Fritz Braun, Dr. Friedrich Krebs, Dr. Heinz F. Friederichs, Dr. Adam Heldmann, Dr. W. H. Ruoff, Milton Rubincam, F. A. S. G., and John I. Coddington, F. A. S. G.; Civil Affairs Guide; *Archival Repositories in Germany*, War Dept. Pamphlet No. 31-180, 15 May 1944; Marion Dexter Learned, *Guide to the Manuscript Materials Relating to American History in the German State Archives* (1912); Archibald F. Bennett, *A Guide for Genealogical Research* (1951), pp. 255-256 (German Record Sources). Grateful acknowledgement is made to Dr. Ernst Posner, Chairman of the Department of History, The American University, Washington, D. C., for reading this chapter and making many suggestions for its improvement.

deutsche Personen- und Familiengeschichte (Central Office for the History of German Persons and Families) at Leipzig.

The periodical literature in the field of German genealogy is especially rich. The American researcher who has the patience to examine it will often find it rewarding. The Zentralstelle für deutsche Personen- und Familiengeschichte has long been a leader in this field. In 1903, it commenced the publication of a magazine, *Familiengeschichtliche Blätter*, which, until its discontinuance in World War II, contained important articles on families, individuals, sources, etc. Each volume is indexed by surnames. From 1900 to 1938, the Zentralstelle issued the *Familiengeschichtliche Bibliographie* (Family History Bibliography), which is an important "locator" for genealogical material, whether in book form or in periodicals. Five years ago the Zentralstelle resumed publication of the *Bibliographie,* the printing being done by Degener & Co., Neustadt-on-Aisch, Bavaria. In 1929, the Zentralstelle began the compilation of a card index of German emigrants. Since 1 February 1957, the Zentralstelle für deutsche Personen- und Familienforschung in Leipzig is under the State Archives Administration of the German Democratic Republic.

Another important genealogical magazine was *Der Deutsche Herold*, published by the Herold Society at Berlin from 1870 to 1943. A current periodical of value is the *Senftenegger Monatsblatt für Genealogie und Heraldik,* published since 1951 by Karl Friedrich von Frank, F. A. S. G., of Schloss Senftenegg, Post Ferschnitz, Niederösterreich, Austria. Although it deals primarily with Austrian families and source-materials, it contains much information on families in Germany and on German emigrants to colonial America.

Throughout Germany there are local historical and genealogical societies which are performing real services to the cause of genealogy by the publication of magazines and books. Among them are the Gesellschaft für Familienkunde in Kurhessen und Waldeck (Society for Family Study in Electoral Hessen and Waldeck), the Gesellschaft für Familienkunde in

Franken (Franconia), the Bayrisches Landesverein für Familienkunde (Bavarian State Association for Family Study), etc. Most of the societies are represented in the national organization, the Arbeitsgemeinschaft der genealogischen Verbände Deutschlands (Co-operative Union of Genealogical Associations of Germany) at Hannover. A list of German genealogists, family associations and foundations, and genealogical associations is contained in *VdFF: Verzeichnis der Familienforscher und Familienverbände, Familienstiftungen und Familienkundlichen Vereinigungen,* edited by Erich Wasmansdorff (4th ed., Glücksburg/Ostsee, 1956): It is supplemented by a quarterly publication, *Praktische Forschungshilfe* (since 1956).

One of the most difficult feats is to establish the German home of an American settler in colonial times. Unless a Bible record, letters, diaries, and other contemporary documents have survived that will identify the town in Germany whence the family came, it is almost impossible to know where to begin the search. Within recent years articles have appeared in American periodicals giving data about emigrants from Germany as shown in the archives of that country. Dr. Friedrich Krebs, of Speyer, Germany, has been especially active in this connection; his articles on emigrants from the Palatinate have appeared in *The Pennsylvania Dutchman* (Lancaster, Penna.), at intervals since 1953, and he has published articles on colonists from Zweibrücken (*Pennsylvania German Folklore Series,* vol. 16) and from Baden-Durlach (*National Genealogical Society Quarterly,* vol. 45, 1957). The last-named magazine carried an article in 1941 by William J. Hoffman, F. G. B. S., F. A. S. G., on settlers from the countship of Nassau-Dillenburg. In 1953, the Pennsylvania German Society published a booklet entitled, *Emigrants from the Palatinate to the American Colonies in the 18th Century,* compiled by Dr. Friedrich Krebs and edited, with an Introduction, by Milton Rubincam, F. A. S. G. This work demonstrates the unusual quality of many records in Germany. Names of immigrants, dates and places of their birth, if known, sometimes names of their parents, names of wives, dates of marriage, names, dates, and birthplaces of their children are shown. It provides a commentary on the morals of the times—the Brandstetter girls, for instance, were occasionally loose with their affections, although it must be admitted that their connections were legalized by subsequent marriages to their lovers. As so many American families are descended from Palatine settlers, it should be noted that information about emigrants from the Palatinate may be obtained from Heimatstelle Pfalz, Kaiserslautern, Stiftsplatz 3.

Primary Sources.—

Church Registers. The most important sources of genealogical information in Germany are the parish registers (Kirchenbücher, church books). The earliest Protestant registers go back to the first half of the 16th century; the earliest Catholic registers date from an order of the Council of Trent, 11 November 1563. A few 16th century registers are extant, but most of those which have survived wars, fires, and other forces of destruction date from about 1650. The parish registers are usually found in the custody of the local clergymen, but many of them have been placed for safe-keeping in state or church archives. The registers not only contain records of baptisms, marriages, and burials, but often statements concerning families' emigration to America and elsewhere. As an example, the church registers of Thaleischweiler, in the Palatinate, stated that Johann Heinrich Daude (Daute) "left for Pennsylvania with wife, children, and the son-in-law, and the wife and children of his son-in-law, 1765, the 7th May." Other records are not as complete as this one; some state simply, "has left for the New Country"; in other cases, only the single word "America" indicates the area to which the family has migrated.

Other ecclesiastical records of value are the banns (registers of intentions of marriage), lists of confirmations and communicants, etc. Many churches have catalogs of fees collected, and even pedigrees. For instance, the State Archives at Marburg, Hessen, has *Listen der Pfarreiangehörigen* (Lists of Parishioners) of families living within the parish of Reichensachsen in 1646 and 1647; these tables were drawn up at that time by the pastor of Reichensachsen.

The Deutsches Central Archiv (German Central Archives) in Potsdam, Stalinallee 98-101, took over the records of the former *Reichssippenamt* (which may be translated freely as State Family Office) and hence possesses a vast collection of church register materials, namely, 3,900 originals, 2,400 volumes of photocopies, and 16,500 microfilms.

Civil Registers. A national law, effective 1 January 1876, made compulsory throughout Germany the civil registration of all persons, including vital statistics and personal status. These records are to be found in the respective *Standesämter*, (singular, *Standesamt*), or registration bureaus in the places where the families lived. Some areas had introduced their own systems of civil registration at earlier dates—the Free City of Frankfurt in 1533, the German territories subject to France in the Napoleonic period in 1798, and the duchy of Nassau in 1817.

Archival Holdings. Each state in Germany has one or more State Archives *(Staatsarchiv)* and many towns and cities have municipal archives *(Stadtarchiv)*. They are a veritable treasure-house of genealogical information. They contain citizenship lists *(Bürgerbücher)*, tax lists, tithe registers, wills and inventories, petitions, registers of real estate transfers *(Grundbücher)*, census records (in a few states where census enumerations were made), military records, passport registers, lists of emigrants, manumission records, etc.

The last-named record group needs explanation. When an individual in the 18th century wished to emigrate to America or elsewhere, he applied to his ruler for permission to go, and paid a stipulated fee in order to obtain his "manumission", *i. e.* freedom from his feudal obligations. The manumission document identified his home in Germany and gave particulars about him, his family, and his property. Examples of manumission records are contained in the Introduction to Volume III, Strassburger and Hinke's *Pennsylvania German Pioneers* (1934). These records are important for the genealogist, but it must be remembered that the manumission refers only to persons who emigrated with the ruler's knowledge and permission. Thousands of persons thought it expedient to leave the country quietly, without bothering the ruler for his always-reluctantly-given permission.

As examples of the material to be found in archival establishments, we may note that the Stadtarchiv at Augsburg, Bavaria, has tax books from 1346 to 1717, and the Stadtarchiv at Bochum, Westphalia (now in the State of Nordrhein-Westfalen), has citizenship lists from 1519 to 1800. The Stadtarchiv at Gross Bieberau, Hessen, possesses real estate records which describe the history of every piece of property and every change of ownership, and give the names of the grantors, the grantees, and the owners of adjoining properties, and the sale price. The Staatsarchiv at Marburg has muster rolls of the Hessian troops who fought for Great Britain in our Revolutionary War.

During World War II many archives and libraries in Germany suffered heavy losses. To select one of many illustrations, the Allied aerial attack on Kassel in 1943 resulted in the destruction of 15th and 16th century documents, the old citizenship lists, and the parish registers from 1750. Fortunately, the parish registers of Kassel prior to 1750 were in the Staatsarchiv at Marburg, which not being a strategic target, was spared and, consequently, its treasures are available for researchers. A great many archives escaped destruction during the war.

The Genealogical Society of the Church of Jesus Christ of Latter-Day Saints has been active in Germany, so that many records are preserved on microfilm at Salt Lake City.

It should be noted that, archivally, the "Iron Curtain" divides Germany into two parts, namely: (1) the Federal Republic of Germany, with the Federal Archives in Koblenz and the State archives in the various *Länder* (states); and (2) the German Democratic Republic, with the German Central

Archives in Potsdam and a number of State archives, all controlled by the State Archives Administration of the German Democratic Republic.

The Study of German Local History.—
A knowledge of the history of the German areas whence came our ancestors is essential for the genealogist. Germany, as we know it, did not exist until 1871; during the colonial period of our history it was known as the Holy Roman Empire of the German Nation, under the nominal rule of the Habsburg Emperor at Vienna. The Empire lasted for a thousand years, from the coronation of Charlemagne in the year 800 until the abdication of Emperor Francis II in 1806.

During this millennium boundaries changed frequently, and states were sold, exchanged, and conquered. As an illustration, the town of Wanfried never moved from the banks of the Werra River, but from 1650 to the present it has been successively in Hessen-Kassel, Hessen-Rheinfels, again Hessen-Kassel, Electoral Hessen, the Prussian province of Hessen-Nassau, and the present State of Hessen. The composite parts of principalities is indicated by their names—Saxe-Meiningen, Saxe-Weimar, Schwarzburg-Rudolstadt, Hohenzollern-Sigmaringen, Nassau-Weilburg, and Nassau-Dillenburg. The duchy of Nassau was incorporated in the Prussian province of Hessen-Nassau in 1866, and since 1945 has been in the State of Hessen. Thus, although Nassau is now in Hessen, its archival repository is not at Marburg (the repository for old Hessen-Kassel) but at Wiesbaden, which was formerly in the duchy of Nassau. It will be seen, therefore, that only by studying the history of an ancestral locality can we determine where our genealogical search should commence.

The indispensable tool for exploring the history of an ancestral locality is Heinrich Karl Wilhelm Berghaus's *Deutschland seit hundert Jahren; Geschichte der Gebietseinteilung und der politischen Verfassung des Vaterlandes* (Leipzig; 5 vols., 1859-62, Part I, 2 vols: *Deutschland vor 100 Jahren;* Part II, 3 vols., *Deutschland vor 50 Jahren*).

CHAPTER VII

THE NETHERLANDS

The following pages are devoted to a general discussion of genealogical research in the Netherlands. It refers to conditions as they existed before the recent war had devastated this peaceful country. Whether any or how much of the valuable records have been lost cannot be determined at this time and the information is, therefore, based on pre-war conditions.

The genealogical literature contains much material about the old settler families from the Netherlands. Many of them became prominent and their descendants are to be found in all sections of this country. Consequently, not only were these descendants interested in the history of their families since their arrival on these shores but also in trying to determine their antecedents in "The Old Country".

Unfortunately, the first attempts to trace the ancestry of families of Dutch descent in the Fatherland were made at a time when scientific research was the exception. Investigations were undertaken either by well-meaning amateurs, who, however, lacked in most cases the necessary knowledge for such a task, or it was put in the hands of (in many cases) unscrupulous professionals who wanted to please their clients and submitted a glorified pedigree which cannot stand investigation judged by our present standards.[1] With very few exceptions [2] all that has been published during the 19th and the first years of the present century should be discounted

---

[1] Among the worst, to cite only a few: *A Founder Family of New Netherland and their ancestry in Holland* (Van Deuzen family), see *New York Genealogical and Biographical Record*, 1934, 62; *History of the Sloat Family of the Nobility of Holland*, by Mrs. Geo. Washington Holland; *The Schenck Genealogy*, see *New York Genealogical and Biographical Record*, 68 p. 114. *The Van der Veere Family in the Netherlands. 1150-1660 and 1280-1780*, see *The American Genealogist* July 1945.

[2] An excellent genealogy is: *The Earliest Cuylers of Holland and America*, by Maud Churchill Nicoll.

until a thorough investigation has proved the reliability of the facts as presented.

In the last thirty years a different attitude toward genealogical research has produced some excellent results and many well authenticated reliable articles have appeared in various magazines, books and family publications. However, the field has by no means been exhausted and, in the present writer's opinion, with the proper approach, the Old World ancestry of many settlers from the Netherlands may be definitely established.

Before embarking on such a quest it is important to determine beforehand the chances of finding the desired data.

First, there are families who came here with family names already established. The genealogies of these families have for the greater part already been determined. However, there are still quite a few which offer excellent prospects for a search (ten Eyck, Verno(o)y, Van Loon, etc.). But, at this point, there should be given a warning. Similarity of family names is never a proof of relationship, unless the family names are exceptional. The most common mistake in all publications is in trying to connect the family in America to one with the same or even a similar name in the Netherlands without any further proof than a similarity of surnames.

The second group comprises the families whose place of birth in the Netherlands is evident from the records in America, such as passenger lists, marriage records, orphan chamber records, and the like. Such leads are in many cases sufficient to warrant making an investigation. When the families apparently only used patronymics, and most of them did, the search is not an easy one but is worth undertaking, the results depending entirely on the place of origin, whether their home was in a large city or a small village and whether the patronymic and given names were rather unusual or very common given names. Each individual case should be judged on its own merits.

When no place of origin is known and only patronymics were used, a search in most cases is hopeless. But there may be indications in which direction to conduct the search, such as the family name used at a later date, the names of sponsors at baptisms, etc., these may give a clue.

The available Dutch printed source material in this country has been searched thoroughly by the various investigators, including this writer, and the possibility of finding any real clues therein is quite remote. Few libraries outside New York City and the Library of Congress in Washington, have any of these books on their shelves. Only one thoroughly versed in the Dutch language is able to consult them intelligently with any hope of success.

An extensive list of printed source material of the Netherlands is to be found in *Repertorium van Gedrukte Genealogieen*, by Jhr. Mr. Dr. E. A. van Beresteyn, published in the Netherlands in 1933. This lists the names of all Dutch families on which information had been published up to that time with reference to the publications in which it had appeared. (A copy of this *Repertorium* is in the Library of Congress, the New York Public Library, the New York Genealogical and Biographical Society, and probably others.) The book contains a list of all the genealogical and historical publications which have been consulted. Only a rather limited number of these, however, is available in American libraries.

Failing to find any clue in this printed source material, an investigation has to be made in the Netherlands. One can consult either a professional genealogist in this country with connections in the Netherlands or employ a Dutch genealogist of good standing and turn the search over to him or her. But in case one desires to make the search personally by writing to various depositories of source material, the following outline is submitted regarding the method of making a search.

There are in the Netherlands the (Federal) General Archives located at The Hague, and in the capitals of each of the eleven provinces, a State Depository of the old provincial archives. In addition, the larger cities which could afford fireproof vaults and buildings to give adequate protection to the valuable records, have their Municipal Archives. Some of the larger libraries have manuscript collections which contain documents of value to the genealogist. The Royal Library at The Hague is one of the foremost among these. All such institutions are managed by a competent staff with special training for this kind of work, and the writer has found them courteous and efficient. In practically all instances a charge is made for answering an inquiry, the amount depending on the scope of the work to be done. None of these institutions, however, do extensive research for others.

WHAT KIND OF SOURCE MATERIAL IS AVAILABLE AT THE ARCHIVES?

Church Records

All old vital church records before 1811 have been deposited —ordered by law—in the various archives as enumerated above. In other words, the churches do not have the old vital church records in their possession. The writer does not know of any complete church records which have been published such as has been done in England and in the United States.[3] The original records have, therefore, to be searched at the archives in which they have been deposited. This is a laborious task and can only be undertaken by one versed in reading the old script. Few of these registers have been indexed. Rotterdam is one of the best in this respect. Amsterdam marriages have been indexed in groups of five years on the Christian names of the persons (old indexes). Amsterdam, the place of origin of a large number of settlers, is a very difficult city in which to find marriage and especially baptismal records. It was a large city, the third in Europe during the 17th century, with quite a number of churches, each with its individual records, and it may take days to

---

[3] A limited number of some very old records have been published; also excerpts from the records of a few cities have appeared in genealogical magazines. These selected entries covered those concerning ministers, military men, artists and the like. A complete list of all available church records (as of 1880) appeared in *Algemeen Nederlandsch Familieblad*, Vols. 1, 5, 6, 7, 8, 9 (available at New York Public Library and New York State Library). In volumes 1887, 1888 and 1889 there appeared the Dutch Brazil records.

locate a single entry. In addition, the fees for consulting the registers are quite high.

There is another important custom to consider. When one or both parties contracting a marriage did not belong to either the Dutch Reformed, Walloon or Presbyterian churches a civil marriage had to be contracted before schepens (see below) and special registers were kept for these marriages.

From the foregoing, it is evident that even to make a search in as simple a source as the church records may require a trip to various provincial or municipal archives and, what is essential, a thorough knowledge of the old script, considerable time and, consequently, a large amount of patience.

Add to this the fact that other source material is much more difficult to search and it is little wonder that the number of active genealogists in the Netherlands is not large and limited to those equipped with the necessary knowledge and perseverance. The amateur who has to search for days at a time in the old script registers is soon discouraged and selects another hobby. An important result, however, is that whatever is published is of excellent quality and based on original work and not just taken from printed source material.

Notarial Archives

These form other important records for genealogical research. Some years ago (12 December 1905) a law was passed directing all still-existing notarial records dating from before 1811 to be surrendered to the various archives. An index is being made in most archives in order to facilitate searching these thousands of volumes. Here one finds wills, settlements of estates, contracts, affidavits, in short a real treasure house of information. A very large number of notarial records have been lost during more than two centuries of private ownership, but many are still available in the various archives.

Orphan Chamber Records

These are also of great importance. Unless the chamber was excluded by will and guardians appointed therein in case there were surviving minors, it was necessary to file an inventory of the estate of the deceased parent with the Orphan Chamber. This institution protected their rights, especially in cases when the surviving party contracted another marriage. (Note: There are still notarial records and Orphan Chamber records in existence of New Amsterdam and Albany dating from the Dutch Colonial period.)

The Court of Schepens

This was an institution unknown in England, but it dates back to the Middle Ages in the Netherlands and other parts of the Continent. In its early existence its members were appointed from the nobility of the district, but upon the growing importance of the cities the members of the court in the cities were appointed from its influential burghers. In the country, the nobility and large landowners continued their hold on its membership much longer but were gradually replaced by the smaller landowners and substantial farmers.

The number of Schepens which made up the court varied in accordance with the size of the city or district under its jurisdiction. One of the members acted as president; attached to the court was a secretary. Their term of office was limited to a few years. In many instances, they could not fill the position for consecutive terms and had to be out of office for at least the duration of a term before being eligible for another appointment.

When sitting as a Court of Law they dealt with both civil and criminal cases. The bailiff or sheriff acted as prosecuting attorney. The secretary, in most cases trained in legal matters, saw to it that the provisions of the law were followed and kept the records. Besides holding court the schepens attended to many other duties. They appointed receivers in bankruptcy, attested to inventories, powers of attorney and various other legal papers, and committed the afflicted to insane asylums. One of their most important functions was that they acted as registrars of deeds and mortgages, for such instruments had to be passed by their board and recorded by them. Schepen records, therefore, form one of the most valuable sources of information for the genealogist. But they can only be properly consulted by skilled searchers, thoroughly familiar with the old script and the legal terminology. They are as a rule poorly indexed and searching these records is a very laborious task but for building up a pedigree they are of the greatest importance.

Another important function, mentioned above, was that all civil marriages had to be performed by their board (see under Church Records).

The schepens also made the appointments of several minor officials and issued certain ordinances. As a matter of fact, their position was one of great importance and in the cities was only surpassed by membership in the City Council—a life job—and the higher municipal, provincial and federal offices held by its members such as burgomasters, delegates to the States General, Provincial Estates, Admiralty Board, etc.

Land Tenure Records

The land was for the greater part owned by the large feudal landowners, be they individuals, associations or religious institutions. Their stewards kept records of the holdings, entering the name of the holder under the description of the various properties.

Such records are extremely valuable in proving a pedigree. Upon the death of the holder the successor had to take the oath of fealty and this fact was entered in the records under the description of the property in question. In many instances, the relationship between the successive holders was indicated or is evident from the patronymics. When the property was held for a long time by the same family the entries may contain the proof to establish a line for several generations. These records, therefore, are of the greatest importance for genealogical research. But again they are only for the experienced searcher.

Several of *Leenakten Boeken* (Land Tenure Registers) of the Province of Gelderland and a few others have been published. These are available at the New York Public Library and the New York State Library at Albany. They are to be found among the publications of the Society Gelre. Excerpts from others are scattered in various other publications.

Notes by other Searchers

In practically all archives there are to be found manuscripts left by former searchers. During bygone centuries a number of famous antiquaries collected data about the leading families of their day. Some of these notes are excellent, others have to be used with caution, and again others should be left alone. The writer has been able to use such manuscripts in a few instances, mostly in connection with determining the arms used by families under investigation. Those in attendance at the various archives are familiar with these manuscripts and are able to advise which to consult.

Guild Registers

In the cities a large number of records kept by the various guilds have been preserved and these contain in many instances entries helpful in building up a pedigree. But they need to be consulted by an experienced searcher.

The Records of the West India Company

These records are on deposit with the General Archives at The Hague. They have been thoroughly searched by competent searchers. Such information as they contain has for the greater part been published, that is, used in the history of the Company. They have not disclosed any important material in connection with genealogical research.

Passenger Lists

The writer has often been asked whether there are passenger lists available. The only ones in existence have been published in the Holland Society *Yearbook* of 1902. They are not really passenger lists but accounts enumerating those passengers who owed the Company money for their passage. Others who sailed on the same ships but had settled their accounts are not listed. Other lists of immigrants of a later date, practically all Germans, are contained in "The Book of

40,000 names". The Amsterdam and Rotterdam Notarial Archives have been searched for passenger lists for these were the principal ports of embarkation for the New World, but no such lists have been found.

Genealogical Society

Het Koninklijk Genootschap voor Geslacht en Wapenkunde De Nederlandsche Leeuw (The Royal Society for Genealogy and Heraldry, The Netherlands' Lion) is situated at The Hague and has an excellent library and manuscript collection. A well-informed staff will answer simple questions or will refer you to a competent genealogist who might be willing to undertake a search. This Society is reliable in every respect and should not be confused with some genealogical agencies in this country which claim to have extensive connections abroad.

* * *

This is in broad outline the genealogical source material available in the Netherlands. Various districts have in many instances special registers and when once a search has been started these should be used when a search in them looks promising. Again, any search has to be undertaken by a person with experience in this kind of work.

CHAPTER VIII

FRANCE

Printed Works

The genealogist of French families will find a vast amount of printed materials at his disposal. Within the limits of this chapter we can mention only a few of the more noteworthy publications. It must be remembered that these are secondary works, and that the authors are not free from error. But they serve the useful purpose of providing clues for further research and, of course, much of the information they present is reliable.

The first of the long series of volumes of the *Dictionnaire des Familles Françaises, Anciennes et Notables, à la Fin du XIXe Siècle,* by Chaix d'Est-Ange, made its appearance in 1903. The families in this work are arranged alphabetically. From 1923 to 1930 Baron de Woelmont de Brumagne published, in eight volumes, *Notices Généalogiques;* each volume has its own index, and in 1928 the compiler issued a book containing additions and corrections to the first five volumes.

A convenient reference for French families is the series known as *Les Vieux Noms de France,* by Maurice Léo d'Armagnac del Cer, Comte de Puymège, of which the first volume came off the press in 1939, and the latest (so far as the author of this chapter can ascertain) in 1954. It consists of brief historical sketches, which vary in length according to the importance of the family and the available material on each family.

André Guirard published *Les Anciennes Familles de France, Leurs Origines, Leur Histoire, Leurs Descendances* in three volumes (1930-35). Generally, the work consists of historical sketches with an account of living members of the families but frequently long genealogies of the families are included.

André Delavenne began the publication in 1954 of a work

devoted to the French middle class, *Recueil Généalogique de la Bourgeoisie Ancienne*, in each volume of which the families are arranged alphabetically.

Periodicals which devote attention to genealogy include the *Bulletin de la Société Héraldique et Généalogique de France* (6 vols., 1879-87, each volume being thoroughly indexed), the *Bulletin Généalogique d'Information*, the quarterly organ (first issued in 1956) of the Centre Généalogique de Paris (Genealogical Center of Paris), and *La France Généalogique*, of which the first number came off the press in January 1959 as the bi-monthly organ of the Centre d'Entr'aide Généalogique (Center of Genealogical Assistance), edited by Dr. du Chalard of Villaines-la-Juhel (Mayenne).

Of prime importance for students of French Huguenot (Protestant) genealogy is the long series of volumes, *Publications of the Huguenot Society of London*, which contain transcripts of the registers of the Walloon Church at Canterbury, Returns of Aliens from 1503 to 1597, registers of the French Church of Threadneedle Street, London, letters of denization and acts of naturalization of aliens in England and Ireland, and other records which have a bearing on the Huguenots in England and colonial America.

The Armorial Général.—

Not to be overlooked by genealogists of French families, especially the noble houses, are the works of the famous d'Hozier family. Pierre d'Hozier, Seigneur de la Garde (1592-1660), *juge d'armes* (Judge of Arms) of France (an office approximating that of Garter King of Arms in England), left at his death 150 volumes or portfolios of documents and papers relating to the genealogy of the principal families of the Kingdom. His younger son, Charles René d'Hozier (1640-1732), who succeeded his brother, Louis Roger (1634-1708), as *juge d'armes* in 1675, established (1696) the General Armory (Armorial Général) of France. This vast work included not only the coats-of-arms of noble families *but also the armorial insignia of commoners entitled to bear arms.* The collection is incomplete, however; in spite of a royal edict requiring the registration of arms, many families refused to comply. His nephew and successor as *juge d'armes*, Louis Pierre d'Hozier (1685-1767), published *Armorial Général, ou Registres de la Noblesse* (10 vols., 1738-68), which, unlike his uncle's great work of similar name, dealt only with noble families and was not an official publication. The tremendous genealogical and heraldic collections of the d'Hozier family are in the Bibliothèque Nationale (National Library) at Paris.

Primary Sources[1]

PARISH REGISTERS AND REGISTERS OF THE CIVIL STATE.—A few parish registers date from the early part of the 16th century, a few more from the 17th century, but the majority of extant registers are from the 18th century. The custodian of the registers was the curé, or parish priest. Occasionally, from the 17th century, but more especially from the beginning of the 18th century, the priests deposited duplicates of their registers with the *Greffe du Tribunal* (Office of the Clerk of Court). When the Revolution swept over France in 1789 the priests were required by law to transfer all of their registers to the town hall (the *Mairie*); they then became known as the *Registres de l'État Civil* (Registers of the Civil State). In the various localities these registers of births, marriages, and burials are preserved either in the *Bureau de l'État Civil* (Office of the Civil State) of the *Mairie*, or in the *Archives Communales* (Municipal Archives), or in the *Archives Départementales* (Departmental Archives). (France is divided into 89 departments, corresponding generally to our States.) The registers prior to the Revolution contain an index, usually by surname but for the older registers by Christian name, at the end of the volume or end of the year. For the registers after the Revolution, except for the earlier years, there are indexes (alphabetically, by surname) compiled every five or ten years. Unfortunately, in Paris, both

---

[1] This section is based on H. L. Rabino di Borgomale, "Genealogical Research in France", *The Genealogists' Magazine* (London), vol. 10, Sept. 1946, pp. 1-7.

the original and the duplicate registers up to 1860 were lost by fire. An attempt has been made to reconstitute the État Civil before 1860, but these records are, of course, fragmentary. The Archives of the Department of Seine (*Archives du Département de la Seine*) contain card and alphabetical indexes for the Paris État Civil after 1860.

NOTARIAL RECORDS.—In France, as well as in other European countries, the records of notaries public are highly important for the genealogist. The notaries drew up wills, deeds of purchase and sale, marriage contracts, and other documents that provide much information on individuals and families. These records are frequently in the possession of successive notaries of a locality, but early in this century they were authorized to deposit their papers which they no longer required with the National Archives at Paris or the Departmental Archives. The volumes of notarial records are often indexed, but in cases where they are not provided with this finding aid it is virtually impossible to conduct researches.

MILITARY AND NAVAL RECORDS.—The records of French soldiers and sailors are maintained at Paris in the *Archives Administratives du Ministère de la Guerre* (Administrative Archives of the Ministry of War) and the *Archives du Ministère de la Marine* (Archives of the Ministry of the Navy). For the period before the Napoleonic Empire, the records of officers are kept alphabetically in boxes, but since that time an alphabetical index of officers has been maintained.

The Public Archives [2]

The National Archives at Paris and the numerous departmental archives possess a well-nigh inexhaustible fund of material of genealogical as well as historical value. Here are maintained the charters of the Middle Ages, the registers of feudal dues, tax-registers, obituaries, decisions of the *Conseil du Roi* (Council of the King) and of the Law Courts, etc. In

---

[2] This section is based in part on Rabino di Borgomale, *loc. cit.*, and *Archival Repositories in France*, compiled by Dr. Ernst Posner for the Committee of the American Council of Learned Societies on Protection of Cultural Treasures in War Areas, and issued by The National Archives, Washington, D. C., December 1943.

many cases printed inventories of the holdings of the departmental and municipal archives are available. Card indexes in the muniment rooms of the archival establishments are of help to researchers.

A few examples of the importance of archival holdings may be given. The *Archives Communales* at Abbeville, Département de la Somme, owns an impressive collection of records of the city authorities from the 12th to the 17th centuries and treasurers' accounts from 1340 to 1775. The *Archives Municipales* at Bordeaux lost many of its records by fire in 1862, but among the documents that survived the conflagration are numerous chartularies from the 13th century, 900 volumes of vital statistics, and many family archives. The *Archives Départementales* at Colmar, Département du Haut-Rhin, holds the records of the authorities of the *ancien régime* (Old Regime) prior to 1790, including the archives of the Counts of Ribeaupierre, the archives of religious institutions and corporations, and the records of the Revolutionary period, 1790-1800. One of the richest depositories in France is the *Archives Départementales* at Dijon, Département de la Côte d'Or, where are preserved the records of the ancient Duchy of Burgundy, as well as records created by various authorities in later periods. The *Archives de la Ville* (Town Archives) of Montbéliard, Département de Doubs, has records of privileges and franchises from 1283, citizenship lists from 1316, notarial books from the 16th to the 18th centuries, and guild records.

CHAPTER IX

SWITZERLAND *

Switzerland is a Federal Union of 19 cantons and six half-cantons, as follows: *German,* Zürich, Bern, Luzern, Uri, Schwyz, Obwalden and Nidwalden (half-cantons comprising the Canton of Unterwalden), Glarus, Zug, Solothurn, Basel-Stadt and Basel-Land (half-cantons making up the Canton of Basel), Schaffhausen, Appenzell Inner-Rhoden and Appenzell Ausser-Rhoden (half-cantons composing the Canton of Appenzell), Sankt Gallen, Graubünden, Aargau, and Thurgau; *Italian,* Ticino; *French,* Fribourg, Vaud, Valais, Neuchâtel, and Geneva. The majority of the population speaks German, with smaller percentages speaking French and Italian. There is a fourth official language in the Union, recognized as such a few years ago—Rätoromannic (Rhaeto-Roman), spoken by about one percent, namely, the mountaineers of Graubünden (Grisons) and the headwaters of the Rhine. It is a historical survival of the Latin spoken by the Roman legions in ancient Switzerland. The cantons have alternative German and French names; for example, German Luzern is French Lucerne; German Zug is French Zoug; German Graubünden is French Grisons; German Solothurn is French Soleure; French Vaud and Valais are German Waadt and Wallis; Geneva is Genève in French and Genf in German; and so on.

Printed Works

Genealogical studies in Switzerland are of comparatively recent date. Before the 19th century chroniclers and his-

---

* This chapter is based, in part, on W. H. Ruoff, "Concerning Genealogy in Switzerland", *Genealogical Research in German-Speaking Lands: A Symposium* (Special Publication No. 19, National Genealogical Society, 1958). pp. 18-20; *Dictionnaire Historique et Biographique de la Suisse,* vol. 3 (1926). p. 349 (article, "Généalogie") ; Albert B. Faust. *Guide to the Materials for American History in Swiss and Austrian Archives* (1916); Archibald F. Bennett, *A Guide for Genealogical Research* (1951), pp. 262-263 (Swiss Record Sources).

torians established genealogies of families of dynasts and of middle-class families grouped according to their localities. These old genealogies were not necessarily intended to contribute to a knowledge of Swiss history, but rather to support territorial pretensions of certain families. This was especially the case in 1707 when genealogical tables accompanied the manifestos of the pretenders to the sovereignty of Neuchâtel.[1]

Although two centuries have elapsed since its publication was begun, Hans Jacob Leu's *Allgemeines Helvetisches Eydgenössisches oder Schweizerisches Lexicon* (General Helvetian Confederated or Swiss Lexicon) (20 vols., 1747-65) is still a standard reference. It is a historical, topographical, biographical, and genealogical work, and its subjects are arranged alphabetically. A supplement was published in six volumes (1786-95) by Johann Jacob Holzhalb.

Among other useful publications in the field of Swiss genealogy are Galiffe's *Notices Généalogiques sur les Familles Genevoises* (7 vols., 1829-95), dealing with families of Geneva; *Recueil Généalogique Suisse* (Swiss Genealogical Collection) (3 vols., 1902-18, also dealing with families of Geneva); and *Recueil de Généalogies Vaudoises* (Collection of Genealogies of the Canton of Vaud), published by the Société Vaudoise de Généalogie, which was founded at Lausanne in 1910. In 1905 was published volume I of the *Schweizerisches Geschlechterbuch* which bears the alternative French title, *Almanach Généalogique Suisse*. This is perhaps the best all-around work thus far produced on Swiss families; volume XI of this series was issued in 1958.

The noted genealogist, Johann Paul Zwicky, of Zürich, published *Sammlung Schweizerischer Ahnentafeln* (Collection of Swiss Ancestor-Tables) (1938 to 1942). This well indexed

---

[1] The present Canton of Neuchâtel was ruled for centuries by its own line of counts; in 1707, the King of Prussia successfully prosecuted his claim with the result that he and his successors were Princes of Neuchâtel until 1857, when Prussian rule was terminated. From 1806 to 1813, one of Napoleon's marshals was Prince of Neuchâtel, but as the Napoleonic empire was coming to an end the sovereignty reverted to Prussia.

volume takes some of the families back to the 16th century. On pages 65-66, it shows the American connections of one Swiss family, namely, Belsterling, Markley, Preston, Heisler, and Carlile, of the Philadelphia-New Jersey area.

A most useful reference work is the *Dictionnaire Historique et Biographique de la Suisse* (Historical and Biographical Dictionary of Switzerland), which also was published in a German edition, *Historisch-Biographisches Lexikon der Schweiz* (7 vols., 1921-34). It gives brief accounts of thousands of Swiss families, including many which have branches in America, such as Bürgi, Feer (Fehr), von Graffenried, Has(s)ler, de Saussure, Tschudi, Tschumi, and Zollikofer.

The National Genealogical Society in Washington published *Lists of Swiss Emigrants in the Eighteenth Century to the American Colonies*, by Albert Bernhardt Faust and Gaius Marcus Brumbaugh (2 vols., 1920-25). Volume I gives details about the emigrants from Zürich to Carolina and Pennsylvania, 1734-44, and Volume II provides similar data concerning the emigrants from Bern, 1706-95, and from Basel, 1734-94. This work is indispensable for students of Swiss colonists in America.

Societies

There are several societies in Switzerland that are engaged in preserving their genealogical records. In addition to local societies, on a national scale are the Schweizerische Gesellschaft für Familienforschung (Société d'Études Généalogiques), or Swiss Society for Genealogical Studies, and the Schweizerische Heraldische Gesellschaft (Société Suisse d'Héraldique), which devotes itself to heraldic studies. There is also an association of Swiss professional genealogists, the Verband Schweizerisches Berufs-Familienforscher.

Parish Registers

In Switzerland for centuries there were only two recognized churches, the Reformed and the Roman Catholic. The Reformed church registers are the older, having been instituted by the great reformer, Ulrich Zwingli (died 1531). The Catholic registers date from an order of the Council of Trent in 1563. The types of records contained in the parish registers are baptisms, marriages, burials, and confirmations. Of equal importance are the *Jahrzeitbücher*, which contain data on legacies set aside for masses of the dead. Names of parents and grandparents of decedents are often included, and even landed property is frequently designated. In some parts of Switzerland these books date from the 14th century.

By a national law of 24 December 1874, it was ordered that the ancient parish registers were to be preserved (either originals or copies) by officers of the civil state. Many of them are found in the various State Archives (*Staatsarchiv* in German cantons, *Archives de l'État* in French cantons, and *Archivio Cantonale* in the Italian canton). A large number of registers are still in the custody of the parishes. Many registers are on microfilm at the Genealogical Society in Salt Lake City.

Notarial Registers

Records kept by notaries, which contain records of wills, inventories, etc., are for the most part in the custody of the state archives of the cantons.

Civil Registration

The French canton of Vaud commenced civil registration in 1800, but the other cantons did not follow suit until required by a national law effective 1 January 1876 (the same day that civil registration in Germany started). These records of births, marriages, and deaths are preserved by the respective civil registration offices *(Zivilstandsamt)*.

Citizenship Lists

The *Bürgerbücher* (citizenship books) have been kept for many centuries. A number of *Bürgerbücher* have been published. The original volumes are preserved in the municipal archives (the towns and villages have their own archival establishments) or in the civil registration offices.

Census Records

The first general census of Switzerland was in 1841, but these records are not widely used because of the completeness of the parish registers. It should be noted that in 1764 the canton of Bern was so concerned about Bernese emigration to England and America that a census of its population was ordered in that year.

Real Estate Registers

These important registers of landed property, dating from the late Middle Ages to modern times, are preserved in the various archives. Included with them are the *Zinsbücher* (tribute books), containing names of serfs who paid dues to the manorial lords.

Emigration Records

The State Archives of Switzerland contain abundant information on emigrants in the 17th, 18th, and 19th centuries.[2] The Staatsarchiv at Zürich has many documents relating to people going to the Palatinate, Swabia, the Netherlands, Alsace, America, and elsewhere; some of these records date from 1651. In 1702, there was compiled a list of persons who were "not at home in that year". The Staatsarchiv at Glarus has records of landed property transferred to its former inhabitants living in America (1837-67). The Staatsarchiv at Basel has petitions from the Junt and Rieger families which wished to emigrate to Virginia in 1771. The Staatsarchiv at Schaffhausen has records (1735, 1741, etc.) of persons from that canton who went to Carolina and Pennsylvania. The Staatsarchiv at Bern has documents relating to the 18th century Swiss settlements in Lancaster County, Pennsylvania, the

---

[2] The statement in *Genealogical Research in German-Speaking Lands* (1958), p. 19: "It is noteworthy that there are almost no records of emigration—a matter of importance when one attempts to trace the Swiss ancestry of an American family" is incorrect. As the illustrations in the text, selected at random, demonstrate, the Swiss cantonal archives possess many documents bearing on emigrants to America and other countries, from the 17th century on. It should be noted in passing, that in addition to the State Archives of the cantons and the archives of towns and villages, the *Bundesarchiv* (Federal Archives) was established at Bern in 1798. It is comparable to our National Archives.

19th century settlement at Vevay, Switzerland County, Indiana, and other Swiss colonies in this country. At the Staatsarchiv and Stadtbibliothek (Municipal Library at Bern) are many papers dealing with von Graffenried's settlement at New Bern, North Carolina.

CHAPTER X

SCANDINAVIA

Printed Works

In recent years there has been an ever-increasing interest in genealogy in the Scandinavian countries and Finland. Several books and magazines containing articles on family records, handbooks on genealogy, etc., have been published in those countries.

Sweden was one of the first nations in the world to publish statistics, and the idea of preserving and organizing manuscripts is old there. Unfortunately, in many instances, fires have destroyed church archives as well as other manuscript collections, and other sources, therefore, become doubly important.

In Sweden, genealogical research was aided and facilitated several years ago by Professor Odhner, the well-known historian, who was instrumental in having a law passed that all records and manuscripts in the custody of Swedish churches should be assembled in certain central archives. Several of these district archives were established throughout Sweden. Some of the churches in the Province of Dalarna refused, however, to part with their valuable records. Finally, it was decided that churches not willing to send their church books to the central archives should be allowed to keep them, provided the churches constructed fireproof vaults for the safekeeping of their manuscripts. A list of these churches is found in Ella Heckscher's *Sex Kapital om Släktforskning*. An excellent little folder, *Finding Your Forefathers*, was published by the Swedish Foreign Office Press and Information Service in 1957. It contains a wealth of information useful to the genealogist searching for Swedish ancestors.

In Denmark, Frabritius and Hatt published *Haandbog i Slaegtforskning* (Handbook on Genealogical Research) (Copenhagen, 1943), which "covers the entire North."

In Finland, we find one of the best books on the subject, *Släktforskning. Praktisk Handbok för Finland*, by Alfred Brenner (Helsinki, 1947). It, naturally, concerns Finland especially, but it contains much information for Swedish and even Danish and Norwegian genealogists.

Brenner gives a list of the provincial archives, including the National Archives, and he describes their general content. He publishes facsimiles of the alphabet and of the handwriting of the 17th and 18th centuries, and he explains certain signs and expressions which occur in church books that must be understood if a genealogist is to make headway. He completes certain common abbreviations in Latin and the native language, found especially in the early church books.

For Norway, we have *Aett og By. Festskrift til Finne-Grønn. Om Nordisk Slegtforskning og Oslo Byhistorie* (a title which may be translated briefly as "On Nordic Genealogical Research"), by several writers (Oslo, 1944).

The books listed above all describe methods and sources of genealogical research in the Scandinavian countries. A large number of books and periodicals dealing with families have been published. The most important of these are listed as follows:

DENMARK: *Danmarks Adels Aarbog* (Yearbook of the Nobility of Denmark); *Dansk Historisk Tidskrift* (Danish Historical Journal, which often contains articles of interest for the genealogist); *Genealogisk og Biographisk Archiv; Genealogisk Tidskrift; Genealogiske og Personalhistoriske Meddelselser* (1925); and *Personalhistorisk Tidskrift*.

FINLAND: *Ättertavlor för de på Finlands Riddarhus* (pedigree book of the families matriculated in the Finnish House of Knights); *Finlands Riddarskaps Adels Vapenbok* (Book of Coats-of-Arms of the Finnish Knighthood and Nobility); *Finsk Historisk Bibliografi* (Finnish historical Bibliography), by J. Vallinkoski and H. Schuman (contains sections of genealogical and historic-genealogical works for Finland and Sweden); *Finsk Historisk Bibliografi, 1901-25*, by A. Meliniemi and Ella Kivikoski (valuable); and *Genos*, a magazine published by the Genealogiski Samfundet (Genealogical Society of Finland).

NORWAY: *Historiske Samlinger* (Historical Collections); *Norsk Slekthistorisk Tidskrift* (Journal of Norwegian Family History; also occasionally contains articles on Finland and the other Scandinavian countries); *Norske Stamtavler* (Norwegian Pedigrees), by W. Lassen; *Norske Slegter* (Norwegian Families), by H. K. Steffens; and *Norsk Tidskrift för Genealogi* (Norwegian Genealogical Journal).

SWEDEN: *Äldre Svenska Frälsesläkter* (Old Swedish Gentry), by F. Wernstedt (1957); *Den Introducerade Svenska Adelns Ättartavlor*, by Gustaf Elgenstierna (9 vols., 1925-36 —index in vol. 9; valuable record of all present as well as extinct Swedish noble houses); *Ny Svensk Släktbok* (New Swedish Family Book), by K. A. K. Leijonhufvud; *Svenska Släkter*, Swedish Families), by T. Uggla and V. Ljungfors (4 vols., 1908-15); *Sveriges Ridderskaps och Adels Kalender* (Calendar of the Swedish Knighthood and Nobility; a yearbook).

Original Sources [1]

Most of the works listed above can be found in the Library of Congress in Washington, the New York Public Library, and other large libraries. But, after the printed works on Scandinavian genealogy have been exhausted, the researcher must turn to the primary sources in the countries themselves. Such sources often offer difficulties for the genealogist who is not thoroughly familiar with the languages and, in many cases, even if he knows the languages well. This is especially so in Finland, where the researcher must know both Swedish and Finnish if he is to be successful. In Finland even a person who has a complete command of the two languages often encounters great, even insurmountable, difficulties in tracing a

---

[1] This section is based for the most part on Archibald F. Bennett's *A Guide for Genealogical Research* (1951), pp. 246-248 (Denmark), 252-255 (Finland), 259-260 (Norway), and 261-262 (Sweden); Dr. Ernst Posner's *Archival Repositories in Enemy Occupied Countries of Northwest Europe* (The National Archives, Jan. 1944), pp. 36-42 (Denmark and Norway).

Finnish name. Due to the patriotic spirit often found in certain Finnish circles many people, especially among the educated, have changed their Swedish names (and in some cases other foreign names), or translated them into their Finnish equivalent, as has been done in some cases in this country (for example, Sjöstrand is now Seashore). There is still another difficulty that besets the genealogist who works in Finnish sources. We find names of places that once existed but are no longer printed on the maps, thus necessitating the use of old maps and books and histories of many localities.

DENMARK: The earliest parish registers (Lutheran) in Denmark date from 1572; only a few were kept prior to 1641. By 1685, approximately half the parishes maintained such records, and from the 18th century all of the parishes were doing so. The entries included infant baptisms, confirmations, engagements, marriages, burials, membership lists, etc. The parish clergyman recorded all births in his register, whether or not the persons concerned were of the Lutheran faith. The original records from the earliest period to 1890 are in the Riksarchiv (State Archives) at Copenhagen, and the Provincial Archives at Aabenraa, Odense, and Viborg. The registers since 1890 are in the custody of the respective parishes.

Census enumerations were taken in Denmark and her possessions in 1787, 1801, 1834, 1840, 1845, 1850, 1855, 1860, 1870, 1880, 1885, 1890, and every ten years following 1890. The schedules from 1787-1840 inclusive listed each person in the family, giving his name, address, family position, age, marital status, and occupation. In later years, additions were made to these records, such as birthplaces, church affiliations, and dates of birth. Census returns after 1890 are not available to the public, but the earlier returns may be consulted at the State Archives in Copenhagen.

The military levying rolls were begun in 1788, and the navy levying rolls in 1802, although the island of Fyn had the latter as early as 1796. Here were listed each male individual, his father, his own place of birth, age, height, residence, etc.

The *Skifteprotokoller,* or probate records, were maintained as early as 1574, but it was not until 1683 that probate records were generally kept in Denmark. These records are as valuable as the parish registers for the data they provide on deceased persons and their families.

A very few records of land tenures (Jordebøger) were kept as early as 1500, but they were maintained in considerable number after 1600, and by 1660 the provinces kept such records generally. These records give the names of the copyholder, sometimes his parish of birth, the names of the former copyholders, and their relationships to former holders of the land.

The marriage license records *(Kopulationsprotokoller)* exist for the city of Copenhagen only, and cover the period 1735-1868.

The originals of all of the above records can be found in the State Archives at Copenhagen. Fortunately, The Genealogical Society of the Church of Jesus Christ of Latter-Day Saints has been extremely active in Scandinavia, with the result that all of these records, generally down to 1860, have been microfilmed and are available to researchers in Salt Lake City.

A little-known archival establishment in Denmark is The Emigrant Archives at Aalborg, where are maintained letters, diaries, and autobiographies of Danish emigrants, together with many of their portraits and pictures of their houses, farms, and places of business.

FINLAND: Finnish parish registers begin in 1648, and they contain records of births, baptisms, proclamations, deaths, and burials. Another type of ecclesiastical record is the group known as house examination records, which were started in 1667. They list the families of the parish, including all members of the household, dates of birth and death, where they came from, where they moved to, etc. The parish minister is the custodian of a variety of records—the church registers, the house examination records, the confirmation records, the change of residence records (started in 1686, but the oldest extant records date from 1722); the church accounts, and the private parish inventories (records of widowers and widows in connection with marriage proclamations).

The Central Government Archives at Helsinki (Helsingfors) has on deposit the transcripts of church records from 1648 to 1850 (they are owned by the Genealogical Society of Finland), old account records, 1538-1634 (information about land owners, persons employed in the collection of state taxes, etc.), new account records, 1635-1809 (military lists, records relating to ownership of land, etc.), census records, 1810-present (these records are really tax lists), court records, 1620-present (wills and inventories when involved in court cases, dates of sale of farms and houses and legal confirmation of their possession with some data about family relationships, marriages, guardianships, etc.), and the General Register of Inhabitants of Finland, 1539-1809 (general index of genealogical data based on the accounts and church records in the Central Government Archives).

All of the above-mentioned records are available on microfilm at The Genealogical Society at Salt Lake City.

NORWAY: The earliest parish register, that of Andabu, begins in 1623, but generally such registers do not commence until 1700. The original registers are in the *Statsarkiv* (State Archives) at Oslo, from the beginning until 1850, and the Provincial Archives at Bergen, Christiansand, Hamar, and Trondheim.

The census returns were really tax lists; they were taken in 1664, 1701, 1801, 1865, 1875, 1890, and every ten years thereafter. Returns from 1664 to 1865 are in the State Archives at Oslo, but those for later years are in the various Provincial Archives.

The Norwegian probate records *(Skifteprotokoller)* date from about 1550, in the cities, and from late in the 17th century in the rural areas. The originals are in the Provincial Archives.

The Provincial Archives also have the mortgage books, the earliest of which date from before 1700; they are arranged chronologically by sheriff's offices, of which there are about 60. These records provide information about estates, sale contracts, mortgages, freeholders, etc.

The rent roll books for 1660, 1723, and 1838 are in the State Archives at Oslo, and give data about land ownership, their possessors, inhabitants, domestic animals, etc.

Microfilm copies of these records are on file at The Genealogical Society, Salt Lake City.

SWEDEN: The Swedish parish records *(Kyrkoböckerna)* include church registers, house examination records, removal records, and biographical records and obituaries. The earliest such records date from 1622, but it was not until 1686 that laws were passed requiring parish ministers to keep them. They are kept in the various Provincial Archives.

The National Archives at Stockholm have in their custody census records and land records, although a duplicate copy of land records may be found in the Provincial Archives.

Microfilm copies of these records are available also at The Genealogical Society, Salt Lake City.

Part 5

SPECIAL FIELDS OF INVESTIGATION

CHAPTER I

HERALDRY

Definition

Technically, the study of coats of arms, or Armory, is a branch of the larger study, Heraldry, which includes all that pertains to the duties of heralds, such as the conduct of tournaments, the establishment of precedence, the marshaling of coronations and other ceremonies, etc.; but since heraldry, in popular language, means the study of coats of arms, the word is here used in that sense.

Limitation

In order to be heraldic, a design must fulfill three requirements: (1) It must be displayed on some article of military equipment, such as a shield, flag, helmet, etc.; (2) it must be hereditary; and (3) it must conform to the standards of design set by custom.

The pennon attached to the lance was very probably the first object to be thus decorated because it would best serve the purpose of making a rallying point for the soldiery enlisted under one overlord; but the broad surface of the shield offered a favorable means of display, and the garment of the knight, armorially decorated, explains the use of the term *coat* of arms. The military use, which was the first, is reflected in the German term for a coat of arms, "Wappen", etymologically related to the word weapon, as well as to the later German word, "Waffen", which means the same thing. At first purely military, the coat of arms was soon adopted into ecclesiastical and secular use in general.

The hereditary feature distinguishes the coat of arms from arbitrary shield decoration which is probably as early as the use of the shield itself. We find it among the ancient Greeks and Romans, the ancient Peruvians, and even today among African tribes.

There is something to be said in favor of the very first

coats of arms having been territorial rather than personal, and something of this has come down to our times. Thus, the arms of the King of England are not his personal, family arms, but those of his realm, and on the Continent the much divided arms of the higher nobility are composed of territorial coats with the family arms placed on a small shield in the middle. Such arms went with the land, and when one dynasty was succeeded by another, all that was needed was a change in the family arms which occupied the middle shield.

The design on a knight's shield naturally became a family symbol cherished by his sons and daughters, so that it became customary for them to use it in their turn, often with some minor alteration to distinguish the son from the father, as well as the different sons from each other. As time went on and associations gathered about the family symbol it was jealously guarded against use by others, and such misuse became the subject of legal trials and personal combat.

Early custom established what was and what was not appropriate as the design of a coat of arms. It is true that in the period of decadence many "horrible examples" have had official sanction; but this does not justify classifying as coats of arms, merely because they are enclosed within the outline of a shield, the many state and municipal symbols, to say nothing of trademarks. The town of Crewe, in Cheshire, England, for example, rejoices in a shield divided into four quarters each showing a different mode of transportation —a canal boat, a stage coach, a pack horse and a horse with two riders—and the crest is a locomotive! A dispenser of toilet paper in Boston, Massachusetts, used a shield divided into three fields, each displaying the form in which his product was to be had—in rolls, in boxes and in pads; above the shield is a royal crown with the name KING in large letters on the circlet. It would be hard for the student of heraldry to whip up much interest in such productions.

Rules

The rules of heraldic design are not a formulated code; they are those rules which have become set by actual usage because they have been found valuable, and the term is used in the sense that we say that something is true "as a rule."

The fundamental purpose of a shield-design of an armorial nature is its identification at a distance, which is why the design should be in large contrasting masses and colors. This gave rise to the rule that is known to everyone, that color must not be placed on color nor metal on metal. The heraldic pigments are white, yellow, red, blue, black and green; rarely, and in small amounts only, orange, purple and crimson. The latter mixed colors are too easily confused, especially if faded by sunlight and discolored by time, with their components, so they are generally avoided. White and yellow (the "metals") are light in comparison with red, blue, black and green (the "colors"); so, in order to obtain distant visibility, the light is used in contrast to the dark, and, as any sign painter can testify, black on yellow carries further than blue on green. Otto Hupp, the great German authority who died not long ago, has made an interesting observation: That shields with a green field, although common in the earliest times, soon became very unusual—presumably because they were not easily seen at a distance against the green of fields and woods. In the painting of small details, such as the tongue and claws of a lion, the rule is disregarded; a gold lion on a blue field is generally shown with a red tongue and claws. Though they would not be distinguishable at a distance they are wholly unimportant to the picture as a whole, and painting them red enlivens the design when seen nearby.

Vocabulary

Like any other subject, heraldry has its own terms, which are largely derived from the French in the case of English heraldry, because French was the court language when heraldry arose. There is really no need of saying gules instead of red, azure instead of blue and sable instead of black; the common words answer just as well and are always used in German heraldry. The case is different in the subject of the designs; surely there is no advantage in saying "a blue shield crossed diagonally by a yellow straightsided band running from the upper left corner to the lower right side" when heraldic shorthand says it all in "Azure a bend gold." This brings up the matter of heraldic right and left; the point of view from which it is determined is that of the bearer of the shield, not the observer, just as stage right and left are determined from the point of view of the actor and not of the spectator; consequently, "dexter" means the observer's left and "sinister" the observer's right hand. In Tudor times, when euphuism became fashionable, some of the earlier books on heraldry were written; and it was but natural, when every subject had to become a "mystery", that heraldry, especially since it was so closely associated with court life, came to be overloaded with all sorts of absurd rules and expressions, so much so that one of the heralds declared that it was "a study which loads the memory without improving the understanding." Quite true, in his time; but this deterrent factor is fast being thrown into discard and no serious student of heraldry of today will maintain that if a roundel is blue it must be called a hurt, if black an ogress, if red a torteau, etc.

Period

Heraldry was unknown at the time of the first Crusade; it was in full bloom by the time of the second. The reason for its sudden appearance and its immediate use in all Christian countries is attributed to the need of distinguishing symbols when, for the first time, warriors from so many different countries assembled under common leadership. In spite of the apparently heraldic decoration of shields and pennons in the Bayeux Tapestry (1066) no true heraldry is shown there; the same warrior appears in different sections with different shield designs, and the designs there borne did not become hereditary. The first Crusade was from 1096 to 1099 and the second in 1147; between these dates, in about 1135, we find seals displaying shields with designs which we know become hereditary. Seals are our first and best pieces of evidence. Not only have all of the original objects—helms, shields, surcoats, etc.,—on which heraldic designs were first shown long since moldered away; but in that age, when only clerics knew how to read and write, a man's seal was his *alter ego;* it actually represented the owner himself. This explains the great perturbation which followed the accidental loss of the matrix of a seal, for it deprived the owner of any way of authenticating documents, since he could not sign his own name. When Richard I's chancellor, with the Great Seal hung around his neck, was drowned at Rhodes, the king declared all documents sealed with the lost matrix to be void, so that all who had them had to bring them in and obtain new charters sealed with the new seal—a considerable source of revenue to the spendthrift king!

The Middle Ages embrace all of the heraldic period—its beginning, its development, its burgeoning and its decadence, though its time of real decay came about a century ago. It began as a military necessity, at first limited to the higher nobility, but very soon became a social custom among the gentry, spreading in its use to ecclesiastical and secular foundations, municipalities, societies and guilds. Its study, therefore, really necessitates some knowledge of the life of the Middle Ages, and its usage needs to be interpreted from a mediaeval point of view. What followed the Middle Ages is of interest, of course, but it forms, as it were, an appendage rather than a subject in its own right.

Source Material

The very earliest source material which has survived to our times lies in the seals preserved on old documents, and secondly, in the pictorial embellishments of mediaeval documents; included among the latter are those highly interesting collections of coats of arms, pictorial or descriptive, occasionally both, of those who were present on some particular occasion or which the compiler had reason to wish to remember. The latter are known as rolls of arms, and exist in many lands —England, France, Germany, Scotland, etc.

The old sealing wax, made of bees' wax, has astonishing powers of endurance when guarded against excessive heat and against pressure. It is wholly different from the brittle modern sealing "wax" which is really a lacquer. For this reason, it has endured when the documents to which it was attached have been destroyed by damp and by decay; means have also been devised for the faithful reproduction of all details in durable materials so that copies of the same seal may be in the hands of many scholars. The advent of photography has spread abroad in book form accurate pictures of ancient seals, so that the student no longer has to rely on the intrepretation of the engraver.

The poets of the 13th century seem to have been impressed by the splendid appearance of the knights at military musters, at sieges, at tournaments, etc., and have left us descriptions of the shields and flags displayed on those occasions. The heralds, too, had occasion to make records for their own reference purposes, and many of these, especially in England, have been preserved and are today the subject of painstaking study.

The earliest known treatise on heraldry is the "Tractatus de Armis" by "Johan. de Bado Aureo" (ca. 1394); Evan John Jones, in his *Mediaeval Heraldry* (1943) offers evidence to show that the author was John Trevor, Bishop of St. Asaph. The next was the "De Studio Militari" by Nicolas Upton (ca. 1441). Both of these dates antedate the invention of printing and the two works were first printed (in one volume) by Edward Bysshe, Clarenceux King of Arms, in 1654. The first printed work on heraldry in the English language was *The Boke of Saint Albans,* anonymous, printed at Saint Albans in 1486; its source material appears to be the work of Nicolas Upton as well as a French manuscript. A facsimile reproduction was brought out by William Blades in 1901.

The Title to Arms

There can be no doubt that from the earliest times coats of arms were merely assumed at will by those to whom they were useful. They were, it is true, the mark of a certain social class; and yet, since the right to bear them is hereditary and since families suffer vicissitudes, it is equally certain that the right exists in the case of individuals in very humble circumstances. It was not long before the reigning powers discovered that the right to bear arms was looked upon as a privilege which they could make useful, so that they began to grant arms to those who wished to have them from an official source, and were willing to pay for the privilege. Hence has arisen the erroneous belief that any given coat of arms must have been granted, in the first place, because of some distinguished service to the prince or the state; whereas, in fact, it was probably first assumed because it was needed. Bearing a coat of arms has been compared to wearing a gold watch; it is true that gold watches are presented by firms and corporations to individuals who have served them long and well, but the wearing of a gold watch does not prove any such service—it may have been inherited from father and grandfather, and it may have been bought, when his circumstances allowed it, by the man who carries it.

On the Continent the right to assume a coat of arms has been called by a competent writer the very cornerstone of heraldry but, of course, the new coat must not conflict with any other coat.

In England there has never been, so far as I know, any act of Parliament regulating the bearing of coat-armor. Nevertheless, an officer of the College of Arms has stated in a recent publication that "Entitlement to Arms is created by Letters Patent of Arms, the Arms being granted, under Warrant from the Earl Marshal, to an individual and his descendants in the male line, according to the Laws of Arms." This statement is based on recent legal decisions in the courts in England, so it appears that there the right of the College of Arms to regulate the use of arms is recognized in spite of the absence of any act of Parliament.

In Scotland, the matter has long been regulated by Parliament; nobody in Scotland may bear arms until they have been matriculated in the Lyon Office (corresponding to the English College of Arms) which stipulates the exact design.

Many people in the United States imagine that the use of a coat of arms is in some way undemocratic. It is true that we do not use titles, but a coat of arms does not presuppose a title. By assuming a coat of arms a man does not claim high lineage; he merely adopts a convenient and picturesque mode of marking his possessions in place of the bald use of lettering. George Washington inherited and used his coat of arms on his book-plate. Thomas Jefferson believed that his family had a coat of arms and had a search made for it in London. Even Benjamin Franklin used arms, though it must be confessed that his right, not to arms per se, but to the design that he used, has never been shown.

In Switzerland, that most truly democratic of countries, there are coats of arms for every canton and for the great majority of the towns, and any Swiss individual has a right to use arms, whether inherited or personally assumed.

Application

Coats of arms have been used in almost every imaginable way. They first appeared, as has been said, on the pennons, shields, helms and surcoats of the military; then on seals; their use was extended to buildings, carved over the gate on the outside and over the mantel in the inside, as well as in stained glass windows and on furniture and furnishings; on tombs both within and without the churches; later painted on coaches and on chinaware and engraved on silver; and more recently embossed on letter paper and printed or engraved on book-plates. In this country, private arms are seldom seen publicly displayed, and perhaps their greatest field of use is on book-plates where they are seen only by the owner and his friends. Since, according to ancient usage, the arms stood for the man himself a coat of arms is far more appropriate for a book-plate than is a picture of the owner's house, a library interior, or a composition indicating all the subjects in which he is interested. Theoretically, the use of a coat of arms makes unnecessary the name of the bearer; but so few of us are generally known by our arms today that in the case of a book-plate, the addition of the owner's name is advisable.

Armorial Design

The earliest coats of arms were very simple. Two strongly

contrasting pigments, red and white, blue and yellow, etc., laid on in two or three large areas worked best for distant visibility and identification. As time went on and designs multiplied greater elaboration is found. By the period of the Tudors, when many "new men" came to the fore and had to have new coats, symbolism also became popular and the shield became more of a show piece than a military necessity; so we find much overloading with many charges and a consequent loss of the simplicity which had once been so important.

In an elder day it had been found that allusions to name, estate or office in the design of the arms furnished a useful jog to the memory; for instance, the family of Bolles had a blue shield with three silver bowls, and the branch of this family whose seat was at Swineshead added a golden swine's head set into each bowl. The elaboration of Tudor times is well illustrated by the arms of Thomas Cardinal Wolsey; the reasons for its design are set forth in *Historic Heraldry of Britain*, by Anthony R. Wagner, Portcullis Pursuivant (now Richmond Herald): "It was reasonably conjectured by Everard Green, Somerset Herald (*The Nineteenth Century*, June 1896), that we see in Wolsey's Arms 'the sable shield and cross engrailed of the Uffords, Earls of Suffolk'; Wolsey being the son of an Ipswich butcher; 'in the azure leopards' faces those of the coat of De la Pole, Earls of Suffolk; in the purple lion, the badge of Pope Leo X; in the rose, the Lancastrian sympathies of the builder of Cardinals' College (Christ Church) Oxford; and in the choughs, the reputed or assigned Arms of St. Thomas of Canterbury—argent three choughs proper. Thus, in the cardinal's coat we see his county and its history (i. e., its two earldoms), his religion and his politics, his Christian name and his patron saint." Such allusive heraldry, instead of aiding the memory, requires an intimate knowledge not only of the person but of the times and the places where he lived.

Just as the earliest armorial designs were simple, so were their earliest illustrations. The mantling, in particular, was merely a simple scarf which covered the top and the back of the helm, designed to protect the knight from the heat of the sun. As heraldic illustration advanced, the mantling became more and more profuse, convoluted and slashed, reaching its apex of beauty in the hands of Albrecht Dürer in the earliest years of the 16th century. In his work, however, we see the beginning of the decadence of heraldic painting. The design on a shield was painted; consequently it was flat and not modelled, and in representing it this should be shown. Dürer, however, was too great an artist to stop when he should; his pencil tempted him on, and his designs of shields generally have all the beauty and modelling of a finished painting of an object. Thus, in his well-known Coat of Arms with a Skull, the effect is what would have been obtained had he taken an actual skull, cut it in two vertically, and then affixed the front half to the shield. The Germans have always kept more or less of the mediaeval in their heraldic work, but in England there developed a daintiness of design, which, although in itself pretty if not actually beautiful, was unsuited to heraldic illustration, which should always be vigorous, masculine and bold. A reaction set in in the 1880s which at first went too far, even to the grotesque, but the heraldic design of today in the hands of competent artists who follow the mediaeval usages is at a very high level.

Differences

Today, except in Scotland, a coat of arms is looked upon as a family possession and all members of the family may bear the same arms. In Scotland, each individual member, on reaching maturity, is expected to have his arms matriculated in the Lyon Office, where some alteration is made to distinguish his arms from those of the other members of the family.

In early heraldry, this was frequently done, sometimes by a change in the colors, by a change in their disposition, or by a change in the number of the charges. At a later period, the shield of the eldest son bore a "label", i. e., a narrow strip crossing the shield near the top with (generally) three tags hanging from it. Still later, the younger sons marked their position in the family by means of small added marks, such as a crescent, a five-pointed star, a "martlet" which was a swallow-like bird, etc. The position and the color of these small marks was generally left to the discretion of the artist, so that in a description of a coat of arms we often see at the end "a crescent for difference" and nothing more.

Common Errors

The earliest coats of arms were merely assumed by their bearers, and this has always continued to be the practice except in Scotland, where since the 17th century the matter of using arms has been regulated by Act of Parliament, and in England, where the Court of Chivalry has jurisdiction. For this reason, it is a mistake to suppose that one's family has a right to a certain coat of arms because it was granted to an ancestor for important services to the state, military or otherwise. It is far more likely that when he reached a certain social grade he assumed a coat of arms as a matter of course, just as Samuel Pepys sported a sword when he felt that his position warranted it.

Everybody knows, or thinks that he knows, that illegitimacy is shown by a "bar sinister". "Sinister" indicates that the charge is shown in the opposite way to its usual position, in other words as if seen in a mirror. Since a bar is a charge which crosses the field horizontally, its mirror picture would be unchanged; moreover, a bar is not used singly. The confusion arises from the French word "barre" (which is also used in Scotland) meaning what is in English heraldry called a bend, that is a band which crosses the shield diagonally from the upper dexter (observer's left) corner to the lower sinister (observer's right) side. A bend sinister takes the opposite course; and even this is not the badge of illegitimacy. If its ends are cut off, so that it does not reach to the upper corner or to the lower side, it is called a baton and not a bend; and the baton sinister is one of a number of indications of illegitimacy.

Another misconception is that certain charges have certain meanings, for example, that a scallop shell indicates that the bearer went on a pilgrimage—preferably, of course, a

Crusade. Some might have been chosen for such a meaning; but, as Oswald Barron has pointed out, scallops are much more likely to mean that the bearer came from the part of England where the great family of Scales bore the six scallop shells which alluded to their name; in the same way, the noticeable prevalence of chevrons in English heraldry has been supposed to point to the enormous holdings of the great family of Clare, whose arms were three red chevrons on a golden shield. Some reason there doubtless was for the original choice of a charge, and in many cases, a great many cases, it may be shown to have been allusive to name, estate or office, like the three silver pence of Penn; the six "fountains", divided by a bend, of Stourton whose park pale had on each side three fountain-heads which together formed the river Stour; or the checky coat of Stewart pointing to his stewardship over the exchequer.

Another common error is the belief that every family of respectable social standing must have a coat of arms if only it could be found. Nothing could be further from the fact. In the course of time families pass through vicissitudes, and in both directions; the prominent families of today may come from people of humble station at the time of the immigration, and thus have no hereditary arms, whereas it may be that today's day laborer may be a descendant of some old English county family which figures in a Visitation. Linked with this error is the other which assumes that identity of name presupposes identity of family, so that if there is a coat of arms borne at some time by someone of the same name it is right to assume that anyone of that surname may use the arms in question. Even if the name is unusual and is found, let us say, in England in only one small locality where there was an arms-bearing family of the same name, it is not correct to assume relationship; for the right to a given coat of arms is a species of property and its descent generation by generation must be proved in order to establish a claim. In many cases, family tradition tells that an old armorial seal, painting, piece of silver, etc., was brought to this country by the first-comer. The style of the work usually makes it possible to approximate its date. So far, I have seen just one water color armorial painting which I believe to have been imported by the 17th-century immigrant; and I know of an oil color hatchment to which the usual tradition is attached, but its design is just that of a well-known heraldic artist who was working in Boston as late as 1744 when a member of this family died, for whom the hatchment was in all probability painted.

Value to the Genealogist

Heraldry has been called the hand-maiden of history because a knowledge of the subject has often led to the clue which unravelled some problem, and there have been cases where the unbroken use of a certain coat of arms has led to the recovery of property. Certain forms of design are common in certain districts, because of the tendency (abovementioned) of men to incorporate in their arms some allusion to their overlords, and hence to the place from which the family came; thus, a knowledge of the arms borne by a family may furnish a clue which will indicate place of origin and through that lead to finding the ancestry.

Among the early settlers in America there was still a good deal of class consciousness, and there is a discernible tendency for the men who bore arms to choose their wives from arms-bearing families; such a tendency cannot be magnified into a rule, of course, yet it may incline one to believe that a wife of unknown ancestry is to be looked for among the arms-bearing lines of her surname.

Heraldic phrases are not often found in colonial records and letters, but Alice Morse Earle quotes the words of John Dunton, the bookseller who came to Boston in 1686, speaking of a grass widow, Madam Toy, whose husband was at sea, as "Parte per Pale." When the arms of husband and wife are shown on one shield it is longitudinally divided down the middle—"party per pale"—with the husband's arms on the dexter and the wife's on the sinister side. Dunton's meaning apparently was that just as her arms were parted from her husband's by the "party per pale" division, so was she for the present parted from her consort.

Early American Heraldry

Some of the colonists brought with them armorial seals, and in at least three cases pedigree charts ornamented with painted coats of arms—Chute, Miner and Scott. Heraldic display, however, seems to have been neglected, which is quite natural in the case of new colonies planted in the wilderness. The most natural place for it would be on gravestones, and a number of early gravestones bear heraldic devices.

By the end of the first quarter of the 18th century there was a distinct upsurge in the fashion of displaying coats of arms, but by this time, about a hundred years or three generations from the time of the first comers, their use cannot be said to prove anything. Many families which occupied a humble position at the immigration had prospered and must show coats of arms to be in the fashion, so they adopted the arms of some English family of the same or a similar surname, taking them out of the heraldry books of the period.

Besides seals and gravestones there may be mentioned hatchments, arms painted on a black background, in the form of a square which was hung by a corner, used at funerals; the "scotcheons" so often mentioned by Judge Sewall as hung on the hearse or on the horses; paintings, occasionally shaped like hatchments but not so used; and embroidered arms which were often designed like hatchments and were perhaps copied from them. The embroideries were presumably home products; but there sprang up a profession of arms painting, certainly in Boston, Salem, Marblehead and Newburyport, Massachusetts, and presumably elsewhere in New England. The majority of these paintings are about 14 x 10 inches in size, painted in water colors on laid paper, and framed under glass; sometimes the old frames with "French putty" decorations have been preserved which are, for some occult reason, attributed to Chinese workmanship.

Samuel Mather, writing the *Life* (Boston, 1729) of his father, Cotton Mather, describes as no "matter of much consequence" the family arms, making just the same mistakes that are found in what appears below a painting of the arms of "Mather of Salop" which hangs in the rooms of the American Antiquarian Society in Worchester, Massachusetts, which he probably had before him when he wrote. Instead of being the arms of Mather of Shropshire, however, they turn out to be those of Madder of Staffordshire, which adjoins Shropshire on the east, and it may be that Mather and Madder are variants of the same name. Our Mathers came from Lancashire, which lies some miles northerly. To those who own these old paintings an article about them in the *Transactions of the Colonial Society of Massachusetts 1942-1946* may be of interest.

The Committee on Heraldry

In 1864, a standing Committee on Heraldry was appointed by the New England Historic Genealogical Society. Its purpose was to look into the validity of arms used in this country and to discourage the use of unauthorized arms. For long, it was the feeling of the Committee that no arms should be looked upon as valid unless they could be traced back to a Visitation, which proved descent of the immigrant to America from the Visitation family. Such a restriction narrowed the number of valid arms to so small a number that it was the expressed opinion of the Committee that it was better for Americans not to use arms at all.

In 1914, with the introduction of some new blood into the Committee, there was a change of front, and criteria were established which have been in use ever since, namely.

"For the purposes of the Committee, the word 'proof' means:

(a) The filing with or exhibition to the Committee of the original document or thing relied upon.

(b) Reference to published books the authority of which is recognized by the Committee. (Burke is not accepted as an authority.)

(c) Copies or photographs of documents, seals, tombstones or other objects relied on, together with affidavits or certificates made by Justices of the Peace or Notaries, or by other responsible persons. In every case, the evidence must be such as to satisfy the minds of the Committee.

"Proof of the descent of the immigrant from a family rightfully bearing the arms claimed is the best.

"Proof that the immigrant brought arms with him from the old country, either painted, embroidered, engraved or upon a seal, would probably be sufficient.

"Other forms of proof may, of course, be sufficient.

"The Committee cannot accept statements as to pedigree or the right to arms often found in family genealogies merely because such statements are in print."

There was a gradual accumulation of records, and the Committee decided to publish the arms which had been registered in the form of a continuing Roll of Arms, in parts. The first part appeared in 1928 and to date seven parts have appeared. It is hoped that the continued support of those who are sufficently interested to apply for the registration of their own arms or the arms of others will enable the Committee to continue publication.

Recommended Reading Matter

There is probably no subject about which so much "engaging nonsense" (as it was called by that great authority on the Middle Ages, the late Oswald Barron) has been written as heraldry; we know of no writing about it until the social custom had been in existence for about two centuries, and the writers of that time could not imagine a time when it did not exist. There being no one to say them nay, they felt quite at liberty to invent arms for Alexander the Great and for Julius Caesar, for the Virgin Mary and for Noah and Adam and Eve, for such shadowy figures as King Arthur and his knights, and Prester John. The following works, though perhaps disappointing in flights of the imagination, may be strongly recommended.

ON THE SUBJECT IN GENERAL.—

"Heraldry". The article on this subject in the *Encyclopaedia Britannica*, 11th edition (1911). This was its first appearance, and in later editions it was abbreviated. Though anonymous, it was written by Oswald Barron.

A Grammar of English Heraldry. By W. H. St. John Hope. Cambridge University Press and G. P. Putnam's Sons, New York, 1913. "A small but important manual" (Horace Round). Recently re-edited by Anthony R. Wagner, Richmond Herald.

Historic Heraldry of Britain. By Anthony R. Wagner, Portcullis Pursuivant (later, Richmond Herald). Oxford University Press, London, New York and Toronto, 1939. The subject matter is the heraldic exhibition at the World's Fair in New York of that year, but the book contains as well an excellent article on heraldry.

Heraldry in England. By Anthony R. Wagner, Richmond Herald. Penguin Books Ltd., London and New York, 1946. A condensed little manual of much usefulness and beauty.

ON SPECIAL ASPECTS.—

The Ancestor. A Quarterly Review. Edited by Oswald Barron, April 1902 to January 1905. Archibald Constable & Co., Ltd., Westminster. A mine of useful information, with articles by various authorities including the editor.

Heralds Heraldry in the Middle Ages; An inquiry into the Growth of the Armorial Function of Heralds. By Anthony R. Wagner, Portcullis Pursuivant (later, Richmond Herald). Oxford University Press, London, Humphrey Milford, 1939. A piece of original research which throws new light on the duties of the mediaeval heralds.

ON HERALDIC ART.—

Heraldry as Art. By G. W. Eve. B. T. Batsford, London, 1907. By the well-known designer of heraldic book plates.

Decorative Heraldry. By G. W. Eve. First edition 1897. Second edition 1908, George Bell & Sons, London. Well written and illustrated.

Heraldry for Craftsmen and Designers. By W. H. St. John Hope. The Macmillan Company, New York, 1913. The most generally useful book in this field, by a well-known authority.

CHAPTER II

GENEALOGY AND THE LAW: COURT REPORTS

During the year 1201, when King John's Justices in Eyre journeyed to Cornwall and held court in the Hundred of Powdershire, they found a curious case to try as disclosed by Select pleas of the Crown.[1]

"William de Ros appeals Ailward Bere, Roger Bald, Robert Merchant, and Nicholas Parmenter, for that they came to his house and wickedly in the king's peace took away from him a certain villein of his whom he kept in chains because he wished to run away, and led him off, and in robbery carried away his wife's coffer with one mark of silver and other chattels, and this he offers to prove by his son, Robert de Ros, who saw it. And Ailward and the others have come and defended the felony, robbery and breach of the king's peace, and say that (as the custom is in Cornwall) Roger of Prideaux, by the sheriff's orders caused twelve men to come together and make oath about the said villein, whether he was the king's villein or William's, and it was found that he was the king's villein, so the said Roger the serjeant demanded that (William) should surrender him, and he refused so (Roger) sent to the sheriff, who then sent to deliver (the villein), who, however, had escaped and was not to be found, and William makes this appeal because he wants to keep the chattels of Thomas (the villein), to wit, two oxen, one cow, one mare, two pigs, nine sheep, eleven goats. And that this is so the jurors testify. Judgment: William and Robert in mercy for the false claim. William's amercement, a half-mark. Robert's amercement, a half-mark. Pledge for the mark, Warin, Robert's son. Let the king have his chattels from William. Pledge for the chattels, Richard, Hervey's son."

The case is interesting not only because of the early date, the three generations of genealogy, and the human interest involved, but because it is illustrative of the origin of court reports.

A court report is the result of an appealed court proceeding, the opinion of the justices of the appeal court being printed in book form. The records and files of a trial court should not be confused with court reports. The records and files

---

[1] *Select Pleas of the Crown*, Vol. 1 A. D. 1200-1225, Selden Society, London 1888.

of the trial court, which include such documents as complaints, petitions, answers, wills, and so forth, remain with the clerk of the trial court. The judges of the appeal court after reading the briefs on appeal and hearing oral argument of the lawyers for both sides of the controversy write an opinion as to why they are affirming or reversing the judgment of the trial court. Subsequently, these opinions are printed and appear in book form in public and private law libraries.

Inasmuch as court reports are the source to which a lawyer goes to find precedents, it is obvious that the reports were created for the benefit of the legal profession and not genealogists. However, when a case pertains to real property, will contests, and a multitude of other matters involving families, the inclusion of genealogical data in reported decisions cannot be avoided.

A genealogist in making a visit to a law library for the first time cannot help but realize that hidden away in the law libraries throughout the country, lies concealed the solutions to many ancestral enigmas that have been plaguing genealogists for many years.

The large law libraries in the United States such as the Library of Congress, and the Los Angeles County Law Library, in addition to collecting the American and English court reports have very complete foreign sections. A person interested in French, German, Spanish or genealogy of any other country will find a fertile source in the larger law libraries; however this chapter will be confined to American and English court reports.

Many law libraries have court reports for the Dominions and colonies of the British Empire, and the information given here will apply, to a great extent, to their use.[2]

English Court Reports

Among the oldest court records are the "Year Books", the reports of cases from the reign of Edward I to Henry VIII,

---

[2] *A complete list of British and Colonial Law Reports and Legal periodicals.* Third edition. W. Harold Maxwell and C. R. Brown, Toronto, 1937.

which were taken by the prothonotaries or chief scribes at the expense of the crown and published annually, hence the name "Year Books". The Selden Society commenced publication of the Year Books in 1903; volume 17 of the Selden Society publications contains volume one of the Year Books. It is suggested that a thorough examination be made of all Selden Society publications, as they contain an abundance of genealogical detail. All volumes contain a name and place index which greatly aids the search.

Shortly after 1500, near the close of the Year Book period, Dyer's Reports appeared, which were the first collection of cases called "Reports", rather than "Year Books". These were followed by Plowden's and Coke's Reports, which are comparable to a great extent to modern reports. The work commenced by Dyer, Plowden and Coke, has been continued from their day down to the present time.

All of these early reports, together with those more recent, have been reprinted in what is called *The English Reports*, consisting of 176 volumes. Except for minor errors in printing, *The English Reports* are as dependable as the original reports, but they are not as easy to use as the Selden Society's "Year Books", as they are not as well indexed. *The English Reports* do have a table or index of cases in two volumes that lists all of the cases in the work by surname. Thus, if a person was interested in the Hilton family, the table of cases will refer the researcher to cases in which the Hilton family was involved as *plaintiff* only. Unfortunately, the names of defendants are not arranged alphabetically. Tables of cases are also found in volume 24 of *Mew's Digest*; volumes 45 and 46 of the *English and Empire Digest;* and in volume 35 of *Halsbury's Laws of England.*

The "Table of Cases", of the above mentioned reports, and the indices to the "Year Books", are used in the same manner as any index. For example, assume that you are interested in the de Maulay family. An examination of the index of volume 17, Selden Society, which is also volume one of the Year Book Series, discloses considerable information about the de Maulay family, in addition to other information on page one:

"Peter, son of Peter de Maulay, Roger of Kerdeston and Juliana of Gaunt, by their attorney, demand against Joan, wife that was of Robert of Driby, the third part of two parts of the manor of H(undemanby). Gilbert of Gaunt the elder, father of said Juliana and grandfather of said Peter and Roger, whose heirs they are, gave to Gilbert of Gaunt, the younger, and Lora his wife, and the heirs of their bodies begotten, and which after them, Gilbert and Lora ought to revert to the said Peter, Roger and Juliana by form of the said gift for that said Gilbert of Gaunt the younger and Lora his wife, died without heirs of their bodies."

No comment need be made relative to the value of the information given in the case of de Maulay v. Driby. Of course, a person encounters difficulties when the name is very common, in which event it is necessary to examine a considerable number of cases to see if the cases involve the family under consideration.

American Court Reports

The reports of the courts of appeal of the various states offer excellent opportunities for solving ancestral tangles. The difficulty in their use is not lack of material, but rather the lack of adequate indices to make the information readily available. The closest approach to an index for the entire United States is the table of cases in the American Digest System, particularly the table of cases in the Decennial Edition of the *American Digest,* published by the West Publishing Company, found in volumes 21 to 25, inclusive, and entitled: "A Complete Table of American Cases from 1658 to 1906." This index or table of cases is particularly valuable when the place where the family came from is not known, and the surname is uncommon. To use the table of cases is like using any index, as it is just a matter of looking according to the surname. A reference in a table of cases such as: "Avery v. Ray, 1 Massachusetts 11," signifies that Avery's suit against Ray will be found reported in volume 1 of the Massachusetts reports, at page 11. An examination of this case discloses this was an action of trespass against Alpheus Ray brought by Horace Avery, an infant under twenty-one years, who sued, by his father and guardian, Miles Avery, for an assault and battery alleged to have been committed on **February 4, 1803.**

The table of cases found in the *American Digest* is far from satisfactory as an index, as only the surnames of the plaintiffs are arranged alphabetically.

A digest of the case law has been compiled for most states, and included as a part of such digests is a table of cases. It is, therefore, suggested that the table of cases of the digest for the state in which the researcher is interested be examined first.

Following is a list of digests which contain a table of cases for the states indicated:[3]

Connecticut Digest, 1785 to date. By Richard H. Phillip (1945) vol. 3, p. 2261.

Delaware Cases, 1792-1830. Ed. by Daniel J. Boorstin (1943), 3 vol. p. 341.

District of Columbia Digest, to date. (1937) vol. 12, p. 313.

Encyclopedic Digest of Georgia Reports. (1910)

Callaghan's Illinois Digest. By George F. Longsdorf (1926) vol. 15. (Covers period subsequent to 1819.)

Callaghan's Indiana Digest. By Jess C. Weaver. (1934) vol. 16. (Covers period subsequent to 1817.)

The Annotated Louisiana Digest. By Edward F. White and William Kernan Dart. (1917) vol. 7, p. 423. (Plaintiffs only.)

The Maine Digest. By Fred F. Lawrence. (1916) vol. 2, p. 1273.

Maine Digest Facts and Law. By Charles H. Bartlett and Harry Stern. (1932) p. 613.

The Massachusetts Digest. (1906) vol. 8.

Mississippi Digest. (1912) Vol. IV, p. 279.

Digest of Decisions of the Courts of Missouri to December 1904. vol. 10.

Digest of Cases Determined in the Supreme Court of New Hampshire from 1816 to 1920. By Crawford D. Hening. (1926) p. 1677.

New Jersey Digest 1790-1931. (1932) vol. 12.

Abbot's New York Digest, 1794, to date. (1942) vols. 40, 41.

North Carolina Digest, 1778 to date. (1938) vol. 20.

---

[3] Space does not permit the listing of every state in the Union. States with the oldest court reports are covered.

Vale Pennsylvania Digest, 1682 to date. (1939) vol. 44.

The Rhode Island Digest, 1828-1911. By John A. Tillinghast. (1913) p. 2484.

South Carolina Digest, 1783-1886. vol. 2, p. 871.

Michie's Digest of Tennessee Reports. (1940) vol. 17.

The Vermont Digest. (1789-1910) vol. 3.

Mitchie's Digest of Virginia and West Virginia Reports, vol. 10.

In some instances it is easier to go through each volume of the court reports of the state in which a person is interested. This is particularly true when the residence of the family is known, or if a certain period of years is desired to be covered. It goes without saying that if the family were domiciled in New Hampshire in 1795, the reports for the state around that year would be the logical starting place. Every volume of court reports contains an index or table of cases, and this applies to every state in the Union. Generally the cases are indexed according to both plaintiff and defendant; this is an advantage over the table of cases in the American Digest System.

The various volumes of Court Reports, arranged by states and chronologically under each state, are listed in Appendix III of *Materials and Methods of Legal Research,* by Frederick C. Hicks (1942), which volume will be in any law library containing the volumes of Reports. By reference to it, the applicable volume for the state and period desired can be readily determined.

A few additional volumes (not included therein) may well be mentioned. These may be found in general as well as law libraries.

Records of the Court of New Castle on Delaware, Vol. I, 1676-1681 (1904); Vol. II, 1681-1689, Land and Probate (1935).

Statute Law of Kentucky. By William Littel. 5 vols. (Vol. 1 (1809) contains a name index. Although these volumes are all statutory law, not court reports, they are mentioned here as they contain considerable early genealogical data.)

Maine Province and Court Reports, 1636-1711. 4 vols. (1928-1958).

Proceedings of the Maryland Court of Appeals, 1695-1729. Ed. by Carroll T. Bond. (1933)

Journal of the Courts of Common Right and Chancery of East New Jersey. Ed. by Preston W. Edsall. (1937).

The Burlington Court Book: A Record of Quaker Jurisprudence in West New Jersey, 1680-1709. Ed. by H. Clay Reed. (1944)

Minutes of the Commissioners for Detecting and Defeating Conspiracies in the State of New York. 1778-1781. 3 vols.

Minutes of the Executive Council of the Province of New York, 1668-1673. Ed. by Victor Hugo Paltsits. (1910)

Select Cases of The Mayor's Court of New York City, 1674-1784. Ed. by Richard B. Morris. (1935)

Records of the Vice-Admiralty Court of Rhode Island, 1716-1752. Ed. by Dorothy G. Towle.

South Carolina Chancery Court Records, 1671-1779. Ed. by Anne King Gregorie. (1950)

County Court Records of Accomack-Northampton, Virginia, 1632-1640. Ed. by Susie M. Ames. (1954)

In addition to the court reports of the states to be found in every law library, there are some valuable reports which are generally not available in many law libraries. Some of these volumes are rare books, and when a law library does have them, they are often segregated and so may escape attention.

In the *Lawyer's Reference Manual of Law Books*, by Charles C. Soule (Boston, 1884), some valuable sources are given. If a researcher will take the time to follow up the rare items Soule mentions in the footnotes, he will be richly rewarded for his efforts. For instance, on p. 29, footnote 2 refers to *The Militia Reporter,* which contains reports of four trials by court martial between 1805-1810, published in Boston in 1810. Also mentioned is Whitman's *Massachusetts Libel Case of 1828.*

Unfortunately, the tables of cases in Court Reports list only the names of plaintiffs and defendants; the names of other persons (not parties to the suit) are not indexed. Therefore, a page by page examination of each volume is necessary if a thorough search is to be made. This may often be well worthwhile.

The general belief is that persons of moderate or no means

would not be involved in a case appealed to a Supreme Court. That belief is not true. Particularly in early days, the economic or social status of the parties was not a factor; the legal principle involved was important.

In using a table of cases as an index, particular attention should be paid to cases where one political subdivision is suing another. Such cases often involve paupers or other questions of domicile, or matters of jurisdiction; the facts brought out may be of considerable genealogical value.

CHAPTER III

A STUDY OF SURNAMES

A. BRITISH SURNAMES

The studies of genealogy and inherited surnames are inseparable for neither can be perfected without the other. Every person acquired one or more descriptions or epithets distinguishing him from his fellows, and formerly these identifying labels were known as surnames, a title which is now applied only to those of an hereditary nature. The nickname, formerly an eke-name, i. e., added name, has also changed in signification and is today no more than "a dispensable appellative of an individual used as an alternative to his personal name or surname or both". To the failure to adopt such limitations in definition much misunderstanding and controversy has been due.

During the past two millenniums various races have inhabited and ruled the British Isles, resulting in alterations of language, more particularly among the landed gentry, professional classes, and city dwellers. The Romans did not impose either their speech or elaborate system of nomenclature upon the Celtic natives, and with the departure of the legions in the 5th century, these innovations passed out. The indigenous Cymry and Gaels remained satisfied with single names although they added a wealth of genealogical data not so much for personal identification as for its practical value in emphasizing rights to land tenure. These miniature pedigrees maintained through the centuries finally led to the great number of Welsh surnames in *ap-*, Scottish, in *mac-*, and Irish in *O'*, and *mac-*.

The withdrawal of the Romans made possible the incursions of various Teutonic tribes and these continuing steadily, by the 9th century, in the eastern half of Britain, had resulted in the establishment of names and language now known as Anglo-Saxon or Old English. The individual designations, usually compound words having no appropriate reference to their bearers, are of special concern to the present subject because many survived or were revived as first names to become family labels centuries later. All attempts to substantiate the belief that any of these personal descriptions, before the Norman Conquest (1066), had become hereditary and therefore true surnames have been discredited by further inquiry. A pleasing feature of interest to genealogists is that one family might take a liking to one alphabetical character, the name bestowed upon each child having the same initial letter providing a clue to parentage.

Ireland was not troubled by invaders until the end of the 8th century when bodies of Northmen (Danes and Norwegians) came to stay. Both England and Scotland likewise supported prosperous colonies of Vikings.

One-third of the forces of William of Normandy at the Battle of Hastings are said to have been Bretons returning to the land of their forefathers and who, for a brief time at least, remained active in East Anglia. The principal languages, then, to be heard in the British Isles, besides Norman-French and Anglo-Saxon, were the six Celtic tongues, Welsh, Cornish, Breton, Gaelic (Scotland), Manx, and Irish, and these, all except Breton, survived until the time when patronymies were becoming settled. The influence of the Northmen must not be overlooked, for surnames, particularly from the Orkneys and the Isle of Man, evidence undoubted Scandinavian provenance. The nomenclaturist, who essays to divine the origin of an obscure appellative, is faced with wide possibilities on language alone and the importance of the genealogical investigation in determining the original habitat is apparent.

The Norman introduction of the feudal system, by which fiefs were held under the Crown in return for services, naturally led to feoffees becoming indicated by the names of their estates and these distinctions passing in time to sons and grandsons had the earliest chance of becoming recognized as the birthright of descendants. There was, however, no property in a territorial or, in fact, any other designation and in later years those of great seigniories were not infrequently borne by menials. Had the original drafts for Domesday Book been preserved valuable data would be obtainable, but the fair copy, finished in 1086, omitted most of the secondary descriptions then of little or no consequence, although a few undoubtedly became transmitted to succeeding generations. Half a century later, as an analysis of several thousand entries in the Crown muniments, temp. Hen. II, shows, 83 percent of persons were given secondary epithets, that is, on parchment, but few of these are traceable elsewhere as hereditary surnames. Sometimes on an official roll from one to four alternative descriptions may be found attached to a single baptismal name.

No precise date can be assigned for the adoption of surnames in Britain and actually the now general usage derived from a gradual process continuing for centuries and serving no very weighty purpose except in the denser populated districts. There the greater headway is observed. The earliest legal announcement is found in 1267 when the verdict of a London jury in the Court of Chancery expressed the view that a man's "true name" was that borne by his father.[1] Many years passed before this practice became accepted custom and it has never been insisted upon by jurisprudents, and even in course of time when people were prepared to look upon second names as heritable property the law denied the right. To determine whether a description has become a permanent family name, a pedigree is absolutely essential.

In the 14th century the unsettled nature of second names continued, as an analysis of the entries on the Poll Tax Rolls, 1377, demonstrates. It is seen that 24 percent of the epithets employ *filius, de, le, atte (at the)*, etc., evidence that not many more than 76 percent of persons could have had hereditary second names. From very early date a few manifold descriptions are noticeable. By the 14th century what look to be multiple font or family names may be found in documents, but more often as the result of clerical omission of a prepo-

---

[1] Calendar of Inquisitions, Misc. (Chanc.), I, 183.

sition or an alias. A ludicrous misuse of a quadruple name occurs in Shaw's 15th-century drama, *Saint Joan,* and appearance of a double addition in a pedigree may give a strong suspicion of fictitious interpolation, as in a recent prominent Howard genealogy.

One of the most important factors adding enormously to the possibility of error in location has been the eastward movement of the Celtic races. Documentary search in the archives of the Public Record Office has revealed that persons bearing descriptions associating them with Wales, Brittany, and Ireland had as early as the 13th century spread into every county in England.[2] A little later, Cornishmen can also be traced as being as widely dispersed. Welshmen went further afield and in 1890, for instance, it was ascertained that in Ireland there were 50,000 persons claiming the names Wallace, Walsh, and Welsh.

Fifteenth-century records dealing with the taxation of strangers yield a useful indication of the counties most fancied by the immigrant representatives of Continental races, from which it may be gathered that French, Normans and Flemings favoured Devonshire, Wiltshire and Kent. Dutchmen and Hollanders had a liking, doubtless, on the ground of contiguity, also for Kent and other eastern counties. In the 16th century, London had become a chief resort of refugees, the Subsidy Roll for 1540 certifying no fewer than one-third of the population as being aliens.

The polyglot difficulties touched upon must have been greatly increased by this influx, which long continued, but comparatively few of the foreigners can have been able to impose their appellatives in native purity on the officious English scribes, who had no hesitation in modifying them until they sounded familiar, and many incomers had also accepted English equivalents. The letters of denization and Acts of Naturalisation collected by the Huguenot Society supply some thousands of names, the majority closely resembling English and providing an illustration of how wrong

---

[2] The lists have been given in *The British Race—Germanic or Celtic?*

it is to assume from an old-time surname a long line of domestic ancestry. Here may be seen such distinguished names as Carowe, Cotton, Spilman, Wyman, Lever, Poole, Trumper, Ingram, Jenner, Putnam, Garrett, etc.

Perhaps the most astonishing migration has been that of Irishmen, the census returns for 1861 showing that no fewer than 4 percent of the inhabitants of England gave Ireland as the country of birth and they had been also pouring in for centuries to become assimilated in countless thousands. They have likewise added considerably to the names of Scotland, as the directories evidence. Notwithstanding much obfuscation of racial identity, the student of British surnames must ever be alive to the possibilites of Celtic and Continental provenance.

In determining the genesis of a surname, the first step is a search of bygone records to obtain the successive changes of orthography with dates and localities. The earliest of these will provide a possible clue to language and signification. A derivation unbacked by progressive documentation is in most cases guesswork leading to such absurd popular origins as those attributed to Turnbull, Vinegar, Gosbeck, or Metcalf. The onomatologist obtains no aid from a context as does the glossarian who gleans from literary sources, and he is unable to view a site like the philologist, who determines the purport of an archaic place-name. Moreover, in the case of a widespread appellative the primitive form may well have existed in more than one word base. That a modern orthographic or phonetic variant may be germinated in several roots independently is as certain as that several names may be traced to one and the same root.

Useful clues to surnames may be obtained from repetitions in any one manuscript or from duplicated lists or from a series of documents. For instance, Abouen, in an eastern county in 1330, does not convey much assurance of Celtic blood, but followed by Waleys it is safe to conjecture ab Owen, now Bowen. In many cases where full documentation is obtained it will be gathered that the primary vocable has undergone an evolutionary process which may be by initial, medial, or final expansion, contraction or internal development.

The number of formations is considerably increased by suffixes. For example, Richard reduced to its pet forms and modified by epithesis gives upwards of one hundred further surnames. Besides the founding of new varieties by regular and recognizable grammatical processes, corruption of orthography has supplied a remarkable series of puzzles which have baffled all inquirers. There are upwards of one hundred different ways of representing the thirteen English vowel sounds, and diphthongal equations abound. Irregular use of the aspirate provides many other deviations sometimes altering the signification. Consonantal equations are many. To name a few: $b=m$, p and v: $d=g$, k, r, and t: $f=p$ and v: $l=n$ and r. Faulty ear or misreading may be responsible for the freaks. Welsh and Cornish mutations are not to be overlooked, nor the wide distinctions in spelling and pronounciation in Irish names.

The number of orthographic modifications of any one name obtainable from old scripts and registers is often astonishing, several genealogists having compiled lists of one to five hundred. The present writer actually found his own name spelled with from three to nine letters (Uen-Hewghinge).

In searching the contemporary manuscripts the nomenclaturist should remember that he is at the mercy of the court clerk, who at best could only glean first or second-hand from illiterates. A description in Latin often served two or more variants, thus *marisc'* might cover Marsh, Marish, or Marshall.

A constant possibility of false lineage is due to foundlings being dubbed with fanciful distinctions, as Marlborough, Richmond, Ridley, Milton, Bacon, Drake, Nelson, Hogarth, etc., leading to later claims of kinship to these notables. Another source of difficulty arises from "change of name", a practice permitted to anyone.

Of particular importance to genealogists is the doctrine of synonymous change. An addition being looked upon as an identification label, words having or appearing to have equal signification were considered interchangeable without adverse comment. Thus, in 1509, an alias of Edward Doucheman was Frise. One Cristemasse had the alternative Yool registered in 1386. "De la Guttere" was also officially entered as "atte Strete". A 14th-century taxpaper enrolled as le Charpentir in 1327 appears five years later as le Wryth. All four classes, characteristic, local, genealogical, and occupational are here represented. Occasionally, the synomymous change might be from one class to another or from one language to another as Evans to Jones. Playnamur was likewise Trewelove (Essex 1360). A Smith could be Faber (Lat.), Angove (Corn.), Gow (Gael.), or le Feure (Fr.), as most in keeping with his district.

There are two classes of Inherited Surnames and two of Acquired Surnames. Of the former (1) Characteristic (6 to 10 percent) answers: What is his personal peculiarity? (2) Local or Locative (40 to 50 percent): Where is, or was, he located? (3) Genealogical (30 to 40 percent): Who is, or was, his most important kinsman? (4) Occupational (12 to 20 percent): What is his vocation? There are eighteen subclasses, some of our common surnames as Bell or Cock falling into two or more. Descriptions answer to the same interrogatories and follow the same classification as the family name. The scope for name composition and multiplication by derivation and corruption is so wide that probably it is an underestimate to put 100,000 as the number of surnames in the British Isles. The Complete System of Descriptions and Surnames is as follows:

Group I. INHERITED SURNAMES

Class 1. *Characteristic Surnames*

(a) From Appearance, e. g., as Fairfax, Augwin (the white), Foljambe, Shortneck, Kicks (dried up).

(b) From Character, i. e., mental and moral attribute or peculiarity, perhaps Simple, Yepe (sly), Sage, Quant (O. F.), Dolittle.

(c) From Physical Attribute, e. g. as Armstrong, Lefthand.

(d) From Possession, e. g. Sanzaver (*sans avoir* "without property"), Chefdor (heraldic).

(e) From Action or Habit, e. g. Plauntesoyl, Sweetmouth, Pothardy.

(f) From Condition or Quality, e. g. Jeune (Fr. "Young"), Baseson, Freeman.

(g) From Relationship, i. e., consanguinity, kinship, Eam (uncle), Ayell (O. F. "grandfather"), Noy (Corn. 'nephew').

(h) From Race or Sept., e. g. Fleming, Picard, Lamont, Ju.

Class 2. *Local Surnames*

(a) From Place of Residence or Work, e. g. Wardrobe, Scawen (alder tree), Culverhouse.

(b) From Late Place of Residence, e. g. Kent, Fife, Cardigan, Cork.

Class 3. *Genealogical Surnames*

(a) From Personal Name of Male Parent, e. g. Fitzpatrick, Widow (Guy), Pugh (ap Hugh).

(b) From Personal Name of Female Parent, e. g. Sybilson, Liquorice.

(c) From Personal Name of other Relative, e. g. Gilbertmagh, Musefader.

(d) From Description or Surname, e. g. Scotson, Vikercosyn.

Class 4 *Occupatioal Surnames*

(a) From Office or Profession, e. g. Dempster, Sturtivant.

(b) From Mock Office, e. g. King, Dragon.

(c) From Military Rank, e. g. Bower, Squire, Marrack (soldier).

(d) From Trade or Vocation, e. g. Faraday (chapman), Crowder (fiddler), Caleyx (lime-burner).

Group II. ACQUIRED SURNAMES

Class I. *Self-assumed Surnames*

(a) Of Ecclesiastics. An Archbishop Tibold took the name of Sudbury.

(b) Of Theatrical Artistes. Stage names, Wyndham, Irving, became surnames.

(c) Of Authors—none.

(d) Of Business Men, e. g. McCall changed to Almack.

(e) Of Private Persons are common.

(f) Of Slaves or Apprentices, who having no name took their late master's, as du Boulay.

(g) Of Refugees, e. g. Carrington to Smith during civil war.

(h) Of Aliens, e. g. Rose from Rosenbaum.

Class 2. *Reputed Surnames*

(a) Of Bastards, who commonly became known by name mother.

(b) Of Foundlings, e. g. Goldfinch, Coalhouse, Found, Parish, Portobello.

For an original study of surnames of the United Kingdom there is no lack of excellent material in both public and private archives and particularly in the British Museum and the Public Record Office. A large proportion of the oldest documents has been printed and indexed by order of the Government or learned societies and several hundred volumes are available for reference. This magnificent series of transcripts is not, however, infallible, for instance in one case (1066), the ancient name of Chinchen is made to read Climehen. In the leading libraries the printed surveys on the subject show little of a scientific nature. The first attempt to date and cite each change of form was that of Canon C. W. Bardsley, but lack of library facilities prevented him from using records prior to the Hundred Rolls (c. 1275) and the result in many instances is superficial and speculative; nevertheless the dictionary of 1901 is perhaps the most valuable reference for names other than Celtic.

For a first approach to the study the following works may be suggested:

Bardsley, C. W.;	*A Dictionary of English and Welsh Surnames*, London, 1901.
Black, G. F.;	*The Surnames of Scotland*, New York, 1946.
Ewen, C. L.;	*A History of Surnames of the British Isles*, London, 1931. This work contains a bibliography.
Forssner, Th.;	*Germanic Names in England*, Uppsala, 1916.
Harrison, H.;	*Surnames of the United Kingdom*, London, 1912-8.
Moore, A. W.;	*Manx Names*, London, 1903.
Redin, M.;	*Studies on Uncompounded Personal Names*, Uppsala, 1919.
Searle, W. G.;	*Onomasticon Anglo-Saxonicum*, Cambridge, 1897.
Woulfe, P.;	*Sloinnte Gaedhael is Gall*, Dublin, 1923.

With these nine books a beginner, well warned of pitfalls, may make a very fair start, but let him remember to take any derivation not completely documented with "a pinch of salt".

(Note: Possibly there should be added to this list a recent book, *A Dictionary of British Surnames*, by P. H. Reaney (1958). Ed.)

B. EUROPEAN SURNAMES [1]

Surnames first came into use in Southern Europe, especially in Spain and Italy. They were instituted among the patricians of Venice in the 11th or 12th century. In other parts of Europe they were first borne by the nobles, who took them from their castles and estates. From them the custom descended to the retainers, and finally to the tradesmen, farmers, and common people in general.

From Italy the use of surnames crossed the Alps and became widespread in Switzerland and in the upper Rhine Valley in the 12th century. They were not frequent in North Germany until the 14th century, and were not widely adopted in the Netherlands until the 18th century. In Trieste, in northern Italy, many families had no surnames until the beginning of the 19th century. Surnames were borne in Sweden by noble families in the 16th and 17th centuries, but were not in general use among the lower classes until the 18th or even the 19th century.

European surnames, like their British counterparts, fall into four categories, as follows:

(1) Personal characteristics, such as German *Schwarz;* French *Lenoir,* both meaning black.

(2) Geographical: German *Rosenberger,* one who lives at or near a hill of roses; French *Picard,* a native of Picardie.

(3) Genealogical: i. e. surnames derived from patronymics (or, more rarely, from matronymics, or mothers' names): Norwegian *Olsson,* son of Ole; Swedish *Johansson,* son of Johann; Spanish *Sánchez,* son of Sancho. To this category also belongs surnames derived from nicknames, such as German *Theiss,* from Matthias.

---

[1] Albert H. Gerberich, Ph.D., F. A. S. G., "Geographical Aspects of Pennsylvania German Genealogical Study", *National Genealogical Society Quarterly,* vol. 34, Dec. 1946, p. 113; Joseph G. Fucilla, *Our Italian Surnames* (1949), p. 13; studies by Milton Rubincam of Swedish noble and middle-class families, based on Elgenstierna's *Den Introducerade Svenska Adelns Ättartavlor* (9 vols.), and Örnberg's *Svenska Ättartavlor* (14 vols.) China adopted surnames centuries before Christ (Smith, *The Story of Our Names,* p. 126).

(4) Occupational (including professions and offices): German *Zimmermann,* French *Charpentier* (Norman-Picard form, *Carpentier*), both signifying carpenter; German *Bischof,* bishop; French *LeMoyne,* monk.

To these we may add a general category:

(5) Miscellaneous, which serves as a wonderful catch-all for names of other origins, such as those derived from animals (French *Cochon,* pig), and coats-of-arms (Swedish *Oxenstierna,* so named because this famous noble house bore the head of an ox on its shield, and *Natt och Dag,* meaning "Night and Day", because the upper part of its shield was gold, and the lower part blue). (See *Nordisk Familjebok* (1931), vol. 15, p. 467, for *Oxenstierna,* and vol. 14, p. 786, for *Natt och Dag.*)

Some genealogical enthusiasts assume that because a family shares the same surname with a noble house the two lines are descended from the same mediaeval ancestors. It is quite likely that the family is derived from a retainer or laborer on the lord's estate, and took, or was given, the place name as a surname. For instance, the fact that Johann Heinrich Schwalbach, a mid-18th century German arrival in Philadelphia, bore the same name as the ancient Hessian noble family von Schwalbach, does not necessarily make him a descendant of that house. Schwalbach (officially, Langenschwalbach) is a place-name, that of a famous health resort in Hessen. There are cases, of course, in which plebeian families can be traced in the male line to a younger branch of a noble house, *but no assumptions of noble ancestry should be made merely on the basis of identical surnames.* Each family must be independently investigated.

Names can be misleading. One who has a knowledge of German might assume that the Jewish name *Dreyfuss* has the meaning "three feet". Actually, it does not. In 1555, the Elector of Trier, Johann IV, Count of Isenburg, expelled the Jews from Trier (French Trèves). They fled mostly to France and to Lorraine. As they had no surnames, they were inscribed in the municipal records with their given names, to which was added the Latin adjective, *Trevus*, meaning "from Trèves" (Trier). In France, Trevus became *Trefousse*, and in Lorraine *Dreyfuss*, and both surnames are found among Jewish families to this day.[2]

It must not be assumed that because an American name of German origin has a "von" in it, that the family is of noble lineage. Many American families with this particle can trace to noble ancestors, such as von Lossberg (the name of an American Foreign Service officer at Johannesburg, South Africa), and von Schweinitz of Pennsylvania and North Carolina. But again each family with this important little word of three letters must be investigated and stand on its own merits. For instance, the American family Fonderberg originally was *von der Berg*, from the mountain. Fondersmith was once *von der Schmidt*, from the smithy.

A similar word of caution must be given in connection with French names beginning with "de", which can either be the noble particle or a preposition. A French family named de Mière prides itself on being of noble stock, and in that mistaken belief so uses that form of the name. But in its origin the name "de Mière" is derived from the words *demierre, demiere, dimier*, which are traceable to Old French *dymierre*. The last-named word is from Latin *decimator*, in French *percepteur de la dîme* (*disme*, in the 12th century), or, in plain English, collector of the tithe.[3] Thus, the "noble" family of "de Miere" has swiftly fallen to the relatively obscure rank of tax-collector! As one writer has expressed it, "the use of the preposition *de*, uniting a place-name with an individual name, was formerly as frequent among those of plebeian origin as among the nobles."[4]

In Switzerland, in 1783, the Sovereign Council of the Republic of Bern went a bit further, granting authority to all middle-class families to assume the particle "de" "*if such was*

---

[2] Gerberich, *loc. cit.*, p. 114.

[3] Pierre Chessex, *Origine des Noms de Personnes* (1946), p. 112.

[4] *Ibid.*, pp. 110-111, quoting Ernest Muret: "L'usage de la préposition *de* unissant un nom de lieu au nom individuel était jadis aussi fréquent chez les roturiers que chez les nobles."

their good pleasure."[5] Thus, Swiss families having this so-important little word prefixed to their names may or may not be sprung from patrician stock. Only a careful investigation will disclose the facts.

The old Dutch families of New Amsterdam (New York) assumed surnames from the same general sources as other European families: (1) Personal characteristics, such as *Vroom, Vrooman* (wise or pious man), *Stille* (silent), *Krom,* (bent or crooked, in the sense of crippled), *de Lange* (tall man);[6] (2) Geographical: *de Noorman* (the Norwegian), *van Doorn* (from the village of Doorn, province of Utrecht), *van Rensselaer* (name of a farm-estate), *Hoogland* (high land), *Beekman* (man from the brook); (3) Genealogical: *Jansen* (Johnson, of Long Island, descended from Barent Jansen, *i. e.*, Barent, son of Jan Barentz van Driest), *Rutgers,* of New York City, and *Rutsen,* of Ulster County, N. Y., (both descended in the male line from Rutgers Jacobsz or Jacobsen); (4) Occupational: *Kuyper,* cooper (descended from Claes Jansen *de kuyper,* the cooper), *Smid or Smit* (the Smith), *de Clark* (the clerk).[7]

The old Spanish families of the present United States have names which in translation sound odd to English ears. The oldest family of European origin in our country is Solana; it has been at St. Augustine, Florida, since before 4 July 1594, when Vicente Solana, formerly of La Vila, in the Spanish province of Navarre, married Marìa Visente at St. Augustine.[8] *Solana* means "strong sunshine, sunny place." Pedro Robledo, whose death on 21 May 1598 gave him the dubious distinction of being the first European to die in New Mexico, bore a name (*robledo, robledal)* which means oak grove or wood. Several New Mexican families named Madrid obviously lived at one time in that Spanish city. In California are two related

---

[5] *Ibid.*, p. 111.
[6] In Dutch, *de* is the definite article.
[7] See Rosalie Fellows Bailey, *Dutch Systems in Family Naming: New York-New Jersey* (1954).
[8] Information from John I. Coddington, F. A. S. G., and Walter C. Hartridge, F. A. S. G.

families, dating from the 18th century there, *Verdugo* (which means executioner, among others), and *Carrillo* (small cart).

The unwary genealogist is often misled by surnames. An American family with a good English surname may turn out to have a European origin. As examples, the Seeley family of upstate New York was originally French *Usilié*, the Carpenter family of Philadelphia was once *Zimmermann* (of which "carpenter" is the English translation), a number of Baker families were formerly *Becker*, etc. In Louisiana, where German families settled as early as 1720, a family now named *Labranche* came originally to that French colony from Germany, and was surnamed *Zweig*, which means the same thing (branch). Another Louisiana family bearing the very proper French name of *Fauquel* is of German descent, its original name having been *Vogel*.

German names especially undergo odd transformations. The families of Rubincam of Pennsylvania and Revercomb of Virginia are descended from the same immigrant ancestor who landed in Philadelphia in 1726; both are variants of German forms, Rubincam coming from High German *Rübenkamp*, meaning "turnip field", and Revercomb from Low German *Rövekamp*, which also means "turnip field". Sounds are frequently interchangeable, such as "b" and "p", "g" and "k", "d" and "t", "f" and "v". Thus, we have Dambach-Taumbaugh, Voight-Focht, Gebhard-Kephart, etc. The Brumbach family has become *Brumbaugh* in some lines and *Brownback* in others, while in one Federal census record *Achenbach* has been disguised as *Achingback!*

The reader will find the following bibliography of European surnames helpful for a further study of the subject:

EUROPEAN (GENERAL):

Smith, Elsdon C.: *The Story of Our Names* (1950).

Smith, Elsdon C.: *Dictionary of American Family Names* (1956).

DUTCH:

Bailey, Rosalie Fellows: *Dutch Systems in Family Naming—New York and New Jersey* (Genealogical Publication No. 12, National Genealogical Society, 1954).

French:

Chassex, Pierre: *Origine des Noms de Personnes* (1946).

Dauzat, Albert: *Les Noms de Famille de France* (1945).

Dauzat, Albert: *Dictionnaire Étymologique des Noms de Familie et Prénoms de France* (1955).

German:

Heintze, Albert: *Die Deutschen Familiennamen.* Edited by Prof. Dr. Paul Cascorbi (1933). (This work is known generally as Heintze-Cascorbi.)

Gottschald, Max: *Deutsche Namenkunde* (1954).

Italian:

Fucilla, Joseph G.: *Our Italian Surnames (1949).*

Swiss:

Les Noms des Familles Suisses. Familiennambuch der Schweiz. I Nomi di Famiglia Svizzeri. Edited by the Swiss Society of Genealogical Studies (2 vols., 1940).

THE AUTHORS

In addition to the usual abbreviations for academic degrees (Ph.D., etc.), the following abbreviations are used for special honors: C. V. O.—Commander of the Royal Victorian Order; F. A. S. G.—Fellow of the American Society of Genealogists; F. G. B. S.—Fellow of the New York Genealogical and Biographical Society; F. N. G. S.—Fellow of the National Genealogical Society; F.R.Hist.S—Fellow of the Royal Historical Society; F. S. A.—Fellow of the Society of Antiquaries (London); F. S. G.—Fellow of the Society of Genealogists (London); K. C. V. O.—Knight Commander of the Royal Victorian Order. Two periodicals frequently mentioned in the following sketches are represented by TAG—*The American Genealogist* (New Haven, Conn.), and NGSQ—*National Genealogical Society Quarterly* (Washington, D. C.).

REV. ARTHUR ADAMS, A.B., A.M., S.T.M., PH.D., F.S.A., F.R.HIST.S., F.S.G., F.A.S.G., 42 Pinckney St., Boston 6, Mass. President Emeritus, American Society of Genealogists. Editor, *New England Historical and Genealogical Register*, 1949-59. Contributing Editor, NGSQ.

HAROLD BOWDITCH, M.D., F.A.S.G., 12 Pine St., Peterborough, N.H. For many years Secretary, Committee on Heraldry, New England Historic Genealogical Society. Authority on heraldry.

MRS. MARY GIVENS BRYAN, Atlanta, Ga., Director, Georgia Department of Archives and History. Contributing Editor, NGSQ. Author of articles on Georgia genealogical sources. President, Society of American Archivists, 1959-

JOHN INSLEY CODDINGTON, A.B., A.M., F.A.S.G., 11 Walnut Street, Bordentown, N. J. Formerly a member of the history faculties of Harvard University and Olivet, Swarthmore, and Haverford Colleges. Contributing Editor, TAG and NGSQ. Lecturer, Institute of Genealogical Research, Washington, D. C.

MEREDITH B. COLKET, JR., A.B., M.A., F.A.S.G., 2263 Lamberton Rd., Cleveland Heights, 18, Ohio. Director, Western Reserve Historical Society, Cleveland. Director, Institute of Genealogical Research of The American University, Washington, D. C., Contributing Editor, NGSQ.

WALTER G. DAVIS, B.A., LL.B., F.A.S.G., F.S.G., P. O. Box 230, Pearl St. Station, Portland, Me. President, American Society of Genealogists, since 1958. Past president, Maine Historical Society. Contributing Editor, TAG and NGSQ.

LEON DEVALINGER, JR., A.B., M.A., Hall of Records, Dover, Del. State Archivist of Delaware. Director, Delaware Historical Society. Co-Founder, Society of American Archivists and Delaware Swedish Colonial Society.

JOHN FREDERICK DORMAN, M.A., F.A.S.G. Vice-President, National Genealogical Society (1958-59), Librarian (since 1959). Associate Editor, NGSQ. Editor, *The Virginia Genealogist*. Treasurer, American Society of Genealogists, 1959-.

DAVID C. DUNIWAY, A.B., A.M., Salem, Ore. State Archivist of Oregon. President, Marion Co. (Ore.) Historical Society. U. S. Delegate, International Congress on Archives, Florence, Italy, 1956.

C(ECIL) L'ESTRANGE EWEN, F.A.S.G., Paignton, Devon, England. Author of *History of Surnames of the British Isles*. Died in 1949. His section on "British Surnames" (see Part 5, Chapter III, Section A), was completed on his deathbed.

MARGARET DICKSON FALLEY (MRS. GEORGE F.), B.S., F.A.S.G., 999 Michigan Ave., Evanston, Ill. Contributing Editor, NGSQ. Lecturer, Institute of Genealogical Research, Washington, D. C. Recognized as the leading American authority on genealogical research in Ireland.

SIR FRANCIS JAMES GRANT, K.C.V.O., C.V.O., LL.D., F.A.S.G., Edinburgh, Scotland. Lord Lyon King of Arms and Secretary of the Order of the Thistle, 1929-45. Author of *The Manual of Heraldry*, etc. Contributor to *The Scots Peerage*. Died in 1953.

MARTHA WOODROOF HIDEN (MRS. PHILIP WALLACE), F.A.S.G., Newport News, Va. President of the Order of First Families of Virginia, and of other organizations. Author of books and articles on Virginia history and genealogy, Died in 1959.

THE AUTHORS

WILLIAM J. HOFFMAN, M.MECH.ENG., F.G.B.S., F.A.S.G., Laplume, Pa. Contributing Editor, TAG. Compiler of *An Armory of American Families of Dutch Descent* (1933-41). Died in 1955.

WINIFRED LOVERING HOLMAN, S.B., F.A.S.G., 275 Concord Ave., Lexington, Mass. Vice-President, American Society of Genealogists, 1957-59. Contributing Editor, TAG and NGSQ. Author and editor of numerous genealogical works.

DONALD LINES JACOBUS, M.A., F.A.S.G., P. O. Box 3032, Westville Station, New Haven, Conn. Editor-in-Chief, TAG. Honorary Member, National Genealogical Society. Contributing Editor, NGSQ. Honorary Director, New Haven Colony Historical Society.

AMANDUS JOHNSON, A.B., A.M., PH.D., 400 Master St., Philadelphia, 22, Pa. Founder and Director, American Swedish Historical Museum. Founder and President, New Sweden Historical Association. Knight Commander, Order of Vasa, and Knight, Order of the North Star (Sweden).

GÉRARD MALCHELOSSE, F.A.S.G., 5759 Ave. Durocher, Outremont, Montréal, P. Q., Canada. Past President, Bibliographical Society of Canada. Author of numerous books and articles dealing with French-Canadian genealogy and history.

G. ANDREWS MORIARTY, A.B., A.M., LL.B., F.S.A., F.S.G., F.A.S.G., Ogunquit, Me. Vice-President, New England Historic Genealogical Society and Chairman of its Committee on English and Foreign Research. Contributing Editor, NGSQ. Authority on English feudal genealogy.

MILTON RUBINCAM, F.A.S.G., F.N.G.S., 6303-20th Ave., W. Hyattsville, Md. Past President, National Genealogical Society and Pennsylvania Historical Junto. Editor, NGSQ. Contributing Editor, TAG. Lecturer, Institute of Genealogical Research, Washington, D. C.

HERBERT F. SEVERSMITH, B.S., M.A., PH.D., F.A.S.G., F.N.G.S., 4708 Bradley Blvd., Chevy Chase, Md. Past President, National Genealogical Society. Contributing Editor, NGSQ. Compiler of a monumental work on Long Island and Connecticut families, of which vol. 5 is in preparation.

WALTER LEE SHEPPARD, JR., M.S., F.A.S.G., 923 Old Manoa Rd., Havertown, Pa. Secretary, American Society of Genealogists. Contributing Editor, TAG.

MARY J. SIBLEY (MRS. HENRY O.), B.P.H., M.PH., PH.D.., Syracuse, N. Y. Authority on Upstate New York genealogy. Died in Portland, Ore., several years ago.

JEAN STEPHENSON, J.D., M.P.L., LL.M., S.J.D., F.A.S.G., F.N.G.S., 1228 Eye St., N. W., Washington 5, D. C. Formerly Editor, NGSQ, and Chairman, Genealogical Records Committee, N.S.D.A.R. Lecturer, Institute of Genealogical Research.

NOEL C. STEVENSON, LL.B., F.A.S.G., Wasco, Calif. Contributing Editor, TAG and NGSQ. Member, State Bar of California. Author, *Search and Research* (Revised Edition, 1959). Editor: *The Genealogical Reader* (1958).

JAMES J. TALMAN, PH.D., London, Ont., Canada. Chief Librarian, University of Western Ontario. Past President, Canadian Historical Association and Ontario Historical Society.

ANTHONY R. WAGNER, D.L.H., C.V.O., F.R.HIST.S., F.S.A., F.S.G., F.A.S.G., London, England. Richmond Herald, College of Arms. Secretary, Most Noble Order of the Garter. Author of numerous books and articles on heraldry.

EDWARD H. WEST, F.A.S.G., 802-4th St., Laurel, Md. Past President, National Genealogical Society. Author of books and articles on historical and genealogical subjects.

THE AMERICAN SOCIETY OF GENEALOGISTS

The American Society of Genealogists was founded in New York City 27 December 1940, and was incorporated under the laws of the District of Columbia 30 March 1946. The Society's Constitution limits the number of Members, known as Fellows, to fifty, chosen "on the basis of the amount and quality of their published genealogical work."

ROLL OF FELLOWS

Following is the complete Roll of Fellows from the Society's inception to the present time, together with the offices held by them in the organization. The office of Treasurer was combined with that of Secretary from 1940 to 1952, but since 1953 they have been separate offices. The numbers before the names signify the order of the Fellows' election. The asterisk (*) denotes those who are deceased; a dagger (†) denotes Fellows Emeriti.

1. REV. DR. ARTHUR ADAMS, Boston, Mass., *Founding Fellow*, 1940. President, 1940-58. President Emeritus, 1958-60.*
2. JOHN INSLEY CODDINGTON, Bordentown, N. J., *Founding Fellow*, 1940. Secretary-Treasurer, 1940-41. Honorary President for Life, 1969.
3. MEREDITH B. COLKET, JR., Cleveland, Ohio, *Founding Fellow*, 1940. Vice President, 1940-41. Secretary-Treasurer, 1941-51. Honorary President for Life, 1969.
4. DONALD LINES JACOBUS, New Haven, Conn.*
5. COL. LOUIS EFFINGHAM DEFOREST, New York, N. Y.*
6. DR. HAROLD BOWDITCH, Peterborough, N. H.*
7. MILTON RUBINCAM, West Hyattsville, Md., Vice President, 1946-49, 1959-61. Secretary-Treasurer, 1951-52. President, 1961-64.
8. MISS ROSALIE FELLOWS BAILEY, New York, N. Y., Secretary, 1953-57.
9. GEORGE ANDREWS MORIARTY, JR., Ogunquit, Me.*
10. WALTER GOODWIN DAVIS, Portland, Me., Vice President, 1941-46, 1952-57. Secretary, 1957-58. President, 1958-61.*
11. MRS. GEORGE U. G. [MARY CAMPBELL LOVERING] HOLMAN, Brookline, Mass.*
12. DR. EARL GREGG SWEM, Williamsburg, Va.*

GENEALOGICAL RESEARCH

13. RUSSELL BRUCE RANKIN, Newark, N. J.*
14. DR. MARCELLUS D. A. R. VON REDLICH, Chicago, Ill.*
15. HARRY WRIGHT NEWMAN, Washington, D. C. *Resigned.*
16. RICHARD LEBARON BOWEN, Rehoboth, Mass.*
17. JOHN COX, JR., New York, N. Y.*
18. MRS. JOHN RUSSELL [KATHARINE BAGG] HASTINGS, Santa Barbara, Cal.*
19. MRS. FRANK RILEY [WINIFRED LOVERING HOLMAN] DODGE, Exeter, N. H., Vice President, 1957-59.
20. MAJ. GEN. EDGAR ERSKINE HUME, Washington, D. C.*
21. CONKLIN MANN, New York, N. Y.*
22. CLARENCE ALMON TORREY, Boston, Mass.*
23. MRS. GARNER P. [LILA RUSSELL JAMES] RONEY, New York, N.Y.*
24. REV. CLAYTON TORRANCE, Richmond, Va.*
25. REV. DR. GILBERT H. DOANE, Newport, R. I.
26. MRS. PHILIP WALLACE [MARTHA WOODROOF] HIDEN, Newport News, Va.*
27. PROF. WILLIAM J. HOFFMAN, LaPlume, Pa.*
28. WILLIAM HERBERT WOOD, New Haven, Conn.*
29. HOMER T. BRAINERD, Amherst Mass.*
30. MISS SYBIL NOYES, Saco, Me.*
31. DR. HERBERT F. SEVERSMITH, Chevy Chase, Md.*
32. MRS. LOUIS CARLETON [CAROLYN ROGERS KEMPER] Newport News, Va.*
33. DR. GAIUS M. BRUMBAUGH, Washington, D. C.*
34. HIRAM E. DEATS, Flemington, N. J.*
35. SAMUEL COPP WORTHEN, New York, N. Y.*
36. CHARLES CARROLL GARDNER, Madison, N.J.*
37. DR. EDWIN JACQUET SELLERS, Philadelphia, Pa.*
38. DR. JEAN STEPHENSON, Washington, D. C., Secretary, 1961-66.
39. CAPT. JOHN BENNETT BODDIE, Mountain View, Cal.*
40. WILLIAM PRESCOTT GREENLAW, Boston, Mass.*
41. FLOYD WILLS SYDNOR, Richmond, Va.†
42. EDWARD H. WEST, Laurel, Md.*
43. H. CLIFFORD CAMPION, JR., Swarthmore, Pa.*
44. DR. ALBERT HORWELL GERBERICH, Bethesda, Md.*
45. WALTER LEE SHEPPARD, JR., Havertown, Pa., Secretary, 1958-61, 1966-67. Vice President, 1967-70. President, 1970-73.
46. CYRIL L'ESTRANGE EWEN, Paington, Devon, England.*
47. ALFRED TREGO BUTLER, London, England.*

ROLL OF FELLOWS

48. SIR FRANCIS JAMES GRANT, Edinburgh, Scotland.*
49. W. BLAKE METHENY, Philadelphia, Pa.†
50. SIR ANTHONY RICHARD WAGNER, London, England.
51. DR. JOHN GOODWIN HERNDON, Haverford, Pa., Vice President, 1949-52.*
52. HAROLD MINOT PITMAN, Bronxville, N. Y., Vice President, 1963-64. President, 1964-67.*
53. GEORGE HARRISON SANFORD KING, Fredericksburg, Va., Secretary-Treasurer, 1952-53. Treasurer, 1953-59.
54. WALTER CHARLTON HARTRIDGE, Savannah, Ga.†
55. GERARD MALCHELOSSE, Montreal, P. Q., Canada.*
56. HOWARD STELLE FITZ RANDOLPH, La Jolla, Cal.*
57. ARTHUR SOPER WARDWELL, Brooklyn, N. Y.*
58. LEWIS D. COOK Philadelphia, Pa.
59. GEORGE VALENTINE MASSEY, II, Dover, Del.
60. GEORGE McKENZIE ROBERTS, San Francisco, Cal.
61. REV. DR. FREDERICK LEWIS WEIS, Dover, N. H.*
62. NOEL C. STEVENSON, Los Angeles, Cal.
63. DR. GEORGE E. McCRACKEN, Des Moines, Iowa.
64. MRS. GEORGE F. [MARGARET DICKSON] FALLEY, Wilmette, Ill., Vice President, 1961-63.
65. SIR CHARLES TRAVIS CLAY, London, England.
66. BARON KARL FRIEDRICH von FRANK, Post Ferschnitz, Austria.
67. GEOFFREY H. WHITE, London, England*
68. MRS. JOHN E. [FLORENCE HARLOW] BARCLAY, Whitman, Mass., Vice President, 1964-65.
69. DR. ROBERT H. MONTGOMERY, Cambridge, Mass.
70. GERALD JAMES PARSONS, Syracuse, N. Y.
71. DR. RALPH DORNFELD OWEN, Springfield, Pa.†*
72. BRIG. GEN. JOHN ROSS DELAFIELD, New York, N. Y.*
73. JOHN FREDERICK DORMAN, Washington, D. C., Treasurer, 1959-66.
74. MRS. LEWIS T. [ANNIE LASH] JESTER, Tabb, Va.
75. DR. KENN STRYKER-RODDA, South Orange, N. J., Vice President, 1965-67. President, 1967-70.
76. MRS. F. SPENCER [HANNAH BENNER] ROACH, Philadelphia, Pa.
77. DR. ARCHIBALD F. BENNETT, Salt Lake City, Utah.*
78. CAMERON HARRISON ALLEN, Newark, N. J.
79. LUNDIE WEATHERS BARLOW, Richmond, Va.*
80. PAUL W. PRINDLE, Darien, Conn., Secretary, 1967-68. Treasurer, 1968-

GENEALOGICAL RESEARCH

81. CHARLES W. FARNHAM, Providence, R.I.
82. MISS RACHEL E. BARCLAY, Whitman, Mass. Assistant Secretary, 1972-
83. DR. RAYMOND MARTIN BELL, Washington, Pa.
84. MACLEAN W. McLEAN, Pittsburgh, Pa.
85. DR. MALCOLM H. STERN, New York, N. Y., Treasurer, 1966-68. Secretary, 1968-73; Vice President, 1973.
86. GEORGE OLIN ZABRISKIE, Honolulu, Hawaii.
87. DR. AMANDUS JOHNSON, Philadelphia, Pa.†
88. FRANCIS JAMES DALLETT, Villanova, Pa.
89. MRS. BERT HENRY [MARY E. McCOLLAM] HARTER, Key West, Fla. Secretary, 1973.
90. DR. CLAUDE WILLIS BARLOW, Worcester, Mass.
91. MRS. LEON J. [VIRGINIA POPE] LIVINGSTON, Chester, Va., Vice President, 1970-73; President 1973
92. THE HON. FOLKS HUXFORD, Homerville, Ga.
93. DR. NILS WILLIAM OLSSON, Minneapolis, Minn.
94. SIR IAIN MONCREIFFE OF THAT ILK, Perthshire, Scotland.
95. JOHN D. AUSTIN, Jr., Glens Falls, N.Y.
96. WINSTON DEVILLE, New York City and New Orleans, La.
97. DR. DAVID HUMISTON KELLEY, Calgary, Alberta, Canada.
98. MISS LUCY MARY KELLOGG, Brighton, Mich.*
99. DR. KENNETH SCOTT, Douglaston, N.Y.

4 311TF BR1
08/93 24-950-00 5665 GBC

DATE DUE